Mapping Histories

Essays presented to Ravinder Kumar

Also by Neera Chandhoke:
Beyond Secularism: The Rights of Religious Minorities (1999)
State and Civil Society: Explorations in Political Theory (1995)

Mapping Histories

**Essays
presented to Ravinder Kumar**

Edited by Neera Chandhoke

Anthem Press
London

Anthem Press is an imprint of
Wimbledon Publishing Company
PO Box 9779
London
SW19 7QA

This edition first published by Wimbledon Publishing Company 2002

First published by Tulika, India, 2000

British Library Cataloguing in Publication Data
Data available

ISBN   1 84331 050 3 (hbk)
       1 84331 036 8 (pbk)

1 3 5 7 9 10 8 6 4 2

Printed by Newton Printing Ltd, London, UK.   www.newtonprinting.com

Contents

CONTENTS

v i

Preface

Despite the fact that many scholars are uneasy and somewhat impatient with postmodernity, the postmodern moment, in my consideration, has touched all of us in two basic ways. One, we have become much more self-conscious of our cognitive, evaluative and epistemological modes. Consequently, this self-consciousness throws into sharp relief the methods by which we appropriate the social and political world. Two, the postmodern moment has inculcated a healthy sense of respect for those modes of analysis that may not be our own. This is not to say that we should accept or justify relativism; it is merely to suggest that other ways of appropriating the social and political world may be perhaps just as legitimate as the ones we espouse. Of course, in a basic sense, these other modes should be acceptable to our considered convictions—to our ethical and political commitments—and to our projects of what we want to do with scholarship. Those congnitive modes that violate our sense of cognition and evaluation or our ethics and politics cannot be considered acceptable, irrespective of what some of the 'postmodern excesses' suggests. Let me clarify that when I speak of 'our' political and ethical commitments and projects, I am not advocating subjectivity. I am speaking of moral arguments that, even as they appeal to our considered convictions, meet the test of both moral justification and political viability.

Therefore, we have come to understand that other ways of appropriating the social and the political world may prove valuable because all theories, analyses and frameworks provide only partial glimpses into the complexity of social and political life. Consequently, in order to acquire a nearly adequate picture of the social and political world, in order to acquire some sense of what the world is about, we need to look at other ways of looking at the world. More importantly, we need to respect them. If the postmodern moment has achieved anything at all, it is to make social and political theorists modest about their own ability to provide either a final, unqualified or comprehensive insight into the messy but occasionally creative world we live in. If it has managed to achieve anything at all, it is to inculcate a sense of respect for other theories and modes of knowing, viewing and evaluating the world. It is in this sense that the essays in this volume— each of them providing a window to a collage of events and images superimposed upon each other, that we call the social and the political world—provide partial but rich glimpses into this world.

The essays are arranged in a broad chronological sequence, from ancient history to the present, and the subjects they deal with cover diverse categories, from historical understanding to contemporary history to cultural studies to feminism, among others. They offer readings on how we understand our past or, conversely, how we bring an understanding of the past into comprehending our present.

NEERA CHANDHOKE

Ravinder Kumar

Neera Chandhoke

Professor Ravinder Kumar, who headed the Nehru Memorial Museum and Library, New Delhi, for almost seventeen years with considerable distinction as director, and who founded the Centre for Contemporary Studies where most of the contributors to this volume have been or are fellows, is well known as an institution-builder. Under his able guidence, the Centre for Contemporary Studies developed into a prestigious research centre, offering to several academics from a variety of disciplines—history, anthropology, sociology, education, economics, literary and cultural studies, political science, ecology, law—fellowships ranging from three to five years. During this period, they were able to devote themselves wholly to research projects leading up to a publication at the end of their stay at the centre.

Professor Kumar not only provided the fellows with felicitous conditions for independent research work, he personally directed the building up of a vibrant and lively atmosphere for academic discussion and engagement. They were able, through presentation in seminars of both work in progress and finished research papers, to get the response of an exceptionally lively academic community. The Centre for Contemporary Studies acquired national and international prestige as a centre of academic excellence, and several acclaimed publications emerged from the research work carried out in the environs of the Nehru Memorial Museum and Library.

The fellows at the centre carried out empirical as well as theoretical research on themes that hold relevance for the understanding of postcolonial societies in general and India in particular. Much of this could take place because Professor Ravinder Kumar brought to his directorship of the centre immense personal prestige as a scholar of eminence. His own research work has been hailed as

1

pathbreaking in the historiography of modern India. And yet his early education was in the physical sciences rather than history. His academic biography from physical scientist to historian is of some interest because it highlights the impact of historical and personal events on the evolution of scholarship.

Born into a Kashmiri pandit family which had settled in Lahore, Ravinder Kumar spent the first fourteen years of his life in what is now Pakistan. The partition of India in 1947 brought the family, whose head was an academic teaching chemistry in the university, to Delhi, Kumar's father was a man of deep intellectual commitment. Involved with the Society for the Promotion of Scientific Knowledge and with literary and social activities, he was also a connoisseur of poetry. Under his influence, Ravinder Kumar took to the study of chemistry at the University of Delhi. But questions relating to the history of nineteenth and twentieth-century India in particular, and the world in general, had already begun to preoccupy the mind of the young scholar.

His vocational trajectory was deeply influenced at this stage of his life by a bout of serious illness. During his convalescence, he found himself drawn to an exploration of the political processes of Indian society, to the social anomie that he discovered around him, and to the possibilities of social transformation in the revolutionary mode. Influenced by Marxist thought, he was to hereafter devote his scholarly pursuits to the human sciences. Taking up the study of history as a discipline, he acquired an M.A. degree in 1956, and then explored the possibility of a doctoral dissertation on issues pertaining to social and economic transformation in peasant societies like India.

It was during this time that he came in contact with Professor Anthony Low, and English academic who was engaged in the process of creating a research group on South Asia at the Australian National University in Canberra. Low, by then well known for his research on African societies, possessed the intellectual disposition of social historian drawn to the Annales school. He had subsequently turned his attention to the processes of decolonization and nationalism in South Asia. Ravinder Kumar was greatly influenced both personally and academically by the vision of a mature scholar like Low, and proceeded to work for a doctorate under his guidance in Canberra. A sustained academic partnership and lifelong friendship followed, nurtured by a common intellectual commitment to social causes.

Ravinder Kumar successfully completed his doctorate at the University of Canberra and was appointed a fellow at the Institute of Advanced Studies of Australian National University. A relatively young scholarly formation at the time, the ANU provided facilities for stimulating academic exchanges between scholars. Here Kumar, in the company of gifted intellectuals like W.K. Hancock, Barry Smith, Robin Gollan, W.H. Passmore, P.H. Partridge, Eleanor Searle and Eugene Kamenka, all of whom were grounded in 'Annales' historiography, was encouraged to explore the creative interaction between different disciplines of the social sciences. The practical result in the shape of doctoral dissertation, which was transformed subsequently into a book—*Western India in the Nineteenth Century,* was to gain acclaim as a work of significance. And Kumar came to be known widely as a historian of considerable potential.

His study of Maharashtra in this book demonstrated the complexity of British colonial domination over South Asia. Far from a simple exploration of economic exploitation of the colonial subject, the argument focussed on how the British attempted to create a rich peasant society in western India, which the magic of private property and the rule of law would transform into a stable social and economic base for the colonial regime. Kumar argued that tied to this rural economic strategy was the creation of an intelligentsia that was sympathetic to the liberal discourse even as it came to be linked to British colonialism through ties of interest and sentiment. However, the same processes that created a rich peasantry, he argued, also resulted in the impoverishment of other sections of the peasantry. A nuanced portrayal of the social consequences of colonial rule, the book put forth the thesis that the creation of a kulak-like rural class ruled out the prospect of social transformation in India along the lines of the revolution in Russia or China.

The book was hailed as a pioneering work, and Kumar was elected to a chair in history at the University of New South Wales in Sydney. This was followed by a visiting professorship to the University of Sussex in the United Kingdom in 1971. Subsequently, Kumar's research interests reached out to the themes of 'history from below', the crystallization of working-class politics, popular nationalism, the fabric of plural societies, and secularism in South Asia. He also wrote extensively on the philosophy of history and historiography. His work on the civilizational character of Indian society as the most profitable point of entry into an exploration of the history of contemporary India, is regarded as a major attempt in understanding the complexities of Indian society.

Returning from Sussex to his university in Sydeny, Kumar renewed his activities in lecturing and research. But his stay in Australia ended in 1978 when he decided to return to India as a professor in modern history at the University of Allahabad. Soon after, in 1980, he was offered directorship of the Nehru Memorial Museum and Library. And, as stated earlier, under his able guidance an archival library was transformed into a centre of historical research, and a new tradition of research was built up, encouraging academic investigation across disciplines in order to understand the past and the present of Indian society.

During this period, the 1980s he published two volumes of essays—*Essays in the Social History of Modern India* and *The Making of a Nation*—which reveal both the wide vision and the reflective turn of his mind. His essay on the social history of Lahore on the eve of the Rowlatt Act satyagraha has been recognized as a seminal work by social historians. His definition of India as a 'civilization-state' rather than a 'nation-state' marked a decided shift in conceptualizations of India as a plural and culturally diverse nation. He also focussed on the fact that Indian society was integrated through a creative interplay between an apex high culture, a broad-based middle tradition of devotional theism, and innumerable localized cults and sects. His continued preoccupation with historiography and the philosophy of history is reflected in his contributions to two books edited by him: *Philosophical Theory and Social Reality* (jointly edited with D.P. Chattopadhyaya) and *Science, Philosophy and Culture: Multidisciplinary Explorations.*

Ravinder Kumar's many friends and admirers know him equally as a formidable intellectual with tremendous vision and knowledge, and as a generous human being. His contributions to academic exchanges, his piloting of several prestigious seminars, his informed though informal discussions with the fellows at Teenmurti, his humanism, the elegance of his language, his wit, are all generally admired. The doors to his office-room were always open to friends and strangers alike, and he was ever ready to exchange ideas over a cup of tea. He is respected as much for his skill in building an institution as for his deeply compassionate spirit. It is for these reasons that several of the fellows of the Centre for Contemporary Studies decided to come together to pay their tribute to him through this volume.

Kalidasa in the Nineteenth Century in Europe and in India[1]

Romila Thapar

The assessment of a literary work is frequently restricted to the literary tradition from which it comes, as has often happened with works in Sanskrit. This is legitimate but limiting, because literary works have a historical context and when seen in the light of a historical moment, their meaning and function can be enhanced. Where such a text is translated into another language, the context expands to include the intellectual concerns of the society whose language is used in the translation. Similarly if, many centuries later, there is a revival of interest in the original text within the same society, then the changed historical context becomes significant. The literary text takes on a life of its own and may be seen as showing some characteristics of what might be regarded as a historical event. I would like to illustrate this by narrating the reception of Kalidasa's play, the *Abhijnana-Shakuntalam*, in nineteenth century Europe and India.

Kalidasa wrote the play in the early centuries AD, when the literary genre of the *nataka*/drama, the context of the story and of the audience, was entirely within the frame of Sanskrit literature and the society of early India. Fifteen hundred years or so later, the play was translated into English and soon after into German, and emerged almost as a kind of mast-head of German Romanticism: a turn of events which may well have bewildered Kalidasa had it been predicted to him. In this changed historical situation, the translations and their treatment give the play a variety of new incarnations. There is a shift from discussions about the play itself, as in earlier Sanskrit literary theory, to the impact of the translations on perceptions of the Indian past and present.

The eulogistic reception of the German translation by Goethe is frequently quoted as an indication of the high quality of the work.

5

Yet its quality did not require this testimony as it had been established many centuries earlier within the Sanskritic literary tradition. What is perhaps more fascinating is the way in which it became a symbol within a European literary movement at the start of the nineteenth century, and faded out by the end of the same century with the decline of Romanticism. But by this time it had also become an icon of what was being projected as Indian national culture, drawing its legitimacy as much from the earlier Sanskritic tradition as from the pride which the Indian middle class took in the praise for this icon in Europe. The *nataka* itself, as it were, began to play multiple roles. The story of what might be viewed as the conversion of an icon into a historical event, begins with the first translation of the play into a European language.

At the end of the eighteenth century, Sir William Jones and other officers of the East India Company at Calcutta were busy translating texts relating to law and to religion from Sanskrit and Persian and from other Indian languages, in an effort to understand the high culture of the colony which they were governing. An assertion of power also required a knowledge of the history and culture of those now in a subservient status. Such translations were partly a response to intellectual curiosity and partly an aspect of the practical function of the East India Company officials in India. Jones was impressed by Sanskrit literature and Hindu mythology and some internalization of ideas from these is evident in his poems, such as 'Hymn to Camdeo', 'Hymn to Narayan' and 'The Enchanted Fruit', composed in 1784–85, and in a number of essays published in *Asiatic Researches*. These grew out of his readings of the Puranas and his attempt to find parallels with Graeco-Roman religions and biblical chronology.[2] The poetry and the essays came to be reflected in the imagination of the poets of the Romantic movement.

One may also ask whether William Jones was not subconsciously influenced by what has been called the hunt for the Welsh past with its revival of bards, druids and nature worship.[3] The involvement of his family with Welsh nationalism would have familiarized him to it. Welsh was supposed to hold the secrets to man's primitive language, consequently links were sought between Noah and the Welsh. This was an ambience in which myths, far from being dismissed as fantasy, were instead believed to incorporate statements about the past.

Jones' writing touched many chords: the supposedly

primitive and spontaneous poetry of the orient, its origins in emotion and imagination and the emphasis on the lyric form.[4] His intention of translating a Sanskrit text was however more ambitious. Jones had heard about the genre of *nataka* and thought it was a kind of history, but Pandit Radhakanta who advised him on such matters clarified its meaning and defined it as being similar to the plays performed by the English in the cool season in Calcutta. This was a very perceptive observation. When asked to suggest a play, Radhakanta referred to what was regarded as the best in the tradition, Kalidasa's *Abhijnana-Shakuntalam.* Jones' other advisor was a *vaidya* from Nadia who endorsed this selection and helped Jones with the translation. Jones was much enthused on reading the play and decided to translate it. He saw it as demonstrating the high quality of Indian civilization and thought that it was all the more remarkable as it was written at a time 'when Britons were as unlettered and unpolished as the army of Hanumant'. His description of Kalidasa as 'the Indian Shakespeare' has since come to stay.[5]

His initial translation was into Latin since he felt that the structural similarities of Sanskrit and Latin would facilitate such a translation. From the Latin he translated it into English and published it in 1789 as *Sacoontala or The Fatal Ring.* He explains in the introduction to the text that he faced two problems: translating it into a foreign idiom although the translation was not the most felicitous; and his wish to convince readers of the greatness of Indian civilization. The latter led him to tone down some of what he perceived as the more erotic passages, which he assumed would unnecessarily result in English hostility towards the Sanskrit classics. He was anticipating possible criticism on these grounds from the perspective of European views on erotica in literature.[6] That it was an initial venture in translating Sanskrit literature into English is evident from the additional phrases here and there which Jones incorporates in order to clarify the meaning.

William Jones was not averse to literary Romanticism, as is evident from his own poetry. Doubtless one of the attractions of the play for him was a theme central to Romanticism, namely, the evocation of nature. This was the period when the debate on Nature and Culture had begun to convulse the literary scene in Europe. But perhaps his personal inclination was still more towards Neo-Classicism and he sees Shakuntala as a 'rustic girl', the term he frequently uses, rather than as a 'child of nature', which was the phrase used by the German Romantic poets. Although embarrassed by the eroticism of some of the verses in the play, he does not however make moral judgements on the characters of the play. Nevertheless, it would seem that Jones was anxious that the play not be performed in its entirety to a Calcutta audience of the East India Company officials and their wives, nor that the full version be read in England.

What were viewed as erotic passages had been perceived differently by Indian audiences in the past, and the nineteenth-century European view of erotica seems a trifle absurd to us today. Thus the term *jaghanagauravat,* meaning heavy hips, was thought to be erotic. Jones translated it as 'elegant limbs' and later translators referred to the 'graceful undulation of her gait' (Monier-Williams) or the 'weight of rounded hips' (Edgren), and some omitted it altogether.[7] Yet such descriptions had not only been acceptable to Indian audiences but had also been regarded as essential to the creation of the emotion associated with love and the erotic. Such embarrassments with what was judged to be erotic affected many European versions and Jones' reluctance was repeated, for instance, by A.L. de Chezy when he rendered the play into French.

Jones' translation in fact took Europe by storm. It was in turn translated into virtually all the European languages including Icelandic, and some more than once during the nineteenth century and some at fourth remove: from Latin to English to French to Italian. This enthusiastic acclamation for the play was also due to Georg Forster who, in 1791, published a German translation of the text by Jones. Forster had been interested in Tahiti and his reading of Jones' translation led him to believe that there might have been a link between Tahitians and Indians. His fascination with the play arose from 'the fact that the tenderest emotions of which the human heart is capable could have been as well expressed on the Ganges by dark-skinned people as on the Rhine, the Tyber or the Ilissus by our white race.'[8] Forster maintains that the childlike and unspoilt relation which the Hindu has with nature has been lost to the modern European and the latter has to be reminded of it through Indian literature.[9]

Forster sent his translation to Goethe who praised it almost to excess in spite of his otherwise contemptuous comments on the many-armed deities of Indian religion. His well-weathered verse on the play, an instant reaction, hardly bears repeating:

Would'st thou the young year's blossoms and the fruits of its decline,
And all by which the soul is charmed, enraptured, feasted, fed,
Would'st thou the Earth and Heaven itself in one sole name
    combine?
I name thee, O Shakuntala! and all at once is said.

Yet, even later, his comments born of reflections in tranquility support his earlier enthusiasm, an enthusiasm which doubtless encouraged its being highlighted by German Romanticism. In a letter to A.L. de Chezy in 1830, he wrote:

> Only now do I grasp the extravagant impression that this work excited in me. Here the poet appears to us in his highest role, as a representative of the natural state, of the finest way of life, of the finest moral striving, of the most dignified majesty and the most earnest contemplation of God: at the same time however he remains lord and master of his creation; he can dare common and ridiculous opposites which nevertheless must be considered as necessary links in the whole organism. . .[10]

In each decade of the nineteenth century there was yet another translation in yet another language.[11] Not only was the play read and occasionally performed but it also provided the story for a number of minor operas and ballets such as the poet Theophile Gautier's ballet pantomime *Sacountala,* with music by Ernst Reyer, in 1858, or the opera by Franco Alfano in 1921. Frans Schubert's opera of 1820 remained incomplete and is now lost. The sculptress Camille Claudel is said to have been deeply moved by the play, an emotion which she might have conveyed to Rodin. Both in France and in Russia it was taken up by the Symbolists. Alexander Tairoff had it staged in 1914 in Moscow as an expression of the Symbolist Movement.

Romanticism was the predominent perspective in European literature and the arts during the late eighteenth and nineteenth centuries. It was in part a reaction to the neo-classicism of the previous period which had enthused over the discovery of the Greco-Roman tradition and in literary theory had submitted to the dictates of Aristotle and Horace in particular. If the English Romantic poets drew inspiration from the writings of William Jones, German Romanticism of the nineteenth century saw a new vision in this play. The imagery evoked was stunning to a European readership. The Shakuntala of the play became the ideal Indian woman, encapsulating the beauty of all women. But more than that it was her portrayal as the child of nature which most attracted German Romanticism. The identification of the heroine with nature was seen as an appropriate counter to the crafted women of neo-classicism.

Interest in Greek drama had preceded this new enthusiasm for Kalidasa. It was part of the earlier Greek Renaissance and by the nineteenth century it was avidly discussed in literary and philosophical studies. Goethe, for example, was reading Greek tragedy and was much taken up, as were others, with *Antigone* of Sophocles, at the same time that he was ecstatic about Shakuntala. Quite how a romantic comedy was juxtaposed to a tragedy of the dimensions of *Antigone*, and both described as representing the ideal in drama, is rather puzzling. Holderlin, Hegel and Schelling wrote extensively on *Antigone* and A.W. Schlegel saw it as epitomizing high morality and absolute purity.[12]

Romanticism preferred the less orderly aspect of the Graeco-Roman past and looked for the exotic, the unusual, the irrational, the emotional and the imaginative as against the typical, the rational and the real. The availability of literature from the 'orient' revealed another world. It was a move away from the known European civilization to the imagined fantasies of societies outside Europe and from times long ago. Folk tales, fairy tales, poetry from various parts of the world and mythology contributed to its perception of what literature is about. Novalis sums it up in his statement: 'The world must be romanticized. In giving the usual a noble sense, the ordinary a mysterious experience, the well-known the dignity of the unknown, the temporal a perennial aura, I am romanticizing.'

The creation of what has been called the ideal of India in German Romanticism was also conditioned by a simmering of ideas rooted in early Greek views of India and being drawn upon in European writings on India of the fifteenth century and after. Throughout the earlier centuries, Greek and Latin authors had nurtured the stories of the supposed conversations between Alexander of Macedon and the 'gymnosophists' of India, by which was meant brahmins, Buddhists, ascetics, philosophers and a variety of religious teachers. The conversations were thought to have explained the essentials of Indian philosophy—metampsychosis, non-duality, the unity of man and nature, the meaning of renunciation—to Alexander or to later Greek visitors. They became central to the ideas of the Neo-Platonists, who believed that much that was essentially the alternative to Judaeo-Christian and mainstream European thought was derived from Indian sources. The articles of William Jones had been used to suggest the identity of Vedanta with Pythagorian and Platonic philosophies and endorsed the importance of Vedanta in Indian philosophy, encouraging comparative studies of language and religion. These theories now interested the Romantics. The departure from the dependence on such views for knowledge about Indian thought came with the possibility of studying Sanskrit texts in the original in Europe rather than relying on the hearsay of earlier writers. That such readings would still be coloured by European perceptions of the texts was not recognized.

Romanticism, therefore, was not merely a reaction to Neo-Classicism. It was to some degree a part of the parallel tradition which continued to question ideas and perspectives based on Judaeo–Christian thought and the Enlightenment. One ancestral strand in Romanticism, apart from many others, was perhaps the persistence of Neo-Platonism. This can be seen in the earlier fascination for Roman culture giving way to the Greek, which was thought to be closer to the ideals of Romanticism. Familiarity with Greek culture inevitably encouraged a further investigation of the debates around Pythagoras and Plato and their possible indebtedness to Indian thought, a debate which is equally apparent among the English Romantic poets.

J.G. von Herder referred to the Kalidasa play as a rare masterpiece which challenged Aristotle's theories and could be used to question the hold of the classical literary canon in European writing. Shakuntala to his mind represented the fairy-tale atmosphere of the childlike Indian, the flower fantasy which (like the Indians themselves) breathes the blissful peace of paradise. Shakuntala is compared to a flower unfolding its innocence in a holy retreat.[14] He adds that the play has given him more insights into the true and living concepts of the Indians' way of thought than have all the Upanekats (Upanishads) and Bhagavadams.[15] Herder, in his foreword to the second edition of the Forster translation published in 1803, defines the image of India as a contact of spirits, where everything is touched gently and tenderly and perhaps to that extent is an illusion.[16]

The brothers Frederick and August Wilhelm von Schlegal were initially both enthusiasts of Sanskrit and of things Indian. This is

11

apparent from their statements in setting forth the principles of German Romanticism in 1798–1800. The unity of poetry and mythology so central to Romanticism was said to be characteristic of Sanskrit literature which, they maintained, embodied through its sensuality, the childhood of mankind. The hermitage of Kanva where Shakuntala grows up is the idyllic settlement, even as Kashmir is the earthly paradise. There was a childlike innocence of the golden age associated with Indians, the noblest people of antiquity. Hinduism and Christianity were said to have an affinity, and the allegorical basis of Hindu mythology according to Frederick Schlegel was unique.

This was also the period just prior to the coming of comparative philology in which the links between Sanskrit and Greek and Latin were regarded as the revelation of earlier ancestral links between peoples and cultures. The Semitic languages became the point of contrast. The enthusiasm of German Romantics for aspects of Indian literature was furthered by the discoveries of comparative linguistics.

A major figure of German Romanticism, F. Von Hardenberg or Novalis, was important to the early phase of the movement when the return to antiquity and its values was regarded as essential to the construction of culture. For him, Sanskrit held the secrets of the universe and among the mysteries which he invoked was the symbolism of the Blaue Blume—the Blue Flower, which drew into itself many ideas and was associated with India.[17] It is thought that possibly somewhere he linked it to the blue lotus, the *nila kamala*. Endorsing the image of Shakuntala in terms of German Romanticism led him to call his fiance, Sakontala!

By way of contrast, the English Romantic poets were less overtly enthusiastic about Kalidasa and the literature of the Sanskrit classics although they drew in varying degrees from Indian sources or, more correctly, from Orientalist scholarship, and occasionally from reading some Indian literature in translation. Most were familiar with what William Jones had written and admired him for revealing a new civilization which gave direction to some of the ideas they were formulating. Jones' hymns to various Hindu deities were part of this revelation. It is thought that Samuel Taylor Coleridge's references to the god who floats upon the lotus in 'The Triumph of Loyalty', was to Vishnu. 'Kublai Khan' may also have been influenced by Jones' essay on Tartary.[18] Shelley is also known to have been reading Jones among others writing on India, and the impact of this reading has been traced in 'Prometheus Unbound' as also in 'Queen Mab'. Robert Southey's poem, 'The Curse of Kehama' is said to have been indebted to Jones.[19] The debate on whether Pythagoras received his ideas from Indian philosophers and the close parallels between Neo-Platonism and Vedanta were also discussed in these circles.

A review of a later translation of the play, (by Monier-Williams) appeared in *The Edinburgh Review* of July 1858, and touched on many of these notions.[20] The author of the review describes dramatic poetry as the peculiar glory of the Indo-Teutonic race. He goes on to say that India was a nation of dreaming mystics such as those met by Alexander's companions, and Kanva's *ashrama* where Shakuntala grew up is the kind of grove where Alexander discovered the gymnosophists. The enterprising reviewer was attempting to give some historicity to the play and this was a small departure from the purely Romanticist reaction.

Blackwoods Edinburgh Magazine, although reflecting Victorian England, evokes the imprint of Romanticism:

> It is delightful to sink away into those green and noiseless sanctuaries, to look on the brahmins as they pass their whole lives in silent and reverential adoration—to observe virgins playing with the antelopes and bright-plumaged birds among those gorgeous woods—and, as the scene shifts, to find ourselves amid the old magnificence of oriental cities, or wafted on the chariot of some deity up to the palaces of the sky.

The reference to virgins playing with antelopes is of course very evocative of medieval European Romance literature, where themes such as the well-known virgin with a unicorn run through it like a thread, sometimes becoming the dominant theme as in the magnificent tapestries associated with the monastery at Cluny. Parallels between the Indian and the European past were seen as manifestations of Indian culture being reminiscent of the infancy of Europe.

Acclamation for the play by German Romanticism has other, perhaps not so tangential, aspects as well. The projection of Shakuntala as nature's child would have been reminiscent of other children of nature such as the nymphs of Greek literature, water spirits and fertility spirits, who inhabited springs, woodlands and hills and had loving relationships with men although never permanent. This recognition of the nymph in the *apsara*, made the *apsara* less alien. The departure

13

of Shakuntala for the court is a farewell to the innocent joys of a life in nature and the coming of years of incomprehensible tribulations associated with the mores of life at the court.

It has been said that the Oriental Renaissance was in its initial phase the checkmating of Cartesian absolutism, although the western image of India moved from incredulous amazement to condescending veneration.[21]

It can be argued that the insistence on seeing a Sanskrit classic as a eulogy on nature also carries, in the nineteenth century, some racist undertones. Those close to nature were the primitive peoples, primitive in the nineteenth century sense of being at the start of the evolutionary scale, a notion which has a trace of contempt. The reference to childlike Indians was not entirely complimentary. Max Muller's description of India as consisting of idyllic village communities where people were gentle and passive and spent their time meditating,[22] evokes the *ashrama* of Kanva. Supplementing this was the eroticism of the play, where eroticism was also linked to the primitive. The language was beautiful in itself but the erotic thoughts which it expressed were less noble. This reflected the weakness of Indian civilization. It was more appropriate, therefore, to delete such passages. If Indian society in its closeness to nature represented the infancy of human society, as many thought it did, then there would also be support for the idea that the present of India was similar to the lost, utopian past of Europe.

The Romanticist celebrations of human creativity have in various ways set up an oppositional parallel to positivist, materialist, teleological and other universalist schemes.[23] Where the first was attempting to understand the world, the second was concerned with explaining the world. But the two were not demarcated finalities and there were points of overlap. Even Enlightenment rationalism was neither unified nor uncontested. These were in part conditioned by the way in which culture, language and society were linked.

For Herder and Schlegel, the interlocking of language and culture was crucial to the human being for language endows humans with consciousness, and this combination is best seen in the dynamic interaction of language and culture as in Sanskrit, German and Celtic which were vibrant languages. This made the Indian image important to the argument. The mechanical, non-dynamic languages were English and Latin.[24] Such ideas also fell happily into place in the racist theories of the nineteenth century. Herder argued for the concept of the *volk*/the people and the uniqueness of each *volkgeist*/the spirit of the people which, like fundamental truths, could not be analysed through rational enquiry. The concept of the *volk* with its roots in primitive beginnings and a closeness to nature, remained vague, but could be borrowed by a variety of later movements searching for identity and descent. German Romanticism is believed to have provided some germinal ideas to the later theories of cultural nationalism.[25]

Such views coincided with a search for a new experience different from that of Europe and the hope that the Oriental Renaissance would bring other dimensions as yet not experienced, as had the earlier Greek Renaissance.[26] The Oriental Renaissance was viewed from two different perspectives. One was the belief that it would reveal connections with the ancient past of Europe. The sons of Noah were said to have migrated in diverse directions including the orient, and the theory of such migrations was sought to be strengthened by the idea of a monogenesis of languages, encouraged duly by the new-found theories of an ancestral Indo-European language. The assumption was that all cultures ultimately could be traced back to the Bible. The other understanding was that this Renaissance would lead to new experiences of mind and emotion, vastly different from those familiar to Europe—a hope which still rises periodically in western societies. The intensity of this expectation was largely an escape from what was viewed as the degeneration in the quality of life in Europe largely because of industrialization.

Enthusiastic translations of the play into various European languages did not prevent an inability to grasp the perspective of Sanskrit poetry and of Kalidasa.[27] Aristotelian poetics were debated but there was no interest in investigating theories of poetics relating to Sanskrit literature. The translations amended the text in accordance with the norms of the literatures of the languages of the translations and the social mores of their societies. The concept of drama in Sanskrit literary theory was very different from that of Aristotle, familiar by now to European literary theory. The erotic in the Sanskrit play becomes a barrier and moral homilies, both spoken and implied, enter the language of the translation. This contradicts the trend in nineteenth-century European literature of introducing an erotic sensibility which becomes, according to one view, the mainspring of works of the imagination.[28] The mysterious bond between pleasure and suffering enters the inheritance of Romantic and decadent sensitivities. This should have resulted in the unquestioning approval of the *Shakuntalam*, but possibly its erotic sensibility, coming as it did from an alien culture, reduced the approval. The centrality of duty takes a different form from the original and the irrational is equated with fate, introducing strands of pessimism in the European interpretation.

The projection of the Indian world as a place which could host the fantasies of Europe, declined in the late nineteenth century with the more aggressive European articulation towards the world in the form of imperialism, theories of race and Social Darwinism. But the image created by the Romantics with all its ambiguities remained an undertone, nurtured on the memories of the earlier reception. In a sense the Kalidasa play had performed its function and had now, in the post-Romantic period, been relegated to a curiosity of European Romanticism. It was however at this point that it became important to the emergent Indian middle class in the latter half of the nineteenth century in India. This process however was seized through a colonial experience and this was inevitably different from the perceptions of the Romantic movement.

To return to the British and India. Jones' enthusiasm was of course not shared by the English Utilitarians who had always found him too sympathetic to Indian culture. James Mill, whose endorsement of the Utilitarian philosophy led him to being extremely critical of the Indian past, was one for whom Sanskrit literature was the literature of a self-indulgent society.[29] It is only nations in their infancy who produce literature which is in praise of the pastoral, for such societies are fettered by despots and they can only indulge in light romances rather than analyzing their condition. There was much in the narrative of the play which, he argued, signalled Indian degradation.[30] Irrationality was for Mill a characteristic of Indian civilization. Such a perception was far distant from the enthusiastic reading of Shakuntala as the child of nature. It was, to the contrary, a statement of culture having superceded nature, if it is viewed in terms of the juxtaposition of the two.

What may be called the cultural imperialism of the Utilitarians was a major shift in focus and should be differentiated from the more sympathetic Orientalism of the early scholars of Sanskrit. The Utilitarians refused to study the Sanskrit or Persian texts from India but nevertheless denigrated them and argued for imperial culture as superior in every way and the avenue for radically altering colonial society which required, according to them, fundamental alteration. In part this was the result of the East India Company earlier having maintained that its authority was legitimized by its conforming to local laws, but now having to adopt in effect an aggressive assertion of authority which included violence and conquest. The establishing of colonial rule required that matters of cultural articulation also be formulated and be given direction.

More ambiguous than Mill were the attitudes of other scholars working as administrators in India. This ambiguity arose from many features. It was necessary, they felt, for those who governed India to be familiar with Indian culture, as indeed it had been the policy of earlier scholar-administrators to educate Europe as well in this area. It was also their policy now to rediscover the Indian past for the Indian and to formulate or to revive, as they perceived it, Indian culture as defined by Orientalist scholarship. Not only was the emergent middle-class Indian to be made aware of this culture, but it also required the imprinting on his mind of the interpretation given to it by Orientalist scholarship. This was another strategy of control. [31] Thus, whereas the pastoral beauty and lyrical charm of the play was appreciated, nevertheless the unabridged play was not approved of as a text for teaching Sanskrit in schools and colleges because it was said to support immorality and impurity.[32]

This is demonstrated in the next major translation into English of the play, that of Monier-Williams, published in 1855, entitled *Sakoontala* or *The Lost Ring*. Monier-Williams was associated with the Boden Chair at Oxford and was Professor of Sanskrit at Haileybury College where those who were to be posted out to administer India were being trained. His was clearly an influential point of view. His intention in doing a new translation was motivated by the thought which he expresses in the introduction to the translation, that:

> A great people, who, through their empire in India, command the destinies of the eastern world, ought surely to be conversant with the most popular of Indian dramas, in which the customs of the Hindus, their opinions, prejudices and fables; their religious rites, daily occupations and amusements, are reflected as in a mirror.

Apart from the fact that this was good copy for his own translation, one wonders whether he really thought that most Indians in the past lived either in forests or in royal courts. The play was seen as a vignette of Hindu life. That there was a distance of at least fifteen hundred years between the time of the original writing of the play and these translations did not not seem to matter, for it was believed that Indian society has been a static society and not registered much change from early times.

The reading of the play was beginning to shift from Shakuntala being the child of nature or the 'rustic maiden' of Monier-Williams, to her innocence being subverted by passion. Nature and culture were no longer in oppositional juxtaposition, for nature had receded and what were perceived as the mores of culture were being foregrounded and would gradually become essential to assessing the actions of Shakuntala. The nineteenth-century concern with the morality of the woman was in itself a critique of nature, that is, of those beyond the confines of settled society. The subject of morality comes to be conceptualized in a variety of ways, each underlining the importance of this issue.

Monier-Williams' translation soon became standard and was extremely popular. The publication of the play gave it a huge audience and doubtless further encouraged the translations of the play from Sanskrit into the Indian regional languages, which increased the audience. In the eighth edition published in 1898, Monier-Williams reiterates the two-way policy of acquainting Europe with Oriental ideas and reviving Indian culture for its own people. He states:

> a literal translation . . . might have commended itself to Oriental students, but would not have given a true idea of the beauty of India's most cherished drama to general readers, whose minds are cast in a European mould and who require a translator to clothe Oriental ideas, as far as practicable, in a dress comfortable to European canons of taste.

He adds: 'The English student at least, is bound by considerations of duty, as well as curiosity to make himself acquainted with a subject which elucidates and explains the conditions of the millions of Hindus who owe allegiance to his own sovereign, and are governed by English laws'. This is followed by a little self-congratulation: . . . 'youthful English-speaking Indians—cultured young men educated at the Universities of Calcutta, Madras and Bombay—have acted the Sakoontala in the very words of my translations'.[33] As proof of this last point, he includes in this edition of the book a letter from V. Padmanabha Aiyer of Trivandrum dated 1893 and referring to such a performance. The letter states:

> The Hindus have a great liking for this play and not one of the enlightened Hindu community will fail to acknowledge your translation to be a very perfect one. Our object in acting Hindu plays is to bring home to the Hindus the good lessons that our ancient authors are able to teach us.

Evidently the Indian middle class in some areas was reading the play in English translation and performing it likewise. Was this to encourage the British in India also to attend the performances and be educated in 'Hindu culture' especially where the offending passages had been expurgated? By now there were just a few who still had the enthusiasm of William Jones. Such performances were advertised in the newspapers and a short summary of the story was included. Or was there in the larger towns already a cross-section of the Indian middle class speaking different regional languages and therefore attending performances in English? The Parsi Elphinstone Dramatic Society founded in 1861 in Bombay staged plays in English. There were also the Kalidasa Elphinstone Dramatic Society and the Victoria Natak Mandali, both performing the plays of Shakespeare and Kalidasa, the latter either in Sanskrit or in translations into Marathi, Gujarati and Hindi. In 1867, the Monier Williams translation was staged.

The first printed edition of the play in Sanskrit dates to 1791. Translations from Sanskrit into the regional languages of India were published in the latter part of the nineteenth century. Presumably, prior to that the Sanskrit version was better known and translations into other Indian languages would have remained in manuscript form. The nineteenth-century translations were received with enthusiasm and the narrative came to be incorporated into dance forms as well. The play was assessed as a gem from what was now being called 'the classical age of Indian culture', and the fact that it had been so widely appreciated in Europe, added to its prestige in Indian eyes.

What is most noticeable in these comments and the reception of the play at this time is that there was a shift to viewing the play as specifically a representation of Hindu culture, and according to Monier-Williams it provided a glimpse of the Hindu subjects of the British empire. This was a somewhat different argument from that of

William Jones who saw it as encapsulating a different civilization. For Jones, the Hindus of earlier times represented the condition of human society prior to its dispersal; therefore they were part of the pre-history of human history. Nevertheless, even for him, Indian culture was Hindu and he warned against following 'the muddy rivulets of Musalman writing in India instead of drinking from the pure fountain of Hindu learning'.[34] Inevitably, from this period, texts such as the play came to be viewed as Hindu texts *per se.* This was a new perspective on the narrative, for, in the literary analyses of the major figures of Sanskrit literary theory such as Abhinavagupta or Raghavabhatta when writing specifically on *Abhijnana-shakuntalam,* the religious identity of the play is incidental.

Where William Jones was curious and even adulatory, Monier-Williams is condescending and imperious and this represents at one level the change from Company rule to Imperial rule. The Mills and the Macaulays and the Evangelicals had left their imprint. Appreciation of what was projected as Hindu culture had to be spelt out for the Indian middle class. Cultural articulations which could be controlled were, from the colonial perspective, preferred, for they reduced such articulations to a kind of neutrality in which both the colonizers and the colonized could interact comfortably. The literature of the Indian past was being accepted but with appropriate deletions. The latter were seen as necessary to prepare Indians to move towards a society sanctioned by Victorian values.

In 1871 Ishwarachandra Vidyasagar had published the play and this became the standard text[35] for students learning Sanskrit. Therefore that which was thought to be erotic and indelicate was deleted. This new fastidiousness, both imposed on and expressive of the Indian middle class, was a radical change from the audiences of earlier times who read the play or saw it performed and were not embarrassed by the amorous scenes. This 'moral' tone was partly borrowed from the more recent Orientalist scholarship and was endorsed from the appropriating of Victorian views. In terms of Victorian values the connotation of virtue was substantially that of sexual chastity. Where British Orientalists may even on occasion have conceded erotic freedom, their Indian counterparts would by this time have become fearful of embarrassment and ensuing denigration. The imprint of what is believed to be virtuous can be severe.

The moral tone was also partly derived from family life

requiring the subordination of women. This is not to suggest that in earlier periods the daughter, the wife and the mother in the family were liberated women, but at least concessions to human relationships could be made in the fantasy world of literature. It would also have had to do with the fact that these texts were now published, were taught in schools and colleges, and were read by young men and women. The censoring of the text avoided giving publicity to situations and relationships which were considered transgressions by late nineteenth-century codes of social behaviour. The printing of a text makes it available to a large and varied audience. Therefore in the early stage of printed texts it was thought necessary to exercise a considered choice in what was printed. This is particularly the case when there are also the pressures of attempting to construct a homogenous national culture.

By the end of the nineteenth century, the life of the play was to move in yet another direction. A national culture for India was being chiselled. In this the early past was envisaged as a utopian period and the more idyllic descriptions from literature were quoted as reflecting a different reality from the present. *Abhijnana-shakuntalam* was a major text in this perspective, marking both a quality of life that was superior as also a much appreciated literary achievement, the appreciation being both from the Sanskrit and the European traditions. The reading of the main character of the play, Shakuntala, was from a nineteenth-century perspective and related therefore to the perceptions of the ideal woman as defined by the Indian middle class, and was clothed in sentiments which drew not just from indigenous sources but also reflected the views of Orientalism, Romanticism and Victorian England. She was no longer the child of nature of German Romanticism, for her love in its natural form had to be chastened by suffering, as Tagore saw it.[36] The woman who emerged was the ideal woman: romantic but essentially submissive. Thus, the play, as a historical event, was to take on yet another reading.

Notes and References

[1] This essay is drawn from a more detailed study of the narrative of Shakuntala at various points in time.

[2] G. Canon, *The Life and Mind of Oriental Jones,* Cambridge University Press, Cambridge, 1990.

[3] P. Morgan, 'From a Death to a View: The Hunt for the Welsh Past in the

Romantic Period,' in E. Hobsbawm and T. Ranger, *The Invention of Tradition*, Cambridge University Press, Cambridge, 1996 (rpt).

4   M. Abrams, *Natural Supernaturalism*, Columbia University Press, New York, 1971, pp. 87–88.

5   S.N. Mukherjee, *Sir William Jones: a study in Eighteenth Century British Attitudes to India*, Cambridge University Press, Cambridge, 1968, p. 105. This label encouraged a variety of comparisons in the late nineteenth century between Shakuntala and the heroines of Shakespeare such as Miranda and Desdemona.

6   G. Canon and S. Pandey, 'Sir William Jones Revisited: on his translation of the Shakuntala,' *Journal of the American Oriental Society*, 96, 4, 1976, pp. 528–37.

7   Ibid.

8   Quoted in W. Liefer, *India and the Germans*, Shakuntala Publishing House, Bombay, 1977.

9   A. Leslie Willson, *A Mythical Image: The Ideal of India in German Romanticism*, Duke University Press, Durham, 1964.

10   Ibid., p. 69. Translation and quotation.

11   M. Schuyler, 'The Editions and Translations of Shakuntala,' *Journal of the American Oriental Society*, 22, 1901, pp. 237–48.

12   G. Steiner, *Antigones*, The Clarendon Press, Oxford, 1984.

13   A. Leslie Willson, *Mythical Image*, p. 148 ff.

14   Ibid., p. 49 ff.

15   *Werke*, XVI, 85–91. Quoted in J. Sedlar, *India in the Mind of Germany*, Washington 1982, p. 26 ff.

16   Leslie Willson, *Mythical Image*, p. 221 ff.

17   Ibid., p. 148 ff.

18   H. Drew, *India and the Romantic Imagination*, Oxford University Press, Delhi, 1987.

19   Ibid., M.J. Franklin, *Sir William Jones*, University of Wales Press, Cardiff, 1995, p. 9.

20   *The Edinburgh Review*, July 1858, Article X, p. 253 ff.

21   R. Schwab, *The Oriental Renaissance: Europe's Rediscovery of India and the East, 1680–1880*, (trans.) Columbia University Press, New York, 1984.

22   Max Muller, *India, What Can it Teach Us?*, Longmans Green and Co., London, 1883, p. 101.

23   T.B. Hanson, 'Inside the Romanticist Episteme', *Thesis Eleven*, 48, 1997, pp. 21–41.

24   Ibid.

25   H. Kohn, *The Idea of Nationalism: A Study of Its Origins and Background*, Macmillan, New York, 1944.

26   Schwab, *Oriental Renaissance*.

27   D.M. Figueira, *Translating the Orient*, SUNY, Albany, 1991, p. 25 ff.

28   M. Praz, *The Romantic Agony*, London, 1933.

29   *History of British India*, II. 2., Chelsea House Publishers, New York, 1968 (5th edn), p. 111.

[30] G. Visvanathan, *Masks of Conquest*, Columbia University Press, New York, 1989, p. 121 ff.

[31] Ibid.

[32] Ibid., pp. 5–6; p. 27 ff.

[33] Monier-Williams, *Sakoontala*, Routledge and Sons, London, 1898 (8th edn), pp. vi, vii, xv.

[34] *Asiatic Researches*, III. p. 65; I. pp. 223–24 ; II. pp. 58–63.

[35] D.K. Kanjilal, *A Reconstruction of the Abhijnana-Shakuntalam*, Sanskrit College, Calcutta, 1908.

[36] R. Tagore, 'Shakuntala, Its Inner Meaning', *Modern Review*, 9, 1911, p. 171 ff.

Is Buddhism the Answer to Brahmanical Patriarchy?

Uma Chakravarti

Is Buddhism the answer to Brahmanical patriarchy? Perhaps it is, given the crucial connection between patriarchy and caste in Hindu society. Due to the fact that Buddhism does not provide religious sanction to the caste system like Brahmanism does and, indeed, is critical of birth-based identities and privileges which are regarded as a creation of the Brahmanas to ensure their own dominance, makes Buddhism a crucial intervention in understanding caste. Since caste is a secular institution, created by human beings, it can also be destroyed by human agency. The specific characteristic of Brahmanical patriarchy is that it is a set of rules and institutions in which caste and gender are linked. Each shapes the other and women are crucial in maintaining the boundaries between castes. To the extent that Buddhism, or Buddhists, rejects caste not merely at the ideological level but can break the connection between caste and gender in practice, Buddhism can be one kind of answer to Brahmanical patriarchy. However, we need to explore the practice of Buddhism in societies like Sri Lanka where a diluted form of caste system exists and where different patriarchies are prevalent, including those within the Buddhist *sangha*. What needs to be stressed is that an enabling ideology at a given point of time in history needs to be interpreted along radical lines continuously, through people's struggles, for it to be a useful counter to a deeply hierarchical ideology—which Brahmanism and Brahmanical patriarchy certainly are. But this is not enough because hierarchies in India operate not only at the level of ideology; they are premised upon a sharply stratified material structure. Therefore, struggles to transform social relations, including a wholesale rejection of caste and endogamous marriages, must accompany any move towards the adoption of a more humane ideology. This paper explore some of these issues.

Anyone who is not a high-caste Hindu male in Indian society or being one, does not want to be part of a privileged structure, should be expected to look for alternatives to Brahmanism and Brahmanical patriarchy in order to make it possible to step out from some of the oppressions experienced by the relatively less privileged. Perhaps that is what impelled me to examine Buddhism as an alternative to Brahmanism as an ideological formation. Growing up in the first decades following independence, I was aware of the humanist impulses of the post-independence era and the celebrations commemorating 2,500 years of Buddhism in India. I was also somewhat vaguely conscious of the mass conversion of the dalits, led by Ambedkar, to Buddhism in 1956, although as an adolescent of fifteen I did not understand the radical import of the event. Nevertheless, an interest in Buddhism had been awakened and inevitably I was drawn to researching the social milieu that had given birth to Buddhism for my first piece of academic work. Looking back, I can see that what those of us who found the hierarchies of caste and gender unacceptable were trying to do, was to find something enabling in a tradition which we were always being told to adhere to but which we were, for the most part, at loggerheads with.

My research led me to two conclusions. First, the Buddha is the greatest social philosopher that India—perhaps the world—produced, at least in my view. Second, unless we *historicize* him and go beyond him and his ideological formulations we will not be able to address the complexities of our society or work towards a transformation of social relations, including the social relations of production, and make an intervention in the politics of our times.

To begin with, let me try and historicize the Buddha.[1] Scholars of early India have been struck by the vitality and proliferation of ideas in the sixth century BC, the era in which Buddhism, Jainism, Ajivikism, materialism and a host of other less fully worked out philosophies made their appearance. Scholars have also pointed to the historical context, the material and social milieu in which these ideas were generated and the overwhelming experience of change; it is no wonder, then, that Buddhism has been described as the metaphysics of perpetual change. This sense of continual flux, *anicca*, may have influenced women and men to experience a sense of alienation and perhaps this explains the wide-ranging search for the meaning of human existence, best epitomized by the personal search of the Buddha himself. But

25

what precisely was the historical context that created the sense of uprootedness, of anomie?

I have described elsewhere the political, economic and social changes noticeable in the age of the Buddha. The shift towards an intensive agrarian economy in the Ganga valley and the appearance of private holdings of land, some large enough to require the labour of a great number of *dasa-kammakaras*, servile labourers, made for a basic distinction between those who wielded control over land and those who laboured. The Buddhist texts are replete with juxtapositions of the rich with the poor, the great and the humble. Even the graphic and sensitive descriptions that we see of poverty and the use of the word *dalida* (Pali for destitute) appear for the first time in Indian literature and, perhaps for the first and last time, poverty is included in any philosopher's frame of reference. Descriptions of power as well as its despotic and arbitrary nature in the hands of individuals who are accountable to no one are also unique to Buddhist literature. Apart from economic stratification between those who control the means of production and those who labour, there is evidence of social stratification between those who are regarded as low and those who are regarded as high, corresponding to those who work for themselves and those who work for others, in the schema adopted by the Buddhist texts. At the same time the Brahmanas were claiming superior ascriptive status by virtue of birth. There was stratification along gender lines too and a sexual division of labour was firmly in place. Inheritance was patrilineal and control over female sexuality was well established. In sum, there were broadly two classes of people: those who had power and those who were subordinated, a dramatically different situation from the earlier less sharply stratified communities.

Being a witness to such changes, certain concerns for the Buddha such as *dukkha* (sorrow) and *tanha* (desire, greed) were organically linked to the society of the sixth century BC and have historical roots. Even though they are metaphysical rather than social concepts, social concerns have inevitably shaped the centrality of *dukkha* as a metaphysical concept and imbued Buddhism with a deep humanism.

Apart from the metaphysical level, the Buddha also responded more directly to the social contradictions playing themselves out in the society of his time. But first a word of caution before proceeding further. Buddhism, it must be remembered, originated in a society that was rapidly changing but had not yet revealed the fully developed formation that the hierarchical Indian system was to become. Only the direction could be seen and this did make it possible for the Buddha to be dialectical in his approach to the problems of his day even without the precise contours of the new formation and the extent of the ramifications being clear. The Buddha's social intervention was dual in its thrust: the really radical solutions to the problems of his day were applied in the world of the *sangha* (the Buddhist monastic order) through the creation of an egalitarian structure where birth-based or property-based distinctions were abolished, and where all members of the *sangha* shared the resources that the community placed at their disposal. The *sangha* was an imaginative recreation of the prestratified, community-based clan political formations, the *gana-sanghas* of his day which were then being swamped by the new aggressive monarchies of the Ganga valley. The world outside the *sangha*, a world of individual property holders—Gahapatis and Brahmanas, and power wielders—kings and Khattiyas (Pali for Kshatriya) was humanized through appropriate modifications. Poverty was to be eradicated but for a society where inequalities of economic and political power were already well entrenched and outside of the Buddha's direct ambit, he provided codes of civilized interpersonal conduct. Kings, landholders, labourers and householders, both men and women, were all advised to follow certain codes of responsibilities to achieve a civilized and harmonious society. This society was to be humane even if inequalities of wealth, power and status remained. Social conflict was to be managed rather than resolved through eradication, by whatever means, of existing inequalities. Even the very visible tense relationship between Buddhism and Brahmanism as articulated in the Buddhist texts, especially the *Jatakas* and the *Therigatha*, suggests that conflicts emanating from the caste hierarchy, which were unambiguously opposed by the Buddhists, were to be resolved decisively mainly on the intellectual and philosophical plane rather than through social strife.[2]

One major lacuna in early Buddhism was that neither in theory nor in practice was the question of gender-based inequality *seriously* addressed. Initially women were not even admitted into the *sangha*. It was only after Ananda, the Buddha's closest disciple, intervened on their behalf that women were permitted entry into the *sangha*, and even then they were not granted equality with the monks. In fact, the *bhikkhunis* were placed under the authority of the *bhikkhus* and the Buddha was unrelenting on this rule even though the *bhik-khunis* resented its imposition. Thus, Buddhism failed to incorporate a critique of gender inequality into its framework even though it abolished birth-based and wealth-based distinctions within the *sangha*.[3] Perhaps this gender bias in the original framework of Buddhism has made for the slide to a full-scale accommodation with patriarchies in countries such as Thailand and Sri Lanka where Buddhism became dominant. In Sri Lanka, even the entry of women into the *sangha* died out by the thirteenth century and women today are fighting a battle for its restoration.[4]

A significant aspect of society at the time of the Buddha from the standpoint of this essay is that caste as a system of 'graded inequality'[5] was yet to reach its full-blown form; in fact, the Buddhist texts reflect a simple two-tier system of stratification rather than the complex system of ranking presently associated with caste. Early in the first millenium AD, despite the support of individual kings and considerable popular support for Buddhism, the Brahmanic social organization as reflected in the *Dharmashastras*, especially Manu, seemed to be gaining a firm footing in the agrarian areas of the subcontinent. The most striking feature of Manu's prescriptive text was its discussion of the *varna-sankara*, or the mixing of castes. Devised as a theoretical tool to provide for caste elaboration and the proliferation of caste groups, *varna-sankara* made possible a triangular structure, which was narrow at the surplus-controlling top and broad at the labour-providing base. The low castes were many at the base and the high castes were few at the top.[6] The system of graded inequality was such that each caste in a given area was higher and lower than others in an ascending scale of reverence and descending scale of contempt, as aptly described by Ambedkar.[7] Each caste was also a closed, bounded group and the whole structure relied on endogamy to reproduce itself. Caste was also linked to class and production relations although it was not entirely congruent to it. Further, state power was necessary to reproduce the system—no wonder, then, that the king plays a critical role in the Brahmanic Hindu social organization and Manu devotes a number of clauses to the duties of the king.[8] As the structure became firmly entrenched, local dominant groups reenacted kingly power to reinforce caste and gender inequality, as I have shown elsewhere.[9]

It should be fairly clear from the preceding paragraphs that the understanding of caste as an *ideological* system, based on the irreconciliable opposition of the principles of purity and pollution as outlined by Dumont[10] and now dominating the discipline of sociology, is completely unsatisfactory, especially from the point of view of those who have been condemned to occupy the bottom rungs under degrading conditions of existence. Apart from being Brahmanocentric, it is totally unmindful of the very material dimensions of the caste system. Caste for me is not the opposition between pure and impure; more fundamentally, it incorporates other kinds of oppositions such as domination and subordination, exploitation and oppression based on unequal access to material resources, and is close to the formulations of Joan Mencher and Gerald Berreman[11] and especially to Claude Meillasoux for his ability to build class into the framework of caste. In a masterly formulation Meillasoux argued that the notion of the impure was required to keep the low in a state of subordination.[12] Denial of knowledge was a crucial part of the ideology of the caste system and it was one of the most elementary forms and formulations of inequality in traditional India.[13] Not only did it succeed in crippling the exploited castes but it also led to the Brahmanic ideology of the social order becoming hegemonic—the only knowledge system to explain caste for all time, leading directly to the Dumontian framework of today.

Meillasoux's outlining of the relationship between caste and class as it developed over the centuries is useful from the point of view of this essay because it helps to bridge two major moments in history: the move from a pre-Manu social formation, well-delineated in the early Buddhist literature and broadly reflecting the period from the fifth century BC to the third century BC, to the structure outlined by Manu in the first or second century AD; and from the structure reflected in the *Dharmashastras*, including Manu (roughly second century AD to sixth century AD), to contemporary social reality. This will enable us also to understand better the problem that we posed at the beginning of this essay—is Buddhism the answer to Brahmanical patriarchy? But we can now expand it to: Is Buddhism the answer to the caste system itself, which after all is the basis of Brahmanical patriarchy?

Meillasoux begins his insightful essay by taking a strong position against the structuralist analysis of caste led by Dumont. He argues that an enveloping (and we may add static) concept of caste conceals a complex and heterogeneous social reality which is continually shifting and which the structural analysis of caste does not, indeed cannot, capture.[14] Drawing from prescriptive texts, myths and literature, systems of representations are imposed by structuralists upon social reality by ideologies and doctrines rather than by drawing from the social reality itself. In the real social process it is the relations of production and reproduction that define social groups and not the other way around. The representations of the Brahmanical prescriptive texts, thus, must be confronted with *lived social reality* which is sometimes hidden, but which an analysis of material relations can make clear.[15]

Some of Meillasoux's formulations are borne out by the evidence of the Buddhist texts where the Buddha is often depicted as *contesting* the claim of the Brahmanas to inherent superiority by virtue of their birth as Brahmanas. Apart from demystifying the birth-based superiority claim by showing the similarities in the biological processes of birth, the Buddha also points out that the Brahamanical claim to the services of other castes was invalid, as anyone who had wealth, regardless of their origins, was in a position to buy the services of others; there was no inherent right to the labour of the Sudras, as the Brahmanas were demanding. He also argued that in the north-western parts of the subcontinent there were *aryas* and *dasas* and their positions were mutually reversible.[16] Subordination was not everlasting and it was certainly not a factor of birth-based, fixed identities in the age of the Buddha. This description of wealth and the capacity to buy the services of others suggests the flexibility of class rather than the fixity of caste. Such class relationships, becoming reified, had depended less on birth than on the possession of land, and threatened the social order being sought to be consolidated by the Brahmanas. To move from such flexibility to fixity, the manipulation of relationships between various categories of people through marriage was a crucial factor. (Marriages between the twice-born could be endogamous or hypergamous but marriage between twice-born men and Sudra women, even though hypergamous, was forbidden by the early Brahmanical prescriptive texts.) Marriage prohibitions thus 'distinguished the dominant classes from the subject class'.[17] Over the centuries the fixity was further facilitated through severe punishment for hypogamous relationships between women of the upper castes and men of the lower castes on pain of death to the erring man. Servility was thus *enforced* upon a whole group of people through a series of coercive moves. Barred also from knowledge, the conditions imposed upon the lower orders were those of an 'alienated and depersonalized class—a class kept in subjection by being denied any participation in the society of men, and kept as a group apart, a group of social defectives, by means of religion and force.'[18]

Finally, when the structure was complete, Brahmanic Hinduism froze a historic moment by codifying definitively the privileges, prerogatives, functions and duties of each class and imposed them with the force of a religious ideology. As Jakubowsky puts it, they are only 'the atrophied forms of relationships of production which had developed organically'.[19] In contemporary society the historic developments are manifested as a situation where there are 'two kinds of castes: those who hold the land and those who do not.'[20] The land-holders represent the dominant class but they are also the dominant castes of the sociologists which wield political power and reproduce the royal function at the village level, monopolizing authority and dispensing justice. The largest other social group in the village is the group of exploited castes who are today kept in servitude through loans: as Kosambi recognized, there was no need for largescale slavery in India, as the same function of providing a pliant labour force was performed by the caste system[21] and debt bondage. The entire exploitative structure was of course sustained by religious ideology, or more aptly religious *terrorism* in the words of Meillasoux, but also by violence.

What is additionally notable in the processes of transition outlined earlier is the resolution of another tension depicted in the Buddhist texts between the Brahmanas and the Khattiyas, evident also in earlier Brahmanical texts such as the *Satapatha* and *Aitareya Brahmanas*.[22] In the status order, though entitled to a share of the surplus, the Brahmanas were clients of the Khattiyas and dependent on them. However, they gradually obtained from their 'protectors', through land grants, direct rights on the lands which enabled them to establish, to their profit relations of production, and to escape their economic subordination as clients. In this way they came to exploit the populace directly and to assume protective and administrative functions as the dominant caste in many parts of the subcontinent.[23] Evidence of this through the practice of the grant of land is available in the Buddhist texts but reaches its full articulation in the post-Gupta era. Summing up his arguments, Meillasoux states that in the present Indian society, according to the system of castes, the idea is to pile into a vertical linear hierarchy groups that have a basic organic relationship with the economic structure, where the dominating and dominated are ranged at

31

the top and bottom of this hierarchic scale. Linked to values, this formal hierarchic framework was capable of embracing any new group whose labour the top layers could use by inflicting any of its abstract cultural criteria upon the group. The ideological representation of Indian reality *having a historical and dialectical basis* was able to thus facilitate the shift between changing relations of production and the fixed principle of the status hierarchy of *varna* which reflected the class structure at a given moment in history. The caste system represents for Meillasoux the perpetuation and adaptation of status relationships and status ideology within a class society that was constantly changing under the impact of internal and external forces, as a means of domination of the social groups at the top of the production system.[24] Kosambi has also recognized that the principal function of the caste system now is its *negation of history*; the caste system in his view is designed to preserve Indian society in a static mould,[25] and thus, preserve the domination of particular groups in Indian society.

The principle of pure and impure is strongly critiqued by Meillasoux who exposes its inconsistencies and its failure to explain the low status of certain occupations such as those of the boatman or the potter. Further, the killing of men and the meat-eating of Khattiyas did not reduce them to the status of butchers or fishermen, whose status as landholders and wielders of political power put them at the top of the class hierarchy. Rejecting the 'crude symbolism' of the purity–impurity dichotomy, Meillasoux argues that 'in reality impurity was one more weapon in a repressive ideological arsenal used in one direction only, arbitrarily and opportunistically, as a means of discrimination, oppression and exploitation'. The notion of impurity was used *opportunistically* as the most powerful means of protection against social contamination and to *codify and reinforce pre-existing relations of subordination and alienation* (emphasis added). Meillasoux draws our attention to the importance of alienation from the means of production, since 'one must be alienated if one had to accept being impure'. This is why the caste system cannot be terminated through acts of subversion in which the low use their pollution as a weapon against the higher castes. Those at the top continually back up the purity principle by persecution, denial of access to material resources, and violence to keep the lower orders in their impurity.[26]

From the point of this essay the whole of this complex formation was contingent on Brahmanical patriarchy; so to that we must now turn. To understand the significance of Brahmanical patriarchy we need to recognize that it is not merely a routine variant within the framework of the subordination of women but is a structure unique to Hinduism and the caste order. The term Brahmanical patriarchy is a useful way to isolate this unique structure of patriarchy which is by now dominant in many parts of India. It is a set of rules and institutions in which caste and gender are linked, each shaping the other, and where women are crucial in maintaining the boundaries between castes. Patriarchal codes in this structure ensure that the caste system can be reproduced without violating the hierarchical order of closed endogamous circles, each distinct from and higher and lower than others. Further, Brahmanical codes for women differ according to the status of the caste group in the hierarchy of castes, with the most stringent control over sexuality reserved as a privilege for the highest castes. Finally, it incorporates both an ideology of chaste wives and *pativrata* women who are valorized, and a structure of rules and institutions by which caste hierachy and gender inequality are maintained through both the production of consent and the application of coercion. In sum, Brahmanical patriarchy implies the model of patriarchy outlined in the Brahmanical prescriptive texts, to be enforced by the coercive power of the king or those who act on behalf of the king. This set of norms has shaped the ideology of the upper castes in particular. It continues to be the underpinning of beliefs and practices extant even today among these castes, and is often emulated by the lower castes, especially when seeking upward mobility. What the lower castes doing so have not recognized is that since Brahmanical patriarchy is structurally integrated into the caste system the distinctive cultural codes for upper and lower-caste women in terms of marriage and sexuality are also closely linked to the appropriation of the labour of the lower castes by the upper castes. This explains the ban on remarriage of the upper-caste woman at one end and, sometimes, the enforced cohabitation of the lower-caste woman at the other. *The larger 'rationale' of the caste system as a system of labour appropriation has shaped the codes of gender to further the ends of the upper castes.*[27]

From the discussion above it can be seen that Brahmanical patriarchy is a mechanism to preserve land, women and ritual quality within it. If we add to this the necessity of ensuring a labour supply to work the land, we can see that caste and patriarchy in the social formation of early India required not only control of women's reproductive power of the upper castes through whom the closed structure of land and ritual quality was to be preserved, *but of all castes to ensure an adequate labour supply*; This was achieved through the unique form of demographic control described above.

Under Brahmanical patriarchy, women of the upper castes are regarded as gateways—literally, points of entry into the caste system. The lower-caste male whose sexuality is a threat to upper-caste purity of blood has to be institutionally prevented from having sexual access to women of the higher castes, so such women have to be carefully guarded. Miscegeny or *pratilomic varnasankara*, hypogamous relationships, represents the breakdown of the elaborate edifice of social order, epitomized in the anxiety about *kaliyuga*—a time when families are broken, rites are forgotten and women are defiled. When women and lower castes do not conform to the rules, that is *kaliyuga*.

Given the fact that the caste system and Brahmanical patriarchy work to the advantage of very few men at the top of the order, all others who are *complicit* in this system only ensure the reproduction of this very unequal structure. It is ironical, therefore, that Brahmanical patriarchy's obsessive concern with controlling female sexuality and ensuring the reproduction of pure blood—the earliest evidence we have for an abhorrent form of genetic engineering—has survived across all caste groups, high and low, in a way that changes in legal forms and even liberal ideologies have not been able to break. What is tragic is that the lower castes too, especially in north India,[28] strongly monitor female sexuality for purposes of exogamy but also more generally, thus reproducing the bio-genetic map of inequality *without being conscious that these norms are derived from the very structures that oppress them in other ways.*

In its fully worked-out form following Manu, *varnasankara* theory, untouchability, caste-based patriarchal codes and a certain kind of production relations in an agrarian society with state power backing both the caste system and patriarchal practices, we have a very complex formation operating in India. Can the humanism and ethical codes of Buddhism break this complex structure, so contingent upon endogamy and so entrenched in India even today? Without creative interpretation and radicalizing inputs it is unlikely, particularly when we recall that the more radical solutions in terms of production and reproduction had been provided for by the Buddha in the *sangha*, where the *bhikkhu* and *bhikkhunis* abstained from both, not in the

34

world of social relations. This is a crucial failure, especially because the world of production and reproduction in the social world outside the *sangha*, both of which were contingent on endogamy, was left without *radical* alteration. On hindsight it might even appear that the humanism of Buddhism failed to *intervene* in a process where caste was yet embryonic but was expanding as a formation because its humanism alone was not effective enough to create a decisive impact on the direction of change. Perhaps we may even argue that because it was focused at the level of ideology and the creation of parallel institutions but did not address itself to transforming material structures it could not become hegemonic—Brahmanism was more successful at becoming the hegemonic ideology because it rationalized caste, and the caste system enabled a particular mode of production and labour relations to expand to different areas—and so it was of greater use to those in power. Humanist solutions cannot break social relations and are not a substitute for class struggle—in India it would have to be caste-cum-class struggle given the connection between caste and class here.

Thus, when it comes to the inequalities prevalent in contemporary society, how effective can Buddhism be today in combating this complex formation where caste, class, gender and power are so intertwined and where women of the upper castes and men and women of the lower castes are all complicit in marriage arrangements? We need first to *critically assess the historical experience of Buddhism.* As I have argued earlier, the Buddha was a product of his times and was concerned about the nature of the changes the people in his society were experiencing. As a sensitive, humane, and above all, rational human being, he responded to these changes by providing humane solutions to the problems of inequality. But being concerned with the end to human misery at the metaphysical level his creative energies went in shaping the *sangha*, the necessary base for those who were pursuing the goal of *nibbana*, which was the ultimate end of every Buddhist. For those who want to see an end to inequality in the social world, in the world of lived social reality, the humanity and creativity of Buddhism can be enabling but not anywhere near enough: one would have to engage in struggles to radically transform social and material relations which no social philosopher in India, not even the Buddha, has to date made the central focus of their attention. On the issue of gender subordination we would have to go much farther than the Buddha did, but gender relations are a part of social and material relations as we will readily recognize now. The very complexity of the formation that I have tried to outline here indicates that no philosophy that is engaged with a system in-the-making can provide all the solutions to the social contradictions of a vastly differentiated society.

In any case, how useful is religion in dealing with the social relations between men and men and between men and women? Besides, an ideological shift means very little without real struggles on the ground to change social relations, and that Buddhism did not centrally build into its framework of ideas. To transform contemporary social relations we will also have to draw on socialism, feminism and anti-caste movements of the nineteenth and twentieth centuries.

I do not, however, want to give the impression that the mass conversion of many sections of the dalits to Buddhism in the last few decades is futile. Apart from the very important political import of the conversion which rejects the degradation, exploitation and inhumanity of caste so intrinsic to Hinduism (however much its apologists might try to disentangle the religion from its social practice), which I wholeheartedly support, it represents the search for a code of ethics and a larger culture which provides everyone with dignity and can, therefore, fill a crucial vacuum in the lives of those who adopt Buddhism. Further, because Buddhism does not provide 'religious' sanction to hierarchies of caste, class or even gender, but clearly regards them as purely secular arrangements which societies create, it also recognizes that these can change. And also, because Buddhism upholds *kammavada* and regards human beings as agents of their own destinies, it provides tools which can be built upon by those looking for more radical solutions than the Buddha himself was able to formulate for his own society. The whole edifice of caste and its linkage with class, as well as its peculiar manifestation of gender in the form of Brahmanical patriarchy needs to be eradicated *in its entirety*. Obviously there are no easy solutions, but as a beginning, we must have conceptual clarity. We also need to distinguish between what could be enabling and what if used uncritically could be disabling. If this paper can contribute in any way to a clarification of the basic issues that it has tried to address, some of the concerns that led me to research the age of the Buddha would be fulfilled, at least in part.

This paper was first read at a seminar organized by the Department of Political Science, Poona University, on Ambedkar and Buddhism: Revisioning the World, at Pune in

October 1998. I am grateful to the participants for their lively discussions on my presentation as well as others; these discussions have helped to shape the arguments in this version of the presentation.

Notes and References

1   I will rely on my published work on Buddhism, particularly the following, for the arguments that I am making in this paper: Uma Chakravarti, *The Social Dimensions of Early Buddhism*, Oxford University Press, Delhi, 1987; 'The Social Philosophy of Buddhism and the Problem of Inequality', *Social Compass*, 33 (2–3), 1986, pp. 199–222; 'Women, Men and Beasts: The Jatakas as Popular Tradition', *Studies in History*, 9 (1) n.s. 1993, pp. 43–70; 'Buddhism as a Discourse of Dissent: Class and Gender,' *Pravada*, 1(5), May 1992, pp. 12–18.

2   Chakravarti, 'Women, Men and Beasts,' p. 68.

3   One major point of distinction between Buddhism and Brahmanism in the context of women is that the Buddha accepted that the goals for men and women were the same, the pursuit of a higher life ending in *nibbana*, the blowing out of an individual human existence and the cessation of the cycle of birth, death and rebirth. Women were not promised salvation by mere devotion to husbands. Consequently, many women left what one Buddhist woman in the Therigatha described as the drudgery of the pestle and mortar, the misery of kitchen-work, to become *arhats*, those who had achieved the highest status of a Buddhist (Uma Chakravarti, 'The Rise of Buddhism as Experienced by Women', *Manushi*, no. 8, 1981, pp. 6–10).

4   Kumari Jayawardena, 'Sinhala Buddhism and the "Daughters of the Soil", *Pravada*, 1(8), May 1992, pp. 24–26.

5   Oliver Herrenschmidt, 'Ambedkar and the Hindu Social Order', paper presented at seminar on Ambedkar and Buddhism, Poona, October 1998.

6   S.J. Tambiah, 'From Varna to Caste through Mixed Unions', in Jack Goody, ed., *Character of Kinship*, Cambridge University Press, Cambridge, 1973, pp. 191–229.

7   Herrenschidmt, 'Ambedkar and the Hindu Social Order'.

8   *Manudharmashastra*, translated and edited by Wendy O'Flaherty and Brian Smith as *Laws of Manu*, Penguin Books, Delhi, 1991.

9   Uma Chakravarti, 'Wifehood, Widowhood and Adultery: Female Sexuality, Surveillance and the State in 18th Century Maharashtra', in Patricia Uberoi, ed., *Social Reform, Sexuality and the State*, Sage Publications, Delhi, 1996, pp. 3–22.

10 Louis Dumont, *Homo Hierarchicus*, Paladin Books, London, 1972.

11 Joan Mencher, 'The Caste System Upside Down, or the Not-So-Mysterious East', *Current Anthropology*, 15(4), 1974, pp. 469–93; Gerald Berreman, 'The Brahmanical View of Caste', *Contributions to Indian Sociology*, n. s. 5, 1971, pp. 16–23.

12 Claude Meillasoux, 'Are There Castes in India', *Economy and Society*, 2(1), 1973, pp. 89–111, p. 107.

37

13 Sheldon Pollock, 'Deep Orientalism? Notes on Sanskrit and Power Beyond the Raj', in Carol A. Breckenridge and Peter van der Veer, eds., *Orientalism and the Post-Colonial Predicament: Perspectives on South Asia,* University of Pennsylvania, Philadelphia, 1993, pp. 76–133, p. 109.

14 Meillasoux, 'Are There Castes in India', p. 92.

15 Ibid.

16 Chakravarti, *Social Dimensions,* pp. 98–100; *Majjhima Nikaya,* translated by I.B. Horner as *The Middle Length Sayings,* Vol. II, Pali Text Society, London, 1975, p. 341–42.

17 Meillasoux, 'Are There Castes in India', p. 97.

18 Ibid., p. 98.

19 F. Jacubowsky, cited in ibid., p. 110.

20 Ibid., p. 100.

21 D.D. Kosambi, 'On a Marxist Approach to Indian Chronology', in A.J. Syed, ed., *D.D. Kosambi on History and Society: Problems of Interpretation,* Department of History, University of Bombay, Bombay, 1985, pp. 79–91, p. 82.

22 R.S. Sharma, *Material Culture and Social Formations in Ancient India,* Macmillan, Delhi, p. 81.

23 Meillasoux, 'Are There Castes in India', p. 96.

24 Ibid., p. 105.

25 Kosambi, 'Caste and Class', in Syed, *D.D. Kosambi on History and Society,* p. 128.

26 Meillasoux, 'Are There Castes in India', pp. 107–08.

27 The discussion on Brahmanical patriarchy is a summary of some of my earlier published work, namely: 'Conceptualizing Brahmanical Patriarchy in Early India: Gender, Caste, Class and State', *Economic and Political Weekly,* 28 (14) 3 April 1993, pp. 579–86; 'Gender, Caste, and Labour: The Ideological and Material Structure of Widowhood', *Economic and Political Weekly,* 30(36), 9 September 1995, pp. 2248–56.

28 See for example Prem Chowdhry, 'Enforcing Cultural Codes: Gender and Violence in Northern India', in Mary E. John and Janaki Nair, *A Question of Silence: Sexual Economies of Modern India,* Kali For Women, Delhi, 1998, pp. 332–67.

The Story of Draupadi's Disrobing

Meanings for Our Times

Rajeswari Sunder Rajan

Among the chief narrative legacies that modern India has inherited in the cultural-religious sphere is the ancient Sanskrit of the *Mahabharata,* with its many variations and revisions to the present day.[1] It is the story of its heroine, Draupadi, and in particular the famous episode of her disrobing, that I subject here to feminist examination and reinterpretation. My interest lies primarily in discovering the resonance of this story in contemporary India and its implications for women. In the latter part of this essay I undertake, consequently, to show how the 'uses of tradition' in postcolonial societies may be understood, drawing upon contemporary social practices and a wide range of modern texts that are connected to the 2,500-year-old story of Draupadi's sexual humiliation.

How to justify such a proceeding, either as history or as criticism? My representation of Draupadi's story is tendentious: I shall confess to reading 'only along the grain of our pressing cultural and personal needs,' a proceeding which Gillian Beer describes as 'hermeneutic retrenchment.' But if such a reading 'brings sharply into focus a pattern of debate within the work hitherto little understood, or marks discursive elements unfulfilled at the historical moments of the text's production,' it may have 'a sound political function,' she grants.[2] Such at least would have been my intention.

The resonance of the *Mahabharata* and its different plots, subplots and episodes is evident from the numerous adaptations, commentaries, revisions, dramatizations and retellings it has undergone in Indian cultural history. Read as psychobiography (Gayatri Spivak's term),[3] we have in the Draupadi story a text that serves as resource for operating relations of power. I do not mean to propose some timeless and unchanging condition of women's oppression in India based upon

39

the wide contemporary currency of the epic's narration of Draupadi's humiliation. On the contrary, it is precisely the potential and the fact of its appropriation by opposite ends of an ideological spectrum—from the patriarchal legitimation of the control of women by inflicting punishment upon them, to claims on Draupadi as a proto-feminist cultural heroine—that claim our attention and that I shall be outlining in what follows.

The first I see reflected in the ubiquity of the phenomenon of that peculiarly Indian form of male sexual behaviour known as 'eve-teasing', most prevalent in the larger metropolitan cities but becoming increasingly an aspect of small-town Indian life; and in its rural counterpart, the practice of women being stripped and paraded naked in public. In the second part of the paper, I discuss these as actions aimed at the sexual humiliation of women—hence as expressions of misogyny or as methods of social control rather than as a pathology of sexual violence, as such. Following this, I point to both the 'moral' that popular cinema draws from its representations of women in such situations, as well as to the language of the law's prohibition of these actions. The concluding section of my paper contains reflections upon recent feminist appropriations and critical 'uses' of the figure of Draupadi.

I

It will be necessary to briefly recapitulate the Draupadi story and its context in the epic to begin with. The disrobing scene occurs in the second book of the *Mahabharata* which narrates the struggle between two clans, the Kauravas and the Pandavas, for the possession of a kingdom. Draupadi is the joint wife of the five Pandava brothers. The Pandavas have successively lost all their possessions, including their kingdom and their own selves, in a gambling match with the Kauravas. They are urged to stake Draupadi in a last throw of the dice. Yudhishthira, the oldest brother, does so and loses. Draupadi is sent for to appear at the court, even though as a Kshatriya woman and a princess, she would not appear in public thus; further, she is menstruating and hence ritually impure. She refuses to obey, and tells the messenger instead: 'Go and ascertain from the gambler whether he lost himself, or me, first.' She is thereupon forcibly dragged by the hair and brought to the hall by Duhshasana, one of the Kaurava brothers. Again she repeats her question: did Yudhishthira have a right to stake her if he

40

had already become a slave? Her question is disregarded. Karna, on the Kaurava side, orders her to be stripped since, being married to five men (contrary to custom), she may be regarded as a 'whore'. Duhshasana begins to pull off her garments, but miraculously more and more of them appear to clothe her, and he stops, exhausted. The blind old Kaurava king is persuaded to cry a halt to this injustice and he offers Draupadi three boons to compensate for the insult inflicted upon her. With these she frees her husbands. The Pandavas, in response to Draupadi's rage at her humiliation, vow revenge on the Kauravas. After losing at another gambling match, and serving thirteen years in exile, the Pandavas return to wage war against them. The great *Mahabharata* war is fought, however, not to avenge Draupadi's insult; the 'righteous war', the occasion of the *Bhagavad Gita*, is fought to settle the long-standing struggle between the clans for political power. Finally, the Kauravas are defeated and killed, the kingdom is restored to the Pandavas, and Draupadi is avenged.

I wish to draw out several strands of speculation from this: first, to observe that the Draupadi 'scene' is structurally similar to other forms of staged spectacle in its transgression of the 'separate' spheres, that is, in the enactment of a private act (here, the display, disrobing and attempted sexual violation of a woman) in a public space (the king's court or assembly). Woman as the sole and singular object of the public gaze in such scenes may ambivalently be the recipient of both admiration and scorn—neither response is free of the overtones of the other, or of sexual significance. The woman's response to the gaze is also ambivalently divided between pride and shame, an aspect of the simultaneous exhilaration and disgrace/danger that attend what I have elsewhere described as women's exceptional entry into the space of the public.[4] As I shall shortly be pointing out, Draupadi too seeks to exploit the public space and public speech that circumstances—however unfavourable—give her access to, with varying degrees of success.

In the *Mahabharata* episode Draupadi explicitly recalls the only other occasion she had been viewed in public—in the *swayamvara* arena where the assembled kings came to woo her—when she had chosen her future husband, Arjuna, for his feats of prowess. So she laments:

> Alas, only once before, on the occasion of the *swayamvara*, I was beheld by the assembled kings in the amphitheatre, and never even

once beheld afterwards. She whom even the wind and the sun had never before seen is exposed to the gaze of the world. I think these are evil times when the Kurus allow their daughter-in-law to be thus tormented.[5]

Then, she had been a cynosure of all eyes. Her appearance—in both senses of the word, her dishevelment as well as her presence in the court—is a very different matter now.

I want to read deeper into her connection of the two exceptional events whose only common point is her presentation to an assembled gaze. I am led to the intuition that what she experiences as trauma is not the shock of the unexpected but the recognition of the familiar. For Draupadi this repetition-with-difference is not merely poignant, it has the quality of nightmare. For, in the scenario of nightmare too, humiliation follows from stripping or some sense of the loss of the familiar accoutrements of identity, the metaphoric isolation of the naked self, exacerbated by the stares of a crowd. And in the dream this is attended by paralysis.

Does this dream-state also explain why women experience such fatalism about sexual violation when it happens? If women are socially and culturally conditioned to expect and therefore accept such violation, might it not be that they have always already experienced it? Not in the sense of literal knowledge or of fantasy (the latter based on the covert or unacknowledged desire for it that they are accused of having), but as a 'memory', from an institutional rather than individual source.[6] This is not to say that women's knowledge of violence is only a subjective experience, but rather to insist that the dynamics of the subjective, here as memory, must enter the space of narration. Draupadi, it is true, is shown to react strongly to her ordeal by speech and action but the epic narrative mode does not provide access to interiority. So it is through Draupadi's rhetorical evocation of the similar-but-contrasted past that we read her cognitive structuring of the present scene of violation—as the expected and inevitable—and the past scene of triumph—as the ordeal of the public gaze, in terms of resemblance.

Both the trauma of publicity and the sanctity of privacy are, for women, products of the ideology of separate spheres. In the narrative of the *Mahabharata*, textual scholars say, it is not so much the disrobing as the forced entry into public space that Draupadi returns to later (in her recurrent allusions to the time), as the source of her shame. Since 'it is the barrier between the public and the private which defines "respectable" and "non-respectable" women,' this transgression enforces her new status as slave woman. Even the disruption of her ritual pollution as a menstruating woman may be viewed as a trespass into 'the private language of the female body'.[7]

There are two cruxes that are usually recognized as being of special significance in the interpretation of Draupadi's agency: the first, her famous question; and the second, the means of her salvation. Her question, did Yudhishthira put her at stake before or after he lost himself, is never answered because it is unanswerable. Alf Hiltebeitel, the noted Draupadi scholar, regards it as a *feminist* question since 'it challenges the men to consider . . . their lordship over and "ownership" of women in contexts of patriarchy.' For him it is a 'class-action appeal' by Draupadi on behalf of women as a group which 'calls into question two kinds of male lordship: that of kinship and family, and that of the dharmic politics of kingship in the *sabha* or men's hall,'[8] The philosopher B.K. Matilal describes her question as the sole and 'unique' unanswered dilemma in the epic. But Matilal too notes a displacement: Draupadi's question is 'more concerned with rights or legality . . . than with the morality of the situation.' From his contemporary location he also concedes that it as a 'point (made by) a social rebel, presumably a non-conformist.' 'If Draupadi's questions were properly answered, it would have required a "paradigm shift" in India's social thought.'[9]

In contrast to these is the scathing comment of Iravati Karve, the author of *Yuganta* (The End of an Epoch), a major modern version of and commentary on the *Mahabharata*: 'Draupadi's question was not only foolish; it was terrible.' 'Draupadi was standing there arguing about legal technicalities like a lady pundit when what was happening to her was so hideous that she should only have cried out for decency and pity in the name of the Kshatriya code.'[10] Though Draupadi's question is not answered to any purpose, complex questions about the responsibility for her staking and about the rules of gambling are nevertheless debated among the men in court (in all this Draupadi's wife/woman-status as property is not in dispute, only the rights of slaves over their women).[11] But the point, as Karve points out, is that, 'no matter what answer was given her position was desperate.' Karve speaks with the bitter irony of a woman who knows that women must obey the rules: 'She (Draupadi) had spoken in the assembly of men, something she should have known she must not do.'[12] Functioning as a powerful verbal marker, especially in a public forum, the *question* bestows authority upon the speaker. But Draupadi cannot claim the authority of prosecuter when she is, simultaneously and contradictorily, criminal as well as a victim of crime. Her demand is an instance, once again, of women's inappropriate because unaccustomed speech —what I have elsewhere described as linguistic *excess*.[13]

In a more recent debate on the feminism of Draupadi's question, Draupadi scholar Janaky, offers somewhat different arguments to counter Shuddhabrata Sengupta's praise of Draupadi's 'feminist' question on the grounds of a 'universal' womanhood.[14] By raising the question of slavery, Janaky argues, Draupadi brings up the class and caste aspects of sexual oppression; and by claiming protection as a the *kulavadhu* of the clan (i.e. on the basis of her kinship relationship), she highlights its political dimension.[15] Draupadi can be recuperated for feminism not by essentializing her predicament as a 'women's issue,' but by remaining alert to the 'sexual vulnerability and political subordination of women *within the larger network of intersections of power and ideology at the multiple levels of caste, race and class*'.[16] (emphasis added).

How are we to reconcile these different interpretations of Draupadi's question: on the one hand, the easy recuperation of feminist rights talk; on the other, the difficult recognition of the limits of such rights? The universalization of her predicament as against the specificity of her historical, social, political identity intersecting with her gender identity/Draupadi's question, in these feminist contentions makes no difference to *her* within the frame of the disrobing scene. However, it may resonate outside that context.

The second crux of interpretation—which is also a textual crux—relates to the means of her salvation. Draupadi rehearses a range of more or less successful strategies to escape her situation, ranging from physical resistance, to recourse to legality, appeals for male protection, curses, threats of revenge, and, finally, to dignified submission coded as moral triumph. Because at the overt level she reacts to her ordeal in such strenuous and resistant ways, she is frequently recuperated as 'feminist' by contemporary scholars and artists. But in the *Mahabharata*, the prevention of her nakedness is attributed to no action of hers, but to the operation of cosmic or universal justice. More importantly, she is subjected to the full extent of her humiliation already by being dragged into court, reviled and manhandled: any reading of 'salvation' after such an ordeal can only be ironically intended.

In most popular versions, including the recent television serial of the *Mahabharata,* Draupadi is saved by Lord Krishna, who appears in response to her prayers (these are most likely later interpolations, according to critical scholarship). It is he who sends forth the endless saris that clothe her when she is being stripped. In the critical edition of the epic, however, there is no prayer and no visible divinity.[17] But it would be fair to assume that in either case it is Draupadi's virtue as chaste wife that produces the miracle, and that divine justice intercedes to protect innocence and prevent the outrage of its violation.[18] Is this too to be read as a sign of Draupadi's 'agency', her independent assertion of virtuous selfhood? But to the tautology of the virtuous woman who is saved because she is worthy to be saved has its inexorable logic: raped women, that is, those who are *not* saved, are unworthy. We can admire the feminism of Draupadi's exceptional salvation only at the cost of the misogyny of that logic.

The 'resolution' of the disrobing scene does not, however, consist of this confirmation of Draupadi's virtue but in what lies beyond and as a consequence of it: the freedom she wins for her husbands by exercising her compensatory boons. Hiltebeitel argues that this is a sign of her greater agential initiative than that of her defeated husbands' at this point—and indeed Karna taunts the Pandavas for their indebtedness to their wife for their release. When the Kauravas had already won the kingdom of the Pandavas and reduced them to slaves, for them to further instigate the staking and attempt the disrobing of Draupadi is a gratuitous insult that leads to a reversal, their moral defeat. Why then does the gambling match proceed to the self-defeating excess of this event? And yet this question is rarely asked, so logical does it seem as structural climax and the violation of women of a defeated territory so routinely claimed as the victor's crowning triumph and as a closure to political deals. The Kauravas are seemingly only indulging in playful, high-spirited celebration in calling for the sport of disrobing Draupadi. Nevertheless, there is unease among the Kauravas themselves about the propriety of the act; the enormity of the transgression of '*dharma*', the norms of kingly conduct, finally strikes home. We are led to recognize that patriarchy is not a monolithic, chinkless ideology, that there is religious, legal, political and humanistic recourse available for women; but also that the holders and dispensers of these institutional remedies are men. Hence the wide distribution of roles among the male actors in the scene—as perpetrators of the deed, outraged but helpless kin, doubters, defenders of *dharma*, legalists, and saviour—and the consequent trivialization of the woman's agency. Hence, too, the overwhelming impression of the single/singular woman in the midst of and against an assembly of men, which displaces the scenario of two opposed clans in which the wife may be seen as aligned with her husbands.

What I have sought to do in my argument thus far is keep Draupadi's story exorbitant to the narrative movement towards a formal resolution: first by structuring her ordeal as a 'nightmare', or reverie; then by stressing her questioning as futile/improper talk rather than active agency within the situation; finally by calling attention to the narrative excess of the disrobing scene, and to her exclusion from the concerns of political conflict. The *Mahabharata* will serve as pretext for other violations but provide the scenario for few instances of salvation. Draupadi's salvation is not only exceptional, it is also, finally, irrelevant. And, as I argued earlier, it must not blind us to the awareness that the mere withholding of some 'ultimate' outrage (e.g., rape) cannot count as 'salvation'.

II

Despite the continuum on which eve-teasing, stripping and the rape of women exist, and the actual continuities between them, it would be useful to separate the first two from rape and mark the more significant differences between them. The most obvious of course is that the first two are performed in open, public places, generally by a group of men, while rape is committed in some degree of privacy, though not necessarily only by a single male. This should mean—but does not, necessarily—that their occurrence is more easily established and consequently punished as crime, than rape, where the question of evidence is a major obstacle to legal conviction. But if they gain their power, and hence sanction and even the protection of invisibility, from being group activities, they have their self-censoring limits for the same reason. Self-righteousness usually dictates that the violation of the woman stops just short of actual rape.[19]

'Eve-teasing' is the male harassment of a woman in public— verbally, physically, or both—a form of taunting with varying degrees of seriousness. The eve-teaser may act alone or in a group of like-minded men, while the victim is usually single. Women in the west experience sexual harassment in the form of wolf-whistles, bottom-pinching and similar expressions of male 'admiration' of the woman in a public place. The quaint term 'eye-teasing,' in India, carries similar connotations of simultaneous gallantry and 'harmless' male mischief, and has passed into accepted usage (figuring also in the title of the law prohibiting such harassment). Nevertheless, as both social behaviour and phenomenon, it is viewed more seriously in a context where women's chastity and (their) men's honour are major values. There are consequently two contradictions that inform the eve-teasing activity in India (which are highlighted by the *Mahabharata* episode as well), which mark its differences from sexual harassment as such: one, that even when viewed as wrong in moral and legal terms it is underpinned by a self-righteous logic of punishment and, consequently, caries implicit social sanction; and two, that in spite of its overt and indeed blatant aggression towards the victim it transparently reveals anxieties about female sexuality, or superior social status, or mobility, or a combination of these.

These contradictions are strikingly revealed in a reader's letter written in response to a newspaper column attacking eve-teasing:

> Your column . . . totally upset me. I don't agree with your views at all. . . . Mostly it's the dress that puts many a young woman in trouble. Why can't they dress decently? 'Here, it's for you', 'Don't just see, take it', 'Hold me!', 'Take me', are the possible gestures they throw at the sterner sex. . . . Did you bother to think on the 'why' aspect? What forced the guy to resort to that unbecoming assault? Simple. She must have humiliated him, . . . double-crossed him, made the poor guy's life miserable. . . . He's finished for life. . . . After initial reluctance, women actually enjoy being raped. Do you have any say in this? Even if the guy ignores the above 'invitations' and goes his way he's immediately branded 'thumb-sucking sissy!' . . . Hope you desist from blowing the silly feminist trumpet of this kind in future.[20]

Uniquely pathological though this diatribe may sound, it in fact echoes the legitimizing logic of 'eve-teasing' and of rape, even as it conveys the confused but genuine belief that 'women want it,' the skewed semiotics of sex in a rapidly modernizing society.

Crime statistics reveal interesting facts: a growing increase in the incidence of 'eve-teasing', not attributable entirely to more women reporting the crime than before; a significantly higher incidence in the northern states than the southern, in Delhi than in other cities; and an equal number of cases in affluent neighbourhoods, colleges and workplaces, as in slum areas. Sociologists attribute these phenomena to different causes, such as urban migration, the destruction of a traditional *mohalla* culture, the sudden upward social mobility of certain caste groups, new wealth, and, above all, the pervasive 'culture' of *purdah* (characteristic of the northern belt that had been subjected to Islamic invasions in the past) that secures women's safety only within doors and makes them fair prey in public places.[21] In an impressionistic book-length account of 'small town India,' *Butter Chicken in Ludhiana*, Pankaj Mishra writes about the city that is arguably the most unsafe for women—Benares. In this ancient Hindu temple town and pilgrimage centre, when men belonging to a traditional feudalistic society confront the 'modern' in the form of the 'west', particularly foreign women tourists, they respond in predictable ways. Mishra is offered the following explanation by a local friend:

> The cruelty is unimaginable. . . . (You may have) become a modern consumer, part of the global market and so on, but your social attitudes have not progressed beyond the eighteenth century. Women are no more than chattel to you, and a foreign woman is even less than that. Unlike an Indian woman, she is not a wife or daughter or sister to anybody. She is a pure and simple object of lust, a 'sex machine' . . . something to be consumed if not owned.[22]

Attitudes to gender and modernity clash in particularly conflictual ways. One tendency in contemporary analyses is to blame 'modernity' comprehensively for its 'intrusion' on established ways of life, never mind if the latter had/have no place for egalitarianism. The other side of the argument, which I am trying to push here, is that women's rights are an important component of modernity.[23]

An even more vicious expression of misogyny is found in the reports from rural areas of women stripped naked and paraded through the village streets, a 'traditional' punishment meted out by men in village councils to women found guilty of sexual offences such as elopement with a person of a different caste, adultery, illicit liaisons etc. or of so-called 'witchcraft'. The modern instances of this action, when investigated, invariably turn out to be retaliation by upper-caste landowners upon scheduled-caste women with whom they are invol-ved in property disputes, especially when the women are either more vulnerable or more independent than others in their community; or upon the men of the community for similar reasons.[24] But disputes can arise from a number of larger factors, such as 'inadequate land reforms, ineffective enforcement of the Minimum Wages Act, continuance of bonded labour,' as the 1979 *Atrocities on Harijans* report points out,[25] and the punishment of women is a familiar form of retaliation.

In a detailed exposition of, and theoretical excursus upon, a case of four Harijan women stripped and paraded naked in Sirasgaon (Maharashtra) in 1963, Anupama Rao questions explanations which mask the operations of power, desire and violence in cases of 'atrocity' such as the stripping of women, pointing to the judicial pronounce-ment in the Sirasgaon case as instance. Despite its 'progressive' sentiments on caste equality and its moral fervour, the judgement did little to locate the stripping of the women within a context of social oppression. Significantly, the case itself was not registered under the Untouchability Offences Act, 1955. 'What would it have meant to call Sirasgaon an "atrocity"?', Rao asks. Among other things, it would involve, she argues, recognition of the contradiction of untouchability in its relation to *physical* violence—molestation, stripping and rape—upon the *untouchable* sexed/gendered/physical body. In 'Understand-ing Sirasgaon' Rao insists upon the need to think the social, the poli-tical and the sexual aspects of the issue together.[26]

If, in both eve-teasing and stripping, the intention to humi-liate the woman/women (i.e. misogyny) is, as I surmise, greater than the motive of sexual gratification, the pathology of voyeurism, sadism and domination nevertheless has strong sexual components.[27] The 'meaning' of these actions directed against women is not, however, exhausted by motive (punishment) or practice (ritual); nor can it be confined to an understanding of the pathology of the perpetrators. In almost every instance the attitude of bystanders is of equal significance: this, invariably, is one of non-interference, whether out of fear of invol-vement, or apathy, or even active complicity with the criminals. The law—as represented by the officers of the law—reflects this attitude. It is within this larger frame of reference, in the context of widespread social attitudes, that explanations in terms of 'culture' have resonance.

49

The Draupadi story, it is needless to say, is not being regarded here either as the source or as the legitimation of these actions. Rather, it serves as a heuristic, a narrative frame for viewing contemporary events. Mere 'culturalist' explanations ignore the complicated ways in which culture and society function in relation to each other. Cultural resources, I wish to argue, are *selectively* appropriated to mesh with the postcolonial nation-state's requirements. In this case the entry of women into the spaces of public life, in particular the workplace, is a sign of social change that goes by the ambivalent name of 'modernization.' Eve-teasing is the new and illegitimate offshoot of the project of the social control of women, a project made urgent by these changes, and is reconciled to as one of the risks that women must run in negotiating public life. Public stripping, by contrast, has 'traditional' sanction for imposing such control—but, like presentday sati, it must now function under the sign of disavowal as a consequence of the modern state's refusal to countenance it legally, even as its logic grows more aggressive.[28]

III

Drawing upon the unfailing impact of the episode of Draupadi's disrobing in producing shock and sexual frisson, popular Indian cinema routinely includes a 'rape' scene in which the villain pulls away the heroine's sari, the point at which the representation of sexual violation generally stops due to censorship restrictions. But the knowledge that Draupadi's salvation is not available to *all* women functions as the clue to the culmination of the scene, off-screen, in rape. In such scenes, since they are explicitly recognized according to the convention of *rape*-scenes, there is no ambiguity about the wrong-doing of the villain or the innocence of the heroine. In contrast, the popular song-and-dance sequences which feature the hero and his friends serenading the heroine operate according to the more complex sexual semiotics of eve-teasing. The girl is rich, proud, fashionably (i.e. sexily) dressed, and 'westernized'. She is waylaid and surrounded in a public place, college, park or street; the lyrics of the song frequently tease and taunt her with innuendo. There is no condemnation of the antics of the young men, but instead explicit self-righteousness: the girl must be taught a lesson in humility, modesty and subjection. She responds by recognizing her 'errors', and falls in love with the hero. Male sexual power effectively levels women's class-superiority, a procedure about which the film may rely on widespread acceptance since the traditional gender hierarchy is thereby restored. In the *Mahabharata*, Draupadi's vulnerability lay in her polyandry but, as we are elsewhere in the epic told, it is also her habitual pride, haughtiness, mockery and assertiveness that call forth the resentment and wish for revenge of the Kauravas. Since she is chaste she is saved, but because she is blameworthy she is subjected to the chastening ordeal. We can see how the moral categories of virtue and wrongdoing are displacements of the *ressentiment* produced by social differences, of class, caste, status across the gender divide.

As in a number of other issues relating to women, the state occupies the moral high ground by passing legislation for the 'protection' of women which overrides traditional practices in favour of democratic and universal human rights; while in terms of executive, judicial and law-enforcement practice it does little to effectively alter the *status quo*: a contradiction reflected in both the laws themselves and in legal judgements. The Indian Penal Code prohibits and specifies punishment for various forms of sexual harassment: Section 354 ('assault or criminal force to a woman with intent to outrage her modesty'); Section 509 ('word, gesture or act intended to insult the modesty of a woman', or 'to intrude upon the privacy of such woman'); Section 294 (obscene acts or songs). Little actual cognizance is taken by the police of any complaints received by them, however, and there are few convictions if a case should be brought to court.[29] Women's organizations on university campuses, in particular, have grim stories to tell of inadequate protection and follow-up police action.[30] The police blame the victims: 'The girls invite trouble by sitting outside on the pavements at odd times.'[31] Since Delhi, the national capital, has the dubious distinction of being one of the least safe of Indian cities for women, the Delhi police are known for brief and sudden spurts of action in response to women's complaints: for example, at times like the Holi festival, or the beginning of the school term, when eve-teasing tends to be aggravated under licence of carnival, they issue threats, or put out public relations posters.[32]

The union territory (now state) of Delhi also passed special legislation in 1984 targeting eve-teasing, the Delhi Prohibition of Eve-teasing Bill, where eve-teasing is defined as consisting of the following actions: 'When a man by words either spoken or by signs and or by visible representation or by gesture does any act in a public place, or signs, recites or utters any indecent words or song or ballad in any public place to the annoyance of any woman'. The specificity of the description, the police argue, makes it easier for culprits to be apprehended; besides which the offence has been made cognizable and non-bailable. Nandita Haksar, a feminist activist lawyer, however describes the bill as 'an eye-wash and a fraud on women'. Sufficient provision for recognizing and punishing such offences is already available under the existing penal code, and by fixing punishment at one week of imprisonment the law only 'trivialized the issue and minimized the offence', she points out.[33]

A similar situation of legal cognizance and prohibition weakened by non-enforcement, exists in the issue of humiliation of lower-caste women in public. The Prevention of Atrocities against Scheduled Castes/Scheduled Tribes Act, passed in 1989, specifically identifies the 'removal of clothes from an SC, ST, parading the person naked, and painting his/her face', as an atrocity. As in the Penal Code, anyone who 'assaults or uses force on a woman with intent to dishonour or outrage her modesty', can also be apprehended under this law. Further, anyone who 'intentionally insults and intimidates with intent to humiliate a member of the SC, ST in public view', is guilty of breaking the law. Stripping can be punished under all three sections. Three national-level commissions have been set up by the government to investigate and recommend action in such cases: the National Commission for SC/ST, the National Commission for Women and the National Commission for Human Rights. The commissions however have limited powers and, having no authority to enforce punishment, may only direct state governments to do so. They have limited resources by way of staff, political backing and support for their work. Instances of such atrocities are actually on the rise, marking the limitations of the existence and functioning of such bodies.[34]

The entire complex issue of the law as a force for social change cannot be gone into here; the usual conclusion, that law is a necessary but insufficient condition for such change, must suffice. What *is* important to notice is that the ground and rationale for the existing laws are directed less towards ensuring women's rights to freedom of functioning in public than towards preserving an ideal of public morality and civic law and order. Given such a reading, both the blaming of women for being in the wrong place at the wrong time and its offshoots—greater restrictions on their dress, behaviour, movements—as well as the benevolent notion of protection, are inevitable.

A proposed draft bill for a comprehensive new set of laws on sexual assault and harassment, formulated by the Centre for Feminist Legal Research in New Delhi, therefore proposes that the terminology of Victorian morality—'indecency', 'carnal knowledge', 'outraging the modesty', etc.—which code women's chastity as value, be replaced by one recognizing their sexual autonomy and rights to bodily integrity. In addition, it recommends that the criminal prosecution of offenders be supplemented by a substantive civil law dealing with sexual harassment and that Section 509 of IPC (dealing with sexual harassment) be rephrased as follows:

> Whoever, intending to insult and sexually harass a woman, utters any word, makes any sound or gesture, or exhibits any object, intending that such word or sound shall be heard, or that such gesture or object shall be seen by such woman, or intrudes upon the privacy of such woman, shall be punished with simple imprisonment for a term which may extend to one year, or with fine, or with both.[35]

In September 1997 the Supreme Court issued guidelines on recognizing and punishing sexual harassment of women at the workplace, following the rape of a *saathin* (voluntary worker), Bhanwari Devi, in Rajasthan. The National Council for Women has also proposed new laws that would bring all sexual violation of women, harassment as well as physical violence including rape, under the broad category of 'sexual assault', so that penetration is not fetishized as the singular or even most serious offence of the many sexual crimes against women.

The examples in the foregoing discussion, of the interventions made by feminist legal activists and the NCW, and the example of Rupan Deol Bajaj, a civil servant who won a sexual harassment action suit against a senior police officer at the end of a much publicized case, are evidence of successful feminist resistance.[36] But if, on the one hand, it is 'western' feminist initiatives in the arena of legal reform and legal action that, in postcolonial political struggles, are successfully marshalled against the forces of patriarchal cultural 'tradition'—here embodied in the Draupadi story—then, on the other hand, that tradition may *itself* be plausibly interpreted for examples of resistance to patriarchal domination. How productive or progressive this may be as feminist *strategy* is a question that I shall now turn to.

IV

Alf Hiltebeitel, the American scholar whose work and arguments I have alluded to and drawn upon, links the Draupadi of the classical Sanskrit religious epic to the folklore goddess of the Gingee region in Tamil southern India, where Draupadi worship culminates in major festivals and theatrical performances every year. This goddess figure of Draupadi is closely related to Kali, the avenging goddess worshipped as the fearful feminine principle. Hiltebeitel argues from this development, which is about five centuries old, that Draupadi's powers to curse, and her vows instigating her husbands to revenge against her molesters, reveal the 'dark and destructive side' of her character in the *Mahabharata*, and represents the 'prefiguration of Kali herself.'[37]

The Draupadi who is insulted in court is undeniably an outraged figure, which response—together with the various trials and tribulations she undergoes which make her 'inauspicious'—does not elevate her to the status of role model for Hindu girls raised on stories of other mythological heroines such as Sita and Savitri, who are more exemplarily obedient and devoted to their respective husbands. If Indian cinema, in conformity with this cultural preference, has for long been content to show the violated woman passively accepting her suffering, or dying, the more recent trend in both mainstream and alternative cinema is towards representing her as an avenging figure. The earliest of such films, N. Chandra's *Pratighaat* (Hindi, 1991), explicitly reenacted the scene of Draupadi's violation in contemporary terms: a big-city mafia group attack a forthright woman college teacher, strip her in front of her house and parade her naked in the streets before her paralysed family and neighbours. The scene is shot in negative: no doubt to honour good 'taste', i.e. to avoid creating participant voyeurism among the audience, and explicitly to forestall censorship cuts as well as to symbolically suggest the inversion of normalcy. *Pratighaat* ends with the heroine murdering the criminal leader with unrestrained violence and gore, wielding an axe at a public meeting. In Shekhar Kapur's *Bandit Queen* (Hindi and English, 1994), Phoolan Devi's experience of being stripped and made to walk naked to the village well is made the explanatory linch-pin of her subsequent career as a dacoit. The scene itself is represented with directness and no obscuring gimmicks; the intolerable silence and suspense which mark its narration, and the high-angled shots that let us view the naked female figure as very small and alone in a vast landscape, create an unprecedented degree of empathy with the woman and of insight into the experience of her violation. Phoolan's subsequent career of vendetta, like the other killings by women in recent Indian cinema, is explicitly filled with the resonance of Kali, the demonic goddess,[38] just as the sexual humiliation—public stripping, insult, rape—is linked to Draupadi's story: and as Hiltebeitel shows via anthropological researches, the link between the two is already established within popular Hindu culture.

The avenging woman—like, and following from, the myth of the female goddess—is undeniably in her energy and anger an empowering fiction for women. Her revenge, in narrative terms, unequivocally establishes the wrong of her violation and institutes justice in an unjust world, and her representation as a being capable of violence, even of killing, is a rejection of eternal victimization. Nevertheless, feminism's embrace of feminist *heroines* and, in particular— in the context of contemporary India's fundamentalist Hindu resurgence—the validation of feminist heroines from the Hindu past, has uneasy political implications that I have explored at greater length elsewhere.[39] Here I shall only want to suggest the following: that like all vigilante action, women's revenge is anarchic in pitting individual revenger against individual perpetrator of crime; that it trivializes the strength of the forces, historical and material, that ground women's oppression; that it reduces female power to a reactive (hence negative) dynamics, i.e. that which only acts in the very terms set by the oppressor; and following from these, that it unquestioningly, and questionably as it seems to me, endorses violence as the (intolerable) solution to social evils. It will be easy to see that what is overlooked in this scenario, from the point of view of feminist praxis, say, in the women's movement, is a structural understanding of violence; the possibilities of collective protest; solutions within the framework of law, reform and civil society; and a radical interrogation of the *social* responsibility for individual/collective violence against women.

There have been other modern re-tellings of Draupadi's story that take a more complex view of her in the light of modern, existential tragedy: Karve's heroine in *Yuganta*, out of joint with her own time; Saoli Mitra's sole protagonist, refusing pliant femininity for difficult intelligence and protest in her dance-drama *Nathabati Anathabat*; Somnath Hoare's sculptures of the writhing female figure in Bronze;

Pratibha Parmar's grand but pathetic heroine in the prize-winning Oriya novel, *Yajnaseni*.[40] In these representations, Draupadi is a 'feminist' to the extent that she questions what happens to her, tragic in that she is doomed to confusion, solitude and ineffectual protest. She is claimed across historical distance, but then surrendered to history.

I shall conclude with a very brief discussion of two stories by Indian women writers that I believe go to the heart of the matter of male sexual humiliation of and violence against women in the form of stripping and eve-teasing. In the first, Mahasveta Devi's *Draupadi*,[41] Dopdi Mehjen, a Naxalite Santhal tribal woman on the run, is finally apprehended by the police and ordered (by Senanayak, the police chief) to be tortured and gang-raped into giving information about her comrades. There is no question of either salvation or revenge here—yet Dopdi is triumphant. The story ends: 'Draupadi pushes Senanayak with her two mangled breasts, and for the first time Senanayak is afraid to stand before an unarmed *target*, terribly afraid.' (196) For Dopdi would not let the policemen wash or clothe her after the night's brutality; that would be to wipe away its signs. Worse, her nakedness is offered as an affront to their masculinity: 'What is the use of clothes? You can strip me, but how can you clothe me again? Are you a man? . . . There isn't a man here that I should be ashamed.' (196) Very simply, Dopdi does not let her nakedness shame her, her torture intimidate her, or her rape diminish her. But this refusal is not to be read as a transcendence of suffering, or even simply as heroism. It is instead simultaneously a deliberate refusal of a shared sign-system (the meanings assigned to nakedness and rape: shame, fear, loss) and an ironic deployment of the same semiotics to create disconcerting counter-effects of shame, confusion and terror in the enemy (what is a 'man'?).

The other text that I shall invoke here is *Teaser*, one of a new collection of short stories by Manjula Padmanabhan, in English, titled *Hot Death, Cold Soup*.[42] It is a brilliant monologue crafted in free, indirect speech, of an adolescent boy's gloating plans for and execution of a typical 'eve-teasing' activity, i.e. accosting a woman in a crowded bus. Padmanabhan takes us from the moment of his waking up in the morning to the power and pride of his sexuality: 'He believed the power to be a manifestation of the divine, made flesh upon his body. A baton passed into his keeping for a brief but sacred period. . . . Out of the void it appeared, fluoresced and passed onward to the void again'

(81–2); to his careful deliberation over the choice of a 'target' on the bus: 'In his experience, the ideal was between the ages of 16 and 23. It would be well-dressed and smart, but not too smart. Over confident targets tended to respond in silly ways. . . . He had no interest in confrontations' (84); to the description of the battle-plans: 'The classic manoeuvre required the bus to be careening along at high speed, so that he could use its motion to lean with ever increasing insistence upon the target. . . Today. . . he wondered if he couldn't go much further than he usually dared. Use his hands for instance. Touch her shoulder. Her hair. Or even turn and breathe directly on her. Anything seemed possible' (93). However—as in 'Draupadi' — a reversal of the envisaged triumphant denouement is in store. The target turns round to confront the hunter: 'The woman reached with her hand and touched him. Touched the curving ridge under the zip of his jeans. With the hard red talon at the end of her forefinger. . . . She was laughing silently . . . looking at the damp patch that had appeared under the waist-band of his jeans, on his shirt. "Silly!" she was saying. "Silly little boy has wet his pants!"(94). Male sexuality, that dreaded weapon, is revealed as a very pitiful and vulnerable thing.

Both stories offer debatable conclusions of course. Are acts of sexual violation against women's bodies only *coded* as debasement? Or do they strike at their very identity? A contemporary fictional heroine debates this desperately while being raped: 'What is in a body, she thought. It is but a shell. "No, it is me. I am my body."'[43] Can women unilaterally refuse or alter the meanings of socially-defined action? Is male sexual violence defeated simply by its demystification, its (literal) deflation?

What the women do in these stories is not, however, offered in terms of 'correctness,' as ideal strategies of resistance/counter-attack, or even as replicable in all or other circumstances. Nevertheless their reasoning raises fundamental questions for feminism: about identity, language, agency, the body and sexuality, violence and justice. The contradictory mode of resistance that women envisage and enact in such situations—responding to male humiliation as violation, while simultaneously refusing shame—is dictated by the double aspect of culture, the material 'real' and the ideological, the first to be contended with, the second contested. It is this valence that explains the feminist preoccupation with Draupadi's story in India.

Notes and References

1   The *Mahabharata* is a narrative in verse, supposed to have been composed by the sage Vyasa, who narrated it to his disciples. An earlier version of it, called *Jaya*, thought to have existed. This underwent changes and acquired additions over the centuries. The events recounted in the *Mahabharata* are supposed to have happened around about 1000 BC, though the oldest existing text can be dated only to the eighth or ninth century AD.

2   Gillian Beer, *Arguing with the Past: Essays in Narrative from Woolf to Sidney,* Routledge, London and New York, 1989, pp. 4, 6.

3   Gayatri Chakravorty Spivak, 'Can the Subaltern Speak? Speculations on Widow Sacrifice', *Wedge* 7/8, Spring/Winter, 1985, p. 123.

4   Rajeswari Sunder Rajan, *Real and Imagined Women: Gender, Culture and Postcolonialism,* Routledge, London and New York, 1993, p. 88.

5   The English translations I have used are Pratap Chandra Ray (trans.), *The Mahabharata,* vol. II, Sabha Parva and Vana Parva, Oriental Publishing Co., Calcutta, n.d.; and Chakravarti V. Narasimhan, *The Mahabharatha: An English Version Based on Selected Verses,* Columbia University Press, New York and London, 1965. This passage is Ray's translation.

6   I am grateful to You-me Park (Bryn Mawr College) for offering me this phrase and for other suggestions for this discussion.

7   See, especially, Janaky, 'On the Trail of the Mahabharatha,' *Economic and Political Weekly,* 12 September, 1992, p. 1999.

8   Alf Hiltebeitel, 'Is the Goddess a Feminist? Draupadi's Question', paper presented at the American Academy of Religion Annual Meeting, Chicago, November, 1994.

9   B.K. Matilal, 'Moral Dilemmas: Insights from Indian Epics', in Matilal, ed., *Moral Dilemmas in the Mahabharata,* IIAS and Motilal Banarsidass, New Delhi, 1989, pp. 2–3.

10 Iravati Karve, *Yuganta,* Disha, Hyderabad, 1991, pp. 99. *Yuganta* was first published in Marathi in 1967; the first English translation appeared in 1969.

11 See S.M. Kulkarni, 'An Unresolved Dilemma in Dyuta-Parvan: A Question Raised by Draupadi', in Matilal, *Moral Dilemmas,* pp. 150–56, for an analysis of the legal points raised by Vikarna in the discussion of Draupadi's staking.

12 Karve, *Yuganta,* p. 101.

13 Sunder Rajan, *Real and Imagined Women,* p. 88.

14 Janaky's article is written as a 'response' to Suddhabrata Sengupta's 'Sexual Politics of Television Mythology', *Economic and Political Weekly,* 9 November, 1991. pp. 2558-60.

15 Janaky, 'On the Trail of the Mahabharatha', p. 1999.

16 Ibid.

17 The critical edition is published by the Bhandarkar Oriental Research Institute, edited by V.S. Sukhtankar. The *Mahabharata* exists in many recensions, and the critical edition is based on the oldest manuscripts available.

58

[18] Karve follows the critical edition in holding that Draupadi 'called on neither man nor God', but 'the power of the universe itself had awakened to protect her' (*Yuganta*, p. 100). Janaky responds to Sukhtankar's 'rational scissoring of the God', by protesting that 'it is difficult for anyone to conceive of the episode without Krishna's timely appearance' ('On the Trail of the Mahabharata', 1997).

[19] The gang-rape of Bhanwari Devi, a '*saathin*' in the Women's Development Programme (WDP), by upper-caste men in Bhateri, Rajasthan, in 1992, combined the elements of punitive motive and flagrancy, which are more often aspects of public stripping, with the protection offered by 'invisible' rape. The accused were acquitted at the Sessions Court.

[20] This letter is reproduced by Kalpana Sharma in her Sunday column on gender issues, 'On being "unfair" to men', *The Hindu*, 21 July 1996. The letter was a response to an article in which she had condemned an assault on a woman university student by a schoolboy which had taken place on the streets of Delhi, and deplored the spectators' lethargy as well as the impropriety of the newspaper that had published a photograph of the victim.

[21] The information and opinions here are drawn from newspaper reports: Anuja Pande, 'Politics gloss over eve-teasing on campus', *The Times of India*, 11 July 1995; Malini Goyal, 'Of culture, power and violence: a tale of Delhi streets', *Economic Times*, 8 August 1995; 'Rape trends break class barriers', *The Pioneer*, 9 September 1997.

[22] Pankaj Mishra, *Butter Chicken in Ludhiana: Travels in Small Town India*, Penguin Books, New Delhi, 1995, p. 27.

[23] See also my 'Beyond the Hysterectomies Scandal', in Kalpana Seshadri-Crooks, ed., *Postcolonial Preoccupations*, Duke University Press, Durham, forthcoming.

[24] Usha Rai, 'From Draupadi to Shivapati: An Unending Saga', *Indian Express*, 13 February 1994.

[25] Prepared by the Bureau of Police Research and Development, Union Ministry of Home Affairs, cited in Upendra Baxi, 'The Rights of Untouchables in India', in his *Mambrino's Helmet*, Har-Anand, New Delhi, 1994, p. 137. The report also suggests that 'in order to constitute atrocity ... it [the offence] should have the background of having been committed to teach a lesson to the Harijans.'

[26] Anupama Rao, 'Understanding Sirasgaon: Notes Towards Conceptualizing the Role of Law, Caste, and Gender in a Case of "Atrocity"', in *Thamyris* 4, 1, Spring, 1997, pp. 103–36.

[27] The misogyny is usually couched in a rhetoric of 'blaming the victim', as I suggest later.

[28] Usha Rai's article chronicles several recent instances of this offence, while documenting the caste and property disputes that underlie them and the politics of cover-ups.

[29] Pande, 'Police gloss over eve-teasing on campus'.

[30] Ibid.

31 Ibid.
32 An advertisement to this effect appeared in *The Times of India*, 30 December 1995.
33 Haksar, quoted in Indu Prakash Singh, *Women, Law and Social Change in India*, Radiant, New Delhi, 1989, p. 107.
34 Rai, 'From Draupadi to Shivapati'.
35 Memorandum on Reform of Laws Relating to Sexual Offences, prepared by Shomona Khanna and Ratna Kapur, Centre for Feminist Legal Research, New Delhi, 27 February 1996.
36 For a discussion of the Bajaj case, and especially the political ramifications of the indictment of K.P.S. Gill, Director General of Punjab Police, in 1996, see Kalpana Kannabiran and Vasanth Kannabiran, 'Gendering Justice', *Economic and Political Weekly*, 17 August 1996, pp. 2223–25.
37 Hiltebeitel, 'Is this Goddess a Feminist'.
38 See the essay by Priya Gopal, 'Of Victims and Vigilantes: The "Bandit Queen" Controversy', in *Thamyris* 4, 1, Spring, 1997, pp. 73–102.
39 Sunder Rajan, 'Is the Hindu Goddess a Feminist?', mimeographed monograph, Centre for Contemporary Studies, Nehru Memorial Museum and Library, New Delhi, September 1997.
40 *Nathabati Anathabat*, written, directed and enacted by Saoli Mitra, was performed in Bombay and Delhi in December 1991; I draw on the review by Shuddhabrata Sengupta, '*Nathabati Anathabat*: An act of female resistance', *Economic Times*, 13 December 1991. Somnath Hore's Draupadi sculptures were exhibited at the Centre for International Modern Art (CIMA) Gallery, in Calcutta, in November 1995; for a review, see Lopamudra Bhattacharya, 'Straight from the art', *Sunday*, 26 November–2 December 1995. Pratibha Ray, *Yajnaseni: The Story of Draupadi*, translated Pradip Bhattacharya, Rupa, New Delhi, 1995.
41 Mahasweta Devi, 'Draupadi', translated by Gayatri Chakravorty Spivak, *In Other Worlds: Essays in Cultural Politics*, Routledge, New York and London, 1988. All quotations are from this translation, and page numbers are indicated in parentheses in the text.
42 Manjula Padmanabhan, *Hot Death, Cold Soup*, Kali for Women, New Delhi, 1996; page numbers of all quotations are indicated in parentheses in the text.
43 Lindsey Collen, *The Rape of Sita*, Minerva, London, 1995, pp. 150–51.

Tracing Akbar
Hagiographies, Popular Narrative
Traditions and the Subject of Conversion

Kumkum Sangari

There were a series of more or less evidential and contemporary accounts of encounters between Akbar and sikh gurus, parsis, jains, jogis, jesuit missionaries; contemporary diatribes against Akbar from muslim and brahminical orthodoxy; recurring and probably fictitious encounters in different registers between Akbar and sants, bhakts, sufis, pirs in seventeenth-century hagiographies, some of them were his contemporaries, others not. Akbar appears to have traversed a large number of available denominational and sectarian spaces.

Historians are usually only interested in determining the veracity of these hagiographical encounters. Yet hagiographies were sedimented oralities marked by the intentionalities surrounding the scriptor, by several unnamed perceptions, and also bore an interactive relation to devotional compositions. The prolonged circulation of these narratives and the retrospective assemblage of Akbar in the seventeenth century could lend itself to another set of questions. Why is Akbar the only king who is the object of such excessive narrativization? Why does Akbar feature with such regularity in hagiography even at the expense of bending dates to make saints inhabit his lifetime? Why is he invoked in and beyond Aurangzeb's era, and what is the content of these invocations? Did these invocations indicate a different horizon of expectation, one that conjoined with a social process and a specific state formation? In other words, did they invoke a singular conjuncture, one not existing in the recent past and receding by Aurangzeb's time, even though some elements pre-existed Akbar and persisted beyond his lifetime? Taken together with other contemporary accounts and diatribes, the hagiographies describe a space for rethinking many questions, most especially those of denomination, classification and conversion.

61

I

Pir Hassu Teli

In the fables recorded by Surat Singh in *Tazkira-i-Pir Hassu Teli* (1652), Akbar is presented as a king with spiritual inclinations in constant search of a true preceptor. He is unable to find such a preceptor due to the machinations of his own courtiers that include religious bigots and protagonists of 'false religion' such as Abul Fazl. Abul Fazl resorts to some tricks in order to deflect Akbar's attention from finding his true preceptor in Pir Hassu Teli.[1]

In this fable, Akbar is eligible for initiation and is sought to be incorporated but being trapped in court intrigue, he is circumstantially, though by no means inherently, doomed to be a failed, frustrated seeker. The pir only manages to 'cure' Abul Fazl of his false faith.

Mira

The encounter with Mira is gendered: empty both of philosophical discussion and miracles. The fact that Akbar is accompanied by Tansen, connoisseur of music, also indexes Mira as a performer, blurring the already fluid line between performance and devotion in Krishna worship. In hagiographies of male saints, Tansen acts as a conduit between vaishnav lyrics and the court—he sings their compositions to Akbar and on Akbar's request, leads him to them. Nabhadas, possibly a contemporary of Akbar, refers obliquely to Akbar visiting Haridas but does not suggest a meeting with Mira. Priyadas introduces it in his early eighteenth-century *tika* on the *Bhaktmal* by Nabhadas:

> *Roop ki nikai bhoop Akbar bhaai hiye*
> *Liye sang Tansen, dekhibe ko aayo hai*
> *Nirakhi nihaal bhayon chavi girdhari lal*
> *Pad sukhlal ek tab he chadaayo hai* [2]

Akbar is entranced by her. Priyadas seems to be placing the encounter in a mode shared by hagiography and romance—*hearing* of Mira's beauty and oral performance is a sufficient catalyst for arousing Akbar's desire to see her. Such desire is natural and unquestioned—to want to see is to want to embody, substantiate, personalize a travelling voice, a reputation. Akbar and Tansen, enthralled by the image of Krishna, offer a verse at his feet.

Dadu Dayal

Jan Gopal identifies himself as an ascetic and a baniya in *Dadu Janma Lila* (*circa* 1620). In Jan Gopal's hagiography, and more so in then near-contemporary enlargement and interpolation, Dadu's low-caste status and possibly muslim origin are blurred, he is divinized,[3] and the encounter with Akbar seeks to establish Dadu's superiority over Akbar.

Akbar, hearing of Dadu and impressed by Dadu's pupil, repeatedly asks him to come to the court. He perceives Dadu as a latter-day Kabir. Raja Bhagwant Das (adoptive father of Man Singh) undertakes to persuade Dadu, who in turn puts the decision on Ram. Getting a favourable answer, he goes accompanied by his disciples and by Jan Gopal. The courtiers—Bhagwant Das, Abul Fazl and Birbal—precede Akbar. Functioning as intermediaries, they greet Dadu and question him about his faith. Dadu rejects what is in fact a complex initiation into the court that involves Birbal and Bhagwant Das as centrally as it does Akbar; he distinguishes himself from sycophantic courtiers and false brahmins (one such brahmin, Tulsi, is said to be in the thrall of *maya* and likened by Dadu to a prostitute), and refuses various court etiquettes.

Dadu professes his faith in the indescribable God with no name, no fixed abode—he is Dayal, Gopal, Allah, Alakh, Sirjanhar, Apar, Ram, Rahim, Mohan, Vyapi. Throughout identified with the tradition of Kabir, Gorakhnath and others, he enters the court under the insignia of Kabir—uttering the names of Ram, Rahim and Allah—further aligning Akbar with that same tradition.

In a sense, Dadu stands in for Kabir, who had his own confrontations with rulers but was not, to my knowledge, hagiographically updated to encounter Akbar. In court, Dadu presents himself as, on the order of his Master, a passive instrument with Ram as musician, and his every action as dictated by his Master—that is, as outside the orbit of Akbar's power.

A question-answer session with Akbar on the six systems concludes (in a brief interpolation) with Akbar folding his hands and bowing his head in admiration. Dadu advises him to give up worldly attachments and sexual desire. Akbar, impressed by his teaching (*updesh*), expresses his eagerness to continue the discussion (*goshti*). Dadu's refusal troubles Akbar. Raja Birbal tries to mediate, telling Dadu that the emperor is seen as an *avataru*, worshipped as a god by both hindu and *turak,* and even Dadu should pay him some respect (p. 101). Dadu refuses; he worships only One.

The raja's own discussions with Dadu lead to his worshipping Ram and culminate in the disappearance of his doubts. He shows Dadu palaces, temples, a palace of mirrors; Dadu unimpressed pronounces them unreal. Their discussions last forty days.

When the raja advises Akbar to just humbly ask for Dadu's blessing, the ruler agrees; Dadu comes but does not greet him. In the ensuing conversation Akbar expresses his willingness to learn, to infuse his heart with truth, to commit himself to the path described so that he too may find *gusaiyan* (p.102). Dadu then blesses him. Akbar begs him to take whatever he likes—gold, villages, parganas, elephants, horses—as a gift to support himself and his followers. Dadu refuses, advising the emperor to give up his empire, wealth and women (*kanak kamini*) and treat all beings impartially (p.103).

Here, a subsequently interpolated set of verses claim that from this moment, Akbar himself stopped hurting living beings, made it illegal for others to do so and considered Dadu his pir. This aroused the wrath of qazis and mullas and they begged the Prophet for a miracle that would put Dadu in his place. Akbar is eager to see where the real power lies. On his orders, a throne is prepared and Dadu is invited. Dadu guesses what is afoot to the amazement of Abul Fazl and Birbal; he does arrive but esconced on a strange, radiant throne that appears in the sky. Akbar is terrified (*dahsati shaai*) and bows, saying Dadu is the master and he the slave—*tum murshid mein garib gulam.* All his doubts about who is the most powerful, disappear (p. 103). The miracle, added later to aggrandize Dadu, has a somewhat browbeating cast and given Akbar's pliability, would be unnecessary if something more than the personal religious allegaince of Akbar was not at stake: miracles enter a competitive logic where 'converting' Akbar through a public and spectacular display is a means of silencing muslim orthodoxy. The qazis and mullas declare that Dadu is the pir of hindus and turks: *Kazi mulla hairaan deshyau aasan kampe praan/Tum baksau dadu bade fakir hindu turak hun ke pir* (pp.103–04).[4]

Dadu agrees to the request to stay on in court, reiterates his rejection of its luxury and of gifts from Birbal. Such an impressive rejection of *maya* further consolidates Birbal's new-found faith. The same drama of persuasion is repeated with Raja Bhagwant Das. Much of the detail of the 'conquest' of these two courtiers is a part of the later

64

interpolations and serves to counterpose the divinization of Akbar by his courtiers through the stratagem of relocating their allegiance to an even higher authority. Significantly, though Abul Fazl too appreciates Dadu, no such attempt is made with him.

These sections cohere with the rest of the narrative where Dadu's miracles change the faith of a range of persons—a muslim, a yogi, merchants and, once again, Raja Birbal.

Though Akbar is de-divinized, his character remains intact, untarnished. Akbar is impressed with Dadu's knowledge and asceticism; he freely/spontaneously offers assent and worship. His questions are at once those of a sceptic and a devotee, and this scepticism, except in the throne episode, is mild and benevolent, it virtually invites conversion. The narrative characterises him as intelligent, able to discern good from evil.

Surdas

In Mahipati's *Bhaktavijay*, Surdas Madanmohan is in the official employment of Akbar in the district of Mathura. Surdas first spends all his own money and then all that is in the king's treasury on hospitality to vaisnav saints. When told about his empty coffers Akbar is enraged and sends his officers. Surdas, after giving them a box of fake jewels and a sealed letter explaining he has spent all the king's money on a worthy object, sadhus and sants, disappears into the forest.

The letter acts as a revelation for Akbar, it shows him the way to the otherworldly; he not only punishes those who had slandered Surdas but is personally grateful to Surdas for showing him, hitherto intoxicated by his royal position, that he should be seeking spiritual riches.

He sends his officers to find Surdas who, when located, comes to Hastinapur (Delhi). The king receives him with honour, embraces him, declares he did not know of the worthy object of Surdas' expenses and wants him to return to his post. Surdas says he has put aside desire for worldly things and does not want to be ensnared by them again. Akbar answers, now that Surdas has become a *virakta* who has cast away illusory thoughts, he can resume his former authority and spend all the money for the well-being of saints since no one other than him is wise enough to serve vaishnavs in Mathura, and he should do so now on the authority of Akbar. Surdas, thinking to himself, 'If I can attain the supreme spiritual riches while still engaged in worldly things,

I should not turn away from doing so', agrees and departs with a written authorization from Akbar to feed the saints.[5] Here Akbar appears as a benevolent, pliable king, relaying his power of distributing largesse.

The blind Surdas had been less amenable in a somewhat earlier hagiography, the late seventeenth, perhaps even early eighteenth century *Caurasi Vaisnavan ki Varta (CVV)*. This was a Pushtimarg hagiology describing Vallabhacharya's own disciples, ascribed to his heir Vitthalnath's son Gokulnath (1522–1641) but probably compiled from oral tradition by Hariray, a great-grandson of Vitthalnath, said to have lived from 1591 to 1711. Hariray included his own commentary called *Bhavaprakash*.[6]

In *CVV*, Akbar is said to have summoned Surdas to his court on hearing Tansen sing his verse and, being very impressed by his spirituality, attempted to reward him with gifts of wealth and land. Surdas, however, scornfully rejected such worldly considerations and curtly forbade Akbar ever to bother him again.[7] In this and other typical tussles with authority he gains a spiritual/symbolic victory.[8] Akbar, the benefactor, is both vanquished and incorporated. But here too, Akbar's wisdom and discrimination are not denied. The commentator's explanation in *Bhavaprakash* softens Surdas' rejection in a profoundly suggestive way that I will return to later.

Tulsidas

The latent aggression of the miracle finds its apogee in Mahipati's hagiographic rendition of Tulsidas in *Bhaktavijay*. Here Tulsidas, said to be the *avatar* of Rishi Valmiki, is born in the house of a wise brahmin named Atmaram who is in the service of Akbar; the early part of the narrative mentions that Tulsidas joined Akbar on his royal tour.[9]

However, before Tulsi encounters Akbar in sant style, his sense of religious boundaries is already fastened to a sharp demarcation between hindu and muslim in the narrative. Tulsidas encounters Maruti in the guise of a brahmin in the forest and asks for the gift of a manifestation of Shri Ram. Subsequently Ram and the monkey army pass in front of the hermitage of Tulsi, who does not recognize them. 'He said to himself "Some Muhammedans are passing by". The monkeys seemed heroic and Shri Ram seemed to be the king of the Muhammedans. Seeing them thus, Tulsidas made them a *namaskar*'.

(p. 39) Maruti returns to tell him he has met Ram. Tulsi denies it and insists that 'the one who passed by my hermitage was truly a Muhammedan. I did not see Ram' (p. 39). Maruti reminds him that he has already been guilty of a series of misrecognitions—he has seen a wish cow as a goat, a clever parrot as a dove, wish trees as ordinary trees, a brahmin as a herder of goats, pearls as glass, swans as crows, and now Ram as a Muhammedan. Tulsi replies:

> O swami, you accuse me unjustly, but Ram who fills all space and pervades the space is invisible. . . . Milk comes from water but one should not call water milk. All water is the same but the chatak bird will not drink the water that is on the earth. So the worshipper of Ram does not consider him as appearing in many forms. The Dweller in Ayodhya, the life of Janaki, was holding His bow and arrow in the same way as Valmiki described him. Show me that appearance.(p.40)

Ram is a bit unwilling, how can Tulsi be given 'a direct manifestation in kaliyuga', but is finally persuaded by Maruti on the ground that Valmiki's *avatar*, born to propagate the worship of Ram, deserves to see him (p. 41). The latent question of identity here that perplexes Tulsi, Ram appearing in the guise of a 'Muhammedan', is one I shall return to in my discussion of Vaishnavism.

Tulsidas settles into his bhakti in Benares, performing many miracles including that of bringing a dead man to life. Akbar is informed and makes an attempt to see the miracles for himself; he asks his ministers to send a learned and articulate brahmin as messenger, one who would incline Tulsi to come to Delhi. The minister goes with several such brahmins, tells Tulsi that the king has heard him to be a 'most extraordinary, god-loving vaishnav bhakt' and wants to see him (p. 50). Tulsi thinks this may be a good opportunity to spread the worship of Ram in Delhi, and goes.

The king comes forward and falls at his feet, seats him on his own throne, whispers a command to his servants not to allow Tulsi to return, and then proceeds to worship Tulsi with the 'sixteen materials for worship'. He tells Tulsi: 'I have heard of your wonderful power and that you have made yourself into a god. You made the stone bull eat food. In the giving of a blessing, you brought a corpse to life. Your deeds seem impossible to me. I do not understand your power.' (p. 50) Tulsi says it is all the doing of Ram. Akbar wants to meet Ram and says he will not allow Tulsi to leave until he arranges the meeting. Akbar retires to his palace thinking: 'If he will show me a manifestation of Ram, then only will I regard Tulsidas as a noble Vaishnav' (p. 51).

Akbar's servants confirm Tulsi's imprisonment. Tulsi invokes Maruti, who performs a miracle; he calls together his army of monkeys and commands them to show their 'natural characteristics' to Akbar (p. 52). The monkeys go on a rampage: they break tiles and trees, they break the noses of some and cut off their ears, twist off the necks of others, snatch the clothes of women going to fetch water and throw them in the Jumna, fasten together the braids and beards of mothers-in-law and fathers-in-law. Those who do not worship Ram or persecute vaishnavs are thrown into stinking drains. The storerooms of evil merchants are looted. They enter the palace and cut off noses and ears; throw dirty water on the five hundred wives and concubines of the emperor; seize evil men—thieves, adulterers—in the palace, lift them and throw them down from above; seize garments and orna-ments and give them to the poor and hungry. They make the poor rich, they rob merchants, beat those who speak the untruth. The orgy of violence is at once arbitrary, ugly, patriarchal, sectarian and utopian.

Wise men advise Akbar to stop persecuting Tulsi, otherwise the monkeys will turn Delhi upside down. Akbar now confesses his fault and injustice. He folds his hands and tells Tulsi: 'I persecuted you, because in my ignorance I did not know what I was doing. Duryodhan suffered humiliation when he persecuted the good Draupadi. So it has happened to me by my persecuting you.' (p. 54) Tulsi answers that Akbar has just seen what is only an advance contingent of Ram's army; after eighteen billion monkeys have arrived, then Ram will follow; Akbar's good fortune has no limit, Ram is indeed coming to see him. Akbar says he has already seen enough of Ram, grasps Tulsi's feet, saying he did not understand Ram's power; if ten thousand monkeys can create such destruction, then eighteen billion will mean the end of the world.

Hearing the king's 'pity-arousing' request, the monkey army becomes invisible and all men worship at the feet of Tulsidas (p. 54). Tulsi then spends a year in Delhi, until all inhabitants begin to repeat the name of Ram, after which he takes his leave of Akbar.

Mahipati lived from 1715 to 1790 in the period of mahratta–mughal conflict, but his hagiographies seem to occupy different temporal locales. The excessive compliance of Surdas is very different from the aggression of Tulsi. In some respects the latter is a reversal narrative; it begins with the father in the emperor's employ and the son a natural hanger-on; it ends with the son vanquishing the emperor.

The narrative's intensification of Akbar's scepticism not only increases his adjudicatory powers but produces ambiguity: impressed, respectful and worshipping Tulsi, he is also the king whose determination to test the true from the false vaishnav (a classic trope in the encounter of the devotee with established power) puts him in the position of an antagonist. In the end he is an emperor humbled by the force of miraculous violence, that seems to induce acquiescence to a superior power rather than spontaneous or rational faith. Significantly, the moment of Akbar's acquiescence is also one of 'mass conversion' and it is his acquiescence that allows Tulsi to persist with his proselytization until he has convinced the whole of Delhi.

At another level, in *Bhaktavijay* Akbar is only one in a series of encounters between saints and kings. Anonymous muslim kings appear several times. An evil muslim king goes to Namdev's *kirtan* and kills a cow—Namdev must now revive it in order to prove he is true worshipper, other wise he too will be killed by the king. When Namdev revives it the king responds with a *namaskar*.[10] In a contest between Sena the barber and another wicked muslim king, Krishna goes disguised as the barber and converts him to the worship of Hari.[11] When Latibshah, a muslim, becomes a pious vaishnav and worships Ram, he is persecuted by a muslim king. The soldiers who come to arrest him are so enthralled with the *Bhagavadgita* that they forsake the king's service. The king arrives and is enraged by the vaishnav ritual, the tulsi altar, and the wall-painting of ten *avatars*. He, however, is converted not to Vaishnavism but to a grudging acceptance by the miracle of a painting coming to life: Radha accepts the *paan* that Krishna is offering, the red mark disappears from the wall.[12] Hindu kings also persecute saints, for instance, Janajaswant, while model kings, like Kashipati, are patrons of vaishnav saints.[13] Saints in turn protect rulers. Because Shivaji comes to visit Tukaram, he is protected by Krishna in his battles, who even disguises himself as Shivaji to defeat 'Muhammedans'. In another story, Shivaji is persuaded to renounce the luxury of sleeping on palatial beds by the ascetic Ganeshnath.[14]

Hagiographic codes

It is evident that in these narratives Akbar is at once a prototypical king, the object of the archetypal, even quasi-allegorical encounter/contest between worldly power and a holy person, and occupies a special space as a preeminently and recognizably *historical figure* who is the multiple object of sought affiliations, of persuasion, of enforced acquiescence and of conversion. The fact that Akbar enters all hagiographies as a historical figure, often accompanied by identifiable and named courtiers, sets him off from the stereotype of the unnamed bad muhammedan king of other hagiographies as in Mahipati's *Bhaktavijay*. What are the nuances and implications of such historicization and personalization of Akbar?

In the discursivities of devotion Akbar comes to signify a more extensive, regionally disparate system of symbolic attribution than any other ruler that I know of. This also suggests a new relation between regional locations and the 'centre' in which the initiative and the power of incorporation seems to rest with both.

Different accents intersect in the 'sign' Akbar but they do not change its fundamental form in the discursive field of devotion. The multiple registers of the narratives remain tied to a directionality. Despite the increased aggression of later combative and browbeating accounts, he never becomes a zealot or religious persecutor. Is this to be attributed to the unifying power of the very structures of hagiography? Or is it that Akbar was invoked in Aurangzeb's time and beyond because he had both popular and imperial legitimacy? Do the hagiographies represent a still widely imaginable range of possibility, a social horizon?

Many stock formulae of hagiography appear, of course. The encounter of holy persons with priestly, monarchical or other figures emblematic of local power, is a recurring motif in hagiographies that record the rise, struggle and self-legitimation of new or heterodox devotional forms/cults. The wrestle between forms of spiritual and temporal authority can be traced back to ancient narratives of brahmins and kshatriyas.

In this perspective Akbar is the formulaic object of the encounter with an authority whose rewards are more often than not rejected, as well as the object of a sought conversion that may or may not be gained. The king's 'surrender' or persuasion too is a sedimented sign of symbolic victory often accompanied, paradoxically, by his patronage, that is, relations of dependence.

And yet, invoking the staple tropes of hagiography does not exhaust the issue. The fact that Akbar continued to be narrativized, retrospectively, in the era of Aurangzeb and beyond, when relations of power had altered and the brahminization of bhakti as well as the renewed influence of muslim orthodoxy were determining hagiographic interpolations, makes of him (in Volosinov's terms) a sign that has not been withdrawn from the pressure of social struggle, a sign that retains a live social intelligibility, around which historical memory and contemporary desire can cluster. If hagiographies are tied to the power of their own generic structures they also excercise another privilege of extended orality: the power of omission and re-interpretation.

Finally, what was the location of hagiographies—were they popular or elite? They do seem to occupy diverse social levels 'below' the court, though these levels and the interaction between 'high' and 'low' have to be determined with far more precision than I can attempt here. To some extent, their figuration of Akbar not only exfoliates from the court but corresponds to it or is continuous with it. The narratives are not pure or wholly autonomous constructions or expressions of a popular *mentalitie* bearing no relation to the courtly/self projection of Akbar. But nor are they fully 'corrupt—that is, permeated by or incorporated into dominant models—rather, they enter into a play of contradictions.

II

Let me, however, first turn to the more or less evidential, recorded encounters.

Chishtis and Other Sufis

Akbar's devotion, reverence and pilgrimages to the chishti *silsilah* are well recorded; occupying an intersection of political loyalty and monetary reward, they were closely tied to pragmatic logics and the legitimation of conquest.

Akbar's desire to make a pilgrimage to Khwaja Mu'inu'd-Din Chishti's shrine in Ajmer was aroused after hearing the songs of some minstrels at Midhakur, near Agra, glorifying the Khwaja.[15] He went first in 1562, then in 1568 after his conquest of Chittor and presented the Khwaja's *khanqah* with a huge cauldron. The wealth from the offerings of Akbar and his entourage resulted in a dispute among the Khwaja's descendants and was placed before Akbar in 1570 when he came to proffer thanks for the birth of his son. Akbar settled the dispute by transferring management of the shrine to Shaikh Bukhari.[16]

71

This same powerful royal arbiter also melted, effortlessly, into a humble pilgrim. He had made that special pilgrimage from Agra to the Ajmer shrine on foot to fulfil his vow of thanksgiving for the birth of his son. Salim, later known as Jehangir, was born in Ajmer in the house of a Chishtiya sufi, Shaikh Salim, and named after him.[17]

Akbar's relationship to several chishtis was marked by munificence,[18] reciprocity, loyalty. Shaikh Jalal Thaneswari of the Chishtiya order was an ecstatic who usually refused to meet noblemen. When Akbar visited him on his way to Kabul in 1581, he was aroused from an ecstatic state by his disciples; informed of the presence of the emperor, he ordered them to help him stand so that he might perform his obligation to his *khalifa*, that is, to Akbar, and then proceeded to recite prayers for the successful outcome of the emperor's expedition.[19] One of Salim Chishti's disciples, Shaikh Taha Chishti, was visited by the defeated but still rebellious Sultan Muzaffar of Gujarat; the sultan asked the Shaikh to dress him in his armour as a sign of his blessing. Taha replied that god had assigned Gujarat to Akbar and therefore he had no power to interfere. The sultan threatened to have the mystic killed before Akbar arrived, but finally agreed to wait a week before ordering his execution. By that time the war was over, the sultan was killed and Gujarat belonged to Akbar.[20]

Akbar is said to have been skilful in his use of influential sufis both to further his schemes of conquest and to systematize his rule. Those who chose to live as ascetics were however offered stipends and non-taxable land grants. But he was also careful to moderate the power of those sufis and ulema who could be potential opponents.[21] Sufi attitudes too were not uniform. Babur's conquest gave an impetus to the development of the Naqshbandiya order; later many migrated to Akbar's court, obtaining high posts in civil and military administration. They were generally loyal to Akbar and supported the broad-based policies that he introduced after 1579, but some Naqshbandiya pirs did oppose his religious policies.[22]

The royal arbiter could also function outside the canopy of devotion. The succession dispute of Shaikh Hamid's sons—Shaikh Abdu'l-Qadir and Shaikh Musa—for their father's *khalifa* came to Akbar's court for decision. Musa's political foresight gave him an edge over his brother and Abdu'l Qadir retired to live as an ascetic in Uch. Moreover, one evening in Fatehpur Sikri Abdu'l Qadir had annoyed Akbar by declaring it was unlawful to consume poppy seeds or their oil; and on another occasion in the same place, after performing congregational prayers, Qadir began his own supererogatory prayers in the *diwan khana* or audience hall. When ordered by Akbar to conduct his prayers in his own quarters, the shaikh answered pertly that in the realm of prayer the emperor's decrees were irrelevant. Greatly annoyed, the emperor declared him 'ignorant' and demanded he leave the empire; Qadir stormed from the hall and immediately resigned his *madad-i-ma'ash*.[23] The succession controversy continued; in Uch and Multan, Qadir was recognized as father's successor while Musa was honoured in this role in Delhi and by court scholars. Musa remained loyal to Akbar and was also a friend of Abul Fazl and Faizi.[24]

Thus, not only was Akbar an established arbiter of disputes, but this incident indicates why Abul Fazl could be perceived as standing in the way of true knowledge for Akbar in the story of Pir Hassu Teli.

However, not all the meetings desired by Akbar materialized and he did not unilaterally impose his will. Shaikh Dawud was a passionate sufi who wandered in Multan and Punjab, and settled down later. Hearing of his fame from dervishes travelling in Punjab, Abdul Qadir Badauni visited him at Shergarh, and wrote that every day fifty to a hundred persons came to see him and were converted to Islam.[25] Though Badauni exaggerated the number, the miracles attributed to Dawud did, it seems, prompt some hindus and members of tribes living near Shergarh to embrace Islam. In 1573–74 Akbar sent Shahbaz Khan Kamboh, an orthodox sunni, to invite the shaikh to his court. Dawud refused, arguing that his secret prayers for the emperor were sufficient for his welfare.[26]

Some of Akbar's associations escape the demands of political pragmatism. The pilgrim too could split from the royal arbiter. In 1561 Akbar, disguised as an ordinary citizen, secretly visited the crowd which had assembled *enroute* to Bahraich to visit the tomb of the warrior saint Ghazi Salar Mas'ud, better known as Ghazi Miya.[27] At the festivities of Akbar's circumcision, Shah Birdi Bayat became an ecstatic, resigned his military career, began to supply free water to the people under the name of Bahram Saqqa, and lived for a while in the precincts of the tomb of Nizamuddin Auliya. Akbar visited his *saqqa-khana* frequently as long as he was in Agra, to drink water and listen to his poetry.[28]

Amardas and Other Sikh Gurus

Akbar's meetings with the sikh gurus also speak of an idiom of royal largesse and patronage marked by dialogue and reciprocity both in gift-giving and in receiving blessings for expansion. It is Akbar who enters their territory, and, as an arbiter of local disputes with orthodoxy, he seems to ratify the social space of heterodoxy.

Having heard of his sanctity, and believing that the conquest of Chittor was due to the blessing he had received from Guru Amardas through an intermediary, Akbar went (partly) on foot to meet the guru, partook of the *langar* with great humility, appreciated the guru's singing. He made a gift of villages and/or a vast tract of land to the guru's daughter, Bibi Bhani, for the upkeep of *langar* when Amardas himself refused to accept it. Amardas in turn gave him a gift; so did Guru Arjandev later. Akbar appreciated him too, humbly offered adoration to him and had religious discussions with him in 1598. In 1605 qazis and pandits complained that the *Adi Granth* blasphemed both their religions. Akbar, pleased with and admiring of the teachings of the *Granth*, settled the dispute by dismissing it. The passages from the *Granth* that Akbar is said to have liked critique worldly power, wealth, the rigidities of brahminical and islamic orthodoxy, and this suggests that he was perceived as ratifying this space from 'above'. Akbar is said to have abolished pilgrim tax because of Guru Amardas' refusal to pay it, as well as to have remitted land tax on peasants for a year at a time of famine on the intercession of Guru Ramdas, all of which increased the local popularity of the gurus.[29]

Gosain Jadrup

Akbar visited the famous yogi Gosain Jadrup in 1601. Jehangir continued to visit him and was eulogistic about him. The Gosain's own response to the latter does not name Akbar but has a retrospective resonance that seems to enfold Akbar:

> In what language can I return thanks for this gift of Allah that I am engaged in the reign of such a just king in the worship of my own deity in ease and contentment, and that the dust of discomposure from any accident settles not on the spirit of my purpose?[30]

Shaikh Badi'u'Din Saharanpuri, who claimed he had visited Gosain Jadrup, related how the Gosain had told him the Mujaddid was superior to all other spiritual guides. However, when asked why he did not become the Mujaddid's disciple, he answered that being a prominent hindu saint himself he was not in need of someone else's instruction.[31]

When compared to the hagiographies, these encounters reveal a more variegated spectrum and one more imbued with the pragmatism of empire. But, as is apparent, hagiographic codes too structure the events as well as the recording of these non-fictive encounters: the travelling fame of holy persons fans royal desire; the royal court is omniscient, the deeds and repute of all holy persons reaches its ears; royal munificence is offered and usually accepted; the king either himself travels to meet them or summons them to court. Akbar is an arbiter of succession disputes but not of holiness and, consequently, there are no miracles—these latter two features seem to be more embedded in the structure of hagiographies.

It follows too, then, that conversion should be a more marked feature of the hagiographies. As displays of power, miracles are meant to convert—they can be directed not only at brahmins, common people or kings, but more subtly from a sect to another sect, from sufis to other sufis, from sufis to their adversaries. At a formal level, 'conversion' of the king, whether as outright change in belief, or as patronage, or simply as acceptance, is part of a semantic of conquest of worldly pleasure, a system of subduing worldly authority to spiritual authority, be it vaishnav or sufi.

The question of the social ground of the trope of conversion remains, particularly since it was a recurring motif in the practices of pirs, bhakts, sants, and I will return to it.

III

Let me first summarize the possible axes along which 'Akbar' could become a system of symbolic attributions: the re-narrativization of events, the orbits of charity, an eclectic court, new sources of legitimation from 'below', synchronic 'non-family' or elective communities of saints, his own contradictory personal location, the links between royal self-projection and hagiographic notation, and the difficulty of classifying his beliefs.

Encounter into Hagiography

Obviously, the non-fictive recorded encounters are themselves one such axis, and they provide a bases for extension, elaboration, remodulation, recombination in hagiographies.

Some encounters were later structered into hagiography. Akbar's meeting with the zoroastrian teacher Dastur Meherji Rana became the subject of a popular story and many ballads in Gujarat. The story went: by force of magic a brahmin raised in the sky a metallic tray which resembled a second sun; Meherji Rana brought down the artificial sun by means of his prayers and incantations; Akbar was much surprised by this miracle.[32]

In another variant, a hindu priest named Jugut Guru, deeply versed in magic and sorcery, once performed a miracle in the presence of the emperor and his court by sending up and suspending a large silver plate high in the sky, which looked like another sun shining in the heavens, and challenged the professors of all the religions assembled to take this new sun down and test the power of their faiths. Akbar called upon the ulema to do this and refute the hindu, but they could not do it themselves. Hence they were in anxious search of some one who could do this and digrace the infidel. They were told that a priest in Naosari could do it if he were called. At their suggestion, Akbar sent for him. He came, and by reciting prayers and other incantations he broke the power of the hindu magic, and the false sun came down and fell at Akbar's feet. Akbar was astonished; the priest was received with awe. He expounded his faith to Akbar and convinced him so well as to make him a parsi. This parsi tradition circulated in various forms in prose and verse; some poems about this triumph of Meherji Rana continued to be sung by *khialis* or itinerant minstrels, and others in Gujarat and Bombay.[33]

A *farman* records Akbar's meeting with Udant Nath or pir Bhau Nath, the founder of the Jakhbar *gaddi* of saivite jogis of the Kanphata sect. Local narratives however go much further and claim that Akbar held the pir in deep reverence after he miraculously transported a ber tree from Mecca to satisy the emperor's sudden craving.[34]

The Orbit of Charity

The mughal state continued the practice of several earlier states to institutionalize a relation with ascetic and holy men through charity. Like earlier states, the mughal state too felt bound to notice those who had eschewed its own premises of power and authority; the charity was a form of the state seeking its own legitimacy from those who ignored it, that is, recognizing alternate sources of social authority.

76

The state also classified, subtly arrogating a right to definition as a precondition of its obligation to provide. The most important duty of the *sadru's sudur* was disbursement of state charities and grant of *madad-i ma'ash* to scholars and destitutes. According to Abul Fazl, the following four classes of people were considered worthy and in need of subsistence: those who had withdrawn from all worldly occupations and had made search for true knowledge the sole concern of their life; ascetics and hermits who had left the world to get rid of selfish desires and human passions; the poor and needy who did not even have the strength to busy themselves in search of knowledge; men of noble birth who from ignorance and want of learning were deprived of the means of acquiring money.[35]

Religion was no bar to the grants of *madad-i ma'ash* under mughals; Akbar made land grants to the influential Jogis of Jakhbar starting in 1571, which were confirmed by his successors; he also made a land grant to the Jangambari *math* at Benares, that was confirmed by Aurangzeb in the early years of his reign who at this time also gave other grants to non-hindus.[36]

The politics of the acceptance and refusal of reward in hagiographies could perhaps disentangled not only in relation to the state's idea of charity and to the rejection of the state by some sects, but also to the wider hierarchical underpinning of the idea of charity that was shared across denominational distinctions. The medieval period was conspicuous in lavish gifts and generosity. Charity on the part of social superiors towards inferiors was seen as a virtue by hindus and muslims. The belief prevailed that every gift of charity in this world would be rewarded ten times in value in the next. What is more, frugality displayed meanness of heart.[37]

A Heterodox Court

The patronage of the court extended from translation of Sanskrit to Persian to sanctuary for several heterodox or persecuted persons, including poets; indeed the heterodoxy of the court as a whole dispensed a more personalized and widely dispersed patronage than the religious grants, and also provided after 1576 a space for religious debate in the increasingly cosmopolitan *ibadat khana* or house of worship.

Some poets came to the mughal court because they were persecuted in their homelands for their unorthodox religious views, for instance, Ghazali Meshedi from Iraq and Qasim-i-Kahi who, known for his catholicity, mixed freely with *qalandars*, mystics, free thinkers, and visited different places of worship including Somnath—Badauni said Meshedi had spent his whole life in heresy and impiety! Another poet, Ja'far Beg, was a member of Akbar's Tauhid-i-elahi.[38] Some of Akbar's courtiers—Tansen, Mansingh, Birbal—who liaise between him and saints in hagiographic narratives, themselves patronized a variety of sects and figured independently in some hagiographies.[39] The court's heterodoxy as a whole further diluted the thin discursive divide between the literary, the devotional, the performative, and as is evident in the notation of Mira in *Bhaktmal*, was itself played into an overlapping terrain. Damodar of Jhang, probably a contemporary, refered to Akbar's reign as presiding over the final reunion of Heer and Ranjha after their death in his quasi-mystical rendition of the *qissa*.[40]

Legitimation from Below?

Akbar is simultaneously part of the existing royal practice of patronage of poets and saints—a classic feature of kingship and religious legitimation—and its culmination, but recast in a new mould, since he himself is presented as seeking legitimation primarily from popular worship rather than from brahmins or ulema.

Groups who entered the Indian subcontinent in the early medieval period had often indigenized on the kshatriya model, sought and received brahminical legitimation, a process facilitated by the wide dispersal of brahminical groups who assisted in the reproduction of state and ruling group ideologies. Certain elements of indigenization on the kshatriya model continued during the sultanate and mughal rule but that seems to have been politically insufficient, perhaps because the ulema did not have the reach of brahmins.

By Akbar's time a social process—visible in roving and institutionalized devotional movements, often syncretic and locally influential—was already underway which could provide other axes for the legitimation and reproduction of the state, making it possible for rulers to seek these in disparate modes of worship. This was a contingent, conjunctural phenomena, it was neither reducible to political processes nor did it run in tandem with them; indeed the composite ruling class of the *mansabdari* system never became powerful enough to form a separate force.[41]

It was this phenomenon, combined with heterodoxy, that could interlock with a system of affiliation that I call elective or non-family communities, and allow Akbar to become an 'imaginable' apex figure in a devotional constellation.

Elective Communities

The very fictionality of the hagiographical encounters claimed with Akbar indicates perceived ideological affinities, affinities that are coded as meetings. In the genre, meetings were far more substantive than mere assertions of affinity.

The idea of a non-family community seems to have been initiated by Namdev (1270–1350) as a company of sants who knew each other and sants of the past, cutting across linguistic and regional divisions, and unconstrained by the fact that no such meetings had taken place. This was continued by Eknath who constituted a living tradition of fifty sants based not on meetings but on a knowledge of the stories of their lives.[42]

The oral transmission of hagiographies across linguistic lines may have contributed to the growing power of the idea, as well as the itinerary of pilgrimages that not only took devotees outside their own linguistic regions but produced a spatial catholicity that could become part of a single itinerary. If social practice contributed to the formal assemblage of linked hagiographies, these newly compendious hagiologies implied being born into webs of narratives and interlocution rather than into ascriptive primordialities.

The notion of a company of sants was abstract yet provided a cluster of authority and mode of legitimation that may be related to the socially unprivileged and low caste-character of many devotional movements, which, though dissenting, did not lose their dependence on sanctions. Significantly, the presence of women saints was marginal. The sense of kinship or of being a clan among persons unconnected by any traceable historical lineage, and attached to sant *panth*s, vaisnav *sampraday*s and sufi *silsilah*s has been discussed by Daniel Gold.[43] In spiritual lineages, family trees could contain muslims and disciples from various castes (kunbi, baniya, kshatriya, brahmin), regions, occupations (cultivators, servants, landowners), with hierarchies that often moved upwards and maintained these distinctions in groups of worshippers. Lineages, thus, could contain a great deal of internal variety, local variation and be diffused over various sants, or many *panths* could exist in the name of a dead sant.[44] This speaks for an intricate social networking and geographical mobility which bypasses actual clans and lineages while using their structures!

These elective communities pre-dated Akbar and extended beyond him. A mid-seventeenth-century mughal miniature showing sants and yogis with a group of sufi saints and court familiars watching the ecstatic dance of muslim mystics, set in the Ajmer *dargah* of Mu'inuddin Chishti at the annual *urs* mela, was probably painted under the patronage of Dara Shikoh. Chistis were already closely identified with the mughal dynasty. Many of the sufis are identifiable personalities, long dead, and their presence in a contemporaneous scene suggests the concept of *silsila* or spiritual chain linking gene-ratios of sufis back to Muhammed and god. The identifiable saints are fairly unorthodox: the cobbler Ravidas or Raidas; Pipa (*circa* 1335– 1403), said to have been a raja who abdicated his sovereignty and distri-buted his wealth among the poor, Sena the barber; Namdev; Kabir; Kamal, said to be son of Kabir, a shaivite ascetic, Pir Mucchander, legendary guru of Gorakhnath; Gorakhnath; Gosain Jadrup; Lal Swami; and one unidentifiable figure associated with Vaishnavism. The sants are roughly on the left and yogis on the right at the bottom, above are muslim saints, heads of sufi orders, and in the middle ground there is dancing and chanting accompanied by music.[45]

This crystallized notion of a composite, interactive commu-nity of holy men *across* historical time and space, that is, a *synchronic* community (in which saivites, vaishnavites, sants, Ramanand's disciples *et al* interact with pirs) is significantly not a later liberal inter-polation but a contemporary seventeeth-century imagined/desired horizon. It may be worth remembering that the oral compositions and hagiographies of most of these personages were actually compiled, written or systematized in this period. So the notions of wide-ranging religious affinity, of hindu–muslim kinship and hindu–muslim ani-mosity, *all* occupied the period of Aurangzeb!

Akbar could be one nodal point in the creation of a commu-nity of saints, both metaphorically and literally, as a patron. More significantly, the expansion of empire under him provided some of the material conditions conducive to such non-family bonding, since conquests also enlarged the avenues for mercantile activity, travel, pilgrimage and regional interchange.

A Plebean King?

Akbar's personal location appears to be contradictory. Identifiable with the enlargement of royal pomp since the days of the sultanate, especially in the accumulation of palaces, wealth and women, intensifying the conflation of kings with the principle of worldliness and inviting reform, he simultaneously carried a special plebean, even artisanal aura, compounded with an 'illiteracy'—to which could be ascribed the spontaneous, intuitive knowledge that subversively cut through the corruption of high textuality—celebrated since the early sufis and Kabir.

This latter aura of plebean accessibility attaches itself readily to the incidents recounted by Abul Fazl and others—Akbar visiting fairs in disguise, disfiguring his face with a squint when recognized, watching artisans at their craft, staying in peasant homes, eating at a common *sarai* run by a bhatiyari, wearing a lungi—and is also evident in the account of a contemporary jesuit missionary, Du Jarric, who described Akbar's especial courtesy to men of the humbler classes; his being often seen 'shearing camels, hewing stones, cutting wood, or hammering iron and doing all with as much diligence as though engaged in his own particular vocation'. Du Jarric claimed 'that every man believed the prince was on his side'. [46]

Biography/Autobiography/Hagiography

Again, in contradictory fashion, Akbar appears as the consenting subject of an official biographical divinisation verging on hagiography and as consenting to a denominational unclassifiability that aroused the wrath of orthodox muslims such as Badauni.

Abul Fazl produced a comprehensive ideal of kingship, structured around the unusual dyad of the divine origin of sovereignty and the heterogenous nature of the king's subjects who followed a wide variety of religions. The host of virtues kings customarily possessed—such as magnanimity, benevolence, paternal love, justice, forgiveness, complete trust in god—were now accompanied by a king above religious differences, guided by reason, following the course of enquiry and avoiding blind authority (*taqlid*), adopting universal peace and toleration as the crux of his policy, and *sulh-i kul* or peace with all as the guiding principle of his government. [47]

The king in this account is believer and sceptic, faithful and rational; this mixture of faith and enquiry is not only startlingly replicated in hagiographies but even the spirit of enquiry is implicitly related to the presence of a large number of faiths which make blind authority undesirable.

In *Ain-I Akbari* Fazl's stated problematic was the friction between various religions in India. He attributed this partly to the barrier of linguistic diversity compounded by the insularity of the country from others and the persecution of earnest inquirers that prohibited dialogue; he gave a positive role to the state in ensuring security and making a space for dialogue—almost exactly what Akbar does even in the more aggressive hagiographies.

The posited relation here between a notion of kingship and the relation of the state to religious difference is substantiated in many of Akbar's recorded encounters with holy men and even more markedly in hagiographies (the similarity and difference between them needs more detailed attention than I can give here). So vivid is the triangular relation, even mutuality, between discursive courtly ideal, royal practice and a regionally disparate hagiographic horizon, that it is difficult to reduce this phenomenon to the exfoliation of an image of a benevolent state and emperor from 'above'. It may instead be a clue to the way the terms of the practices and self-projection of state and court are being restructured in relation to needs from 'below.' In other words, the heterodox tendencies in court and in popular culture may have been part of an interactive historical dynamic.

It seems that the personal divinisation of Akbar was the only device available to Abul Fazl through which religions and politics could be made to cohere and to be ultimately subservient to the emperor—the highest court of appeal. He traces Akbar's political wisdom to divine revelations; his political authority is invested with spiritual leadership and the dichotomy between religion and politics was to resolve itself before his all-embracing personality which looked after both the mundane and spiritual affairs of society; Akbar is imagined as an emperor–prophet. The first chapter of the *Akbarnama* describes the 'holy manifestations' preceding his birth, reads like a popular traditional superstitious account of the birth of prophets, and is hardly consonant with Fazl's own critique of the irrational approach of the ulema. Light shines from the brows of Akbar's pregnant mother, light enters the bosom of the nurse; Akbar even remembers everything from the time he was one-year-old.[48]

However, Akbar virtually co-authored the *Akbarnama*. Not only did he take a keen personal interest in its day-to-day progress to see how his biography was being presented, but Fazl's scheme of glorification agreed in all details with his own ambitions.[49] If Akbar was part-creator of his own official image, then the *Akbarnama* occupies an intersection between hagiography, biography and autobiography, giving an uncanny dimension to the continuum between Akbar, the court, some contemporary perception, and hagiographic inscription—almost as if Akbar is actually being seen, at least by some, the way he wanted himself to be seen.

How did this willing subject of hagiography enter the hagiographies of others? Does the aura of divinity that makes him a preceptor in his own right make him less of a king and more of an equal? Is he not merely a king, but himself the architect of a creed and a preceptor in contest with other preceptors? It is evident, at least from the interpolation in *Dadu Janma Lila*, that the divinization of Akbar produced some resistance too, and could have been related to the use of miracles to impress him, though to some extent these are structural to hagiographies. Did the divinisation of sovereignty, involving as it does a system of attributes that imply reciprocity between divine objects and believers, and a semiotic that cuts across boundaries of region and religion, facilitate Akbar's absorption into hagiographies as primarily a benevolent ruler?

In practice, Akbar's divinization was simultaneously fleshed out and undercut by its content, a content that cannot be identified with any single religion and was closer to the refusals in sant traditions. Akbar seems to have fostered the image of inoffensive controlled scepticism and unclassifiability. He seems to have repeated the claim of being neither muslim nor hindu, that resonated in the north for several centuries from Kabir to Dadu Dayal to Bulhe Shah: 'I am neither in the ranks of unbelievers nor of musalmans. I am neither fit for hell nor heaven. What am I to do?'[50] This very ambiguity may have multiplied the range of religious sites he was made to occupy.

Eclecticism and Unclassifiability

Echoing Akbar's contemporaries, historians from the eighteenth century to the present have debated, from different stances, whether or not he was a muslim, whether or not his eclecticism meant deviation from or confirmation of the fundamentals of Islam, whether or not he was anti-islamic, and whether or not he was a believer. This debate seems to assume that denominational classification and religious boundaries were stable, impermeable to historical change, and ignores the pressure for alternate spaces that had come into being. While varieties of 'unbelief' and changes in religious practice are accepted, these are believed to have no effect on the *definition* of religions.

It may be more rewarding to see the cooperative and contradictory play between hagiographies and the court as part of an ongoing social process. The interrelated heterodox tendencies in court and in devotional movements show that there was a conscious and far-reaching contest over defining a more denominationally defiant and flexible third space, critical of established religions. This space was widening at many social levels, ranging from popular devotion and the cosmopolitan court of Akbar (with its comparativist, innovative and intellectual bent) that interacted with those 'below' through patronage, to a 'symbolic' social potential around which popular versions of Akbar were knit. Devotional movements faced difficulties in consolidating this space. If some political and economic changes abetted it, other elite and class interests resisted it.

This space also seems to have a complicated relation to previous puranic and early medieval forms of eclecticism, and to earlier eclectic forms of royal patronage. Both had assisted its unfolding but at the same time continuously reabsorbed it into existing power hierarchies. Maybe that is why, over time, the relation to royal or established power was shaped around a dyad of contest with and incorporation of saints, till it became an established hagiographical trope.

The nature of the space itself was preeminently one that resisted ready denominational classification or identity—a tendency, as is evident in hagiographies, that ran counter to a contrary existing tendency of direct recourse to or incorporation into recognised/sanctioned brahminical and islamic models.

IV

Akbar was not only the (willing) object of a series of failed classifications but also of part-successful or failed conversions from above and below—and these too were linked to questions of classification. He was the object of conversion for three organized religious groups—jains, zoroastrians and jesuit missionaries; all three were, interestingly, trading groups and direct beneficiaries.

Parsis

Akbar entertained and held discussions with zoroastrian scholars, accepted fire-worship and parsi festivals.[51] He gave a land grant to the parsi religious leader Meherji Rana, resident of Naosari, Gujarat, who visited the court and explained the tenets of his religion; his son Kaiqubad also received a grant from Akbar.[52] Later traditions read these as signs of conversion.

Traditional Gujarati songs suggest that Meherji converted Akbar by investing him with *surdesh* (the sacred shirt) and *kusti* (the sacred thread girdle), outward signs of having adopted that faith.[53] The *khial* begins:

> Meherji Rana was a very virtuous man.
> He was a perfect servant of god.
> King Akbar put on the sudrah.
> Look to the display of the Zoroaster religion.[54]

These mutation may have taken place in the late eighteenth century. A manuscript dated 1792, written for a well-known merchant of Bombay, Behdin Jamshedji Kukaji, by Mobed Behram, carries a praise song of the *dastur* and Akbar authored by the celebrated Tansen.[55]

Jains

Akbar entertained and engaged jain monks in prolonged debates in the *ibadat khana*. According to contemporary svetambar jain accounts, they were a persuasive influence. He became an object of jain *prashasti* and panegryrics. His court was a space for upward mobility in administrative posts for some jains, while the encouraging reception of jain ascetics also ensured support of prosperous jains.[56]

Three great jain teachers are recorded as having visited the court of Akbar—Hiravijaya Suri, Vijaysen Suri and Bhanuchandra. It was later claimed that Akbar, under jain influence, forbade animal slaughter for twelve days during the holy Paryushana festival in six provinces of India where they were in residence.[57] He conferred by special *farman* a number of hills, temples, pilgrimage spots on Hiravijaya Suri.[58]

It seems Akbar was also interested in jain philosophy, especially in adopting partial vegetarianism. He appreciated the doctrine that *karma* or human action and not god were the cause of human happiness and unhappiness, and more or less accepted *ahinsa*. In the course of his conversations with jains he began to question the validity of islamic tenets of revelation, resurrection and the day of judgement. The Jain tenets of *karma*, *moksha* and *ahinsa* were debated vis-à-vis both islamic and brahminical tenets.[59]

Jesuits

The European encounter has its own interest. In his negotiations with the Portugese, Akbar came across accompanying jesuit missionaries; he invited jesuits from Goa to his court at Fatehpur Sikri.

This led to an enthusiasm on their part for converting him—it would be a victory for the church since large numbers could then be converted. According to the accounts of these jesuits, he showed respect for the Bible and they felt that his interest in knowing about the Trinity and the incarnation of god as Christ was a sign of real interest in the christian faith; but they were disturbed because his mental disposition did not seem right for conversion, nor did his polygamy—he seemed to them to lack interest in changing his way of life. They decided to persevere since he was well-disposed to the missionaries and had abandoned Islam.[60] Attachment to polygamy was construed as an obstacle to conversion while Akbar's curiosity and long discussions were read as readiness to convert.[61]

One missionary, Acquaviva, put these difficulties into the discourse of pragmatism and ambiguity. He categorically affirmed that the conversion of Akbar was impossible. Some would say he was a hindu, others that he was a muslim. He adds that the emperor conformed himself to all to win the goodwill of all. He was neither a christian nor a hindu nor a muslim.[62] But he thought that it might help if the pope himself wrote to Akbar. Pope Gregory XIII did write in 1582, saying that there should not be great delay in taking the bold step since 'this movement of [Akbar's] spirit' came from god. He asked Akbar to compare the worth of his soul and the salvation promised by Christ against the kingdom, power, sons, subjects and wealth he possessed as the ruler, and suggested that all these were worth nothing compared with the dignity of his soul, and

> an everlasting kingdom compared with one of short duration, perishable and subject to many contingencies; transform your mortal power into undying bliss; prepare for yourself a new family

and treasures in heaven. God will perhaps grant you that, if it be expedient for your salvation, you enjoy also this earthly kingdom.

He suggested that if it were God's will, Akbar could continue holding the reins of the kingdom even after conversion to Christianity.[63]

Acquaviva noticed changes in Akbar—homage to sun and moon, partial abstinence from meat, patronising parsi festivals. This mix of the hindu, jain and zoroastrian confused Acquaviva who was unable to understand him or his continuing friendliness; he claimed that Akbar had himself admitted to him that he, 'was so bewildered as to be unable to establish the truth'.[64] He felt that Akbar's motives for cherishing friendships with Europeans were other than the religious.

In 1590 Akbar celebrated the feast of the assumption of the blessed virgin Mary and her picture was put up for public veneration. The jesuits felt he had finally renounced Islam, and one of them even reported that he had given all his wives but one in marriage to various nobles. Akbar performed the same celebration in 1595 for another set of missionaries and asked them to start a church at Lahore. These missionaries too attributed pragmatic motives to Akbar; and Akbar did indeed have political motives.[65]

The particular jesuit father who was in the court on Akbar's death said: 'He died as he had lived; for, as none know what law he followed in his lifetime, so none knew in which he had died.'[66] According to another jesuit missionary's observation:

> The emperor is not a Muhammedan but is doubtful as to all forms of faith and holds firmly that there is no divinely accredited form of faith, because he finds in all something to offend his reason and intelligence.... At the court some say that he is a heathen.... Others that he is a Christian. Others that he intends to found a new sect. Among the people there are various opinions regarding the emperor; some holding him to be a Christian, others a heathen, others a Muhammedan. The more intelligent, however, consider him to be neither Christian nor heathen nor Muhammedan, and holds it to be the truest. Or they think him to be a Muhammedan who outwardly conforms to all religions in order to obtain popularity.[67]

Another equally confused jesuit father, Xavier, eventually resolved his dilemma by characterizing Akbar as 'a philosopher in search of truth'.[68]

The jesuits work on the assumption that Akbar could belong to only the one or the other religion. In this logic, tolerance or eclecticism becomes deceit or dissimulation, the patina for an undisturbed core of the true belief lying beneath. The unclassifiable is more troubling for jesuits than for most other religious groups, who seem content that Akbar had accepted *some* of their tenets or practices.

Again, as far as the idea of tolerance that takes the shape of such partial conversion goes, the freedom of every religion, logically, impinges on the boundaries of all. This was indeed the jesuit position. As Monserrate put it, Akbar's toleration of all religions in reality violated the law of all religions.[69]

Akbar himself seemed untroubled by the wider possibilities of conversion. The christian missionaries who he repeatedly invited to court received freedom to worship, to make converts, to construct churches, and were given land and cash.[70]

Obviously, the relation between state and religions was complex—royal eclecticism could serve many purposes, while the close relation between mercantile interests and religious groups raises a host of questions. Neither of these can, however, be reduced to pragmatism alone.

The fact that Akbar allows jesuits to convert anyone they wished shows an easy acceptance, a lack of fear of conversion, an understanding that conversions are not unilateral but can come from many directions, while his own practice indicates that they need not even be complete.

This opens into other questions which I cannot do justice to here. First, the hint of a deep and wide-ranging comparativism on pre-orientalist principles, in which no religion seems to have been the first principle from which to evaluate others. Second, the crystalization of profound departures from puranic and pre-medieval processes of religious choice and selection. Third, 'partial conversions' may be a better analytical tool to understand processes of assimilation and syncretism.

V

Akbar's unclassifiability was a source of palpable discomfort for jesuit missionaries. Two vaishnav hagiologies faced with the same difficulty resolved it differently through multifaceted gestures of inclusion and exclusion—that describe some of the trajectories of 'partial' conversion.

Vaishnavism

The question of denominational identity was particularly vexing for vaishnavs since Vaishnavism had been a site of prolonged hindu-muslim interaction in Maharashtra, Awadh, Bengal, Gujarat. *Avatar*s figured as an axis of mutual incorporation and many 'muslims' like Abdur Rahim Khan Khanan, Bairam Khan's son, wrote vaishnav poetry. A number of the translations from Sanskrit to Persian commissioned by Akbar were of vaishnav texts.[71] There is also an unsubstantiated story of Akbar visiting the Krishna temple built by Mansingh in Vrindavan with Akbar's permission.[72]

Several muslims were converted to Vaishnavism. According to Mahmud Balkhi, a Central Asian, who travelled in India in 1624–25 during Jehangir's reign, vaishnav practices in Mathura at the Krishna temple built by Raja Mansingh, were so attractive that they seemed worth conversion. He wrote in *Bah-rul Asrar*:

> Beaming with joy, men and women, without shame mixing together but committing no impropriety, try to outdo each other in performing their rites, *rasoi* and all their false prayers. In the meantime a few thousand pleasure-seekers assemble at the other side of the bank of the river with the object of witnessing the scene, obtain a sight thereof. Such a sense-enticing sight is obtained that one might lose the rein of Islam and become a follower of the Hindus! Verily, from the heresy of the faces, figures and features of these modest blossoming-faced [women], it is no wonder that one's faith may be shaken and the glass of shame broken by stone; all self-control disappears! [73]

He describes twenty-three muslim bairagis in Benares who converted because they fell in love *an masse*:

> I saw a concourse of beautiful women, perfectly decorated and ornamented.
>
> One of the strange affairs of that place that I witnessed was that twenty-three Muslims fell captive to their charms. Having fallen in love they had deserted their religion and accepted their creed.
>
> For some time I held the company of them [the converts] and questioned them about their mistaken way. They pointed towards the sky and put their fingers to their foreheads. By this gesture I understood that they attributed it to Providence and fate.[74]

Karma into Conversion

In the *Caurasi Vaisnavan ki Varta* hagiography of Surdas, Akbar is endowed with wisdom and discrimination. The commentator, Hariray, finds it necessary to explain the fact that a muslim such as Akbar should be sufficiently perspicacious to be able to appreciate Sur's spiritual qualities[75]:

> So the emperor Akbar was endowed with discrimination. How so? He had become a non-hindu (*mlecch*) through a transgression of correct ritual practice; in his previous birth he had been a hindu celibate (*brahmacari*) by the name of Balmukund, and one day when he drank unfiltered milk a cow's hair entered his stomach. And because of that transgression he became a *mlecch* in his next birth.[76]

This is a very complex gesture of inclusion and exclusion. At one level *karma* leads to a weaving in and out of hindu, muslim and other births, giving the soul a complicated and varied social trajectory. A hindu reborn as a muslim never quite loses all his hinduness which seems to cling in the next birth: Akbar remains a benevolent appreciator of vaishnavs. But arguably, if hinduness is not fully lost in a muslim birth, then muslims are affines at a very deep level indeed. At a popular, rather than philosophical, level *karma* and past hindu birth become a way of accommodating muslims as friends, benefactors, patrons. 'Good' muslims like Akbar can be partially incorporated by virtue of having been hindus in earlier lives. The minuteness of Akbar's sin in his past birth is itself remarkable—a completely unwitting transgression of ritual.

Did the need to explain through *karma* arise because a mughal patron of heterodoxy could not be appreciated except through assimilation? Or because cross-religious devotional cults were common enough, but so were the realities of power and concomitant othering—and *karma* could provide a handy explanatory framework for both? *Karma* could become an assimilative form of (retrospective?) conversion that permitted othering.

William Crooke cites another version, presumably popular in the nineteenth century but now unconnected to any saint.

> The emperor Akbar was in a former life a brahmin named Mukunda, who carried out a course of austerities in order to induce Siva to make him an emperor. Siva refused to grant his prayer, but

advised him to suicide at Prayag or Allahabad as a punishment for his overweening ambition. Mukunda agreed on condition that he might remember in a future birth the events of his present life. Siva agreed and Mukunda was allowed to record his memoirs on a copper plate and bury it at the sacred river Jumna. Years after he was reborn in the womb of Hamida, mother of Akbar, who, when he ascended the throne, went to Prayag and dug up the plate, with the tongs, gourd, deerskins, and other properties which Mukunda as an ascetic used.[77]

Akbar is given the previous birth of an ascetic but unnaturally ambitious brahmin. In what appears to be a decisive shift from oral to print transmission and textuality, this past birth is memorialized in writing that survives as archaeological/'historical' evidence subject to retrieval through proper excavation.

The device of *karma* seems to allow a method of genealogizing that is both parallel and tangential to earlier elite rajput or muslim royal genealogies. In this method, as old as the *Jatakas*, the previous births of an individual rather than the history of a family, group or dynasty, were traced. Here it seems to have become a way of mediating contemporary contradictions in systems of power and the identification of individuals. Akbar discovers his karmic lineage as a 'fallen' brahmin at the moment of his ascent to kingship. *Karma* is at once a principle of differentiation and of connection.

Akbar's narrative 'fate' seems to be a cross-hatch of that of Raskhan, traditionally identified as a pathan named Sayyid Ibrahim from Pihani in Hardoi district, who became a vaishnav bhakt of Vitthalnath and probably lived in the second half of the sixteenth century, as described in the vaishnav Pushtimarg hagiology *Do Sau Barah Vaisnavan ki Varta*, with that of a khatri disciple of Vallabhacharya described in *Caurasi Vaisnavan ki Varta*. In the latter, the wife of a devotee from Kannauj named Damodardas Sambhalvare, anxious as to the outcome of her pregnancy—itself granted as a boon by Vallabhacharya—consulted a woman with special powers to discover the sex of her child. Because of the sectarian insistence on the importance of single-minded faithfulness in devotion to the chosen guru, such a consultation constituted the sin of *anyasray*, or resort to another authority, and was punished by Vallabhacharya who declared that the child would be born a *mlecch*—here synonymous with muslim. The child's mother, once aware that she carried a *mlecch* in her womb, desisted from service to the deity; and when the child was born he was disowned to be reared by a wet nurse.[78] The *Bhavaprakash* commentary, anxious to distance the pious parents from the uncleanness of their child, adds that the boy did not actually become a *mlecch* until reaching the age of ten.[79]

This amazing slippage between caste as an effect of birth and the loss of caste as part of punitive othering exceeds even the machinery of *karma*. Normally, a sinner would be born in the next birth as a woman or *mlecch* or sudra, and so belong to the appropriate family; here, in order to punish the mother, a son of hindu family is born a muslim. This bears the potential of seriously disrupting the entire notion of ritual order, caste and community—anyone can give birth to anyone.[80] The punishment is deeply ambivalent both in its social consequences and by virtue of the parental connection between hindu and muslim. A sense of such social and affinal connections also comes out in the way that *Do Sau Barah Vaisnavan ki Varta* refers to muslims as *bari jati*: in fact Shrinathji (Krishna) himself, the mere sight of whose image has turned Raskhan's heart and produced fervent *gopi bhav* for his *mehboob*, speaks of Raskhan as a 'divine soul who has been born in the *bari jati*.'[81] Perhaps othering was not always a unilateral process but accompanied by assimilation, conversion, and other mutually binding identities—only then could being a muslim be figured consecutively as a punitive fate and as the object of Krishna's compassion, camraderie and ready acceptance. The *Bhavaprakash* commentary of Hariray may have been trying to flatten this ambivalence by putting the age of Damodar's son becoming a *mlecch* at ten (implying circumcision?), otherwise how and when would a child of hindu parentage be singled out as a muslim? The word of an angry, patriarchal guru was insufficient by itself to mark the child.

Conversion and Reversion

Having inherited an apocalyptic view of conversion from the stark oppositions set up between Hinduism, Islam and, later Christianity, in colonial and communal historiography, we forget that conversion was embedded in a variety of social relations and a continuous feature of the history of the subcontinent—buddhist, jain, roman catholic, sunni, saiva, vaishnav, tantric, sufi, bhakti—there was no dearth of proselytizers or of persuasion.

There were instances, as yet underexplored, of conversion to Islam and reversion of rajputs and brahmins in several regions, some of which may have been related to the attempt to retighten caste boundaries loosened by Islam in this period; in medieval Bengal it was said that a brahmin could be taken back for 'the fire of brahminical spirit burns in a brahmin up to six generations'.[82] *Bhaktavijay* retails the story of Bahiram Bhatt, a brahmin who converted to Islam and then reverted, a process which left him for a while in grave doubt about his identity and the conviction that he was neither.

The Siyal clan of Jhang district has a tradition that their founder was converted by Baba Farid. Richard Eaton's count of masculine given names in genealogical charts of twenty generations stretching from the early thirteenth century, in which the founder lived, to the nineteenth century, in which the charts were gathered into a book, reveals a remarkably slow shift in the occurrence of muslim names. Until the end of the fourteenth century only Punjabi secular names appear, in the mid-sevententh century there are as many muslim names as Punjabi ones. Punjabi secular names disappear totally only by the early nineteenth century.[83] Was this gradualness of conversion alone or also a tardiness in changing names?

Evidently, till the seventeenth century, conversion, conventionally defined as a sudden shift from one belief system to another, took place across a continuum. It could be enacted through the force and violence that inhered in war and enslavement; or through punitive discriminatory laws (not unlike the practised discriminations based on caste); or be a response to persecution (as in the case of Buddhism). It could occupy pragmatic locales among men of ruling groups and their marriage alliances, and be a facet of lower caste/class upward mobility. It could be allied with state power or be separate from it. It could be 'unreasonable', as in marriages for love. Or it could be the result of reasoned choice and religious debate—as in the (comparativist?) vocabulary of Eknath, Kabir, Dadu and Nanak in which religious practices were compared, contrasted, sifted, praised, condemned, and which consciously sculpted a medium for discussing tension, underplaying origins and upholding their own choices. Conversion was also tied to illumination—the sudden eruption of a new faith through miracles, sight of a holy person, teaching of preceptors, leading to an 'awakening' or immediate transformation.[84] Finally, conversion was often interleaved in individual trajectories of eclectic experimentation, moving from faith to faith through the pathways of intellectual curiosity, spiritual quest, theological attraction, personal friendship or dialogue.

If conversion is also less conventionally defined as including 'partial conversion'—that is, as a qualitative, relational reconfiguration of belief systems that was not necessarily instant or dramatic or finalist but involved alterations in faith and many boundary-crossing, boundary-effacing transactions, in which the multiple modalities of conversion were not mutually exclusive but could occur severally—then at least two other prolonged and subtler historical processes become available for mapping subcontinental belief systems. The first is the adoption of selected tenets, popular local cults, godlings, fakirs, yogis, festivals, rituals or everyday practices that involved partial acceptance of the new and/or partial rejection of the old, some degree of change in belief systems, and at times gave rise to new cults. Such conscious or reasoned selection from and persuasion by different religions must surely have remodulated their interfaces and boundaries. Second, the less selfconscious process of gradual assimilation, permeation, diffusion, accretion, through social interaction, contiguity or absorption into brahminical Hinduism and Islam that attended on vast changes such as the shift to settled agriculture, the expansions in production, trade,[85] travel and settlement. Both processes were seldom entirely unilateral, and produced interaction and layering of cosmologies, theologies, monotheisms, mysticisms, guru-centred cults and modes of worship and, within the combative self-making of sects, created fresh interfaces, compatibilities or links between sects, inventive modes of incorporation, substitution, overlayering, interweaving, adaptation, domestication, re-semanticization and re-manifestation of deities, icons, concepts and practices. They produced not only defined syncretisms but also ambiguous or doubled identities.

In both the conventional and the less conventional meaning of conversion, changes in belief were seldom coterminous with a thoroughgoing transformation in names, dress, bodily practices, rites of access and passage, or social identity. Some boundaries took generations to cross and some were never crossed. Both temporalities of conversion—as instant and as gradual process—thus, have produced 'unfinished' conversion and consequently new overlapping networks. Even temporary conversion and shallow or pragmatic adhesion seem to leave a residue. Finally, the techniques of disavowal or renunciation of a faith, whether atheistic or agnostic, or as a preamble to the choice of another faith, also carved significant pathways in and out of belief systems.

Given the manifold nuances in the alteration of belief, the variations in composite faiths, the continuities beneath partial shifts in belief systems, the multiple agencies and processes involved, the range of temporal transactions differing in duration, intensity, extent, one may question the adequacy of conversion as a concept altogether, or challenge my own expansion of the term to cover what were indeed variegated and specific processes. Until a new and more precise vocabulary becomes available, I feel that as a working notion partial conversion has the advantage of encapsulating and opening these processes to more nuanced analyses, as well as of suggesting that conversion could signal as much a discourse of *relationality, connectedness,* and *bonding* as of a prickly or combative *antagonism.* After all, conversion in all its variety also represented the *porous boundary* between sects and denominations, the difficulty of absolutising religious difference, and was an often inadvertent mechanism for the production of cohering diversities.

As such, partial conversion may also offer a more useful way of thinking about syncretism, both from the point of view of understanding its persistence, for showing up the hiatus between official or orthodox classification and social practices, and the repeated threat it has posed over time to various absolutisms at different conjunctures. For instance, partial conversion was opposed and subject to 'purification' even before forcible conversion to Islam became an issue. The twelfth-century agamic saiva text *Somasambhupaddhati* prescribed a conversion rite from Buddhism, Jainism, Vaishnavism, Samkhya and so on to Saivism. The rite, regardless of which of these the devotee hitherto belonged to, removed the mark imprinted by an inferior/alien religion or philosophical system in the soul of the convert; removed all former religious obligation and all the merit acquired so far by the convertee; the adept had to start from full erasure or from zero, like a new-born child.[86] Partial conversion thus bred not only fecund confusion but also icy clarities, and was itself a terrain of contest, even eradication.

As must be evident by now, several elements from this webbed terrain of sought fixities and practised fluidities clustered around

Akbar. What is more, Akbar regretfully admitted having forced many persons to convert to Islam early in his life.[87] However, in 1562 he abolished the enslavement of families of captives as well as allowed those forcibly converted to return to their former faith.[88] Apostasy in this sense ceased to be crime. Akbar's official permission resonated with or ratified existing practices of moving back and forth 'below'. Significantly, Badauni accused Akbar of being overinfluenced by his hindu wives and practising their rituals; in fact Akbar conducted the marriages of his sons to rajput princesses through both hindu and muslim ceremonies.[89] Evidently inter-religious marriage did not always entail conversion of wives to Islam.

It was also through this other series of attributions—the abolition of forcible conversion, modification of punitive or discriminatory laws, making a space for choice in the legalisation of the reversion of converts, the nuances of partial conversion by wives and others—that 'Akbar' could be made to represent a space for personal choice of a combinatoire.

And since his choosing, combining and selecting from different religions happened without any official change of primordial denomination and without interrupting self-identification, it was possible to pull his syncretic practices into the mobile transactions of partial conversion. The accretion of visible marks and/or practices of many religions were attributed, howsoever temporarily, to Akbar: vegetarianism, *tilak*, *rakhi*, wearing a roman catholic relic and an image of the Virgin Mary, the parsi *sudreh* and *kusti*, jewelled strings on his wrists tied by brahmins.[90] Swetambar jain, sikh, parsi and dadupanthi narratives believe that their tenets were incorporated in Akbar's Tauhid-e-ilahi.

The fact that not all conversions were either finalist or relied on binary definitions (such as hindu or muslim), or presented a very clear definition of what a person was being converted *from* or what the *teleology* of conversion would be, can be glimpsed in the hagiographies. In none of them, with the exception of *CVV*, is Akbar set up as a muslim to be converted: he is the king who comes to worship Dadu or Tulsi or Krishna. The hagiographies seem to settle for instant persuasion or expansion in belief and do not reflect on either long term duration or consequences. The parsis made no attempt to reconcile Akbar's parsiness with the signs of other faiths that he displayed.

The logics of partial conversion could configure one's 'own' religion as mobile, changing, as something that could be adopted by others in a segmented way. Eclecticism and tolerance accrued to partial conversion *from* positions of faith and could involve holding in abeyance, deferring or loosening denominational identity. One person's 'full' truth could be another person's partial truth.

The apparent satisfaction of jains and parsis with the fact that parts of their 'truth' had been incorporated, that is, with the partial conversion of Akbar, suggests not only that in *practice* even 'full' conversions may not always have been thoroughgoing[91] but that the pressures to make them so may not always have been uniform or strident. Partial conversion thus did not have to be mere pragmatism, hypocrisy, something that was superficial, extraneous or on the surface. In a situation where no unified 'hindu' formation existed and where religious sects were constituted through and produced overlaps, even so-called complete conversion may often have signified simply occupying another space within networks of related faiths.

In sum, the ground reality and dailiness of proselytization and conversion also provided a space from which Akbar could be appropriated in the hagiographies and in jain or parsi accounts. In this sense he is the royal, even imperial, crystallization of social practices and processes that exist before and after his time. Akbar is not the solitary object of conversion, he is a bit player in the wider, diffuse dramas of hagiography.

The Conjuncture

Little that Akbar did was new. There were plenty of non-shariati elements, tensions between ulema and rulers during the sultanate, and in some courts heterodox saints were welcomed. Rajput and other rulers also showed eclectic patterns of patronage. But these now come into a unique combination with a new centralized, patrimonial empire ruled by a king with personal authority; a king who as gift-giver, benevolent paternal figure, devotee, preceptor, personalizes this centralized empire; a court that is a sanctuary for heterodox exiles and institutionalizes the protection of holy men; an ongoing social process of religious 'comparativism' and syncretism from positions of belief and devotion (often unitarian of the one god with many names) that are both individual and institutionalized; conversion as part of multiple types of propagation; a series of attributions to Akbar of positions of assimilation, doubt, unclassifiability etcetra which he seems either to have himself assisted or left unchallenged. (Notably, Akbar is never represented as without any faith in divinity.) This system of attributions came from many directions—his orthodox detractors, his loyal biographer, foreign jesuits and so on—became an objective aura, facilitated specific types of recuperation that were in turn tied to wider social processes. In sum, 'Akbar' was a conjunctural phenomenon.

Because the tension between religious elites and kings on the issue of religious authority was familiar, Akbar could be pulled into hagiographic discourse from a number of directions. The sheer number of directions, however, may be related to the emergence of a centralized state formation. Existing sects, denominations, pirs, sants and bhakts who represented popular worship felt they had a claim on him. This wide dispersal and proliferation of the claim was unprecedented. In addition, because conversions were a part of social practice Akbar could be pulled into it in ways both real and imaginary. Every sect, vaishnav, sant, sufi, jogi, could be a proselytizer and display their symbolic agency in converting Akbar.

Mughal rule was not homogenous regarding religion, law, custom, language, culture; there were no fixed continuous policies regarding these. The dialectic of a flexible yet centralized state formation accompanied by personal authority and cultural heterogeneity informs the hagiographic appropriation of Akbar. Even if the ambiguity of some of these was linked to aggression or combative conversion, each claim from below was itself some form of incorporation or conversion.

The popular conversions of Akbar attest to a process of *mutual* legitimation of high and low. If the state was seeking legitimation in new structures and a 'composite' ruling class, new groups seem to have acquired a stake in that state. The Akbari mode of legitimation rested in part on seeking boons from popular worship—such as sikhs and chistis. Popular narrative notations in turn plebeanized the king and legitimated the state; they were a non-elite source of legitimation that metaphorically made many lower groups sharers in the state. Perhaps these narratives indicate that it was not ruling groups alone who had a stake in the state.

Akbar was villainized in other, especially political and puritanical, discourses but to the best of my knowledge not in devotional hagiographies. And the generic discursive constraints of hagiographies, that governed how Akbar would or would not be represented, too emerged from specific social, political and religious configurations. If the oral traditions from which these hagiographies crystallized are an eloquent articulation of those consensualities, those social bases that are silent in written historical records, then social history must begin to take them into account.

This paper was first presented at the Nehru Memorial Museum and Library in 1993, and at the Department of History, JNU, Centre for South Asia, University of Wisconsin; Department of South Asian Languages and Civilisation, University of Chicago, in 1994. The encouraging discussion after these presentations with Ravinder Kumar and Muzaffar Alam assisted in the revision. So did Anuradha Kapur, Indu Chandrasekhar and Ein Lall's comments on the script. The responsibility for any misinterpretation remains mine alone.

Notes and References

1   Cited in Iqtidar Alam Khan, 'Seventeenth Century Assessment of Akbar', ICHR seminar papers on `Akbar and his Age', 1992, pp. 12–13.

2   Nabhadas' text is carried in Narendra Jha, *Bhaktmal: Pathanushilan evam vivechan* (Patna: Anupam Prakashan, 1978), pp. 32, 40. Priyadas is cited in Mahavirsingh Gehlot, *Mira Jivni aur Kavya* (Allahabad: Shakti Kavyalaya, 1945), p. 40.

    Raghavdas' *Bhaktmal* (1720) with a tika by Chaturdas (1800) is fairly similar: *Bhoop Akbar roop sunyo ati, tanhi-sen liye chali ayo/ Dekhi kusyal bhayo chavi lalhi, ek sabad banaai sunayo.* See *Raghavdas krit Bhaktmal*, Rajasthan Oriental Research Institute, Jodhpur nd, p. 100.

3   Winand M. Callewaert, *The Hindi Biography of Dadu Dayal* Motilal Benarsidas, Delhi 1988, pp .21, 31. Subsequent references are to this text.

4   The narrative acquired a hindu cast in some later hagiographies and Dadu (who lived from *circa* 1544 to 1603) acquired the reputation of persuading Akbar to ban cowslaughter. See *Raghavdas krit Bhaktmal*, p. 183.

5   *Stories of Indian Saints*, eds. Justin Abbott and N.R. Godbole (fourth edn 1933, rpt Delhi: Motilal, 1988), part II, pp. 47–48.

6   Rupert Snell, 'Raskhan the Neophyte: Hindu Perspectives on a Muslim Vaisnav' in *Urdu and Muslim South Asia*, ed. Christopher Shackle (Delhi: Oxford Univ. Press. 1991), p. 30.

7   *CVV*, ed. D. Parikh (Mathura: n.p. 1970) in Snell, p. 31. According to Snell if Muslims were seen as outsiders and threats to the sect in *CVV*, then so were other groups such as Shaivites, some other Vaisnavite sects, and non-Pushtimargis (p. 36).

8   In another version of *CVV*, hearing of *Sursagar*, Akbar wonders how he can arrange a meeting with Surdas. The meeting occurs because god wishes it. Akbar tells Surdas that god has granted him the kingdom and all virtuous men sing his praise. He asks the poet twice to sing his praise. Both times

Surdas sings only of Krishna. Akbar realises that Surdas is free from greed and is a man of god. When Surdas does not answer Akbar's questions about how a blind man uses such metaphors, Akbar says Sur's eyes are in god's keeping and he sees through them. He wants to reward Sur but does not make the attempt because Sur is so evidently uninterested in worldly things. See *Chaurasi Vaisnavan ki Varta* (Bombay: Lakshmi Venkateshwara Chapekhana, samvat 1975) pp. 288–91.

Akbar's encounter with Kumbhandas in this version of the *CVV* is more abrasive. As the fame of Kumbhandas' compositions spreads, a musician sings them for the ruler at Fatehpur Sikri. The ruler (*desadhipati*) sends for this *mahapurush*. Kumbhandas rejects the palki sent for him, arrives on foot, reacts against the opulence of the court, sings gurdgingly when asked, and deliberately improvises a song that says Sikri is of no use to bhakts of Hari and that Akbar's face brings sorrow to the viewer. Akbar is angry and says if Kumbhandas wants anything he should sing in praise of Akbar as well. Kumbhandas leaves (pp. 321–24).

After this, Kumbhandas is even more irascible with Mansingh, who appears in *CVV* as a punctilious Krishna devotee. He rejects Mansingh's valuable gifts and tells him not to visit again (pp. 325–30).

9   Abbott, part I, p. 33. Subsequent references are in the text.

10   Abbott, II, pp. 171–75.

11   Abbott, II, pp. 23–27.

12   Abbott, II, pp. 345–47.

12   Abbott, II, pp. 39, 106–07.

14   Abbott, II, pp. 208–14, 332–34.

15   *Akbarnama*, vol II (Calcutta 1879), p. 154, cited in Saiyid Athar Abbas Rizvi, *A History of Sufism in India*, (Delhi: Munshiram Manoharlal, 1976, rpt 1986), vol I, p. 126.

16   Rizvi, I, p. 126.

17   *Tuzuk-i-Jehangiri*, trans. Beveridge, I, pp. 2.

18   Akbar's munificence to the chishtis is well recorded; after Shaikh Salim's death many of his sons and grandsons continued in royal service and rewarded for their loyalty wih high mansabs. See S.A.A. Rizvi, *A History of Sufism in India* (Delhi: Munshiram Manoharlal, 1983), vol II, p. 281.

19   Rizvi, II, pp. 264–65.

20   Rizvi, II, p. 281.

21   Rizvi, II, pp. 371–72.

22   Rizvi, II, p. 181.

23   Mulla Abdul Qadir Badauni, *Muntakhabu't-tawarikh*, vol III, pp. 91–92, in Rizvi, II, p. 60.

24   Rizvi, II, p. 60.

25   *Muntakhabu't-tawarikh*, III, pp. 35–6, in Rizvi, II, p. 61.

26   Rizvi, II, p. 63.

27   *Akbarnama* II, p. 145, in Rizvi I, p. 312.

28   Rizvi, I, p. 474.

29 See M.A. Macauliffe, *The Sikh Religion* (Delhi: S. Chand, 1983) vol II, p. 97; vol III, pp. 82–83; Gurcharan Singh, 'Akbar in Sikh History', ICHR papers, pp. 4–10; Rajat M. Bilgrami, *Religious and Quasi-Religious Departments of the Mughal Period (1556–1707* (Delhi: Munshiram Manoharlal), 1984 p. 63. There is also a strong sikh tradition that Akbar conferred land on guru Ramdas. See B.N. Goswamy and J.S. Grewal, *The Mughals and the Jogis of Jakhbar* (Shimla: IIAS, 1967), p. 21.

30 *Tuzuk-i-Jahangiri*, trans Beveridge, vol II, pp. 52–3, in Rizvi, II, pp. 409–10.

31 Rizvi, II, pp. 410–11.

32 Makhan Lal Roychoudhury, *The Din-i-Ilahi: or, the Religion of Akbar* (Calcutta: n.p., 1952), p. 90.

33 R.P.Karkaria, 'Akbar and the Parsees (1896)' in *Contributions on Akbar and the Parsees*, ed. B.P. Ambasthya (Patna: Janaki Prakashan, 1976), pp. 3–5.

34 Goswamy and Grewal, pp. 6–7, 25.

35 *Ain*, I, pp. 198–99, in Bilgrami, pp. 59–60.

36 Bilgrami, pp. 61–63.

37 K.M. Ashraf, *Life and Conditions of the Peoples of Hindustan* (Delhi: Munshiram Manoharlal, 1970), p. 257.

38 Khaliq Ahmad Nizami, *On History and Historians of Medieval India* (Delhi: Munshiram Manoharlal, 1983), pp. 24–25. There were several others inclined to free-thinking, as well as some who inclined towards the Nuqtawi sect.

39 Thus Tansen appears in Mahipatis' *Bhaktavijay*, not at Akbar's court but in the employ of a pious king of Ujjain, and leads this king to the greatest of all singers—the blind Surdas (Abbott, II, pp. 18–19).

40 Cited in Surinder Singh Kohli, *History of Punjabi Literature* (Delhi: National Book Shop, 1993), p. 66.

41 According to Shirin Mehta the ground for Akbar's liberal outlook and catholicity had already been prepared by the bhakti movement in Gujarat—Raidas, Kabir, Narsi, Mira and others (p. 8).

42 Cited in Eleanor Zelliot, 'Eknath's *Bharuds*: The Sant as Link Between Cultures' in *The Sants: Studies in a Devotional Tradition in India*, eds Karine Schomer and W.H. Mcleod (Delhi: Motilal Banarsidas, 1987), pp. 92, 94–95.

43 Daniel Gold, 'Clan and Lineage among the Sants: Seed, Service, Substance' in *The Sants*, ed. Schomer and Mcleod, pp. 305–06, 315; and *The Lord as Guru: Hindi Sants in North Indian Tradition* (New York: Oxford Univ. Press, 1987), p. 195.

44 Gold, *The Lord as Guru*, pp. 88–93.

45 Described in Elinor W. Gadon, 'Note on the Frontispiece' in *The Sants* ed. Schomer and Mcleod, pp. 415–418.

46 'Episodes in the Life of Akbar: Contemporary Reminiscences', ICHR papers, pp. 15, 20–21, 47, 53, 75.

47 *Akbarnama*, II, pp. 285, 452–53, *Ain*, I, p. 4, in Bilgrami, p. xix.

48 Nizami, pp. 150–51.

49 Nizami, pp. 150–51.

50 Cited without source in Tara Chand, *Society and State in the Mughal Period* (rpt Lahore: Bakhtiar, 1979), p. 99.

51 Makrand Mehta, 'Akbar in Gujarati Historiography', ICHR papers, 1992, p. 2.

52 Bilgrami, p. 63.

53 Karkaria in ed. Ambasthya, p. 3.

54 This was printed in a book called *Gayane Dilchaman* or 'Pleasant Songs' in 1867. See J.J. Modi, 'The Parsees at the Court of Akbar and Dastur Meherji Rana' (1901) in Ambasthya ed. p. 44.

55 Modi in Ambasthya ed. pp. 42–43.

56 Jain traders were profiting from Akbar's policies. See Surendra Gopal, 'The Jain Community and Akbar', ICHR papers, pp. 6, 8; Shirin Mehta, 'Akbar as Reflected in Contemporary Jain Literature in Gujarat', ICHR papers, pp. 2–3, 7, 10.

57 *Bhanuchandra Charitra* ed. Mohan Lal (Calcutta 1941), pp. 7, 78, 79; Mehta, pp. 3–5, 9.

58 Bilgrami, p. 65.

59 Mehta, pp. 4–5, 9.

60 K.S. Matthew, 'Akbar and the Europeans', ICHR papers, pp. 7–10.

61 Roychoudhury, p. 115.

62 Cited in Matthews, p. 10.

63 Cited in Matthews, pp. 11, 24–25.

64 Cited in Matthews, pp. 12–13.

65 Matthews, pp. 14, 17–20.

66 Cited in Matthews, p. 21.

67 Cited in Sushil Chaudhury, 'Contemporary European Accounts of Akbar,' ICHR papers, p. 8.

68 Cited in Chaudhury, p. 9.

69 Cited in I.A. Khan, 'Akbar's Personality Traits and World Outlook,' *Social Scientist* 232–33 (1992), p. 22.

70 Bilgrami, p. 64.

71 M. Athar Ali, 'Translations of Sanskrit Works at Akbar's Court,' ICHR papers, p. 12.

72 See Ganguli, p. 196, 247.

73 Iqbal Husain, 'Hindu Shrines and Practices as Described by a Central Asian Traveller in the First Half of the 17th Century' in *Medieval India* I, ed. Irfan Habib (Delhi: Oxford Univ. Press) 1992, p. 145.

74 Husain, p. 147.

75 Snell, p. 31.

76 *CVV*, p. 48, cited in Snell, p. 32.

77 *North Indian Notes and Queries* (Allahabad, 1891–5), vol V, p. 197 cited in Crooke, *Religion and Folklore of Northern India* (1925, rpt Delhi: S. Chand), p. 151.

78 *CVV*, pp. 30–32, and Snell, p. 31.

79 *Bhavaprakash* cited in Snell, p. 31.

80 The consequences are more evident in another variant of this hagiology. When Damodardas dies, his wife secretly sends his corpse and worldly goods in a boat to Vallabhacharya's temple before announcing the death. Their son, who has become a 'turak' is chagrined by this when he arrives, presumably because he is deprived both of his ritual role and his inheritance. She herself renounces food and drink and dies soon after. See *CVV* (samvat 1975), pp. 30–32.

81 Cited in Snell, pp. 30, 33–34.

82 See Ashraf, p. 110. Dirk H.A. Kolff describes 'temporary conversions' to Islam within soldiering traditions in the 15th and early 16th centuries. See *Naukar, Rajput and Sepoy* (Cambridge: Cambridge Univ. Press, 1990), pp. 57–58, 98–100.

83 Richard Eaton, 'The Political and Religious Authority of the Shrine of Baba Farid' in *Moral Conduct and Authority: The Place of Adab in South Asian Islam* ed. Barbara Metcalf (Berkeley: Univ. of California Press), 1984, pp. 352–54.

84 Many proselytising sufi sects succeeded partly because of their vaunted ability to perform miraculous feats. See Rizvi, II, pp. 427–29.

85 See *D.D.Kosambi on History and Society*, ed A.J. Syed (Bombay: Univ. of Bombay, 1985; Irfan Habib, Medieval Popular Monotheism and its Humanism: The Historical Setting (Delhi: Sahmat, 1993), pp. 9–10; Richard Eaton, *The Rise of Islam and the Bengal Frontier 1204–1760* (Delhi: Oxford Univ. Press, 1991).

86 Hienrich von Stietoncron, 'Religious Identity in Pre-Muslim Hinduism', Seminar on Hinduism: Religion or civilisation Delhi, Max Mueller Bhavan, 1991, p. 81.

87 *Ain*, 111, p. 181, in Rizvi, II, p. 425.

88 Rizvi, 11, p. 425.

89 *Muntakhabu't-tawarikh*, vol II, p. 261, cited in Khan, p. 20; Satish Chandra, 'Akbar and his Rajput Policy: Some Considerations', ICHR papers, p. 12. An eighteenth century historian also located Akbar's catholicity in zenana politics; he attributed Akbar's abolition of enslavement to the influence of a brahmin woman in his harem.

90 J.J. Modi in Ambasthya, pp. 80–81.

91 There is enough evidence of the persistence of previous beliefs and practices among converts, especially tribals, to every religion.

The Homogeneity of Fundamentalism
Christianity, British Colonialism and India in the Nineteenth Century

Susan Visvanathan

One of the interesting aspects of British presence in India is its multifaceted quality. The British had an imagination larger than their isles, and India became a space which they would mould in the image they chose. Eric Stokes' brilliant analyses of *The English Utilitarians and India* (1959) argues that the Industrial Revolution and its aftermath brought along with it the notion of 'a civilizing mission'.[1] Of course, the clearest representative of this dream was Macaulay who prescribed English education and the creation of an indigenous elite who would assist the British to rule India. C.A. Bayly's work *Rulers, Townsmen and Bazaars*, further confirms the cooperation of the merchants of India who tacitly consented to and supported the British in their mode of trade, conquest and administration.[2] The moral tones of a 'civilizing mission' are present everywhere, and with Victorianism this gets compounded in the strident tones of missionary and evangelical zeal. Of course, if one were to read the letters of H.M. Kisch in *A Young Victorian in India,* writing about his work in the famine areas of India from 1874–89, one can only imagine the tenacity and grit of the Englishman striving desperately to keep native deaths and native corruption at bay.[3] All through the text there appears a sense of a duty done, honours received, an empire kept constant in the face of the vicissitudes of seasons, famines and the indigenous population. England's moral claims to rule were apparently given in her nature, in her race, or so the nineteenth century evangelists would have us believe.[4] This expressed itself, as Stokes has so dramatically argued, in 'Free Trade in Evangelicalism and Philosophical Radicalism'.[5] It is with evangelicalism that my paper is primarily concerned. It is true that one can read many biographies of administrators or military men without ever coming across the word Christian or missionary. And it goes without saying that the British in India maintained social hierarchies in their relationship to Indians, and to those of class, gender and occupational status amongst themselves. Interestingly, most colonial writers describe the inscription of hierarchy with the 'arrival of the women'.[6] It would seem that in the early years of the British in India there was much greater liking and affection and even the birth of children between the two races. The 'Mutiny' was to change all that, and with the Victorian era of empire, the clarity of rule ('the Necessary Hell') became strident. What is communicated then is that empires cannot be made without corruption, savagery, guiltlessness. Clive and Warren Hastings were not seen in these colonial reminiscences as 'good' men, but as 'great' men. Further, the great and impoverished mass of Indian peoples, it would seem, were quite indifferent to rule, whether Mughal or British. Not surprisingly, Edwardes quotes a Punjabi proverb 'Plant trees but don't let them touch'. In this manner the British ruled after Cornwallis, for the 'good of the native'. Wellesley described Indians as 'vulgar, ignorant, rude, familiar and stupid'. The Mughal court in decline, described in detail by John Lawrence, was shabby and funny.

> Yet, digging deeper, we find the source of this attitude in fear. The increasing number of women in the European settlement brought with them the materials of a closed society—totems and taboos. The *zenanas* and their 'sleeping dictionaries' disappeared. Surrounded by the black sea of India the English turned away in panic to the careful ordering of position and preferment. The Indians threatened their security in an irrational and frightening way. It was best to keep away from them.[7]

The Empire, it is argued, was created not by bloodshed and oratory but by 'the commonplace, almost casual acceptance of discomfort, boredom and death'.[8] Gravestones in Britain even today carry the epitaphs of the nineteenth century: 'succumbed to the heat of India'. Edwardes, who served John Lawrence, writes:

> It is easy, almost inevitable, to dislike the great names of British India, to be revolted at their cruelties, their indifference, and their shallow minds. But for those unknowns who really made the Empire, the soldiers, the clerks, and the women who lived and died and were forgotten, it is possible only to feel pity. They were no

Empire builders, heavy with plans for expanding frontiers, but wishing only to stay within the confines of the little Englands they brought with them. Their arrogance was actually fear and their pre-occupation with precedence only the ordering of a closed society in which a sense of one's place seemed to give stability to the flux of life.[9]

In this memoir of the Lawrence brothers there is an interesting analysis of *Peregrine Pultuney* or *Life in India* published anonymously by John William Kaye in 1844. The author represents these colonials' wives as bored and cynical, discussing the funeral of Mr Collingwood.

> Mrs Poggleton . . . leant forward, held out her hand for the undertaker's circular. . . . 'Dear me! if it is not the gentleman with that pretty carriage. . . .'
>
> 'Small use to him a pretty carriage now', said Mrs Parkinson, 'the only carriage that he needs is a hearse.'
>
> 'Oh! but' exclaimed Mrs Poggleton . . . 'I have been dying for a long time for that carriage, and now I shall be able to get it. What a nice thing to be sure.'[10]

Kincaid, too, in peculiarly misogynist prose, discusses the civilian women's life in India.

> They sat around in a circle and made languid conversation . . . the talk was almost always of illness or the weather. . . . It was only in the evenings that the ladies seemed to revive or to show signs of animation either at some dance . . . or at one of the formal dinners. . . . When they went back to England for furlough they were often miserable. Lady Lawrence wrote to a friend saying that they had been to the Opera in London, 'We have nothing so bad in India. Did not London fill you with the bewildering sight of such luxury and profusion as we in the jungles had forgotten could exist, and of vice and misery which unless in a year of war and famine could not be equalled here?'[11]

Edwardes saw the nineteenth century in India as an Imperial Tragedy. 'Back in England . . . assiduous clergymen, retired empire builders, missionaries over-flowing with the bowels of some irrelevant compassion were all hard at work creating the mystique of an

106

Empire.'[12] Many of those who went out to India were younger sons of younger sons and when they had made their fortunes, became nabobs, and then returned to their native lands. Many died in the hot seasons and the malarial swamps. They responded to this by writing poetry— 'nostalgia for the fogs of London'—and with the fear of death as ever-present, as in W.T. Webb's poem,

> My fellow exiles, fill your glasses
> We'll sing our song before we die
> The tiger in the junglegrasses
> Has sucked the peasant's life-blood dry
> Go, bind your sons to exile
> To serve the captives' need.[13]

This is the paradox—to capture, to conquer, to enslave and then 'to serve the captive'. The improvement of the life and soul of the Indian became the centripetal force of British life in India.

Honoria, the wife of Henry Lawrence who had spent a secluded childhood by the sea in Ireland, loved the jungle and camping out with her husband. However, she wrote:

> The natives, as far as I have seen, have nothing attractive in their character; indeed as Gil Blas said, when he was with the actors, 'I am tired of living among the seven deadly sins', but those whom we have about us, are, I suppose the worst specimens of native disposition. There is something very oppressive in being surrounded by heathen and Mohammedan darkness, in seeing idol-worship all around, and when we see the deep and debasing hold these principles have on people, it is difficult to believe they can ever be freed from it. . . .
>
> . . . But you will desire rather to know how I find my own spiritual condition affected by this new world. Certainly I miss very much the outward observances of religion, and its public institutions. It is a position to try our motives, for situated as we are, there is nothing to be either gained or lost by religion. . . . But in these wilds, the Bible appears to me more than I ever before found it, the Book. I go into these particulars, for surely if *we look to one home, dearest* Mary and *walk by one rule* we must be interested to know of each other's road, what are its hindrances and advantages.[14]

Earlier, in her journal which she kept in detail, she wrote:

At home, every conscientious person feels responsible to a certain degree for the moral conduct and religious instructions of his domestics, as well as the duty of consulting their comfort. Here the difference of religion does away with the first, and the habits of life in a great measure obviate the second. It is difficult for the master and mistress to recollect that their servants are responsible, moral beings or to think of more than their own convenience. I was surprised to find among Europeans the prejudice of *caste* and that many of them object to a low caste native (simply on that ground) as much as a Hindu would. This is surely contrary to our faith, though I can easily understand the feeling gaining on one. . . . I asked Mrs H yesterday how many servants they had. She replied, 'I am not sure, but we are very moderate people. I can soon reckon.' The number amounted to nearly thirty: a waiting woman, an under-woman, a sweeper, a head-bearer, a mate-bearer, six under-bearers—a khansamah, three table attendants, a cook, a gardener, a water-carrier, a washerman, a tailor, a coachman, two grooms, two grass-cutters, a man to tend the goats, two messengers, a woman to keep off the bodies which float down the stream past the house. . .[15]

Mrs Lawrence was different from the women Kincaid describes with such verve, who if they dropped a handkerchief would 'just lower their voices and say "Boy"!'.[16] A fellow surveyor of Lawrence's team described her 'seated on the bank of a nullah, her feet overhanging the den of some wild animal as she wrote some letters, while her husband was laying his theodolite nearby.'

The Lawrences represented a particular moment in the mid-1800s when the fusion of Christianity and commerce was taking place. The Imperial Hero as, Edwardes shows, was a construction, propaganda which would incite young men to the services of India, to the romance and intoxication of duty. 1857 was the turning point, for 'the lessons of the Mutiny must never be forgotten. Britain might in 1857 have lost India, if it had not been the selfless immolation of its Heroes . . . the Empire could only be cemented by blood . . . the blood of young men steeped in its hagiolatry.'[17] Further,

The Hero of the nineteenth century was either the missionary (for God was always on the tongue of the Victorians if rarely anywhere else) or the soldier. The soldier, frequently with Bible in hand, did

God's work in a more realistic way. A sensible and beneficial partnership between God and Mammon.[18]

How did this fusion happen? How did a nation of merchants turn colonial and Christian without seeing the lapses between these two ideologies? Let us look at the late eighteenth century, when missionary movements to India began to crystallize.

II

In 1793, representatives of the new and zealous missionary societies began to arrive in India. In that year the East India Company's Charter was renewed but the House of Commons Resolution asking the Presidency Governments to consider improvement of the education and social circumstances of the Indians was dropped. By 1813 the missionaries who had till now found it so difficult to enter India were able to appeal to the Board of Control. By 1833 the missionaries had substantially recorded their presence[19] 'and the East India Company's Charter Renewal Act of that year declared that they were no longer required to possess a license in order to set foot in India.'[20] However, the missionaries were not consolidated. They had different styles and made an impact as individuals, not as members of a community.[21] They were tolerated by the East India Company because they were so few and had their uses in a secular capacity. Further, while having been conservative in the early years, evangelism was now in impetus and missionaries worked actively towards reform. The missionaries came in at a time when India was devastated by the degeneration of the Mughal empire, and cross sovereign-wars were being fought. The English had seen the decline of the Portuguese which they understood to be a consequence of ecclesiastical assimilation and miscegenation— the imposition upon the natives of the colonizers' religious manners and law. 'The Indians had their own social organization and the Government's duty was primarily to maintain the peaceful conditions in which that organization could work and trade could prosper.'[22]

Here I wish to delineate the manner in which social conditions allowed for the fusion of Christianity and colonialism. Evangelists and zealots had recognized, in the last decades of the eighteenth century, the necessity to spread Christian ideas. The contribution had first been financial (support for the Danish mission by SPCK). The 'field for the mission houses slowly became the British colonies, not the non-Christian world in general.[23] Then began a period of institutionalization. The Baptist Missionary Society, established in 1792, sent William Carey to India in 1793 the London Missionary Society was set up in 1795; the Church Missionary Society appeared in 1799. Yet the movement was slow and support was negligible, so that in the early years a large proportion of the missionaries were Germans of the Lutheran Church.[24] Other than this apathy was the scourge of the seasons, the vast distances of India and the primeval transport. Deaths were frequent, and the greatest obstacle was the many different languages and dialects of India.

The missionaries encountered the antipathy of not just the natives but also that of the merchant and civilian English who had great power, and on whose patronage they depended upon. Such men might have personally supported evangelism[25] but given the constraints of government, they often wished to delink themselves from the ideological frames of mission. There were differences in the way in which each representative dealt with missionaries. Wellesley, while personally detached from evangelical work, nevertheless praised their translations, made a personal gift of money to enhance their work and 'finally took upon himself the responsibility for permitting two Baptist missionaries to proceed to Agra and Delhi'.[26] Colonel Munro and Lawrence were individually active in propagating Christianity. A mutiny of the Company's sepoys at Vellore in 1807 led to some debate about missionary stances. The Chairman and Deputy Chairman of the Court of Directors of the East India Company, Edward Parry and Charles Grant, both evangelists by disposition, 'wrote a convincing refutation of the missionaries' culpability in a letter to the President of the Board of Control dated 8 June 1807'.[27] These two men played a key role in changing the attitudes toward the missionaries. Minto severely restricted the Baptist Mission Press at Serampore from which violent attacks upon Islam and Hinduism had appeared. He wanted to affirm that the British had no hostile designs against the religions of India. Many in England immediately doubted Minto's attachment to the faith of his country. On receiving 'a sharp letter from the secret committee of the Court of Directors which warned him against tempting the Indians to confuse the acts of individuals with those of government by falling into the same error himself, he realized that his anxiety for good order had unduly influenced his judgement'. After this he became more liberal towards the missionaries ideas.

Since the Court of Directors were more interested in trade than anything else and were afraid that the missionaries would hinder their cause, they were extremely antagonistic. They wanted a tolerant attitude towards 'alien religions' (i.e. the religions of the country which they had entered to trade) and they considered the missionaries to be unfair to condemn that which they did not understand. One might remember the Orientalists in this regard, who were interested in the religions of India.[28] Testimonies against the missionaries and statements in favour of Hinduism were common after the Vellore mutiny. The missionaries saw the merchants' 'interest in religious impartiality' as a 'cloak for their greater interest in dividends'.[29] The missionaries used their great support at home, the subscription of all denominations of Protestant Christians, as the symbol of their hope. They argued that the Company was already unpopular in England, and there were many who were prepared to attack the renewal of the Charter if they felt that the Company was hostile to the evangelization of India.[30]

The debate, as Ingham describes it, could only be swayed by strong individual voices, influential and dominating, for the majority of the House had little knowledge and little interest in Indian affairs and could be persuaded to vote against the Company. In fact, in 1813, a flood of letters to Parliament petitioned for the inclusion of a clause in the Charter Renewal Act admitting the principle of missionary activity in India. William Wilberforce was the chief actor in organizing favourable public opinion. In the House of Lords, Lord Gambier, who was also President of the CMS, played a key role. Wilberforce was able to fuse the Established church and the evangelical organizations. The missionaries, through the debates in Parliament, also received public attention as never before. However, since Indian affairs rarely came up before Parliament, the actual site of intervention was the Board of Control. The latter was less interested in the Company's profit than the Directors' and therefore maintained an impartial attitude towards the missionaries.

What is significant for us to understand is the shift from impartiality to direct intervention, which is the final stage of fundamentalism and empire: one nation and one religion. The effective control that the Board had was, of course, limited; it was the Company's agents in India who actually enacted the policy.[31] The Governor-General was the final authority, and the inconsistent policy on mission in India meant that there was uncoordinated behaviour between the lesser

111

officials. Kenneth Ingham describes the practice as three-fold.

(1) those who enacted the mentality of the Board of Control and derived legitimation from its higher authority.

(2) those who actively helped the missionaries whenever they could.

(3) those whose attitudes depended upon individual encounters and the impact made upon them by individual missionaries.[32]

Missionary societies clearly demarcated the responsibility of their evangelists 'to remember their sacred purpose' and not to engage in political concerns. But the matter of their conscience and their intervention in crimes which could not be seen as secular (*sati,* for instance) blurred the boundaries between religion and politics. The conversion of the east to Christ was, we must underline, a major political plank for imperialism. George Smith, writing in 1893, saw Christianization as the basis for unification of the world, and England was chosen to bring it about.

> Colonization has at last, after the struggle and strife of six thousand years, taken possession of the planet. One language, the English, transcending even the limits of races and nations and governments, as the Greeks never did, has become the ever-growing depository of the highest civilization and the fruitful medium of its unifying extension. The one faith of Christ Jesus, Son of Mary, who said that He came to seek and to serve the lost, prompting science, guiding colonization, and using English speech, is working out the realization of the unity of mankind by the very modern enterprise of foreign missions.[33]

Almost using the language of the alliances of war, the author says

> We together, 100 mission strong, in Europe and America, with the same history, the same tongue, the same literature, the same faith, and therefore the same Christ-commanded duty and assured home, are *set over or over against* the 300 millions of India in the providence of God. (emphasis added)[34]

The author establishes for Indians the Indo-Aryan link through philology and a common descent. 'Our fathers, theirs and ours, dwelt together four thousand years ago. . . . Thus have the English speaking Aryans been trained to become the rulers of India and the

112

evangelists of Asia.' In the reversion of sororotical hierarchy 'The young, of Great Britain and America, have been prepared to serve the elder of India, in the highest ministry of sacrifice.' The language, in its rhetoric, commands that 'The complete conquest of the Brahman and the Mohammedan of India by the cross will be to all Asia what the submission of Constantine was to the Roman empire.'[35]

H.S. Maine, writing in the *Saturday Review* in December 1857, described the historical events that followed as a

> wonderful succession of events which has brought the youngest civilizations of the world to instruct and correct the oldest which has reunited the wings of the Indo-European race which separated in the far infancy of time to work out their strangely different missions, which has avenged the miscarriage of the Crusade by placing the foot of the most fervently believing of Christian nations on the neck of the mightiest of Mahommettan dynasties, will inevitably be read by posterity as the work not of England, but of the English East India Company.[36]

The establishment and the work of the Company was seen to be the base by which evangelization could occur, even though this had taken 'a period equal to that of the Roman Empire between the fall of Jerusalem and the elevation of Constantine'.[37]

The 'Mutiny' of 1857 was seen to be advantageous to colonization and evangelism (described guiltlessly by the evangelists as 'aggressive Christianity'), for the revolt was put down and a new preoccupation of Christian empire came into being. This was not a completely linear movement; there were debates and contradictions, and a particular interpretation of Queen Victoria's proclamation which gave Christian evangelism a strong foothold like it did not have before.

Until the time of the Charter of 1833 passports had been necessary even for a missionary like Alexander Duff. Certainly chaplains had been coming into India for the benefit of the Company's servants who, according to George Smith, had lived in more or less spiritual squalor. But even the chaplains were often venal. Lord Teignmouth had reported to the Court of Directors in 1795: 'Our clergy in Bengal, with some exceptions, are not respectable characters. Their situation is arduous, considering the general relaxation of moral form from which a black coat is no security.' They were poorly paid, so that many of them were engaged in private trade and gambling. They had their salaries raised from £50 to £230 a year, but many of them had shares in Clive's monopolies of salt, betel-nut and tobacco, which allowed some of them to return to England with fortunes upto £50,000.

Meanwhile, the 'outward fabric of imperial order' was being established so that the seed of Christianity could be sown. One of the most interesting analyses of the relationship between Imperialism and Christianity, trade and morality, is Barry Unsworth's novel *Sacred Hunger*. It is, even so, very difficult to analyse the contradictions of nineteenth-century Christianity. The missionaries, while facing the opposition of the merchants and civil servants, were the first to enter the domains of native life. Marshman's wife, Hannah, for the first time began to preach to the women of India. The missionaries, as is well known, used the Bible, the school and healing to spread Christianity.

III

One of the greatest figures who brought about the resolution of the conflict between the Directives of the East India Company and evangelical pursuits was Charles Grant. He was born in 1746 and went to India first as a merchant and then as a civil servant. Calcutta filled him with dread. 'I was brought under deep concern about the state of my soul. There was no person living there from whom I could obtain any information as to the way of a sinner's salvation.' He went to Kiernanden, a missionary whom Clive had invited from Cuddalore to Calcutta. 'I found him lying on a couch. My anxious enquiries as to what I should do to be saved appeared to embarrass and confuse him exceedingly, and when I left him, the perspiration was running from his face in consequence as it appeared to me, of his mental distress.' Grant had brought out with him his wife, her mother and his sister. His sister married William Chambers, who had been influenced by Schwartz. Thus, the family as the space of missionary endeavour was established very early.

Grant desired a mission of evangelists, and eight names were proposed. Grant supported two of the eight missionaries on £240 a year each, with books and teachers. Charles Grant was to become a member of Lord Cornwallis' Council. Cornwallis promised not to oppose Grant's desire for a mission for the natives. 'He had no belief in the conversion of the people of India, they were too bad for that.'[38]

Charles Grant had written a tract in 1797 which was finally

laid before the House of Commons during the Charter discussion of 1813. The preface of the tract reported that:

> In earlier periods the Company manifested a laudable zeal for extending as far as its means then went the knowledge of the gospel to the pagan tribes among whom its factories were placed. It has since prospered to becoming great in a way to which the commercial history of the world offers no parallel, and for this it is indebted to the fostering and protecting care of divine Providence. It owes therefore the warmest gratitude for the past and it equally needs the support of the same beneficent Power in time to come, for the 'chances and changes' to which human affairs are always liable, and especially the emphatic lessons of vicissitude which the present day has supplied many assure us that neither elevation nor safety can be maintained by any of the nations or rulers of the earth, but through Him who governs the whole.

It was, therefore, the Company's duty to spread Christianity in that country where divine favour had protected England's imperial interests.[39] Through the dissemination of printing the Indians 'would see a pure, complete and perfect system of morals and duty, enforced by the most awful sanctions and recommended by the most interesting motives, they would learn the accountableness of man, the final judgement he is to undergo, and the eternal state which is to follow.'[40]

Of course, the underlying principle of this tract is the nature of stratification. It has to be located as much within Max Weber's concept of Puritanism and commerce as well as his reading of honour. Evangelism believed in individual salvation, individual grace *and* hierarchy. The bases of power lay in individual pursuit and divine recognition translated through material success as a symbol of grace. Therefore, if Indians and colonists were separated in this world, it was a logical necessity which needed no explanation other than divine will. What legitimized this difference for both native converts and colonists, however, was the belief in the world to come, when being spirit alone, differences of race, colour, gender, caste or class would not interfere.

The aim of Grant's work was 'the creation of a Christian Church and of a self-governing Christian nation'. That is, commerce led the way, imperialism created the conditions and evangelism was the fulcrum on which Empire must rest with its sense of ultimate satisfaction that the word had been brought to the Indians, and they would be freed from the bonds of hell-fire in the next life, or the cycle of transmigration.

Grant's tract was written in the prospect of the debates in Parliament on a new charter for the East India Company. 'The philanthropists and evangelists of Clapham were led by Grant to work for the Christianization of India from this time forward.'[41] It was in this atmosphere that the young Macaulay grew up, amidst conversations on mission and education.

The shift from the secular to the evangelical took several decades, not without protests from the Indians, as I have shown in *The Christians of Kerala,* where the indigenous aristocracy of Christians as early as 1840 severed all ties from the Missionary Society sensing the change in their stance towards the Syrian community as predatory.[42]

The East India Resolution in its first formulation had stated that it was the duty of the British to adopt such measures that would lead to the 'religious and moral improvement' of the Indians. India House raised such a hue and cry at 'the prospect of the deluge of missionaries and school masters which was to sweep away the Company's rule in the East' that the actual wave of evangelization would take some decades further.

Wilberforce was the chief crusader but his friends in the wave of antagonism deserted him and he wrote, 'India is left in the undisturbed and peaceful possession and committed to providential protection of Brahma.' His last appeal has a curious interest to us in the present day as we face the possible establishment of a state religion in India. He declared that the rejection of the Resolution in practice would be

> to declare to the world that we are friends to Christianity not because it is revelation from Heaven, not even because it is conducive to the happiness of man but only because it is the established religion of this country. Beware how this opinion goes abroad. Think not that the people of this land will long maintain a great Church establishment from motives of mere political expediency.[43]

The important part that the missionaries played in bringing about a change of policy was expressed by a dispatch in the Revenue Department dated 20 February 1833 and addressed to the Governor-General in Council. It was this document which contained the order which set about the severing of the colonial government's connection with idolatry. Till then the British administered the temples and received tax, which was seen by the missionaries as supporting Hinduism for material benefits.[44]

The missionaries contributed substantially to the creation of propaganda against idolatry primarily through their journal and letters printed by missionary organizations which were eagerly subscribed to. The importance of popular support for missionary work in the early nineteenth century can be read through the index of financial support. The Church Missionary Intelligences of 1871 records that

> The East India Company's Charter had in 1814, for the first time a decided Christian stamp on it as the determined voice of England. That year the income of the Church Missionary Society bounded up from £2,831 to £10,691. The next year it was £15,655, in four years more it was £27,440. It had then existed more than twenty years. At the next decade it was £53,200, at the next £65,190. Constant since has been its rise, until now it amounts to over £150,000 besides £20,000 raised and expended in the missions.[45]

The original draft of the 1833 Resolution had been drawn up by the Court of Directors but was, however, scored out by the Board of Control, who then went on to insert the clauses which the missionaries had been advocating for more than thirty years.

It is at this point that the distinction between the secular and sacred interests began to blur. What was truly religious and to be tolerated. What was an obstacle to the creation of a society based on Christian reform?

IV

Sati became one of the central spaces for the discussion between administrators and missionaries. It involved the central questions of life, the other world and deification, pilgrimage and revenue. The missionaries did not conceal their zeal. Missionary societies

> issued injunctions to their agents to remember their sacred purpose and to avoid interference in political concerns. But however desirous of subscribing to these orders the missionaries might have been, the fervour with which they undertook their work, and the reservations they permitted themselves on the grounds of conscience inevitably involved them in secular problems.[46]

117

In this sense their work ran parallel to the colonial government. The latter would legalize change when it became inevitable. The missionaries were catalysts in that they provided motivations and impulses to the possibilities of change. Caste came in for a great deal of attention, particularly in relation to the institutionalization of education, and it is well established that mission schools in the nineteenth century had to clearly develop a strategy for handling inter-caste relations. Race remained a non-problem, as in any theory of evolutionism—people are hierarchically located by the master race, and all social relations are predetermined by difference and antagonism. Ingham documents the variety of missionary attitudes to caste as a dialogue between the various evangelical bodies on the subject. 'It resulted also in a far more frequent and valuable exchange of opinions than was normally customary among them.'[47]

It was clear, however, that neither public outcries nor the arguments with Brahmins could upset the traditional hierarchies of Indian society. Therefore, it had to be through education that a theory of equality could be propagated, and in the case of the CMS in Kottayam, the greatest energies were put into the education of the pariahs so that they could rise in their self-esteem as well as in the view of others.

In the critical fervour of the evangelism with which they arrived in India, both Rhenius and his companion the Rev. J.C. Schnarre had announced their intention of refusing to admit caste into their school, even if it meant having as pupils none but pariah boys. Yet on 3 September 1816, Rhenius wrote to the Rev. M. Thompson, Secretary to the Madras Corresponding Committee of the CMS:

> Experiencing during the existence of our school has brought upon me the consideration that we should make a distinction between the Heathen and Native Christians, it being nearly impossible to demand that heathens as such should enter into the views and principles of Christianity, and that therefore in compliance with their prejudices, we should yield to the desires of the heathen to have Pariah Schools and Tamil Schools separately lest we should hinder them from enjoying the benefits of Christian instruction by which they are first to be brought to think aright and liberally.[48]

The non-missionary and civilian population supported the cautious handling of caste in educational matters. Monstuart

Elphinstone stated in 1824 that unless the missionaries were prepared to tolerate caste hierarchies in their institutions, the result might well be that caste Hindus would ignore the educational opportunities that the missionaries could provide, 'and as a result of this a class of pariahs would develop superior to the rest in useful knowledge but hated and despised by the others.'[49]

In some areas caste demarcations were not admitted to. 'In the CMS schools in Burdwan', Ingham writes,

> the children knew of no precedence save that of merit. At Serampore Mission College, the *pandits* after considerable objection, were induced to teach the sacred classics of Hinduism to a *sudra*. The register of the boys in the free school at Benares, where no distinctions were permitted, contains the names of 142 pupils admitted between June 1824 and May 1833 and includes representatives of innumerable castes ranging from Brahmins to Sudras, Christians and Muhammadans and even to Rajputs.[50]

However, in 1830 A. Lacroisx of the L.M.S. reported that caste was the major hurdle to conversion. The British believed that Christianity provided the possibilities of a less immutable division of society into hierarchies, but that people were divided amongst and between themselves was a given fact of social order.[50]

Quite clearly education lay at the roots of reforming a captive people. The Charter of 1813 laid the base not only of the ecclesiastical structures in the process of 'civilization' and 'Christianization' of India but also for the establishment of educational institutions of the modern kind. The Anglicizing of Native Education of 1835 was followed by the Education Dispatch of 1854, the University Charters of 1857, and the dispatch on vernacular education in 1858.[52] The question of secularism was peculiarly ambiguous.

Smith reports the manner in which Victoria's Proclamation was read from the steps of Government House, Calcutta: 'On Monday the 1st day of November, as the tropical sun neared its setting' the Indians were made direct subjects of the Empire.

> The Act of Parliament had become law on the 2nd day of August. But when the document [of Proclamation] reached the Queen . . . Her Majesty returned it, desiring the Premier to rewrite it bearing in mind that it is a female sovereign who speaks to more than a

hundred million of Eastern peoples on assuming the direct government over them, and after a bloody civil war, giving them pledges
which her future reign is to redeem, and explaining the principles of
her government. Such a document should breathe the feelings of
generosity, benevolence and religious toleration, and point out the
privileges which the Indians will receive on being placed on an equality with the subjects of the British Crown, and the prosperity following in the train of civilization.'[53]

To the new draft the Queen added some phrases in her own
writing, which were suggested by the Consort, presented here in italics.

> We hold ourselves bound to the natives of our Indian territories by
> the same obligations of duty which bind us to all Our other subjects,
> and those obligations, by the Blessing of Almighty God, we shall
> faithfully and conscientiously fulfil ... *firmly relying ourselves on the
> truth of Christianity and acknowledging with gratitude the solace of
> religion.* We disclaim alike the Right and the Desire to impose Our
> convictions on any one of Our subjects. We declare it to be Our
> Royal Will and Pleasure that none be in any wise favoured, none
> molested or disquieted, by reason of religious faith or obscurance,
> but that all shall alike enjoy the equal and impartial protection of the
> law, and We do strictly charge and enjoin all those may be in
> authority under Us, that they abstain from all interference with the
> religious belief or worship of Our subjects, on pain of Our highest
> displeasure ...
>
> When by the Blessing of Providence, internal tranquillity
> shall be restored, it is Our earnest desire to stimulate the peaceful
> industry of India, to promote works of public utility and improve-
> ment, and to administer its government for the benefit of all Our
> subjects resident therein. In their prosperity will be Our strength, in
> their contentment Our security, and in their gratitude Our best
> reward. *And may the God of all power grant to us in authority under
> us, strength to carry out these our wishes for the good of our people.*[54]

The evangelists read this proclamation of secular rights to
Indians to underline that now Christianity was the religion of the state,
of those who were the rulers, and that 'toleration in matters of faith'
was 'a generous concession of multitudinous aliens'. Thus, the Indians

were rendered by this reading to be 'aliens' in their own country, subjects of colonial Christian rule.

Smith, stereotypically Christian colonist, went on to write:

> At this highest and widest the citizenship of Imperial Rome, in which the Apostle Paul rejoiced, was a small thing compared with the gift made to peoples of almost every race, creed and colour, now numbering nearly three hundred millions, and that after mutiny and partial rebellion. From the hour of that concession, the history of the British Empire of India really began. From the day which Christianity, through the avowed faith of the ruling race, in the same equal platform as Hinduism, Parseeism, Buddhism, Mohammedanism, Animism and all other purely human modes of propitiating God, as Christ Himself put it before His Roman judge, the conversion of India to one true and living God became an assured certainty.[55]

The Proclamation, with its signature of Christian belief (with the underpinning of personal prompting from the Consort), led the evangelists to pressurize the government for two more clauses: (1) the state must secure perfect liberty to its Christian servants to discharge their personal service to God in their non-official character; (2) the state must by legislation, on the one hand, remove every obstacle to the unfettered freedom of workshop of all religionists while, on the other, it guards against the danger of indirectly sanctioning and, as it were, fossilizing quasi-religious customs and beliefs which are contrary to humanity, to good morals or to liberty.[56]

Lord Canning had interpreted the Proclamation in 1858 quite differently from the zealous missionaries. He had objected to the distribution of anonymous tracts among the natives near Benares, 'so sensitive was he as to what came to be called the "neutrality" promulgated in 1858.' No doubt there was a sigh of relief amongst the zealots when men like John Lawrence appeared on the scene, fusing in his person the civil and missionary arm of British colonialism. Lawrence was willing to teach the Bible in state schools, and in whatever situations there were Christian teachers, 'in order that our views of Christian duty might be patent to the native people'.[57]

A dispatch recording John Lawrence's contribution says that

> Sir J. Lawrence has been led in common with others since the occurrence of the awful events of 1857 to ponder deeply on what may be the faults and shortcomings of the British as a Christian nation in India. In considering topics such as those treated of in this despatch, he would solely endeavour to ascertain what is our Christian duty.[58]

The Seal of Empire, of unity without difference, a blanket homogeneity with no interweaving or differential patterns, was imposed on India. No wonder that John Lawrence's sister-in-law had written: 'we look to one home, dearest Mary, and walk by one rule'.[59]

This was a stance very far removed from the Despatch of 1853 which had clearly stated with regard to secular institutions of education that:

> The institutions were founded for the benefit of the whole population of India, and in order to effect their object it was, and is, indispensable that the education conveyed in them should be exclusively secular. The Bible is, we understand, placed in the libraries of the colleges and schools, and the pupils are free to consult it. This is as it should be, and moreover, we have no desire to prevent or to discourage any explanation which the pupils of their own free will ask from their masters on the subject, provided such information is given out of school hours.

The same dispatch established on a general basis five universities, but the secular foundation was seen by the evangelists to be problematic.

The Church Missionary Intelligence, Vol. VII of October 1871 carried a strongly worded essay on the 'Dangerous Results of Secular Education'.[60] It began by quoting an Indian writer who had said in the *Indu Prakash* of 16 May 1864, 'The education provided by the state simply destroys Hinduism—it gives nothing in its place. Knowledge alone will not suffice for man, nor material prosperity or good government. Without faith life is without an aim, and death is without hope.' This the evangelists quickly used as an ideal reason for substituting Christian education for moral education: 'the greatest object to be sought in the education of the people of India is their social and moral elevation'. Hinduism had provided a code of moral restraint accounting to them though 'caste and superstition' predominated, 'and in its absence there would be no safeguards except what the Criminal Law provides'. The essay resolved that

> It is considerations of this nature, combined with the far higher views of our obligations as Christians which have led to the formation of the Christian Vernacular Education Society. Composed as it is of the members of various Christian bodies, its sole object is to diffuse by its schools and publications a knowledge of the great fundamental truths recognized by all, and thus to avert this danger.[61]

It would be interesting to re-read Durkheim's powerful essay on 'Moral Education' and the uses of secularism, in this context.

Secular education in the Universities of India had, according to the Rev. N. Midwriter, writing in March 1871, peculiar evils. 'Among the causes that at present operate with power against missions, much stress was laid by some of the members on what may be called Nationalism.' The missionary is surprised by the antagonism of Indians against the British.

> Had we come to the Bengal with the sword in one hand and the Bible in the other, we could have scarcely been surprised if the Gospel, so offered, had been rejected. . . A friend who takes the deepest interest in native progress, tells me he has lately been startled by the frequent use of the word foreigners as applied to Englishmen. It struck him as new, and very significant. The presence of the British Government, with its long train of civil and military servants is an offense to some. And these speak of the 'yoke of the foreigner' in terms which show how completely they have forgotten how much heavier was the yoke of the Moslem, and how much heavier is the yoke of native rule in nearly all the principalities that are still under their own Rajahs. But still more influential is fostering the feeling of nationalism is the want of sympathy between the two races in private life. . . The characters of the two races are so different that I doubt whether either is capable of doing justice to the other.[62]

What the data, so widely disseminated, shows is that the author felt that over three and a half centuries the Englishman had a home in India. What he did not notice was that his blood had not conjoined with that of the Indians because of considerations of race and caste on either side, and that unlike the Muslims who had both subjects and rulers among them and variations in the manner of rule, the English only wanted to rule.

There were antagonists to the missionary attitudes in India

within their own fold. A tremendous sense of shock underwrites the review of a book authored by A.C. Geekie, published in 1871, called 'Are Missions in Wrong Places, to Wrong Races in Wrong Hands?'[63] The affront caused to the reviewer by Dr. Geekie's book, forces him to classify the various types of resistance to mission in India.

> Some have openly scoffed at and derided the exertions and devotion of Christian men in the prosecution of their schemes, others again have argued that the extension of Christianity is adverse to the maintenance of British power, or interferes with British trade and commerce; others in the interests of Rome, have systematically depreciated all the efforts of Protestant teachers, and declared that their work was naught.

Dr Geekie is asked, 'in what department of enterprise have mistakes not been made, *especially in what is most akin to missionary work, colonization, mistakes costing many precious lives and the loss of valuable property.*'[64]

Here, very clearly, shame is put aside, and colonialism and Christianity are seen to be imprinted in the same coin. The reviewer ridicules Geekie's demand that mission should first mould the life and trajectory of the 'influential races'. He scolds Geekie for imposing the dogma that 'charity begins at home' upon the evangelist:

> Will he permit us to remind him that it is another world, not this one, for which they are toiling, and for which they are seeking to prepare their converts. We much mistake them if their cherished object is not rather to multiply the number of those who constitute the Church in heaven, than to establish Churches on earth, or to promote the physical well-being of the races among whom the providence of God has called them.[65]

Here is the clear statement that the matters of the spirit had now entered enumeration, statistical Christianity the ultimate symbol of commerce, of quantity rather than the qualitative and intricate relation between the body intellect and soul that metanoia or spiritual transformation demanded.

It would take many decades before a new vocabulary of dialogic Christianity would crystallize—both in the debates at Tambaram in 1938, the contributions of C.F. Andrews and Mahatma Gandhi to Christian thought and activism, and the coming of a great theological impetus through the life and work of a French Benedictine monk, Swami Abhishiktananda or Henri Le Saux. He was a monastic who lived in India from 1948–1973, upsetting colonialist metaphors and imageries, striving to establish an indigenous Christian form of workshop, and providing the bases of a full bodied dialogue between Christianity and Hinduism in India. It is a symbol of the embodiment of ecumenism and faith that his editor and translator Rev. James Stuart of the ISPCK, should have spent decades making Henri le Saux's work available to us—expressing, therefore, the bridges that can be built between Roman Catholicism and the reformed churches, Hinduism and Christianity, India and the west, the French and the English.

I would like to thank the Charles Wallace India Trust and the British Council for a fellowship to Queens University, Belfast, in 1997, where most of this paper was written. It is a part of work begun at the Centre for Contemporary Studies, Nehru Memorial Museum and Library, New Delhi. The missionary archives at SOAS, London, were very useful and my thanks to the librarians there. Katie Radford, Piera Sarasini, Valeria Lima Passos and many others made Belfast a lovely place to work. Thanks also to Shiv Visvanathan and Mariam Paul.

Notes and References

1 Erik Stokes, *The English Utilitarians and India*, Clarendon Press, Oxford, 1959, p. XIII.

2 C.A. Bayly, *Rulers, Townsmen and Bazars: North Indian Society in the Age of British Expansion, 1770–1870*, Cambridge University Press, Cambridge, 19.

3 Ethel Cohen, ed., *A Young Victorian in India: Letters of H.M. Kisch*, Jonathan Cape, London, 1957.

4 Susan Visvanathan, *The Christians of Kerala*, Oxford University Press, Madras, 1993; 'Missionary Styles and the Problem of Dialogue', Occasional Papers, IIAS, Shimla, 1993.

5 Stokes, *The English Utilitarians and India*, p. XIV.

6 Dennis Kincaid, *British Social Life in India, 1608–1936*, Routledge and Kegan Paul, London, 1973; Michael Edwardes, *The Necessary Hell*, Cassell, London, 1958.

7 Edwardes, *Necessary Hell*, p. 33.

8 Ibid., p. 31.

9 Ibid.

10 Ibid., p. 27.

11 Kincaid, *British Social Life*, p. 184.

12 Edwardes, *Necessary Hell*, p. xvi.

13 Ibid., p. xviii.

14 Ibid., p. 74.

[15] Ibid., p. 72.

[16] Kincaid, *British Social Life*, p. 182.

[17] Edwardes, *Necessary Hell*, p. xx.

[18] Ibid., p. xxi.

[19] Susan Visvanathan, *Christians of Kerala*.

[20] Kenneth Ingham, *Reformers in India, 1793–1833: An Account of the Work of Christian Missionaries on Behalf of Social Reform*, Cambridge University Press, Cambridge, 1956.

[21] Susan Visvanathan, 'Missionary Styles'.

[22] Ingham, *Reformers in India*, p. 2.

[23] Ibid., p. 30.

[24] Ibid., p. 3.

[25] Susan Visvanathan, *Christians of Kerala*.

[26] Ingham, *Reformers in India*, p. 8.

[27] Ibid., p. 7.

[28] Susan Visvanathan, 'Missionary Styles'.

[29] Ingham, *Reformers in India*, p. 10.

[30] Ibid., p. 10.

[31] Ibid., p. 12.

[32] Ibid.

[33] George Smith, *The Conversion of India*, John Murray, London, 1893, p. 32.

[34] Ibid., p. 3.

[35] Ibid., p. 16.

[35] Ibid., p. 85.

[37] Ibid., p. 87.

[38] Ibid., p. 98.

[39] Ibid., p. 100.

[40] Ibid., pp. 104, 105.

[41] Ibid., p. 105.

[42] Susan Visvanathan, *Christians of Kerala*.

[43] George Smith, *Conversion of India*, p. 107.

[44] Ingham, *Reformers in India*, p. 42, Eugene Irschick, *Dialogue and History: Constructing South India, 1795–1895*, Oxford University Press, Delhi, 1994.

[45] *Church Missionary Intelligence*, Vol. VII, 1871, p. 212.

[46] Ingham, *Reformers in India*, p. 15.

[47] Ibid., p. 22.

[48] Ibid., p. 24, Susan Visvanathan, 'Missionary Styles'.

[49] Ingham, *Reformers in India*, p. 24.

[50] Ibid., p. 25.

[51] Dennis Hudson, 'The Life and Times of H.A. Krishna Pillai, 1827–1900: A Study in the Encounter of Tamil Sri Vaishnavism and Evangelical Protestant Christianity in the 19th Century', unpublished Ph.D. dissertation, Clairmont Graduate School, 1970.

[52] George Smith, *Conversion of India*, p. 109.

[53] Ibid., p. 114.

[54] Ibid., p. 114.

55 Ibid., p. 116.
56 Ibid., p. 117.
57 Ibid., p. 118.
58 Ibid., p. 120.
59 Edwardes, *Necessary Hell*, p. 74.
60 *Church Missionary Intelligence*, Vol. VII, 1871, p. 318.
61 Ibid., p. 319.
62 Emil Durkheim, *Moral Education*, The Free Press, New York, 1973.
63 *Church Missionary Intelligence*, Vol. VII, 1871, p. 86.
64 Ibid.
65 Ibid., p. 290.

Colonial Construction of a 'Criminal Tribe'

The Itinerant Trading Communities of Madras Presidency

Meena Radhakrishna

In 1911, the itinerant trading community of Yerukulas in Madras Presidency were declared Criminal Tribes. This was under a piece of legislation called the Criminal Tribes Act, applied to the whole of British India. Under one of its provisions, special settlements could be established where the Criminal Tribe communities could be confined in order to watch and reform them. Missionary organizations— the Salvation Army was the main one—were put in charge of these settlements and were given more or less complete autonomy as far as administration of these settlements was concerned.

In the first part of this paper, in sections I to IV, an attempt is made to identify some of the strands which wove into the ideological perception or construction of a criminal in the early twentieth century, as distinct from actual legislation to deal with criminality on the ground. Attitudes to itinerant communities are discussed in some detail with this aspect in mind, as also the Yerukulas' particular relationship with sedentary communities. In the second part, in sections V and VI, I discuss the main features of a criminal tribe settlement called Stuartpuram where this community lived for decades, and still lives. This part discusses the processes by which the Yerukulas were first sedentarized under the Criminal Tribes Act, then made to work on land owned by the Salvation Army, and finally turned into regular wage workers in a tobacco factory. The last part, comprising sections VII and VIII, describes the way social and cultural aspects of the Yerukulas' community life were transformed in the Stuartpuram settlement under the supervision of the Salvation Army. This seems to have been an inevitable result of the logic of work on land, or in a factory. Section VIII discusses the 'historic memory' of the Yerukulas, and their perception of their ancestors as dangerous criminals. This is done

128

through an analysis of a poem that is a part of their oral culture even today, and which is at complete variance with the 'official' version speaking of a useful, honourable past of the earlier generations.

I

Nomadic communities the world over have always been considered to be more criminal than not, and their 'restlessness' or constant movement is considered a troublesome feature by members of sedentary societies. The relationship between itinerant and sedentary communities has become more problematic in modern times. The more itinerant communities get marginalized to the main sphere of society because of transformative processes, the more they become suspect from the point of view of the sedentary society they interact with. In real terms, their increasing marginality simply compounds the already existing prejudices against them. In Europe, gypsies became gradually marginal to the established system with the processes of industrialization.[1]

In India, the situation was only slightly different: here the British administration's economic policies, aimed at raising revenue, made the itinerant communities redundant and anachronistic. The itinerant community of Yerukulas of Madras Presidency is the focus of this paper, and it is important to first briefly discuss the trajectory they followed in the late nineteenth century, as far as their gradual marginalization to the sedentary society is concerned.

Members of this community were chiefly traders in grain and salt, operating between the coastal areas of the Presidency and the interior districts.[2] They were, at one time, almost the only means of distributing salt in far-flung areas where wheel traffic could not reach. In the 1850s, road and railway networks were established throughout the Presidency, and this community's trade—carried out largely through pack bullocks or donkeys—became largely if not wholly redundant. Further, the famine of 1877 was devastating as far as their salt trade was concerned. Large numbers of their cattle, crucial for carrying their merchandise, died. And as they were *traders* in cattle as well, they suffered huge losses during the decade of the famine. Their grain trade too suffered drastically during this period because of the way famines were managed by the British administration, favouring the bigger grain merchants.[3] Small traders like the Yerukulas found grain totally inaccessible at a time when their cattle were dying in large numbers as well.

129

Forest laws of the 1880s prevented them from collecting forest produce, an important item of barter in their trade, and also did not allow them to collect bamboos and leaves, which they used for making mats, baskets and brooms, etc. Common pastureland and grazing areas were cordoned off, and were no longer available for their cattle.[4]

They were also crucially affected by the new salt policy of the government in the 1880s, which allowed large trading companies to enter the salt trade. A large number of retail outlets were established by the government all over the Presidency on railway routes, where salt was now sold through the agents of large company traders.[5]

As a result of the above factors, the Yerukulas suffered a massive economic setback as far as the period between the 1850s and 1860s is concerned.

II

As they become marginal to the main system, prejudices and myths which already exist about nomads have a fresh lease of life, or come to the surface more explicitly. David Mayall has pointed out some of these in his discussion of gypsy travellers in nineteenth-century England. Some of these apply to itinerant communities in general, and are discussed below.

Most importantly, the nomads' lack of property, and supposed lack of due regard for others' property, is seen to be a threat to the established order.[6] Their independence from the rigid norms and constraints of sedentary societies is found to be equally objectionable. In fact, itineracy is seen as a possible escape route for the so-called outcastes and refuse of sedentary societies—if one is an itinerant, it is probably because he or she was not acceptable to the sedentary society.

There have been other charges against gypsies, migrants, or nomadic people: that they escape from the arm of law, or simply flee from hard work of any kind. In agriculture-based societies, the men resent their escaping the hard work of ploughing and tilling, and the women that, and the harder labour of housekeeping and child-rearing. In short, itineracy is not seen as a chosen way of life, but as an aberration of some sort. In fact, their very marginality to the established system is suspected to stem from a deliberate rejection of that system; this offends the established members of sedentary societies. Accusations of vagrancy, lust for wandering, lack of stability and general purpose in life, restlessness and aimlessness plague all itinerant communities.

In addition, their superior knowledge of the world, acquired during extensive travels, is possibly seen to endow them with greater mental resources and a potential for greater manipulation of others. It is worth emphasizing here that many of the above prejudices are not held so much by the local people, but by the local authorities.[7] In the Indian case, these would mean the British administration, the police establishment, the high-caste sections and the village landlords.

More grievances were added to the standard list of charges against itinerants by the Indian authorities: the lack of predictability of their movement implied a potential lack of control; their shifting abodes meant shifting loyalties to different patrons, and so they were seen to be perennially disloyal; the impossibility of taxing them, or raising any kind of revenue from them, unlike their sedentary counterparts, was probably a major irritant to the administration.[8] In addition, for the keepers of social morality, their lack of visible social institutions implied complete disorder in their community life. Their lack of written codes of conduct and absence of loudly articulated norms of morality implied absolute licentiousness.

At another level, there were more problems. This community had amongst its members acrobats, singers, dancers, tight-rope walkers and fortune-tellers. More and more, like their counterparts all over the world, the street entertainment provided by them was seen to be a threat to public order. Since they always collected a large interested crowd around themselves—and were quite a large crowd by themselves—their presence made the local authorities nervous. The British administration was increasingly inclined to favour forms of recreation which could be supervised by themselves and would not precipitate what they called 'disorderly and riotous behaviour' on the part of the spectators.

It is worth mentioning here that in England, all laws relating to the gypsies were to protect the settled communities from itinerant ones and never the other way around.[9] Large-scale harassment of these communities by members of settled communities was a common feature in Europe, and there is evidence of this happening in Madras Presidency as well.

It is worth pointing out, at this juncture, ambivalences and contradictions in the attitude of sedentary communities to itinerant ones. These are symptomatic of the latter's simultaneous usefulness and marginality to the established systems they have to interact with.

It was, for instance, felt that these communities must be set-tled somewhere, but 'not near us, not here'. This is reminiscent of a similar ambivalence: 'they should visit our village, but should not stay too long'. Further, they were expected to become a part of the main-stream, but were expected also to be segregated from the main society while this was being done, so as not to corrupt it. They were, in fact, romanticized in imagination, especially in English fiction and poetry in the case of the gypsies.[10] This was for their independent spirit; their dark attractive looks (or bright clothes and jewellery as in the case of the Indian Banjaras); their supposedly healthy outdoor life. In general, there was a lot of romance and adventure associated with their travels. However, when confronted in reality, there was fear and dread and they were shunned if not despised. In fact, a number of English ladies in their leisure time in India drew Banjara men and women in a romanticized light while their law-making menfolk made them out to be ferocious criminals. (Banjaras were also declared criminal tribes by the British administration.)[11]

So the important point is that the very nature of the relation-ship between these two different systems, and the gaps in knowledge of each other's real ways of living will lead to myth-making on both sides. Unfortunately, we know little about the myths that the itinerant people have about sedentary societies. At any rate, as far as sedentary societies are concerned, there is an overarching discomfort, a suspicion regarding itinerants which makes for fertile ground for viewing them as established criminals at a later point in time.

III

In the earlier section, some of the general prejudices about itinerant communities were discussed. This section looks into some specific additional charges against the Yerukulas which existed in the minds of the British administrators, and which contributed subs-tantially to their being labelled a criminal tribe. Interestingly, scattered in the official records themselves, there is information collected by the administration for other purposes which contradicts these very charges. However, since the Yerukulas were an itinerant community, the administrators found it difficult to shake off some of the prejudices they carried with them regarding European gypsies, and they seem to have simply superimposed some of these on the Indian counterparts. Moreover, the bulk of their own prejudices were shared by the high-caste, landlord sections, on whom the administration relied for first-hand knowledge of Indian society.

The most important of the accusations was that the Yeru-kulas as itinerants had an 'insatiable lust for wandering aimlessly'. It is important here to point out that their wandering could not have been aimless—they always had fixed trade routes, depending on the demand for their wares; on the cycle of annual festivals and fairs; on availability of raw material for making mats or baskets; and on the season in which forest produce would be available, or stocks of grain, which they used for barter. Their movements also depended on the salt manufacturing cycle, an important item of their trade, or simply on availability of casual work which they did from time to time. Their routes and sche-dules of stopping and moving were fixed and cyclical.[12]

The second of the significant charges was that they were idle, lazy and not keen on hard work. Booth Tucker, the head of the Salva-tion Army in India, wrote of them, 'When we asked them to till the land, or work in a factory, they were shocked. Work? They said, we never work, we just sing and dance.'[13] Now, if they did not work, neither they nor their trade, nor their crafts would have survived for so long. What was being discussed was not whether they worked or not, but the nature of their work. Their work was independent, not time-bound and, most important, not *wage* work.

The third prejudice which had a long life was that of their lack of any social norms, especially regarding their women. Charges of looseness of character, even prostitution, were frequent, stemming from their polygamous practices. Buying and selling of females was another charge, with origins in the bride price which they paid at the time of marriage. The myth of their licentiousness had its roots in their unfamiliar social organization (unfamiliar to the high-caste sections) which included freedom in choosing spouses, easy divorce, widow remarriage, and a marked absence of marriage of girls before puberty. Interestingly, however, this particular view about their women being immoral prevailed with the British administrators as well, possibly because of the polygamy component. Ironically, one of the high-caste commentators in 1948 held the Yerukulas up as the vision of Indian reformers. He stated that since their social norms were what the civil-ized Hindu society was aiming at through legislation, they should, in fact, 'have been left alone'[14] (as far as trying to civilize them was concerned).

133

The final and major charge that plagued the Yerukulas was that of their ostensible criminality. This had two aspects: one, that they had always been criminals—all gypsies supposedly are—and two, that they had become dangerous criminals once they lost their earlier means of livelihood.[15]

As far as proof of the first aspect was concerned, their own alleged folklore were used. It was claimed that 'when they asked their God Subramanya what profession they should follow, he handed them a house breaking implement!'[16] This was supposed to be convincing evidence of their committing thefts and robberies as a profession. In actual fact, crimes attributed to them by the police were seldom proven —this generated another minor myth of their slipperiness and nimble-fingeredness![17]

In the annual crime figures of Madras Presidency, their proportion in the criminal population was always lower than their proportion in the actual population. (In fact, sometimes a high-caste category would account for a much higher proportion of total crime in relation to their proportion in the total population in the region.)[18]

And lastly, the districts through which they regularly passed, or where they stopped for relatively longer periods, did not have a higher proportion of crime than other districts with which they had little contact.[19] Incidentally, when there were genuine crimes committed in areas where they stopped, it was admitted by the police themselves that it was the handiwork of local elements, who got more active whenever an itinerant community was around—these elements were merely using an existing view of itinerants to their advantage, knowing that the crime would be blamed on the itinerants.

However, the second part of this accusation—their *becoming* criminals because they lost their means of livelihood—is more important. This is because part of this assertion was true: they *had* lost their chief means of livelihood over a period of time. As mentioned earlier, they used to be salt and grain traders, taking salt from the coastal areas of the Presidency into inland areas where wheel traffic could not reach, and bartering it for grain or forest produce. The loss of means of livelihood was correctly attributed to a network of roads and railways which had made their trading activities redundant.[20]

However, it is important to point out that salt was a very important source of revenue for the British administration in the nineteenth century, and the Yerukulas were at one time the only means of distributing it in remote areas where only 'pack bullocks' could reach.[21] This is the reason why the British administration officially *recognized* this important aspect of their existence, viz. their salt-trading activities. Similarly, they helped in averting famines in far-flung areas, and that is why their grain trade was acknowledged.

The point, however, is that they were never only salt and grain traders. In fact, they did a number of other things apart from these two major activities. They were cattle breeders and traders; dealers in all kinds of forest and agricultural produce; casual workers; made baskets, mats, brooms and brushes; and as mentioned earlier, were also acrobats, dancers, singers and fortune-tellers. They certainly got marginalized drastically as a result of British policies, but they probably did not become criminals, certainly not as a community. They had too many other resources they could still fall back upon. In the Tamil-speaking region, where they were called Koravars, they continued to be called *inji, kal* or *dabbai koravars,* depending on the work they still did.[22]

The point that is being made so far is that prejudices against itinerants formed a major strand that fed into the Criminal Tribes Act.

IV

The concept of crime and its causes had been changing all through the later part of the nineteenth century, perhaps even earlier, in Europe.[23] There was a strong school of thought, put forward by criminologists and scientists at one point, which held that crime was inherited over generations in a family through a set of genes.[24]

In the Indian context, the concept of a 'hereditary criminal class' remained important and attractive for a long time. This was probably for the reason that this view allowed deflection of enquiries into the causes of crime, and allowed for stringent, arbitrary measures of control. The important point to emphasize here is that the investing of some sections with hereditary criminality was different in the case of India and England. In India it was based not on the notion of genetically transmitted crime, but on crime as a profession practised by a 'hereditary criminal caste'. Like a carpenter would pass on his trade to the next generation, hereditary criminal caste members would pass on this profession to their offspring.[25] In England, a hereditary criminal implied one who had inherited criminality through the genes of a parent or an ancestor.

In India, then, the concept of hereditary crime never really got linked to biological determinism. This happened not because of genuine advance in the field of genetics, but because the Indian caste system seemed to adequately explain to the British administrator the phenomenon of the daunting criminality of at least a section of Indians.

By the end of the nineteenth century, however, it was not the hereditary criminal that the British Indian administrators were looking for any more. Now they were looking for a criminal with more 'scientific' reasons for being one. Clearly, there was a genuine need in these circles to find an explanation for criminality of such large numbers of people in society. By calling the trait hereditary, the problem appeared to be not amenable to resolution or intervention. A genuine social cause had to be identified and dealt with efficiently.

It was in the context of this search that in the first decade of the twentieth century, policies followed by the British Indian administration fifty years ago were blamed for destroying the traditional means of livelihood of a number of communities.[26] Commission of crime was now directly related to lack of means of livelihood, and non-availability of work. (Even in England, lack of 'ostensible means of livelihood' made a person qualify as a potential criminal by now.) This further implied that if honest (wage) work could be found for such communities, they could be weaned away from crime.[27]

And this is how the concept of criminality got linked to a secular cause like loss of livelihood by certain communities due to a set of colonial policies, as discussed in the last section.

It is worth pointing out here that there was the additional input into notions of criminality by the then developing discipline of Indian anthropology as well. This discipline addressed itself to the study of particular sections of the Indian population, mostly indigenous 'tribal' communities and itinerant groups, and contributed in a very substantial way to the conceptual outline of a criminal in the popular mind. By focusing on bizarre or exotic ritual aspects of the social lives of such communities, and at the same time also on their differential anthropometric measurements, the discipline managed to draw fine line between a civilized and barbaric individual. In the popular ethnographic literature of the period, a sketch was drawn of a criminal who possessed not just bizarre social customs, but a strange body and psyche as well, 'which had criminality written all over'.[28]

It is important to mention that the Salvation Army also considerably helped public perception of the criminality of groups with which they worked. In fact they were able to, over a period of time, with some authority, define for administrations all over the world what constituted criminality, and in different social contexts even pointed out who these criminals were—paupers in England, tribals or gypsies in India, aborigines in Australia, New Zealand or North America and so on. The Salvation Army had been working with released prisoners in India a few years before the Criminal Tribes Act was instituted, and this organization was taken very seriously by the government—its officials had evolved categories of criminals like incorrigible, habitual, hereditary, ordinary, worst character, would be good, won't be good, badmash, nekmash and so on, in what they called 'crimdom', and differential treatment was suggested for varying degrees of Indian criminality in a potential 'curedom'. The treatment had to be punitive, deterrent, preventative [*sic*] or curative.[29]

In any case, the general point to emphasize here is that the category of a criminal tribe was not a sudden development—different strands of social and political opinion and considerations had been shaping the general category of an Indian 'criminal' for several decades. The complexity of these converging currents has not been explored here. A criminal could, for instance, be anyone who resisted the British, or even resisted a local oppressive landlord or high-caste member. In addition, the plethora of new legislations that the British introduced created new 'criminals' all the time. These were either people ignorant of the new laws, or those wilfully defiant of the ones which encroached on their traditional rights—for instance, forest laws. To give an example of the broadness and flexibility of the term 'criminal', and the open-ended uses to which the Criminal Tribes Act could be put, it was suggested that the Act could be used profitably 'for combating secret societies, political preachers who might create unrest and so on' to combat the newly emerging nationalist movement.[30]

V

The Yerukulas were declared a criminal community under the Criminal Tribes Act, 1911. Before going into the substantive part of this section, which discusses a criminal tribe settlement called Stuartpuram, it is important to briefly point out a few salient features of the Criminal Tribes Act, and the way it operated in general.

Firstly, before a community was declared a criminal tribe,

'respectable members' of a village were consulted, who were invariably either headmen, or high-caste sections, or landlords; often these categories overlapped. The notified criminal tribe members had to take the permission of the headman before they could enter or leave a village. There is evidence that these headmen-cum-landlords used the Act to extract free labour from the criminal tribe members before they allowed an itinerant community to pass through the village.[31]

Secondly, one of the provisions required the notified criminal tribe members to report to the nearest police station to register their attendance twice a night. These powers were used by the subordinate police for extortion and harassment so widely that it caused some administrative concern.[32]

Thirdly, criminal tribe members were forced to work in mills, factories, mines, quarries and plantations by the police administration as a part of relieving their own vigilance duties, and handing over to the employers extraordinary powers of control under the Criminal Tribes Act. Under this, even ordinary workers could be declared criminal tribes in case their work performance was not satisfactory, and in fact in crucial ways this Act also effectively replaced the Workmen's Breach of Contract Act, especially on the plantations. As far as this particular use of the Criminal Tribes Act was concerned, any low-caste, vulnerable section of the people could be declared a criminal tribe and forced to work in an enterprise; any persons including a manager of an enterprise could be made responsible for their control, and any site including an enterprise could be declared a criminal tribe settlement.[33]

And lastly, a section of those declared criminal could be interned in special settlements set up under one of the provisions of the Criminal Tribes Act. Stuartpuram settlement in Guntur district was one such settlement, and it is here that about 6,000 Yerukulas lived for several decades from 1913 onwards. The settlement was named after Harold Stuart, the moving force behind settlements in general and a senior government official at that time, in charge of the police. The spirit behind these settlements, thus, can be imagined to have been punitive, rather than reformative, contrary to the claims of the administration till much later.

In the 1910s, when the criminal tribe settlements were established in Madras Presidency, itinerant communities were singled out for settling by policy. The official directive was that 'worst characters, especially wandering gangs' must be settled.[34] The Salvation Army was entrusted with itinerant communities, and sedentary criminals were to be the responsibility of the police.[35] Stuartpuram settlement, then, became the literal 'site' where the British administration and the Salvation Army together decided to have what they called an 'experiment in criminocurology'. Since the Salvation Army was responsible for a number of settlements and was, in fact, the main organization working with the supposed criminal communities in India, it is appropriate to mention a few details about this organization, and why it was attractive to the British administration.

The Salvation Army identified itself aggressively with the imperial aims of England of the time. Born in the 1870s, the heyday of British imperialism, it not only called itself the Salvation *Army*, it cashed in on the popular image of romanticized imperialism by adopting marches, flags, brass bands and uniforms for its employees. Their head was called *General* Booth, they had *officers* who signed *articles of war*, their newspaper was called *The War Cry*. They had open air *bombardments*, not meetings. They would not say that they were going to start work in a new region, but *occupy a new territory, and declare war* (on ungodliness or whatever).[36] In short, the Salvation Army was a shadow imperial body—selfconsciously so—and absolutely identified itself with the aims and projects of England of the time.

General Booth had envisaged for the English poor what he called city colonies and farm colonies.[37] For the Indian criminal, however, he decided on 'settlements'. Of course, in this case, this imperial term took on a new meaning—the itinerant communities were to be *settled down* as opposed to being allowed to wander aimlessly.

Stuartpuram settlement was meant to be a settlement for well-behaved, reformed and non-criminal members drawn from another criminal settlement, Sitanagaram, also located in Guntur.[38] However, when the Salvation Army was given land in Guntur to set up this settlement, there were a number of protests, posed in different ways. The landlord sections were particularly infuriated, and charged that criminal tribe members escaped at night from the settlement and committed crime. Thus, this settlement was also declared to be a criminal settlement, and a substantial increase in the police force was sanctioned in the area, to intensify patrolling.[39]

Stuartpuram settlement was planned to have been an agricultural settlement. Five hundred acres of sandy land and one thousand acres of swamp land were handed over to the Salvation Army by the

139

government, free of assessment. However, for a number of reasons, the plans failed. Essentially, the land was of very poor quality and the implements of agriculture primitive. Moreover, the Yerukulas were not keen on tilling the land, and made unenthusiastic agriculturists.

Following is an excerpt from a settlement manager's poetic account of his experiences with making unwilling settlers work on land:

> The Salvation Army found it very tedious
> to convert them into good cultivators industrious
> To work on land they were forced and could not be induced
> Though driven like a flock of sheep, the first crop failed . . .
> No crowbars, no proper spade and no physical strength
> So work turned out did not reach the desired length.[40]

Again,

> In the beginning, I had recourse to a stick,
> I was glad, as it brought the desired result quick.[41]

Most important, there was fierce opposition by the landlords in the area, who objected to the very concept of low-caste communities being given land, in addition to their fear that paddy land, when suitably irrigated, was very valuable.[42] It was revealed that 'the monied folk of Bapatla (had) counted . . . on buying the swamp land at cheap rates and rack renting the actual cultivator whenever a crop could be raised'.[43] This plan was unwittingly foiled by the administration by parcelling out large tracts of land to the Salvation Army. The protest by the landlords was also in a large measure due to their anxiety about losing the services of the Yerukulas as agricultural workers on their own land.[44]

All this opposition took place in an era when landlords were important political allies of the British administration, and on balance, the administration decided not to alienate the landlord/headmen sections any further. Irrigation facilities—plans to make available water from the Krishna river to the settlement—were withheld, and alternative means of supporting the settlement had to be now seriously considered.

It was at this juncture that the Indian Leaf Tobacco Company (ILTD) [a later branch of the Indian Tobacco Company (ITC)] began to be discussed within the administration and Salvation Army circles, as possible alternative employers. The ILTD had existed in Guntur district since 1908 in order to procure local tobacco, as the leaf-wing of British American Tobacco Company and Peninsular Company. By 1925, the factory was said to have employed half of the total adult population of the settlement.[45] Essentially, according to government policy, once infrastructure for the settlement had been provided by the government, the settlements were meant to be self-supporting. Once income from land was found to be not enough, gradually the settlement became very dependent on the factory for the employment of the settlers.[46] The Salvation Army had no other means of finding employment for their charges.

The Company's initial contact with the Stuartpuram settlers seems to have been through the mats made by the Yerukula women. The mats and baskets were, in fact, as essential part of the manufacturing process at the factory, and the Salvation Army was the medium through which the sales took place to the ILTD. Slowly, women came to be employed in the factory as regular wage workers, while the men continued to work fruitlessly on land. The financial situation of the settlement was quite stable for a few years after the women settlers from Stuartpuram began work in the ILTD factory. The ILTD management, the Salvation Army and the administration seemed optimistic about the future progress of the settlement.

VI

In the late 1920s, a process set itself into motion which changed the balance of forces explicitly in further favour of the ILTD and the Salvation Army. This was in the form of availability of more men workers from the settlement for factory work, and more powers of control for the Salvation Army on settlement land.

In 1928, 'natural flow'—fresh water—under the sandy soil was discovered and found to be effective to raise paddy. Water beneath the surface of the sandy soil of the settlement's agricultural land was not brackish, as had been believed all along. This revived the interest of the settlers in cultivation.[47] In the same year, the settlers petitioned the government about being given permanent *pattas* as had been promised.[48] The Salvation Army was firmly opposed to the plan of transferring land to the settlers, and wrote to the officials to this effect.[49] What had happened was that the land had risen enormously in price. 'The place prospered so much that it had its own railway station and villages sprang up like a wild west town after a gold strike.'[50]

The petition by the settlers had been pending for five years before it was turned down on a number of administrative grounds (re-survey of land will have to be done, more village officers will have to be recruited and so on). The most important official argument, however, was that the concept of permanent *pattas* was inconsistent with the running of the place as a reformatory settlement.[51] (Settlers were supp-osed to leave the settlement after their reformation had been achieved, to make place for new criminals.)

Essentially, there had been ominous signs shown by the sett-lers. There was an indication that the settlers had been found to be not totally without resistance to the policies of the Salvation Army, and had in fact organized themselves into a cooperative society.[52] Mem-bers of this society were now preparing to invest their own funds in digging an irrigation channel to improve the land, so that the fruit of the land would then be legitimately theirs and not appropriated by the Salvation Army.[53]

The response of the Salvation Army was to discharge a large number of settlers from the provisions of the Criminal Tribes Act and thus from the settlement itself, and transfer them to a new area called the New Colony near the ILTD factory premises. The official require-ment of a means of livelihood before a settler could be discharged from the settlement was met by finding them employment in this factory.

This plan was fully supported and, in fact, financed by the government. Building a new colony involved digging wells, building huts and providing other infrastructure, and this was done in a great hurry just before the start of the tobacco processing season in 1935, so that the discharged settlers could be immediately employed in the factory. Taking advantage of the situation, the ILTD management decided to expand its operations at Chirala.

The problem of men, hitherto tenants of the Salvation Army, had to be sorted out: these men had to be found work in a factory where work processes had been designed to employ mainly women. But there had been a strike by the 3,000 seasonal workers in 1932,[54] and the ILTD had since then been looking out for a more pliable work-force.

In 1933, the manager of ILTD, Chirala, wrote to the chief ins-pector of factories, requesting him to exempt the workers in the factory from the provisions of the Factories Act, as the factory needed to work for 12 hours a day, and 66 hours a week.[55] The case made out was on the basis of the nature of the processes themselves. The fact which convinced the administration, however, in favour of the exemption of ILTD from crucial sections of the Factories Act was that '*machine room operatives were drawn mostly from Stuartpuram settlement, . . . maintained by public funds*'.[56] The manager of the settlement, a Salvation Army official, had written to the ILTD management, urging that the provisions of the Act should be relaxed to enable the men settlers to work as long hours as possible. The 'concession', according to him, if granted, would benefit the administration of the settlement and indirectly make the task of control of criminal tribe settlers easier and cheaper for the government.[57]

This plea to ILTD, in fact, was not inconsistent with the fact that the Salvation Army wanted to discharge as many settlers from the Stuartpuram land as possible and work had to be found for them in order to make out a case with the government for discharging them. These settlers were soon after, in 1935, discharged and transferred to the new colony near the factory on the grounds that 'to walk 3 ½ miles in the morning for work is not conducive to efficiency'.[58]

The exemption was applied for section 21 (rest periods in factories), section 22 (weekly holidays), section 27 (limiting of working hours per week), and section 28 (limiting of working hours per day). The exemption which was granted was from sections 27 and 28. It applied to *all* machine operatives in *all* tobacco handling and redrying factories.[59] In this way, the Yerukulas were used as an instrument in a major modification of the law, which was to now cover not just machine-room workers from this community in the ILTD factory, but all machine-room workers in all tobacco factories in the Presidency.

By the beginning of 1935, every available man and woman from Stuartpuram was in the employment of ILTD. ILTD, as a result of the new exemptions, was now working double shifts, from 5 am to 1 am the next morning, except on Sundays.[60] The factory manager was reported to have given the government very good accounts of the Yerukula workers. On the whole, these workers were found to be thoroughly satisfactory by the ILTD.[61] They found regular work in the factory for ten months in a year—a pattern which was to continue for many years.

VII

Stuartpuram became a large settlement in terms of numbers, as whole communities—not individuals—were put in at a time. After all, the Criminal Tribes Act was meant to work with the concept of whole communities. In fact, even the Salvation Army said they were embarrassed by what they called 'this rain of riches'. (They explained this phrase to an intrigued government official: 'To others, these criminals may hardly appear in the light of riches, but to us each bears the image and supersubscription of the Divine Mint.')

This large settlement needed an extensive police presence outside to prevent escapes, and inside, the Salvation Army took attendance up to five times a day, including nights.[62] There was strict punctuality and discipline for both children and adults and a system of fines and even corporal punishment to deter disorderly behaviour. Incidentally, virtually no outsiders were allowed into the settlement for scrutiny, and enquiry committees could enter it only in the 1940s, when the nationalists took up this issue seriously.

Stuartpuram settlement, as described earlier, was meant to be an agricultural settlement. Though the official rationale was that it should be so because 'agriculture was the natural profession of all Indians', what comes through clearly in the records is the deep anxiety the British administration had for reclamation of wasteland, forest land and swamp land. In fact, land reclamation was synonymous with reclamation of criminal souls. Once cultivable, the land could start paying revenue. A large tract of wasteland was given to the Salvation Army for cultivation by the Yerukulas. This needed some reorganizing of the community's social and cultural priorities.

A drastic transformation in the lives of the Yerukulas followed. Most important, of course, was the fact that the itinerant mode of existence was suddenly replaced by a forced settled life. The Salvation Army divided the community into families, which now became the new operational social and economic unit—each family was given a small piece of land which it was responsible for cultivating, or else punishment followed.[63] The family was further broken up by removing the children to another part of the settlement. The Salvation Army felt that the 'rising generation' should be kept away from their wicked parents0 and brought up in a more wholesome atmosphere. Separate schools and dormitories were established for these children, and they were allowed to meet their parents only on Sundays during church activities. The two components of criminals' reformation were moral education and work. The Salvation Army concentrated on the children for moral education, and on the adult men for work.

Here it is important to emphasize that the Salvation Army did not normally prepare women for wage work in any of its settlements— they were to be, ideally, trained in feminine virtues and were expected to sew, embroider and cook for their families.

Recent work on Africa shows that missions in general expected women to remain in domestic surroundings and men to earn a wage outside. In fact, in the mid-nineteenth century, a general mission slogan regarding women was: 'Improve the wives of the poor and servants of the rich',[64] meaning that if at all women must work outside, they must again be domestic workers and continue to cook, sew and mind children in their employers' homes.

Coming back to the Stuartpuram settlement, a new division of labour within the family was devised and appropriate gender roles defined. In fact, mat-making, which was a traditional activity of both men and women of the community, was now handed over exclusively to women, to be combined with other indoor activities.[65] Men now ploughed and tilled the wasteland, albeit unsuccessfully.

There were a myriad number of ways in which true women were fashioned out of what the Salvation Army called 'thievish raw material'. For instance, they were taught to pay attention to their appearance. The Salvation Army even held periodic parades of the 'most neatly dressed women' (and gave the winners a prize of one rupee each).[66] The women would also not be allowed to go outside the settlement on a pass if they looked like 'so many vagrants'. The 'before' and 'after' photographs of women in the Salvation Army records show the 'after' version with a completely changed Hinduized appearance, complete with neatly tied saris, oiled hair with flowers and vermillion marks on their foreheads.

Anyway, after more than a decade of such remoulding, something happened: these newly domesticated women were required to work outside their homes for a wage, as the land was found to be unable to support the families. As already mentioned earlier, the government expected the Salvation Army to make the settlements under their care completely self-supporting once the initial infrastructure had been paid for. Now that there was a severe financial crisis, these women were persuaded or forced in hundreds to go and work in the newly established tobacco factory several miles away.

The Salvation Army had so far been systematically inculca-ting in them an indoor culture of house-keeping and child-rearing. Now they were expected to walk a distance of seven miles every day, spend a total of twelve hours outside their homes, earning a wage. In fact, the Salvation Army even asked the government to provide creches for the infants and toddlers in the settlement, so that young mothers could go as well. For the next ten to twelve years, the women alone earned as much as 80 per cent of the entire settlement income.[67]

Ironically, while women were the principal earners in their families, the Salvation Army consolidated the new moral code for them. Unable any more to scrutinize their activities, unable also to adhere to the notion of them as dependent wives, the Salvation Army began to take on a more active role in their personal, marital affairs. This was done in order partly to keep their own control and partly to make sure that economic independence did not confound gender identities, as it had gender roles.

Women used to have the freedom to choose their spouses—the Salvation Army now granted permission for marrying. The Salvation Army officials had always been votaries of proper match-making in the settlements, now they became urgently active on the issue. They wrote to the government wanting 'a voice in the choice of spouses'[68] and got it. They were finding to their alarm that bride price, something they had been trying to suppress as it meant mere selling of females, now rose steeply (sometimes up to as much as Rs 500).[69] The Salvation Army substituted it with dowry, which they gave themselves. It always consisted of saris and vessels for the bride—true symbols of lost domesticity. (Incidentally, in other settlements in the north, the Salvation Army used to insist that the man be able to support his wife before letting them marry—they had to give up that condition here, which they did quite cheerfully.) They also forbade completely what they called 'desertions' by women of their husbands. So, ironically, the women lost their autonomy in marital affairs at a time when they were the principal contributors to family income.

It is important to mention here that the ILTD where the women worked supported the Salvation Army on the severe discipline in the settlement, and their active role in the women's family affairs. In fact, at a later point in time, the ILTD management became quite active itself on the second issue. The discipline—strict punctuality, orderly

146

behaviour and a system of harsh punishments—resonated well with factory life. On the whole, the ILTD management found that these workers were 'less troublesome' than others and much more pliable.[70] The Salvation Army's insistence on an irrevocable form of marriage worked in the company's favour as well, as they could continue to pay a family wage which was much lower that what would have to be paid to an individual man or woman.

As a result of the special exemption from the Factories Act that the government granted to ILTD, whole families from the settlement had come to be employed in the factory from the 1930s. The men were now working up to twenty hours a day in different shifts.

The ILTD, then, had a new interest in keeping families together at the settlement. I came across at least three petitions by Yerukula men in the company records, where the management was requested to intervene and help them in getting their wives to stay with them. The ILTD obliged in all three cases by threatening the women with loss of their jobs in case they divorced their husbands. Interestingly, I did not see any similar petitions by women.

VIII

The earlier sections of this essay have, in effect, dealt with the colonial construction of the Yerukulas' criminality, and the later ones with some of the ways in which their real daily lives were lived out decades ago. It is within this dual context that I shall try and locate this community's current perception of its own past history.

About ten years ago, I met the descendents of the Yerukulas in question, still living in Stuartpuram settlement and working with the very same tobacco factory, the ILTD. When I met them, they were about to be retrenched in thousands, because the factory was going in for a mechanized plant to do the work that these workers had been doing manually. Stuartpuram, of course, was officially not called a Criminal Tribes settlement any more, and the community, Yerukulas, were not criminal tribes any more—after independence the Criminal Tribes Act, under which they had been notified by the colonial administration, had been repealed. The Salvation Army, now a much depleted organization both as far as its authority and the number of personnel were concerned, was still operating there with a hospital, a school and other welfare activities.

I spent a long time with the community, both men and

women, talking about their work in the tobacco factory, the various strikes they had conducted to protest against mechanization and so on. The workers were very eloquent and talked a great deal about their experience with ILTD. They were quite emphatic about the unfavourable partisan role of the Salvation Army in their struggle with the company. They also freely expressed their views on the factory management's mechanization plans which would now make them redundant.

During my stay at the settlement, I noticed that in their leisure time the children and the adults would sing. Sometimes, after the day's work, they would gather together and tell each other long tales with much enthusiasm. I learnt that the stories they told so often were different sagas of how their forefathers were dangerous criminals; how the Salvation Army had worked tirelessly and selflessly for them for decades; how the tobacco factory had weaned their forefathers away from an earlier life of crime by giving them employment and so on. Their songs, I found, were those taught by the Salvation Army in praise of Christ.

I wondered how this had happened. When they were so clear about their present destiny and relationship vis-à-vis the Salvation Army and the ILTD, why were their narratives and songs about their past in such a different tone? I knew by then from official records that this community had been an itinerant one for generations before they were interned in this settlement—in fact, the village community around the settlement remembered their salt and grain trade, and other activities. However, there were no traces of this relatively recent past being part of their memories in any form. There were no songs or folklore which in any way reflected links with their earlier itinerant life, or their earlier work. Their stout denial of an itinerant past intrigued me as much as their assertions of an earlier dangerous criminality —and this phenomenon could not be understood by me till quite recently, when I stumbled upon some official publications of the Salvation Army.

Since I am discussing a community here which was unlettered, and has not left behind any written records, its own folklore (as also folklore about it) becomes an extremely important source to understand a whole range of issues. It also becomes very crucial to pose some of the following questions. Did the components of this folklore originated from inside the community, by and large, or from outside. If the latter, then was it an involuntary, 'natural' or gradual transformation/assimilation of versions of their past, or were some of these consciously or 'artificially' introduced? Is the folklore of the community, in however small a way, a positive reading of its own past, or does the new version/s undermine its confidence or resources to fight its disabilities of the *present*? Have stories or tales about the community, which pass off as its history with outsiders, become a part of the community's own historic memory? And equally, whether subsequent generations of that community keep these narratives alive by making such versions a part of their own oral tradition.

Reproduced here is a poem which appeared in the Salvation Army newspaper, *The War Cry*. It was called 'The Crim as we find him in the Telegu country'.[71] It appeared in 1916, a few years after Stuartpuram settlement had been established. It stands by itself, has no explanation or prose narrative to go with it, and is written by a Major Anandham, a non-Indian Salvation Army officer. (The Salvation Army officials always took on local names, but never from the 'criminal' communities with whom they worked.) Parts of this poem are reproduced here:

> Come listen to me for a moment or more,
> For I am a 'crim', yes, I am a 'crim';
> There are records against me, yes, more than a score,
> I belong to the criminal kind.
>
> I live most by plundering other men's goods,
> For I am a 'crim', yes I am a 'crim';
> My home is in the jungle way off in the woods,
> Oh, I am of the criminal kind.
>
> I watch out for travellers' long lonely bye roads,
> Oh, I am a 'crim', yes I am a 'crim';
> And many a 'hold up' I've done on the road,
> That's the life of the criminal kind. . .
>
> Away to the jungle and off to the fair,
> I'm only a 'crim', I'm only a 'crim',
> There is booty and plenty awaiting me there,
> I belong to the criminal kind.

The reader would have noticed that there is first-person address used here—the 'I' dominates the narrative. The Salvation Army muse here is putting forward the supposed point of view of the Yeru-kulas, but from the point of view of an individual.

Coming to the second edition of the poem which is written about a decade later, it is found to be much edited, changed and added to. It appears in a book of over three hundred pages, written for an international audience by Booth Tucker, now the head of the Salvation Army. The book in which it appears is called *Mukti Fauj or Forty Years with the Salvation Army in India.*[72] It is a part of one of the chapters called 'Criminocurology', and has a long prose narrative before and after. The content of this narrative is almost entirely the unfolding of a success story that Booth Tucker has to tell.

The interesting point about the location of this poem is that it is surrounded with prose which has important details. Here there is discussion of the tremendous resistance that the Yerukulas offered to their sedentarization, conversion to Christianity, work on land or in factories. The poem, however, is quite beatific and ecstatic in tone, as if the Salvation Army just came and conquered. Perhaps the problems could now be talked about, once it is a success story, a story with a happy ending. But still, the lack of any resistance in the poem is inter-esting as this poem, in all essential particulars, represented the myth which the Yerukulas accepted; the resistance which actually took place on the ground was never a part of the myth.

Reproduced here are parts of the poem which are newly added to the earlier version, most likely not by the original author but some more senior bard in the Salvation Army.

I've oft been to prison and tasted their fare,
For I am a Crim, yes, I am a Crim!
Learned more of my business profession while there,
Seeing mine is a criminal mind.

And when I get out into freedom again,
I, who am a Crim, I, who am a Crim!
I fool the police, with their cleverest men,
Oh, I'm of the criminal kind!

The longer I follow, the more I delight,
In this life of a Crim, this life of a Crim!
To rob and to plunder, by day and by night,
This life of a criminal kind.

Here the criminal is shown to be a worse one than in the original version—he fools the police with his cleverness, he even learns new tricks of the trade in prison, and in fact is sadistic about his pursuit of crime—'the longer I follow, the more I delight'.

This is an important development—the criminal is shown to be much more dangerous in retrospect, though he has in fact been steadily reforming for the last decade in the settlement! At one level this is understandable—the Salvation Army has to show their international audience how unpromising the initial raw material was, to heighten the fact of their success with them. Alternatively, maybe the settlers *seemed* more criminal as they were actively resisting the Salvation Army when this poem was being rewritten. But in real terms, the new version was an improvement on the earlier one.

In the second edition of the poem there is an actual break in the narrative when the Salvation Army enters the picture, both symbolically and literally. This break, separating the earlier and later lives of the criminals, is achieved on paper by the device of having the old and the new sections separated by asterisks and it is the newly added section which heralds the new man. It is interesting that this break, symbolic and literal, was absent in the earlier poem written a decade earlier and in some ways shows that even the Salvation Army was aware of the rupture that took place in the interim period, as far as the Yerukulas' past and present was concerned. Thus goes the new section:

> The Salvation Army now comes to our aid;
> With work for the Crim—yes, work for the Crim!
> And for us a pathway to Heaven has made,
> For tribes of the criminal kind. . .
>
> They give us an offer of work we accept
> 'Tis work for the Crim—yes, work for the Crim;
> And soon at our task we become quite adept,
> We tribes of the criminal kind. . .
>
> At last we wake up to the fact, and the thought,
> 'I'm no longer a Crim! I'm no longer a Crim!!
> I'm living by industry, honestly wrought,
> And have changed from the criminal mind!'

The reader will note here that the 'I' of the earlier poem has changed to 'we': there has been great progress in the intervening years.

In fact, the 'we' now includes not only the whole community of say, the Telugu country, but 'we, tribes of the criminal kind'. (There were at least three to four million criminal tribe members in India.) The poem, in fact, is no longer called 'The Crim as we find him in the Telegu Country', but simply, 'The Crim'.

Moreover, the 'we' of the poem now includes not just those who have been reformed but includes the Salvation Army as well:

So all hands to work, through the storm, or the calm—
We will rescue the Crim, we will rescue the Crim—
And rid this fair land from a menace and harm,
The tribes of the criminal kind.

There is not only distancing of the reformed ones from the unreformed ones, there is now total identification the reformed members with the projects and plans of the Salvation Army for all Indian criminal tribe members. The newly reformed man is grateful that the Salvation Army has given him an opportunity to work honestly, and give up a life of crime.

This is quite interesting, as when I spoke to the Yerukulas in the 1980s, I found that the content of the two poems was exactly what they also believed: We were dangerous criminals, the Salvation Army came along, gave us work, and we were reformed!

One can speculate on what happened. Did they really mean what they said ? Were their own stories believed by them? Where were their earlier tales? Why is their present memory devoid of their past? There are several possibilities.

Firstly, the Yerukulas of the 1980s do not have any stakes in their past, so they are not going to intervene in versions of that past; their energies are better deployed in fighting their present, which they were doing. (As mentioned earlier, they were actively engaged in fighting their retrenchment from the ILTD factory in thousands.) Perhaps their emphasis on past criminality is to bring to others' notice their *present non-criminality*—a sign that they are still not free of the stigma of criminality by communities around them. It is also possible that talking about their past dangerous criminality, their ability once to 'hold up' those in power and terrorize them, gives them a sense of power today: 'We were also powerful once'—a sign of their powerlessness in the present. Another possibility is that this is myth-making of their own. Belief in their earlier criminality rationalizes their current situation of vulnerability and poverty: 'Because we were criminals in the past, we deserve our present miserable fate.' There is also a touch of both defiance and relief in their loud assertions of past criminality: 'No one can harm us at least today.' And finally, maybe by resigning themselves to this version of their history they will be left in peace by the Salvation Army, or the ILTD, or whoever might challenge an alternative memory of their history.

These were some possible explanations as far as their assertions of past criminality are concerned. About their inability or refusal to remember their itinerant past, it is probably an expression of their discontent with that way of life. As discussed earlier in the paper, they were becoming increasingly marginalized, and began to be dispensable to the local communities. Even before the Criminal Tribes Act was formally instituted, at least two or three decades before that, they had become vulnerable to police harassment and extortions. Perhaps they finally found peace once they were sedentarized, though it was not in a criminal tribe settlement they would have liked to become sedentary.

These are mere speculations. The explanation for this collective denial of a collective history, and the blanking out of collective memory of their folklore reflecting an earlier life, is probably a combination of all these, but around one major fact: there was a severe rupture in the continuity of their lives once they came to the settlement. Folklore and songs and tales can only survive in a lived community life and one with some continuity, however flimsy, with an earlier life. Under the Salvation Army, in a criminal tribe settlement, their community life was totally broken up and their forced transformation into disciplined wage workers took an absolute toll on their cultural resources.

To repeat here some of what was discussed in an earlier section, firstly and most importantly, from being considered useful if not honourable people, they were officially declared predators on the larger society. Then, their itinerant mode of existence was replaced by settled life. The community as a unit was broken into families, which were now the operational social and economic units. Men's trading activities were replaced by forced work on land and later in the tobacco factory, and the women were first forcedly confined to the home and then forced to become factory workers. Their earlier social practices were considered barbaric and substituted with ones more acceptable to Victorian and brahminical notions of respectability; the women lost their relative egalitarian position in the community and became increasingly subordinated to men.

Moreover, their children were taken away from them—who could they tell tales to, or sing songs to? It was a fractured community life, with broken bonds and ties. The settlement discipline allowed no meetings larger than six people at a time, except under the eyes of the Salvation Army. In any case, there could not be the leisure which must be there for telling of tales or singing of songs—both the men and the women worked up to sixteen hours a day.

In other words, there were several convulsions of engineered and sudden change in the continuity of their lives, and breaches with the immediate past. What remained of the community was more a confederacy, created by the punitive discipline and application of the Criminal Tribes Act. The social and cultural resources gathered over generations were probably irreparably destroyed with the violence of change that each of the breaches implied. The system of relationships and other social balances that communities evolve to sustain themselves seem to have been wiped out in this particular case because of a lack of continuity between the present and the past. Ironically, it was not until both men and women began work in the tobacco factory that some semblance of a collective or community identity began to emerge again, because of a shared environment, however restrictive. By then, however, it appears that their past history had already been rewritten in their memories.

There is a clue to the gradual way in which a rupture from their past took place. Their real lived experience, once they were beginning to be labelled criminals, was at complete variance with their earlier existence as legitimate traders. There was the Salvation Army inside the settlement, and if they managed to escape, the police outside. In fact, the police were a major constituent of their new psyche, as the possibility of a life outside the settlement, if they managed to escape, was clouded with their ubiquitous presence.

> They hunted me, haunted me, hounded me ever,
> I was a 'crim', they said I was a 'crim';
> And my honest intentions were scorned all the more,
> I was branded the criminal kind.
>
> So I gave up my struggle and thought it my lot,
> For I was a 'crim', yes, I was a crim,

With the rest of my fellows, the Sircar I fought,
Being marked as the Criminal Tribe.

The rupture is also expressed tellingly in the amusing manner in which Booth Tucker recounted the following instances to an international audience, fully aware that absconding from the settlement spelt terror for the settlers:

> One of our women officers was conducting a meeting amongst a number of tribesmen. She had been speaking to them . . . about the necessity of resisting the temptations of Satan. 'Who is your greatest enemy?' she asked. 'The Police'. 'But, I mean, your spiritual enemy, the enemy of your souls'. They persisted, however, in repeating the answer. The officer was forced to change the subject and had to give them a chorus to sing instead.[73]

Recounting another instance, he recalled that a Salvation Army officer asked his Yerukula pupils, 'I have a Friend that's ever near—never fear. What does that mean?' 'Don't be afraid of the Police, God will look after you', came the prompt reply.[74]

But the most poignant of all is the way, before the rupture became complete, their prayers which used to be for the peace of their dead and the health of their children changed: 'Spirits of our fathers, help us. Save us from the government and shut the mouths of the police.'[75]

So this was the mental soil on which so powerful a myth, so convincing a version of another history could be sown. The important point to emphasize here is that the Salvation Army had consciously spun it, improved upon it, and intended to plant it years before it was actually made their own by members of the Yerukula community. As indicated earlier, there was resistance on the ground to the components of this version while it was being spun.[76] Now being passed on to new generations, this new history shows no signs of that resistance.

Ironically, the official records of the British administration, the ILTD factory, and the Salvation Army contradict much of what the Yerukulas believe today. These sources not only grant the Yerukulas an 'honourable' past, they speak of the resistance that the community offered to forces which challenged the legitimacy of its existence at various stages. Equally ironically, it is the *official* sources which acknowledge the lack of any real bases for branding the community a

155

criminal one. The *oral* traditions of the community, which are supposed to 'recover' an 'authentic' past, reconstruct over and over again the criminal that the larger society had once invented, by passing on a constructed version of their history to their children and grandchildren. This version, as the paper attempts to show, did not originate from the way their actual lives were lived, but was purposefully introduced into the oral culture of the community about seven decades ago.

It will be appropriate to end with what the 'Crims' in the 1920s were meant to be thinking of themselves and their situation from the point of view of the Salvation Army:

> Now (work) is our watchword, from day unto day,
> There is hope for the Crim; there is hope for the Crim,
> *We wipe from our minds our sad record away,*[77]
> We tribes of the criminal kind.

Earlier versions of this paper were presented at Nehru Memorial Museum and Library, New Delhi, School of Oriental and African Studies, London, Oxford and Cambridge. I am grateful to the participants of these seminars for very useful discussions and comments. Issues raised in this paper have been discussed with a large number of other scholars and friends, some of whom have decisively moulded the final shape. I thank all of them.

Notes and References

All the Government Orders (GOs) at Tamil Nadu Archives and Andhra Pradesh Archives were consulted. The Salvation Army documents were consulted at the organization's archives at the International Heritage Centre, London.

[1] For an excellent account of gypsies in England, see David Mayall, *Gypsy Travellers in Nineteenth Century*, Cambridge University Press, Cambridge, 1988.

[2] For an account of their trading activities, see Meena Radhakrishna, 'The Criminal Tribes Act in Madras Presidency: Implications for Itinerant Communities', *The Indian Economic and Social History Review*, 26, 3, 1989.

[3] Government of Madras, *A Memorandum on the Madras Famine of 1866*, Madras, 1867, Appdx. viii; Government of India, *Report of the Indian Famine Commission*, Parts I, II and III, Vol. I, 1878, p. 49. Also see Sabyasachi Bhattacharya, 'Laissez Faire in India', *Indian Economic and Social History Review*, 2, 1, 1965 and S. Ambirajan 'Political Economy and Indian Famines', *South Asian Studies*, No. 1, August 1971.

[4] Government of Madras, *Administration Report of the Forest Department (Southern and Northern Circles)*, Madras Presidency for 1889–90, Madras, p. 27. Revenue for grazing went up from Rs 40,138 in 1883–84 to Rs

1,43,845 in 1889–90: Government of Madras, *Report of the Forest Commit-tee*, Madras, Vol. II, 1912, pp. 7, 32.

[5] A detailed analysis of the *Report of the Salt Commission*, Madras, 1876, makes this fact clear.

[6] This and the para that follows draw largely from Mayall, *Gypsy Travellers*.

[7] The local people must find the nomads quite useful for the unusual wares they bring periodically. Their various skills of weaving mats or making baskets or playing musical instruments, and more dramatically in the case of acrobats and dancers, make them a colourful and interesting presence, in all probability providing relief and diversion from the tedium of daily routine.

[8] I am grateful to David Washbrook for bringing to my notice the point about taxing.

[9] Mayall, *Gypsy Travellers*, p. 180.

[10] Ibid., p. 87.

[11] The Banjaras were a community much more in evidence all over India, unlike the Yerukulas who operated only in the limited Telegu regions of Madras Presidency. In fact, Banjaras were called 'exporters' of grain and salt to distant provinces and regions by the Madras administration, and Yerukulas were termed 'local' traders. Essentially, Banjaras were a numerically larger community, operating on a much larger scale, traversing a much larger geographic area. For the same reason, they escaped the Criminal Tribes Act for a longer period compared to the Yerukulas, being relatively less vulnerable.

[12] Judl. 239, dt. 24.9.1918.

[13] F. Booth Tucker, *Criminocurology or the Indian Crim and What to do with him—a Report of the Work of the Salvation Army among the Criminal Tribes, Habituals and Released Prisoners in India*, Salvation Army, London, n.d., p. 43.

[14] A. Aiyyappan, *Report on the Socio-economic Conditions of the Aboriginal Tribes of the Province of Madras*, Government Press, Madras, 1948, p. 47.

[15] See Meena Radhakrishna, 'The Criminal Tribes Act', pp. 271–75.

[16] Government of Madras, *Note showing the Progress made in the Settlement of Criminal Tribes in the Madras Presidency upto January, 1925*, Madras, 1926, p. 63.

[17] Ibid.

[18] Ibid.

[19] Judl. GO 1071, Back nos. 51–53, dt. 10.8.1870. IGP to chief secretary to government, Fort St. George, Madras, 19.5.1870, No. 3016.

[20] For a detailed discussion of the process by which the Yerukulas lost their varied means of livelihood because of a set of colonial economic policies, see Meena Radhakrishna, 'The Criminal Tribes Act'.

[21] Ibid.

[22] PWL GO 225L, 26.2.1929.

[23] Clive Emsley, *Crime and Society in England 1750–1800*, Longman, London

and New York, 1987; Anand A. Yang, ed., *Crime and Criminality in British India*, The University of Arizona Press, Arizona, 1985; David Jones, *Crime, Protest, Community and Police in Nineteenth Century Britain*, Routledge and Kegan Paul, London, 1982.

24   Nancy Stepan, *Idea of Race in Science: Great Britain, 1800–1960*, Macmillan, Oxford, 1982.

25   Quoted in Sanjay Nigam, 'Disciplining and policing the criminals by birth, part I: The making of a colonial stereotype—the criminal tribe and castes of North India', *Indian Economic and Social History Review*, 28, 2, 1990.

26   Meena Radhakrishna, 'The Criminal Tribes Act', pp. 271–75.

27   This essentially meant that the CT members, as government policy, were to be parcelled out to owners of mills, factories, mines, quarries as workers, as also to plantation owners. See ibid.

28   For a detailed discussion of some of the currents which went into the making of the discipline of anthropology, see Meena Radhakrishna, 'Colonialism, Evolutionism and Anthropology—A Critique of the History of Ideas 1850–1930', Research in Progress Papers, *History and Society*, Nehru Memorial Museum and Library, New Delhi, June 1997.

29   Booth Tucker, *Criminocurology*, p. 4.

30   Home (Judl.) 2764, dt 23.11.1916.

31   For a general discussion of this issue, see Meena Radhakrishna, 'The Criminal Tribes Act'.

32   W. Bramwell Baird, *The Call of the Jackals*, Salvation Army Archives, London, n.d., p. 281.

33   See Meena Radhakrishna, 'The Criminal Tribes Act'.

34   For an account of the criminal tribe settlements, see Meena Radhakrishna, 'Surveillance and Settlements under the Criminal Tribes Act in Madras', *The Indian Economic and Social History Review*, 29, 2, 1992.

35   *The War Cry*, London, June 1913. *The War Cry* was the official organ of the Salvation Army.

36   Gerald Parsons, *Religion in Victorian Britain*, Vol. I: *Traditions*, Vol. II: *Controversies*, Manchester University Press, Manchester and New York; Vol. I, 1988, p. 22.

37   General Booth had spelt out his plans to salvage the English poor in his detailed work *In Darkest England and the Way Out*, Salvation Army, London, 1890. The criminal settlements in India were inspired by those ideas. See Meena Radhakrishna, 'The Criminal Tribes Act', Appendix.

38   The Salvation Army called Sitanagaram a sieve through which the criminals had to pass and be tested, and 'only those who responded to the treatment could find their Cannan in Stuartpuram'. Judl. GO 3219 (Mis), 21.12.1915.

39   Note on Stuartpuram settlement, *Note, 1925*.

40   M.C. Tiruvenkata Achariar, *History of the Aziznagar Settlement*, Dass Press, Virinddhachalam, 1926, pp. 2, 13. Though the above was said of another section of the Yerukula community in another Salvation Army managed settlement, the same could be said of Yerukulas in Stuartpuram as well.

41   Ibid.

[42] According to the Salvation Army sources, it was Rs 1000 per acre. F. Booth Tucker, *Mukti Fauj or 40 years with the Salvation Army in India and Ceylon*, Marshall Brothers, London, n.d., p. 232.

[43] Demi official letter from Guntur collector to Stuart, member of council, 20.3.1915, in Judl. GO 2509, 14.10.1915.

[44] Notes to Judl. GO 2509, 14.10.1915, comments by inspector general of police.

[45] Government of Madras, *Administration Report of the Labour Department, 1925–26*, Madras.

[46] PWL GO 2394L, 23.8.1929; PWL GO 2338L, 19.8.1930; PWL GO 1313L, 17.6.1932.

[47] The acreage under paddy almost doubled in 1928. Government of Madras, *Administration Report of the Labour Department, 1928–29*, Madras.

[48] PWL GO 1147L, 26.5.1933.

[49] Salvation Army records at Stuartpuram settlement, Bapatla. Letter from manager to deputy tahsildar, Chirala dated 26.8.1930. The policy so far had been that the tenancy of the family was taken away if its members were found to be resorting to crime. This could not be done if the family owned the land.

[50] Bernard Watson, *A Hundred Years' War*, Hodder and Stoughton, London, 1964, p. 145.

[51] PWL GO 1147, 26.5.1933.

[52] This society, called the Stuartpuram Yerukula and Staff Tenants' Cooperative Society, came into existence in 1926 and was free of patronage, unlike other such societies of the Labour Department or Christian organizations.

[53] Government of Madras, *Administration Report of the Labour Department, 1934–35*, Madras.

[54] Government of Madras, *Administration Report of the Labour Department, 1932–33*, Madras.

[55] Devt. GO 1315, 27.10.1933. Commissioner of labour to secretary to the Government of Madras, Devt. Dept. dt 1.10.1933, enclosing letter from the ILTD manager to chief inspector of factories dt 22.7.1933.

[56] Ibid.

[57] Ibid.

[58] PWL GO 2671L, 6.12.1934.

[59] Devt. GO 1315, 27.10.1933.

[60] PWL GO 2726L, 17.12.1935

[61] Government of Madras, *Administration Report of the Labour Department 1934–35*, Madras.

[62] Meena Radhakrishna, 'Surveillance and Settlements'.

[63] Judl. GO 2308, 22.9.1916; *Note, 1925*.

[64] Gaitskell Deborah, 'At Home with Hegemony? Coercion and Consent in the Education of African Girls for Domesticity in South Africa before 1910', in Dagmar Engels and Shula Mark, eds., *Contesting Colonial Hegemony—State and Society in Africa and India*, British Academy Press, London, 1994, p. 121.

65 The notion that this was primarily a woman's job seems to have not been confined to the Salvation Army. It is interesting to note that Yerukulas under a Roman Catholic priest underwent a similar division of labour. Home (Judl.) GO 1534, 14.6.1916.

66 Commissioner Booth Tucker, *Mukti Fauj*, p. 234.

67 PWL GO 1313L, 17.6.1932.

68 Home Judl. GO 1759, 5.8.1918, Booth Tucker to member of council, 12,7,1918.

69 Ibid. As the Salvation Army official put it, girls who had been straightened out and cured of drinking habits were sold to the highest bidder.

70 PWL GO 1654 L, 6.7.1928.

71 *The War Cry*, February 1916.

72 Booth Tucker, *Mukti Fauj*, p. 229.

73 Booth Tucker, *Criminocurology*, p. 13.

74 Ibid.

75 Ibid, p. 12.

76 Even according to the Salvation Army, 'We encountered many difficulties. The tribe was nomadic and resented internment, nor did they like the work in the quarries. . . . In fact, they objected to everything. Even the six hundred donkeys which they brought with them entered into the spirit of their non-cooperating masters.' *Mukti Fauj*, p. 228. Another account speaks of their 'resentful mood', 'arguments and scuffles', 'protestation and threats of violence' towards the Salvation Army officials. W. Bramwell Baird, *The Call of the Jackals*, p. 131. The records at the ILTD factory, Guntur and the official documents record the assertion and resistance of the Yerukulas as workers in the factory, especially after they got organized as the ILTD Workers' Union. Meena Radhakrishna, 'From Tribal Community to Working Class Consciousness: Case of Yerukula Women', Review of Women's Studies, *Economic and Political Weekly*, 29 April 1989.

77 Emphasis added.

Houses by the Sea

State Experimentation on the Southwest Coast of India 1760–1800

Dilip M. Menon

Historical writing on the state in India has an ambivalence about it. There is a tendency to move towards baroque descriptions of centralized states with elaborate bureaucracies or, to argue conversely, that the state was merely a ritual centre. Recent studies on kingship in south India have demonstrated a monarch either apprehensive of the exercise of worldly power or wearing a hollow crown.[1] Such characterizations of the monarchy are often drawn from textual exegeses in which ritual authority seeks to encompass political power through emphasizing the latter's deeply compromised nature. Though the monarchical ideal seems to be an obscure object of desire, the descriptions of processes towards this end are invariably teleological. The emphasis is on a progression towards well-recognized Weberian state forms which manage to set in place structures of taxation and coercion. So while attention may have recently shifted away from the Mughal and Vijayanagara behemoths, it is not without significance that the search is on for 'successor states'.[2] In the shadow of imperial formations, proto-states beaver away at breaking free from the imperial structure on the basis of economic prosperity in 'marginal' zones, individual entrepreneurship and the hijacking of existing revenue structures. The sense of teleology is qualified, at times, through an elaboration of the processes, or suggesting that things could have turned out otherwise, while showing that they did not.[3]

In work done on western India, an augury of the Maratha state is seen in the emergence of 'great households' in the fifteenth century, through revenue-collecting families weaving their webs of kinship in the countryside and judicious acquisition of village headmanships (rather like contemporary property speculators). Alongside this, clerical and administrative skills are distilled into a 'library of categories and techniques', which future kings can consult and rely upon.[4] The reading backwards into the origins of states (an unquestioned trajectory) is somewhat qualified in arguments that suggest that the truth (as one may expect) lies somewhere between 'state' and 'society'. The idea of the proliferation of revenue-collecting intermediaries who emerge as 'portfolio capitalists' in the shadow of erstwhile authority[5]—engaged in war, trade and agriculture simultaneously—seems to suggest the possibility of other trajectories. However, in the logic of the argument these are ephemeral creatures who wilt in the strong light of the centralized state that shall emerge. While the inevitability of their demise may be accepted, the contours of such enterprises need to be fleshed out more thoroughly.

The sense of finality of the emergence of elaborate 'modern' state forms does not allow the recognition of the overdetermination of hindsight. Moreover, such arguments then allow a glossing of the differences between precolonial and colonial state forms—the Company state becomes the highest stage of state formation.[6] Stein's argument about 'military fiscalism' posits thrusting centralization as the signature of eighteenth-century states, involving a freeing of the state from local aristocracy, the creation of an elaborate tax base, and a state organized around war. These elements achieve their fruition in the notion of the 'garrison state' of peers. Despite the details and nuances of these arguments, the trajectory is similar and the emergence of a 'state', a consummation devoutly to be wished for. There is an emphasis on, and a searching in the past for, the lineaments of the modern state: settled agricultural groups, stable revenue organization and bureaucracy, and a monopoly of violence.

In this paper I shall elaborate on experiments in social and political formations on the southwest coast, a parallel to the 'men who would be kings' in the wake of Vijayanagara collapse.[7] These were fragile, transient political forms that emerged in the wake of warfare of the eighteenth century and were a reflection of the sudden availability of a life of war as an avenue for mobility. They were a reflection of the geography of the region, inflected as it was by the fluctuating fortunes of maritime trade rather than the stabler revenues of agriculture alone. The attempts by the Mappila groups in Malabar at creating political formations came in the aftermath of the incursions from Mysore by Haidar Ali and Tipu Sultan between 1766 and 1792. In a region without a 'model' of monarchical centralization, or of an elaborate revenue-collecting structure, aspirants to state formation could not just fit in or hijack; they had to innovate. In that sense, an already existing centre space, assumed by Bayly and Subrahmanyam, had to be created *ex nihilo*. New institutions had to be created out of (in the senses of using both, as well as, outside of) existing ones.

To sum up the argument briefly, Malabar was a region whose history devolved on the ocean. Political institutions that emerged were dependent on the volatile profits of commerce. Kingship, such as it was, consisted of kings perched on the seaface looking out to sea, dependent almost entirely on the duties and imposts of trade. Kings did not have sufficient penetration into the hinterland to collect any form of land tax, and their sway in the interior was dependent on the reluctant allegiance of landowning households that engaged in production for the market. These households maintained themselves through control over land and people; disputes over territory were sorted out summarily through the use of force. Since both kings on the coast and households on the interior had little territory to be controlled, private retinues rather than armies were the norm. The invasions of Haidar and Tipu introduced the rudiments of a military labour market to meet their own need for local conscripts. Moreover, the first attempt to introduce land revenue assessment (the imposition of a tax as well as the creation of an infrastructure for its collection) also generated a new space between the centralizing Mysorean state and the constellation of multiple authorities in Malabar.

State 'experimentation' (rather than formation) happened within this space and built upon the detritus of the Mysorean revenue and military machine. If indeed the character of the Mysorean state was 'military–fiscal' in nature, the effects on Malabar society were curious. The attempts at state experimentation by the Mappilas in Malabar, carried on in the wake of the Mysorean invasions, bore their imprint but attempted a local model. They combined the authority of the large Hindu households with the newer methods of recruitment and revenue collection. Bricolage was the mode in Malabar and it is precisely this which constitutes a unique phenomenon. Studies of ephemeral state forms or aspirations have shown how dependent these were on normative forms of kingship. John Richards' Papadu or Subrahmanyam's Velugoti and Damarla clans drew upon the Vijayanagara monarchical model of conspicuous gifting and other trappings of royalty.[8] The only element of innovation or novelty is in the sheer temerity of individuals—of men who would be king. In this paper, I argue that in the attempts at state 'experimentation' on the southwest coast, monarchy was a form rarely aspired to.

Commerce and Households

Large households in the interior organized production directly on their wetlands with bonded labourers and dependents, or through colonization of the forest by arriving at strategic settlements with tribal groups.[9] Since the principal exports—pepper, cardamom and sandalwood—were forest products, the division between 'settled' land and forest land was an artificial one which varied with international demand for these cash crops. The most spectacular example of colonization of forest and the conversion of other land to cultivating for the market came in the early decades of the twentieth century when Malabar became the foremost supplier of pepper to the European markets. It must be remembered that Malabar remained a secondary supplier and its fortunes were inversely related to the production on the plantations of southeast Asia. The authority of the households over forest lands and their relations with tribal groups varied according to the volatility of international demand. The households were connected to the coast through their relations with Mappila traders who controlled the riverine networks and the coastal trade. In a region whose fortunes were so intimately tied to international trade, the whole system of agrarian rights was inflected by commerce. Land tenures were predominantly of a commercial nature, for improving the land— either raising the yield or converting to cash crops and leasing rights on usufruct.

There is a tendency to conceive of the economies of town and countryside in opposed terms in which commerce and the market are seen as independent of peasant sociology. The rural sphere is seen as characterized by a moral redistributive economy. However, what we have here is a situation in which both the independence offered by the market and *jajmani*-style patronage coexisted largely on account of the volatile nature of the economy. While production on small housesteads offered cultivators a line to the international market, in times of lethargic exports they came to be dependent on the households. Since most of the wetlands were controlled by Nair *tharavadus* and Nambudiri *illams*, when it came to the crunch it was they who underwrote subsistence. Yet again, Malabar was a region deficient in foodgrains for two reasons. First, the fact that cash crops like coconut involved less labour and quick profits meant that from the nineteenth century, there was large-scale conversion of wetlands. Second, in a region inflected by commerce, even rice was exported and there was flourishing coastal trade northwards to Mangalore and around the peninsula to Bengal.[10] Distinctions between cash and subsistence crops are as hard to maintain as those between a market and moral economy. In a continuum from dependence to relative autonomy, households had dependent labourers on their wetlands, tenants on improvement leases and relations with tribal groups as they established branches in the forested regions. Apart from the creation of a sense of community premised on the underwriting of subsistence in times of shortage, households and cultivators were participants in a community of shared worship as well. Brahminical gods, ancestors and tribal gods rubbed shoulders in a shared pantheon of worship.[11] Yet another dimension was the porous boundary between Hindu worship and Mappila Muslim beliefs. Large Hindu households arbitrated in disputes within the Mappila community and households incorporated Muslim folk heroes into their sacred space as much as mosques incorporated Hindu customs like the worship of snakes.[12]

These households were Janus-faced. One face looked seawards to the fragile profits of maritime trade in which they were involved with Mappila traders and financiers. The other face looked to the interior and involvement in production, colonization of land and patronal relations. Large households like that of the Kavalappara Nairs and the Vancheri *illam* were at the centre of a web of authority premised as much on tangible territorial control as on the more intangible imagination of a community of subsistence and worship. These larger households exercised civil and judicial powers as well.[13] When the East India Company took over the region, H.S. Graeme reorganized the administration in 1822–23, mapping revenue and administrative units onto the existing jurisdiction of the large households.[14]

What of kingship, kings or, indeed, a royal model? In Malabar, the kings like the Zamorin of Calicut and the Ali Rajas [15] were largely dependent on revenues from the ports. It is significant that the major 'monarch' in Malabar was termed the Samoothiri (Zamorin), deriving from the word 'sea'; he was the monarch of the waves. They had no revenues except what they derived 'from their own estates and

165

demesnes, funds from customs and other duties, fines on delinquents and 20 per cent of all sums and property sued for under their jurisdiction'.[16] Still, vast areas of the early modern economy were outside the ken of the kings of the coast; the basic trade in rice and cloth could not be regulated or taxed. Moreover, local powers sitting at the nodes of movement of goods from the interior to the coast acted independently in collecting tolls and transit duties. Political authority too was de-centred. If the households in the interior derived sustained revenue from their land and the fluctuating fortunes of international prices, the kings skimmed off the imposts and revenues of trade alone. There was no land revenue in Kerala, nor any revenue-collecting mechanism prior to the Mysorean invasion.[17] When the Joint Commissioners attempted to settle Malabar in 1792, they were unable to find an infrastructure on which they could build. When the first assessments were made in 1774–75 by Tipu's officer Arshad Beg, the 'rajas' of the interior were made responsible for their own collection.[18] The terminology reflected less the existence of monarchs or a royal model in the region and more the importation of a notion from regions where kings exercised the authority that these households did here. The entire revenue establishment—its officers and its vocabulary—had to be thought up in Persian; only the humble menon, or accountant, and other household functionaries existed within the native range of institutions.

It is perhaps possible to argue that in the state of political equilibrium based on access to a wide frontier such as the ocean, centralizing impulses had never arisen. Larger household formations on the coast, like that of the Zamorin, had been content to sit atop the flows of trade from the interior to the coast and beyond. 'Kingship', indeed the history of monarchy in Malabar such as it was, could have emerged in the history of conflict in the ocean. From the sixteenth century, the Portuguese attempted to close off the ocean and monopolize trade.[19] The Zamorin and the Ali Rajas in Cannanore emerged as a political centre to challenge this. Monarchy was the story of an ever-shifting coalition of merchants, naval powers and the emergent court.[20] A telling characterization of this negotiation of monarchy is given in Alexander Hamilton's eighteenth-century account of the Cannanore 'prince':

> His government is not absolute, nor is it hereditary; and instead of giving him the trust of the Treasury which comes by taxes and merchandise, they have chests made on purpose, with holes made in

166

their lids, and their coin being all gold whatever is received by the Treasurer, is put in those chests by these holes: and each chest has four locks, and their keys are put in the hands of the Rajah, the Commissioner of trade, the Chief Judge and the Treasurer; and when there is occasion for money, none can be taken out without all these four be present, or their deputies.[21]

Further south, in Travancore, the emergence of monarchy can be traced to the challenge posed by the Dutch and then the English East India Company in their attempts to control maritime trade.[22]

Swai's discussion of the political formation in northern Kerala is illuminating. In Kolathunad, what he terms a 'political cluster' existed around the dominant household of the Kolathiri who ruled Chirakkal. The Boyanor of Badagara controlled the territory between the Kottah and Kavayi rivers and between the Kavayi and Mahe rivers. Three sets of households—the Achanmar of Randaterra, the Nambiars of Iruvalinad and the Nairs of Kurangoth—stepped on each other's toes within a minuscule territory. By 1760, this loose political cluster had fragmented and each household asserted its own independence.[23] The Kolathunad 'kingship', such as it was, represented the temporary acknowledgement by households around it, of its utility as a node for trade. And with the coming of Mysorean troops under a centralizing monarchy, a few households aspiring to dominance began to look to the royal model. It is significant that the Venganad Nambidis began their transition to 'monarchy' by calling themselves the Rajas of Kollengode in the late eighteenth century.[24] And again there was a flurry of monarchical aspirations as in 1795, when the Chirakkal 'Raja' attempted to hold coronation ceremonies.[25] These attempts at sovereignty came in the interstice of the Mysorean departure and the accession of northern Kerala to Company rule. It was much too late. Once the East India Company had gained control over maritime trade, monarchy was choked and rendered dependent on the subsidy of the colonial state. They were extinguished with a whimper; prefigurations of this were evident when Haidar and Tipu's invasions resulted in a largescale exodus of members of the 'royal' households further south to Travancore.

So what we are speaking about here is not a segmentary state *pace* Stein where the royal court is the centre only of ritual or *dharmic* exchange. The court did not matter here—the households in the interior generated their own aura. It was the arrival of the Mysorean concept of kingship which gave credence to monarchy and its trappings. Apart from a stabler institution based on revenue collection and a standing army, the idea of royal aura was late in coming to Malabar, by which time the age of kings had passed. Further down the coast, in Travancore, increasingly from the seventeenth century, there had been a tendency towards centralized monarchy. Travancore had been for long a part of the constellation of political authority in south India and had at various times been under the suzerainty of the Nayaka formations. Its history of engagement with the idea of monarchy was longer and the thrust towards a centralized coercive formation reached its apogee under Martanda Varma. Even then, the monarchy was considered an expression of hubris as well as immoral. Martanda Varma dedicated his kingdom to the Padmanabha Swami enshrined in the temple and ruled as his *dasa*. The act of appropriating the territories of vanquished foes, as when the *ettu veetile pillamar* were slaughtered, was not considered necessary realpolitik alone.[26] If in Shulman's magisterial work on monarchy, the king is a figure riven by the angst of his existential engagement with power and evil, here the monarch is pressed down less by a larger morality than the very strangeness of his institution.[27] It is an anxiety generated by the emergence of a political formation seen as alien and rather unseemly. Significantly, the myths about the good monarch in Kerala are of the one who left kingship in order to convert to Buddhism or Islam according to variants. Or, in the case of the legend of Mahabali, it was righteous rule by a monarch whose reign was scheduled for extinction.[28] Monarchy on the coast was a superfluous institution. The profits of commerce meant the possibility of the coexistence of multiple authorities; a constellation of households controlling land, rivers and people while kings forlornly looked out to sea. Commerce had generated a political equilibrium which obviated the need for a monarch.

What of the minting of currency, generally seen as a privilege of monarchs and the emblem of sovereignty? The variety in coinage was immense and reflected both the multiple levels of authority as well as the differential engagement with maritime trade. Along the coast there was an immense range in coinage—gold coins carried over from the Vijayanagara period, Venetian doubloons and those minted by the prosperous merchants of Cannanore. Being at the centre of the long routes from southeast Asia to the middle east and Europe, the Malabar

coast was a region where commerce outlived transient political formations. The coinage of dead empires (even the Roman) was kept alive
within the vitality of oceanic transactions. Further inland, there were
the silver coins of various localities and in the interior, every petty raja
coined *casho* or *thutto* of copper.[29] Coinage was most certainly not the
privilege of a king or an overarching political formation. It did not signify sovereignty as much as the exigent needs of commerce, and even
as households or empires flourished and died their coins lived on.

All along the Malabar coast, it is significant to note the number of towns with the suffix *angadi* or market. They were nodal points
on river routes supplying the coastal towns binding together the economy of rivers and ocean. These towns were populated largely by merchants and a host of occupations needed to serve the interests of trade:
headload carriers, moneylenders, boatmen, cartmen and so on. Bayly
has written of the 'commercialization of rights', offices and status following the crisis of imperial authority in the eighteenth century. Implicit in this argument is the proposition that this process is mainly possible whenever political authority is weakened. However, to see the
commercialization of rights as a phenomenon pertaining only to
breakdown is limiting. In Malabar, starting at least from the seventeenth century (and possibly even earlier), *attipettola* deeds transferring
rights to markets, ferries and rivers as well as rights to political and
religious authority were common.[30] The route to respectability was
easy—money could buy the legitimation of status. While larger households consolidated themselves over generations by buying into land,
rights and authority, parvenus could, on the profits of a volatile market, set themselves up even if only in their own lifetime. The processes
tending towards consolidation and fragmentation were coeval and it
was this dynamic which was central to the constellation of multiple
authority. Temples themselves were buying and selling land and were
not dependent on royal favour or secular guilt about involvement in
the machinations of existence. All activity—secular or religious—was
sullied, or enlivened, by commerce, depending on how one looks at it.
Shulman and Subrahmanyam speak about the transition from *brah-
madeya*, the granting of land, to *annadanam,* or charity, with the Sudra
resurgence in the Nayaka period.[31] Even smaller temples in this region
were akin to the corporate Tirupati-style modes of functioning, being
nodes of commerce as much as worship.[32] Commerce also meant there
was considerable social mobility in the region. Alexander Walker, one

169

of the Joint Commissioners appointed to enquire into the affairs of Malabar after its accession to the Company, observed that '[a] considerable degree of hope and emulation has existed among the people of Malabar . . . numerous instances of new families attaining to power and wealth'.[33]

The term 'Nair' acquired the nature of a status category to be aspired to. It has been argued by Susan Bayly that anyone, even non-Malayali military men who bore arms could adopt the title of 'Nair' in this period.[34] Walker speaks of a Pulayan 'bandit' who took on the name of Koolemakeesa Pulayan Canon Nair on acquiring a degree of wealth and power.[35] There is a revealing observation made in this time of turbulence:

> . . . [an] order of men arose in this country, which is not to be found at present in any other part of India. They not infrequently arrived at the authority, if not the rank of princes without assuming any titles. They are distinguished by the emphatic appellation of Nayr, in addition to their proper name, or of their estate. After the power of the titled chiefs declined and they suffered a general degradation, the appellation of 'Nayr' has been proudly assumed. . . . The common and general use of 'Nayr' in this sense is of modern date . . .[36]

Of course, Walker made these observations at a particular conjuncture when society on the southwest coast was in a state of turmoil following the expansion of the frontier of warfare from Mysore. However, it is crucial to note that the general aspiration towards mobility was inflected by the model of the large households of the Nairs and not any monarchical ambition.

What was the nature of political formations that could emerge in this context, considering the absence of a monarchical 'ideal' and the tremendous scope for individual entrepreneurship? We spoke earlier of the twin tendencies: the fragile affluence generated by the market and the consequent dependence for subsistence on larger households. Bayly has an insightful suggestion that within a flexible political economy, the aspect of Hindu caste practice which was most adaptable was that of the *jajmani*-system centred on a dominant group or household.[37] The systematization of revenue extraction was absent, the possibility of coercion was marginal in a decentred polity, only some form of social insurance could form the basis for a cohesive formation.

170

In that sense, the large households which organized production for subsistence and trade and which gathered unto themselves cultivators and dependents as well as an assortment of religious and judicial powers, were the local exemplars. William Logan wrote of 'Nairs of ability' who wrested landholding rights and attracted the 'great body of cultivators' to agricultural production centred on their households. He traced a process of the breakdown of communal rights over land in favour of individual 'familes', beginning from the fifteenth century.[38] It is possible that this process gained momentum in the early nineteenth century with the expansion of land frontiers in the wake of warfare.[39] And, in a sense, even the 'royal' formations can be seen as vastly expanded households, as Arunima has recently suggested.[40] The Kolathiri to the north was split into five branches, the premier branch exercising 'kingship'. The idea of 'palaces', as the Company records in their search for kings record them, were nothing more than branches of a dominant household established in different directions—east, west and so on. The Pazhassi revolt against the Company which was snuffed out in 1806, again represented as a revolt by a 'raja' against English authority, had its origin in a family conflict. The initial fracas was between the Kurumbanad 'raja' and the Pazhassi 'Raja'—a conflict between uncle and nephew over who should succeed to the headship of the matrilineal household.

As Swai has shown, the Company records tended to regard the larger households as 'kingdoms', and the 'rajas' referred to were invariably the eldest men within the largest matrilineal households within a locality. 'Many of these . . . [lesser 'rajas'] possessed in their different districts the same rights as to justice and revenue which the rajas had themselves and were totally exempted from tribute.'[41]

The Joint Commissioners appointed to enquire into the state of northern Kerala, conscious of having defeated one royal challenger, were eager to make a political settlement with a legitimate regional 'royal', preferably Hindu, authority. 'We shall be able to do justice to the Nairs and restore them to their ancient possessions which have been usurped by a race of men naturally hostile to every sect but their own.'[42] Coupled with this was the hatred towards Mappilas expressed strongly by Alexander Walker as a race 'presuming, bigotted and turbulent',[43] and later enshrined in Thomas Strange's reports on the Mappila outbreaks of the nineteenth century. The language of settlement is replete with references to 'rajas' and almost every household was

171

accorded the dignity of royalty. Some of the larger households, like the Vengayil and Kalliattu, were the beneficiaries of this search for monarchs since the settlements gave them almost absolute authority over land. At a later stage, as Arunima has shown, it became important to settle with 'male' authority within the households themselves—the earlier fluidity within matrilineal households where women could succeed to headship was brought to an end by the mid-nineteenth century.[44]

Military Traditions

The discussion in the previous section has thrown doubt on the existence of a royal model and pointed out the absence of a revenue-collecting infrastructure or any notion of land tax. What of the third feature: standing armies and the possibility of sustained coercion? In fact, the argument has been made that the imperative to raise European-style infantry to compete with foreign troops had been one of the major pushes towards the emergence of centralizing monarchies.[45] The demand for cash to pay troops led to more systematized attempts to collect revenue and so on. It is possible to argue that in the case of Travancore this was indeed what happened. The increasing conflicts with the Dutch over the control of coastal trade pushed Martanda Varma towards employing mercenaries, both Indian and European, and finally instituting a standing European-style army trained by the Dutch mercenary.[46] But, as we have argued earlier, Travancore was part of the frontier of warfare and monarchical formation in south India for a longer period. It was this that made the transition to its own consolidation as a monarchy easier. In the case of northern Kerala, it may be possible to argue that the emergence of a military culture or an army was a later event precipitated by Tipu's invasion. The conversion of bands of retainers into a disciplined force proved difficult for indigenous formations, while for Tipu recruiting an army had proved to be a problem because of the non-existence of a 'military labour-market', to use Kolff's phrase.[47] Stewart Gordon, in a suggestive paper, speaks of three military cultures: the Rajput, Maratha and Nayaka.[48] It was the expansion of the post-Nayaka formations which extended the zone of conflict westwards to the coast and the detritus of this conflict which moved as the zone of conflict shifted. We have to understand the transformation on the southwest coast in the light of this phenomenon: the emergence of a shortlived military labour market.

The image of the Nairs of the southwest coast as a martial people may have been determined within two historiographical moments: the travel writings beginning from the thirteenth century and the East India Company records at the time of the conquest of Malabar. Most of the travel accounts of foreign visitors are accounts of the coast; almost none of them ventured inland. Their only exposure was to the 'royal court' of the Zamorin which they were not particularly impressed by. Accounts record his simplicity and lack of opulence. However, the search was for a 'monarch', and they pinned their hopes on available candidates; if not the good Christian king of the east—Prester John—lesser ones would suffice.[49] More important for this discussion are the descriptions of armed inhabitants, particularly Nairs. As for example, Barbosa saying in the sixteenth century that Nairs have no other duty but to carry on war and continually carry arms.[50] This description of armed retainers as would have been kept by any large household or chief cannot be extrapolated to the assumption that all Nairs were martial and that this was indeed their only occupation. Buchanan, writing of his travels through Malabar, wrote of the Nairs as soldiers who disdain industry.[51] It must be borne in mind that he was travelling through the region within a decade of Tipu's defeat. The region had not been settled (the Pazhassi Raja was still leading Company troops a merry dance through the jungles) and not only the Nairs, but most inhabitants, were bearing arms. While the travelogues are speaking about a particular group of people in a specific geographical location—Nair armed retainers on the coast—Buchanan and Company records are speaking of a particular conjuncture when a sword was as much a need for protection as a mark of a profession. For instance, Walker's observation in 1797 that 'the standing army is the nation',[52] or in 1801 Buchanan remarking that it was not unusual to see a man at a plough with a musket on his shoulders.[53]

If we are to argue that the growth of the idea of a standing army and of a military labour market was the result of the expansion of the zone of conflict, then what are we to do with evidence of bodies of armed men? As we have seen, travelogues refer largely to localized retainers. Then there were the *kalaris,* or gymnasiums, attached to individual households. It would be a fundamental misunderstanding to see these as military schools of the upper castes, since elementary education as well was imparted to boys and girls. Moreover, there were Syrian Christian *kalaris* in Travancore and largely Tiyya ones in north Malabar. The only body of literature which gives us a consistent account of the *kalaris* and their involvement in the social and political life of Kerala—the *Vadakkan Pattukal*—dates from the fourteenth to the eighteenth century. It records blood feuds, skirmishes between retainers of households, the employment of individual fighters for protection, heroes championing certain causes and fighting on behalf of righteous patrons.[54] There is no mention at all of a standing army, which is not surprising considering that conflict was both small-scale as well as sporadic. The figures supplied by travellers like Hamilton and the East India Company records (Walker estimates 200,000 armed men in Malabar in 1801[55]) should be treated, *pace* Kolff, as a 'census of probable armed men' than as standing armies.[56] Traditionally, organizations of 300s or 600s, as they were called (these could as well be notional, ideal numbers), composed of four families to each *tara*, or sphere of control of a household, arbitrated and settled disputes over boundaries, lands, water and wasteland. The stakes were too low and too easily negotiated to necessitate a larger armed intervention. Among the followers of Pazhassi raja in his rebellion, on the average there were not more than 50 men under each chief.[57]

The entry of Mysore into the politics of the region upset the equilibrium that had existed on the southwest coast. The constellation of multiple authorities could not face up to the challenge of a centralizing formation which monopolized trade and introduced land tax into a region where earlier land belonged to those in the vicinity who could exercise control over it. In 1763, Haidar Ali entered into an arrangement with the Ali Raja of Cannanore and invaded northern Kerala in 1765–66 aided by Mappila auxiliaries and Mysorean cavalry and infantry. In the four decades between 1766 and 1806, northern Kerala was in a state of warfare. The Mappilas were the first to respond to the creation of a military labour market along with subordinate caste groups which saw in warfare a route to social mobility. Along the coast the conflicts of Mappila traders and seafarers with the Portuguese attempts at monopoly had led to the rise of militancy, best expressed in the rise of the Marakkars of Calicut.[58] Further inland, where the Portuguese did not penetrate, the Mappila communities were less beleaguered. Dale's argument that the Portuguese presence Islamicized and militarized the Mappila community is an unjustifiable extrapolation from the experience of the Mappila seafarers alone. It is not immediately clear why Mappila agriculturists in the interior should have been similarly and as severely affected. Even if we grant Dale's argument of a frontier between Mappila agriculturists and Hindu society, this engendered only skirmishes and outbreaks of collections of individuals. It was Haidar and Tipu's entry into the region which militarized conflict and led to the emergence of a new group among the Mappilas called '*mooppans*'. In ordinary parlance, the word implies overseer or headman but in this specific context they were military recruiters, who as Walker puts it, were heads of small bodies of men, 'like a Roman centurion'.[59] They came up in response to the invasions and the need for soldiers as well as the possibility of acquiring wealth and status through soldiering in troubled times. The entry of the Mysorean forces tipped the balance in favour of the Mappilas against Hindu landlords, though certainly it did not result in the end of Hindu dominance.[60] These Mappila military contractors did not belong to a stable system, they came up in an interstitial period of warfare. With the defeat of Tipu, some of the *mooppans* associated themselves with the brief insurrection of the Pazhassi Raja. The pacification by the East India Company troops rendered them redundant. Instead of locating the militancy of the Mappilas in their religious susceptibilities or a history over the *longue duree* of being beleagured by the Portuguese or Hindu landlords, it may be fruitful instead to look at the origins of militancy in the peculiar circumstances of warfare.

If the Mappilas, or sections of them, responded to the creation of a military labour market, what of the influence on the wider society of the militarization occasioned by the Mysorean invasion? Soldiers from the Carnatic and the north arrived in northern Kerala as the zone of conflict expanded and employers of military labour diminished elsewhere in south India. The Pazhassi raja, while in retreat at Manantavadi, had 112 'Carnaticks' serving with him.[61] The 'kings', or the heads of large ruling households, like that of Chirakkal, the Zamorin and the Palghat Achan, began to train and dress their soldiers in Company style. It is significant that few of them were from Malabar itself; they were nearly all of them emigrants from the Carnatic. Walker further observed that the raja of Cartinaad (Kadathunad) kept a garrison of soldiers 'cloathed in every respect like ours and instructed in all the honorary tricks with which they complimented him. The Chirakkal raja proudly flew the colours of the English presented to him by

General Abercromby.'[62] These farcical efforts were quite unlike Martanda Varma's systematic mobilization and training of the Travancore armies. The Chirakkal raja had 200 men with officers in English uniforms carrying English muskets, British colours and accompanied by drums and pipes. Buchanan records how he was met by an officer of the raja dressed in a blue uniform with white facings, boot and helmet. The response of these men with royal aspirations was to imitate the form of the superior military machine which had defeated them, and to convert erstwhile retainers to the semblance of an army. Walker's diaries record his bemusement as he tracked the elusive and highly professional Pazhassi raja through the forests. Slipping away into the lush greenery, he would leave behind stringed instruments, ornamental spittoons and evidence that his wives were accompanying him, even as he carried on guerrilla warfare.[63] Even the 'king in exile'— Kerala Varma—seemed not to be completely sure of how a king ought to behave.

Apart from these vignettes, it is undeniable that the extent to which Malabar society was militarized was considerable. In 1766, when Haidar Ali made incursions into Kadathunad and Mahe, the armies were secured in the rear by a series of blockhouses called *lakkitikottas*, made of wood. In the period following Tipu's defeat this detritus of warfare could be utilized by aspirants to local power as strongholds. A period of warfare and uncertain political authority, once Tipu's centralizing thrust had been shortcircuited, also meant that the lines of trade were up for grabs. Mappilas controlled the riverine trade and most of the coastal traffic. Now the cesses and imposts which had been levied on them were absent, as were the authorities who could have collected them. In one sense, internal trade had been hit hard by the Mysorean invasion and the merchants on the coast by Tipu's attempts at monopoly. The merchants at Ponnani had for a brief while been turned into agents of Tipu's trade bureaucracy. Once the Mysorean authority was lifted, the sudden opening up of resources meant that the Mappilas could combat Company attempts to control trade quite effectively. The factors at Tellicherry had established round boats to prevent the export of pepper from Kadathunad. Mappila boats out-rowed and outflanked them, rowed by 8–10 men with 4–6 swordsmen. While the Portuguese presence from the fifteenth century had militarized the ocean, the late eighteenth century saw the militarization for a brief period of the inland waterways.

The profits of clandestine commerce were ploughed into attempts at territorial control. Mappila tenants had begun to shift the
burden of the land revenue to the Hindu landlords simultaneously
with the institution of the land revenue assessment between 1774 and
1778.[64] The creation of a revenue bureaucracy by the Mysorean settlement installed Mappila officials within localities previously under the
control of dominant households. Company records observe that the
Zamorin's influence had been 'displaced' by the Mappilas and that
they were trying to 'obliterate Hindu society'.[65] In 1793, the Mappilas
of Koodali applied to the Pazhassi raja for leave to build a mosque.
Earlier Pazhassi had pulled down a mosque built without his prior permission. The building of mosques need not have arisen from an upsurge of religiosity following the temporary incorporation into the
realm of a ruler with Islamic pretensions. In the case of the Mappilas
(both in the early nineteenth century as well as later) mosques became
strategic places of retreat, an easily defensible redoubt when challenged
or pursued. Pazhassi and his followers too were not loath to take refuge
or fight a rearguard action from temples. In an era of warfare, distinctions between sacred and secular had been considerably blurred. Elsewhere in south India, the Srirangam temple housed French troops between 1752 and 1755 and was finally evacuated in 1758. English troops
besieged Srirangam in 1758 by encamping in Jambukesavam temple.[66]
In the late eighteenth century, Jamadar Alap Khan, ruler of Kurnool,
carried away the bells of Srisailam temple and the *mantapa* of Malli-
karjuna temple and manufactured bullets. Cannons were manufactured out of the utensils in the temple; needless to say, the cannon did
not survive the first firing.[67] Athan Gurikkal (of whom there is more
later) sent hill panikkars to buy gunpowder from the local
Malappuram bazaar. A special class of people called *veti gurukkal* or
explosives experts worked for another Mappila rebel, Chembum
Poker.[68] When the Pazhassi raja revolted, several *mooppans* enlisted
themselves to bring Mappilas from the coast. Merchants who dealt in
rice, spices and slaves along the coast began traffic in military men as
well as armaments and gunpowder. In the period between 1760 and
1800, society in northern Kerala had been considerably militarized.
More important for our argument is the fact that, apart from the availability of arms as a route to authority, the rudiments of a centralized
administration had been set in place. In Shernaad, the *adalat* and the
darogas were Mappilas and in the Zamorin's area of erstwhile

authority, Ernad, all the revenue functionaries were Mappilas.

Here we have the interesting contours of a new kind of formation emerging. A number of Mappila entrepreneurs had assumed
control over the networks of trade and had established links with the
merchants on the coast. They had become functionaries within the
rudiments of a revenue administration set up by Tipu. Moreover, they
had gained control over an incipient labour market as military
contractors or access to men through their connections with the coast.
The merchants on the coast had expanded the scope of their operations
from dealing in agricultural produce alone to the currently profitable
supply of men to employers. The detritus of warfare from southern
India was making its way to this unsettled frontier. We can see the
glimmerings of the creatures called 'portfolio capitalists' in the entrepreneurs engaged in warfare, trade and revenue collection. However,
there is a significant difference; they did not come up in a period of
crisis of royal authority. There was no monarch to begin with. Second,
the revenue infrastructure was not hijacked but they were instituted as
its first occupants. In the next section, we look at the political experimentation of Mappilas who would be rulers, but not kings.

The Mappila Rebels

There are markedly different approaches to these Mappila
entrepreneurs in the literature of the time. The East India Company
records see them as brigands and bandits, reflecting the fact that they
were armed bands which engaged in raids and plunders. Since they
were defeated by Company troops and also because they were seen as
the tail-end of Muslim resistance following Tipu's defeat, no wider
ambitions are attributed to them than the immediate gains from
robbery. In Rajayyan's work, on the other hand, they are credited with
an agenda too ambitious. They are inserted into a retrospective nationalist reading of history, where these local efforts are located within a
larger regional struggle of 'Indians' against the 'British'. He attempts
to show that the revolts of the Palaiyakkarars, Pazhassi raja and the
Mappilas were a concerted and coordinated effort. If the Company
records deny that there was any ideology or coherence in the Mappila
actions, Rajayyan attributes a full-blown ideology of national pride to
them.[69] Stephen Dale and Panikkar, to differing degrees, are content
to see them as Muslims, their rebellious activities as tinged by Islam.

178

Dale goes so far as to say that they attempted to create a 'Mappila raj'. There is a certain degree of obviousness in this argument which leads to a simple reductionist proposition: all political efforts by Muslims must be Islamic in nature. Stephen Dale's overall argument is an over-blown one which assiduously traces the growth of a beleagured Muslim identity to 1498, culminating in an apocalyptic expression in the rebellion of 1921. None of these arguments concerns itself with the specific nature of the historical conjuncture—when political authority was up for grabs and economic entrepreneurship thrived—or the specific features of the Mappila experiment. While there is certainly some virtue in a history over the long term, there is always the danger of ignoring the short-term conjuncture and more contingent factors.

What was the context within which these Mappila 'rebels', rather, political entrepreneurs, emerged? Most of the large Hindu households had been displaced; fear of forced conversions had led to a significant exodus. Those that remained had to strike deals with the emerging revenue functionaries, the creations of Tipu's attempts at centralized exaction. They either voluntarily relinquished authority over large portions of their lands or paid protection money to retain what little they had managed to hold on to.[70] From an earlier equilibrium in which a constellation of multiple authorities had obviated the need for one centralizing formation, a new fragile equilibrium was emerging, in which newer entrants were jostling for space and control over men and resources. The earlier demarcations of authority, which had been kept in place by force and recognized over time, were now being challenged by these parvenus. Looting of cattle and grain and the collection of protection money were some of the newer elements in the creation of domains.[71] What is crucial here is the social origin of these entrepreneurs, a factor ignored in the literature so far. A significant number of them were *mooppans*, military labour contractors, left to their own resources after the collapse of the Mysorean military. They were at the centre of a displaced population and land without claimants, besides being in touch with the vibrant economy of the coast through Mappila headload carriers.[72] A life of arms continued to be attractive as a route for social mobility. One of the 'rebels' was someone called Kutty Hussain Mappila, a Tiyya who had converted during Haidar's time and served under Tipu as well. He was employed in command of the infantry and, according to legend, had caused so many

Nairs to be circumcised in 1789 that he was appointed the *amildar* of Poolwaye.[73]

The careers of the four central figures are instructive in their trajectories and aspirations. Athan Gurikkal was a tenant of the 'raja' of Manjeri, one of the largest landowning households of south Malabar. He had lands in Payanad himself and had not made any payments of rent since 1774. While Athan may have come up and made a bid for local power in the wake of Tipu's invasion, it is important to remember that Tipu himself saw no affinity with these parvenus. In 1784, when Athan burned down the Manjeri temple and levelled the raja's home, Tipu aided the raja with whom he had an agreement and Athan was imprisoned at Seringapatam from where he subsequently escaped.[74] Significantly, Athan assumed the name of the household he had displaced and was conscious of succession. He continued to work as a *mooppan* for Tipu and because of his influence, the Zamorin farmed the revenues of Ernad and Malappuram to him. In 1797, 'for motives of policy', the East India Company appointed him head of the police establishment. He managed to combine an insertion into the existing rural hierarchy, by replacing the Manjeri raja, with an incorporation into the revenue and administrative innovations of the Mysorean period.

Chembum Poker was employed by the East India Company as revenue officer in Shernad, but after being accused of bribery was imprisoned at Palghat. He had collected around him 250 armed men when the southern superintendent, Thomas Baber, attacked him. Once he had established himself, several *mooppans* joined him from Shernad and Ernad with 6 to 40 men each.[75] He built a fortified house with small field pieces, probably three pounders, two mounted on his house and two on top of a shrine. He had a retinue of 45 men with muskets and 4 with swords. This was not an inconsiderable number if we remember that the raja of Chirakkal had only 200 armed adherents with him. The merchants on the banks of the Calicut and Mahe rivers supplied him with arms and ammunition. An attempt at a stabler formation is evident in his acquisition of a retinue and a fortified home as also the sending out of palm-leaf *olas* within the locality stating that revenue should be paid to him.[76]

Ellumbullasseri Unni Moota, another *mooppan*, took on the name of the household whose lands he had usurped. He had much closer links with Tipu, had fought with Tipu's army at Travancore and had attacked Munnar with the Mysorean troops. He had set himself against Tipu in his attempt at local authority and had refused an offer allowing him to return to his estates on a pension.[77] Unni Moota had established connections with two rajas of the family of the Zamorin and the Kunji Achan of Palghat in an attempt at local legitimacy. He employed several former sepoys of the Nawab of Arcot as well as merchants and robbers from the coast. He employed a fakir to read Persian, employed two Brahmins to gather intelligence and beat the *nagara* as a symbol of sovereignty. These 'royal' pretensions—a predilection for Persian over Arabic, creating the rudiments of an information system—arose from the Mysorean incursion.

Unni Avaran, another *mooppan*, constructed his house like a fortress—an oblong square of 300 square yards—surrounded by mud wall, 15 to 16 feet in height. There were several houses within the compound for his retainers and pens for the cattle which he had accumulated through raids. He settled several families of artisans around him in the manner of the larger households, replicating *jajmani*-style relationships.

All of them continued within the region as the heirs of the authority of those they had displaced. While Athan Gurikkal's speeches may have spoken of the sufferings of the Mappila community, he never appealed to the Mappilas as Muslims to rise in defence of their religion. There was no natural affinity with the invading Mysorean ruler on grounds of a shared religion: both Unni Moota and Athan Gurikkal opposed the creation of a new capital at Feroke further inland, which shifted the focus away from Calicut (Walker MS 13616). Wanancundy Cunhy Amy, a Mappila 'bandit' leader, hired himself with 85 men to the Pazhassi raja, showing a distinct preference for local affinities over Mysorean ones.[78] While Athan and Chembum Poker fitted into the roles played by the erstwhile Hindu households, Avaran even playing *jajman* to artisans; it was only Unni Moota who seemed to have absorbed to some extent imported ideas of sovereignty. There was no attempt to expand beyond the frontiers of the area of authority that they had taken over. The equilibrium on the southwest coast was maintained and had it not been both for the continuing depredations of these ex-*mooppans*, and the Company's desire for settled revenue coupled with their hatred of the Mappilas, it would have continued even longer. Stewart Gordon, in his article on 'marauding' and state formation, makes the important point that states and bandits are not different in kind but only in the relative degree of success in terms of conquest, revenue collection and infrastructure building.[79] He writes of the 'plunder dynamic' in which 'marauders' try to seize the treasury and standing troops of states while attempting at long-term control of land and revenue. It is their failure to become 'states' which marks them as ephemeral phenomena. What we have in northern Kerala is a similar process of experimentation, but by 'brigands' who do not dwell in the shadow of states and are content with positioning themselves within an existing equilibrium. Had it not been for the presence of Company troops, over time these Mappila parvenus would have been legitimized as households in the interior, situated at the nexus of production, trade and patronage. To say that these were failed experiments is to already accept the logic that a centralized state is the only desirable end of political activity. Even in the arguments made by Dirks and Shulman, the notion of the desirability of the transition to a 'state' form remains. Dirks, looking at the geneaologies in the Mackenzie manuscripts, charts the trajectory of highway bandits to cultured kings. They remain 'little kings' and are always part of a hierarchy headed by a great king which legitimizes them.[80] Shulman similarly argues that the activities of bandits happen within a larger framework: the state incorporates disorder and is founded on the principle of inherent internal conflict.[81]

Fundamental to arguments such as these are two key assumptions. One, of the inevitability (a necessarily retrospective construction) of the emergence of a centralized state with a monopoly of violence and of revenue extraction. Two, a concentration on areas of settled agriculture and hierarchies with a tradition of monarchy dating back at least to early medieval times. Even the straying into areas like forests and wastelands has implicit in it the notion that these constitute 'inner' frontiers which will inevitably be subdued.[82] The persistent incorporation of frontiers and the tension (inevitably temporary) generated by the dialectic between 'settled' and 'unsettled' areas is the history of state formation as it is written now. Implicit in this is a notion of competition over scarce resources—symbolic as well as political and economic. An argument which incorporates a never-to-be subdued frontier, a zone of almost infinite possibility—the ocean—puts a strain on comfortably watertight propositions. On the southwest coast, a political equilibrium was generated by the easy access to the profits of the ocean. A symbiotic relation between households in the interior

182

and merchants on the coast had not necessitated the emergence of larger centralizing formations which would need to extract revenue from the land. Attempts by European powers to control the ocean and make a frontier of it led to a transient monarchical response, a coalition of merchants and the Zamorin in the sixteenth century against the Portuguese. In the eighteenth century, Travancore emerged as a monarchy in its conflicts with the Dutch and the English over control of maritime trade. In the period of the Mysorean invasion, northern Kerala was incorporated within the centralizing experiment of Tipu. Mappila political entrepreneurs emerged basing themselves on plunder, the profits of commerce, access to the newly instituted land revenue infrastructure and, finally, the expansion of the zone of conflict from the Carnatic region. Despite the new variety of resources, they aspired to situate themselves within the older political equilibrium. There were again attempts towards monarchical forms—the Chirakkal raja trying to create an army, the Venganad Nambidis calling themselves Rajas of Kollengode—but the transition to an unarmorial age had begun. While the age of kings passed away in the rest of India, and crowns were rendered hollow, in northern Kerala kingship remained a failed experiment.

Notes and References

[1] N.B Dirks, *The Hollow Crown: Ethnohistory of an Indian Kingdom*, Cambridge Cambridge University Press, 1987; D.D. Shulman, *The King and the Crown in South Indian Myth and Poetry*, Princeton University Press, Princeton, N.J., 1985.

[2] M. Alam, *The Crisis of Empire in Mughal North India: Awadh and the Punjab*, Oxford University Press, Delhi, 1986; R.B. Barnett, *North India between Empires: Awadh, the Mughals and the British. 1720–1801*, Oxford University Press, Delhi, 1987; C. Bayly, *Rulers, Townsmen and Bazars: North Indian Society in the Age of British Expansion*, Cambridge University Press, Cambrridge, 1983.

[3] S. Subrahmanyam, 'The Men Who Would be Kings: The Politics of Expansion in Early 17th Century North Tamilnadu', *Modern Asian Studies*, Vol. 24, 1990.

[4] F. Perlin, *Invisible City: Monetary, Administrative and Popular Infrastructure in Asia and Europe, 1500–1900*, Variorum, Aldershot, 1993; 'State Formation Reconsidered', *Modern Asian Studies*, Vol. 19, 1985, pp. 415–80; 'Proto-industrialization and Pre-colonial South Asia', *Past and Present*, Vol. 98, 1983, pp. 30–95.

[5] S. Subrahmanyam and C.A. Bayly, 'Portfolio Capitalists and the Political Economy of Early Modern India', *Indian Economic and Social*

History Review, Vol. 25, 4, 1988, pp. 401–24.

[6] B. Stein, 'State Formation and Economy Reconsidered', *Modern Asian Studies*, Vol. 19, 3, 1985; D.M. Peers, *Between Mars and Mammon: Colonial Armies and the Garrison State in Nineteenth Century India*, Academic Studies, London, 1995.

[7] S. Subrahmanyam, 'The Men Who Would be Kings'.

[8] V.N. Rao, D.D. Shulman, S. Subrahmanyam, *Symbols of Substance: Court and State in Nayaka Period Tamil Nadu*, Oxford University Press, Delhi, 1992; S. Subrahmanyam, 'The Men Who Would be Kings'.

[9] D. Menon, *Caste, Nationalism and Communism in South India: Malabar, 1900–1948*, Cambridge University Press, Cambridge, 1994; T.W. Shea, *The Land Tenure Structure of Malabar and its Influence Upon Capital Formation in Agriculture*, Ph.d. dissertation, Pennsylvania.

[10] S. Subrahmanyam, *Political Economy of Commerce: Southern India, 1500–1650*, Cambridge University Press, Cambridge, 1990.

[11] D. Menon, *Caste, Nationalism and Communism in South India*.

[12] D. Menon, 'Becoming "Hindu" and "Muslim": Identity and Conflict in Malabar, 1900–1936', in Narayani Gupta et al., eds., *Society, Religion and the State*, Madras, 1996.

[13] M.G.S. Narayanan, *Vancheri granthavari*, University of Calicut, Calicut, 1987; K.K.N. Kurup, *Kavalappara papers*, University of Calicut, Calicut, 1984.

[14] W. Logan, *Malabar Special Commission, Malabar Land Tenures Report*, Government Press, Madras, 1882.

[15] G. Bouchon, *'Regent of the Sea': Cannanore's Response to Portuguese Expansion, 1507–1528*, Oxford University Press, Delhi, 1988; K.V. Krishna Iyer, *The Zamorins of Calicut*, Norman Printing Bureau, Calicut, 1938.

[16] Alexander Walker of Bowland Manuscripts, 1792–1810, National Library of Scotland, Edinburgh, 13825.

[17] W. Logan, *Malabar Manual*, Madras Government Press, 1887.

[18] B. Swai, *The British in Malabar, 1792–1806*, Ph.D. dissertation, Sussex, 1974.

[19] S. Subrahmanyam, *The Portuguese Empire in Asia, 1500–1700: A Political and Economic History*, Longman, London, 1993.

[20] O.K. Nambiar, *The Kunjalis: Admirals of Calicut*, Asia Publishing House, Bombay, 1963; A. Dasgupta, *Malabar in Asian Trade, 1740–1800*, Cambridge University Press, Cambridge, 1976; G. Bouchon, *'Regent of the Sea'*.

[21] A. Hamilton, *A New Account of the East Indies*, London, 1727, reprinted 1970.

[22] M.de Lannoy, *The Kulasekhara Perumals of Travancore: History and State Formation in Travancore, 1671–1758*, CNWS, Leiden, 1997; A. Dasgupta, *Malabar in Asian Trade, 1740–1800*, Cambridge University Press, Cambridge, 1967; G. Bouchon, *'Regent of the Sea'*.

[23] B. Swai, *The British in Malabar*.

[24] P.K.M. Tharakan, *Forest Wealth and Ritual Status: Gleanings from Kollengode Records*, Centre for Development Studies, Trivandrum, 1993.

184

[25] Walker MS 13601.

[26] A.P. Ibrahim Kunju, *Rise of Travancore: Life and Times of Martanda Varma,* Varma History Association, Trivandrum, 1976; M. de Lannoy, *The Kulasekhara Perumals of Travancore.*

[27] D.D. Shulman, *The King and the Clown in South Indian Myth and Poetry.*

[28] W. Logan, *Malabar Manual.*

[29] Walker MS 13825.

[30] W. Logan, *Malabar Manual.*

[31] V.N. Rao, D.D. Shulman, S. Subrahmanyam, *Symbols of Substance.*

[32] B. Stein, 'Economic Function of the Medieval South Indian Temple', *Journal of Asian Studies,* Vol. 19, 2, 1960, pp. 163–76.

[33] Walker MS 13825.

[34] S. Bayly, *Saints, Goddesses and Kings: Muslims and Christians in South Indian Society, 1700–1900,* Cambridge University Press, Cambridge, 1987.

[35] Walker MS 13611.

[36] Walker MS 13798.

[37] C.A. Bayly, *Rulers, Townsmen and Bazaars.*

[38] W. Logan, Malabar Special Commission, *Malabar Land Tenures Report.*

[39] K.K.N. Kurup, *Kavalappara Papers,* University of Calicut, Calicut, 1984.

[40] G. Arunima, 'Multiple Meanings: Changing Conceptions of Matrilineal Kinship in Nineteenth and Twentieth Century Malabar', *Indian Economic and Social History Review,* Vol. 33, 3, 1996, pp. 283–307.

[41] W.G. Farmer to Taylor, Oct. 1792, cited in Swai, *The British in Malabar.*

[42] MDR, Political, 1800, p. 183.

[43] MS 13613.

[44] G. Arunima, *Colonialism and the Transformation of Matriliny in Malabar, 1850–1940,* Ph.D. dissertation, Cambridge, 1992.

[45] B. Stein, 'State Formation and Economy Reconsidered', *Modern Asian Studies,* Vol. 19, 3, 1985.

[46] A. Dasgupta, *Malabar in Asian Trade;* M. de Lannoy, *The Kulasekhara Perumals of Travancore.*

[47] D.H. Kolff, *Naukar, Rajput and Sepoy: The Ethnohistory of the Military Labour Market in Hindustan, 1450–1850,* Cambridge University Press, Cambridge, 1990.

[48] S. Gordon, *Marathas, Marauders and State Formation in 18th Century India,* Oxford University Press, Delhi, 1994.

[49] S. Subrahmanyam, *The Career and Legend of Vasco da Gama,* Cambridge University Press, Cambridge, 1997.

[50] Duarte Barbosa, *The Book of Duarte Barbosa: An Account of the Countries in the Indian Ocean and their Inhabitants,* written by Duarte Barbosa about the year 1518 AD, trans. Mansel Longworth Dames, Vol. II, London, 1921.

[51] F. Buchanan, *A Journey from Madras through the Countries of Mysore, Canara and Malabar,* London, 1807.

[52] Walker MS 13607.

[53] F. Buchanan, *A Journey from Madras through the Countries of Mysore, Canara and Malabar.*

54 K.S. Mathew, *Society in Medieval Malabar: A Study Based on Vadakkan Pattukal*, Jaffe Books, Kottayam, 1979.

55 Walker MS 13612.

56 D. H. Kolff, *Naukar, Rajput and Sepoy*.

57 Walker M.S. 13607.

58 O.K. Nambiar, *The Kunjalis*; S. Subrahmanyam, *The Portugese Empire in Asia 1500–1700*.

59 Walker MS 13799.

60 K.N. Panikkar, *Against Lord and State: Religion and Peasant Uprisings in Malabar, 1836–1921*, Oxford University Press, Delhi, 1989.

61 Walker MS 13605.

62 Walker MS 13616.

63 Walker MS 13612

64 S.F. Dale, *Islamic Society on the South Asian Frontier: The Mappilas of Malabar, 1498–1922*, Oxford University Press, Oxford, 1980.

65 Second Committee 1796, Revenue Diary, pp. 1147–48; Second Committee 1798, Revenue Diaries, pp. 69–70.

66 V.N. Hari Rao, *History of the Srirangam Temple*, Tirupati, 1976.

67 T.V. Mahalingam, *Mackenzie Manuscripts: Summaries of the Historical Manuscripts in the Mackenzie Collection*, Vol. II, University of Madras, Madras, 1976.

68 Walker MS 13613.

69 K. Rajayyan, *South Indian Rebellion: The First War of Independence 1800–1801*, Mysore, 1971.

70 C.K. Kareem, *Kerala under Haidar Ali and Tipu Sultan*, Kerala History Association, Trivandrum, 1973.

71 For instances of 'brigandage', Walker MS 13613.

72 Walker MS 13610.

73 Walker MS 13601.

74 Correspondence on Moplah outrages, iv 101; *Madras District Records, Political, 1800*, pp. 287–88.

75 Walker MS 13608; MDR, Secret 1800, p. 158.

76 Walker MS 13613.

77 Joint Committee, Diary 1794, iii 1158, iv 1243; Supervisor's Diaries, Political 1794, p. 136.

78 Walker MS 13607.

79 S. Gordon, *Marathas, Marauders and State Formation in 18ᵗʰ Century India*.

80 N.B. Dirks, *The Hollow Crown*.

81 D.D. Shulman, *The King and the Clown in South Indian Myth and Poetry*. For a similar argument within Islamic political theory on the subcontinent see A. Wink, *Land and Sovereignty in India: Agrarian Society and Politics under 18th Century Maratha Svarajya*, Cambridge University Press, Cambridge, 1986.

82 C.A. Bayly, *Indian Society and the Making of British Empire*, Cambridge University Press, Cambridge, 1988; A. Skaria, *A Forest Polity in Western India: The Dangs, 1800–1920*, Ph.D. dissertation, Cambridge, 1992.

Competitive Advantage through Contestation

The Indian Shop-floor at the Turn of the Century

Nasir Tyabji

The effect of nineteenth-century working-class struggles in Britain, in spurring technological advances in manufacturing is now a familiar story. Although the struggles were intended to improve working conditions in general, and to shorten working hours in particular, their effect was also to intensify competitive pressures on individual firms. Adoption of better machinery and management practices was the most creative, even if not the most widespread, response to these pressures.

In the Indian context, the diffusion of reforms in managerial practices, initiated in isolated cases as a result of pressures from below, were inevitably long drawn-out processes. Although the Mumbai textile industry had completed the transition from managerial commission on the basis of production to a system of commission on profits by the 1920s, Ahmedabad textile interests continued with the old system for a much longer period.[1] In the textile industry, the jobber's role as a recruiting/disciplining agent remained largely unchanged, though subject to intense workers' opposition during periods of heightened class struggle, up to the late 1940s. The attempt to shorten the working day, the immediate focus of this paper, lasted from 1875 to 1948, when the Factories Act granted recognition of the eight-hour day.[2] Finally, the managing agency, as an organizational form, continued until as late as 1969. The time period which forms the focus of this paper is limited, in that it considers the issue of attempts at the limitation of the working day from 1875 to 1908. In that year, the Indian Factory Labour Commission's Report set in motion the process by which the Factories Act was amended, in 1911, to limit the working period for adult males to twelve hours a day. The paper also examines

187

some of the issues which the limitation of the working hours raised, in terms of its effects on the managerial systems in the mills.

I

One of the most obvious ways in which limitation of the working day was linked to pressures for managerial change was in the prevailing system of managing agency commissions. In the period before 1886, the managing agents in the Mumbai cotton textile industry were paid a commission on mill output regardless of the profitability of the enterprise's operations.[3] This principle of a commission on output began to be replaced by a system of commission on profits in a few mills in the 1890s. However, as late as 1913, of the 59 mills registered under the Indian Companies Act, more than half had still not shifted to a commission on profits.[4]

This prevailing system, according to which the cotton mill agents received a commission fixed on the basis of the weight of the cotton cloth produced, certainly reinforced the tendency towards long working hours in the cotton factories in Mumbai. Attempts, therefore, to shorten the working period, put further pressure towards a change of the basis of the commission.

More generally, as this commission system focused attention on the physical output, not profits, as the object to be aimed at, it encouraged wasteful and uneconomical management of the mills. The management philosophy that was generated by these circumstances also had direct repercussions on the managerial hierarchy. Thus, although the department heads and their assistants were nominally responsible to the (general) manager, they were neither recruited nor removed by him, but by the managing agents of the mill.[5] This implied a rupture in the management system responsible for the technical aspects of production, because the line of authority, from the spinning and weaving masters, looped around the general manager and fed directly to the mill's agent.

There was a further rupture at the level of the jobbers, as the tacklers or foremen were known in the cotton mills. The mill agents saw the jobbers not only as recruiting agents, as is well known, but also as a critical, if not the sole means, of managing shop-floor relations:[6]

> My point is that the jobber is one of them [the workers]. Under
> Bombay conditions the jobber practically comes from the same class

of men as the workman himself and therefore he is naturally in touch. Now the men who are above the jobbers do not belong to the same strata of life . . . and naturally are not in touch with the men . . . You cannot easily get at them [the workers] unless you have some point of contact with them, which those superior officers do not enjoy at the moment.

Thus, the jobbers, by virtue of their designated role in facilitating communication between the workers and the mill agents, had also a direct line of contact with the agents. This provided the basis for a further loop in the line of authority, bypassing all the managerial layers. More critical was the fact that these vertical threads of authority prevented any fusion of efficient practices of machine, raw-material and work-process management at the horizontal level. On the shop-floor, jobbers and departmental assistants had their distinct responsibilities, and these could only be integrated at the mill–agent apex. It is difficult to conceive of a system of industrial management less conducive to generating 'competitive advantage on the shop-floor'.[7]

Given that the tendency of change was oriented towards a commission on profits, working-class struggles could be expected to require a greater attention towards efficient manufacturing operations. An obvious source of efficiency lay in the more direct management of shop-floor processes, necessitating changes in the line of managerial authority. This, in turn, required modifications in, if not replacement of the jobber's role.

The point is that, quite apart from the obvious source of oppression that the jobber's power implied, which was a target for working-class struggles, the removal of the jobber was also the direction through which better coordination of human and material aspects of the production process could be achieved.

II

Although the first cotton mill was established in Mumbai in 1854, official notice of the working conditions in the mills seems to have been taken twenty years later, in the 1872–73 Report of the Mumbai Cotton Department, published in 1874.[8] This was followed, in quick succession, by reports by the Calcutta correspondent of the *London Times*, by the master of the Mumbai Mint, and by the inspector of factories in Britain, all in 1874.[9] The *Times* report was particularly significant, as it also drew attention to the situation in the Bengal jute mills, overwhelmingly under British agencies.

On the prodding of the British government, the Mumbai authorities appointed the first of the factory commissions in March 1875. In the meantime, Lancashire interests had begun publicly raising the issue in parliament, in the House of Commons in February 1875, and in the House of Lords in July of that year.[10]

In spite of this clear indication of the metropolitan government's interest in the matter, the Commission which was formed was largely a sop. With seven representatives of the Mumbai mill owners amongst its nine members, it was not surprising that a unanimous report could not be prepared. The collector of Mumbai, who was the chairperson of the Commission, and a specialist member, an English doctor, were both in favour of a twelve-hour day, prohibition of work by children below 8 years of age, and limiting children between 8 and 14 to eight hours of daily work.[11] However, the Mumbai government took no action on the report, and even claimed that no private member's bill could be introduced in the Mumbai Legislative Council, as the majority of the 1875 Commission had opposed legislation.[12]

It was at this stage that liberal Indian and English philanthropists, notably Sorabji Bengalee and Mary Carpenter, founder of the National Indian Association, began to lobby the legislatures in India and in Britain, in support of factory legislation. Bengalee's letter to the *London Times* asking for Lancashire's direct intervention led to an uproar, and more constructively, pushed the Government of India towards the introduction of an official bill proposing a common factory act for the whole of India.[13]

The first Indian Factory Act of 1881 was largely ineffective. It left adult males (those over 12 years of age) out of its purview. Women's working hours were limited to eleven, between 5 in the morning and 8 at night, while children, defined as the 7 to 12 age group, were prohibited from working more than nine hours. Although the Government of India supported the Mumbai government in favouring an effective act, as did a large section of Mumbai's public opinion, effective opposition, led by Bengal's lieutenant-governor, created a situation in which no step could be taken.[14]

The most important effect of the Act was that it provided a focus to channel the workers' opposition to the conditions in which they worked. N.M. Lokhande, the president of the Bombay Mill-

Hands Association and the editor of *Dinabandhu*, was able now to provide a measure of mass support to Sorabji Bengalee's continued efforts to increase the effectiveness of the Act. When the Mumbai government appointed another Commission in 1884, two meetings of the textile workers were organized by Lokhande, on 23 and 26 September 1884, when 5,500 workers signed a memorandum demanding a weekly holiday, limitation of working hours, payment of wages within fifteen days of the end of the month, and compensation for industrial accidents.[15] Although the details of the nature of the connection remain to be worked out, it is significant that within two years of this demonstration of solidarity, the movement by managing agents from the system of commission on production to commission on profits began.

At that time, legislative safeguards for men had no British precedent, which was always an important defence of attempts to introduce 'British rule' in India. However, the difference between the two situations was well brought out by Sorabji Bengalee's minute of dissent to the 1884 Commission's report, signed jointly with Dr Blaney, who had also dissented from the 1875 Commission. The minute pointed out that 74 per cent of English textile workers were women, 'young persons' and children. The control of women's hours, along with those of young persons and children, effectively controlled the working hours of the mills, including those of the balance, 26 per cent, consisting of adult males above 18. In India, women and children formed, at the most, a quarter of the workforce, and were mostly employed in the reeling and winding departments, which could be separated from the main factory. It was therefore essential, under Indian conditions, to legislate directly for the limitation of men's working hours.[16]

The problem lay in the fact that capitalists in the Bengal jute industry and the fledgling Madras cotton textile industry, largely British at the time, also objected to the attempts to increase the scope of legislative safeguards for industrial workers.[17] The strength of their opposition can be gauged from the fact that even when the Dundee Chamber of Commerce began to support Manchester from the early 1890s, it had little immediate effect.

The general introduction of electric lights in the Mumbai mills led to outrageous hours of work, particularly in 1905. It was then that strikes and other forms of workers' protests led to a renewed series of enquiries, and the eventual passage of the 1911 Act limiting adult workers (only in the textile industries) to a twelve-hour day. The decisive factor for this step was the Report of the 1908 Indian Factories Labour Commission (IFLC), and in particular, the minute of dissent by T.M. Nair, prominent in the non-Brahmin movement in Madras Presidency and mayor of Chennai Corporation.[18]

III

If the 1881 Factories Act provided a focus towards which workers' protest could be oriented, the introduction of electric lights provided the next great impetus to working-class organization and its eventual impact on shop-floor management practices. In effect, while the conditions of natural lighting provided a physical limit to the working day, the introduction of artificial light, theoretically at least, allowed a twenty-four-hour working day. Differences between sections of the Mumbai mill owners on this issue had begun to appear quite early on. Since 1902, most of the mills had used electric lights, and a few mills had begun working for fourteen hours. After 1905 some mills had arranged to work for twelve hours, but workers on a piece rate were obviously unwilling to accept shorter working hours unless their wage rates were raised appropriately, and finally the Millowners Association compromised with thirteen hours.[19]

According to the representatives of major Mumbai textile groups, the problem was that the thirteen-hour day was forced on the owners by the workers both due to their greed, to their (poor) constitutions and habits of work.[20] They argued that although the factory engines functioned for thirteen hours, the workers put in eight-and-a-half or nine hours of work. The intervals taken up (without permission) by the workers in smoking and other forms of idling reduced the actual working hours to a great extent. Unlike the Lancashire workers, the Mumbai workers could not work for fixed hours at a stretch.[21] If the working hours were restricted by legislation, mill owners would have to make up for the time lost by demanding steadier and more regular work; as it was, they had to engage substitutes, when there was already a shortage of workers. Any further strictness or supervision would lead to strikes. Even if the workers agreed to work steadily for a number of hours a day without frequent intervals, under strict supervision, they would soon deteriorate in health, owing to the climatic conditions and old habits of work. It would be a long time before matters became adjusted.

If a twelve-hour day meant twelve hours of actual work, it

was possible they would come to this in time without legislation, argued Currimbhoy Ibrahim. The mill owners were not united on this point, and therefore they had to accept legislation, but there were strong objections in principle to adult labour being restricted.[22]

Japanese manufacturers, with the assistance of their government, had dumped yarn in China at a loss in order to compete with India. Any legislation which would increase the cost of production in India would further lessen India's hold on the China market. [23]

The question of retaining Indian's competitive advantage was viewed therefore as hinging on the capacity of Indian workers to make up for the 'lost time' that shorter working hours would involve, by an increased intensity of work. One view on this question was expressed by Currimbhoy Ibrahim. He had tried a twelve-hour day in the hope of obtaining better production and greater application from the workers, but he had been disappointed, and the workers themselves wanted the same wages that were paid for the longer day. The more advanced view came from the Petit group of mills. They had introduced a higher grade of cotton which allowed both a better quality of yarn to be produced, and the payment of higher wages. In these mills, the daily wage was such as to compare with mills working for longer hours.[24] This appeared to be the only case of a positive attempt to deal with the issue of shorter working hours.

Currimbhoy Ibrahim's experiment of shorter working hours had evidently taken place on an individual mill basis. Speaking presumably on the effects of legislative prohibition of working hours, C.N. Wadia, agent of the Century Spinning and Manufacturing Company, did not think there was anything to be obtained by working more than twelve hours.[25] If the number was fixed, the workers would apply themselves with greater energy and spend less time idling in the compound. A twelve-hour day would benefit the industry as the workers would achieve a higher standard of efficiency and produce nearly as much as during the longer hours. The knowledge that the worker would receive less pay unless he applied himself would stimulate him, and Wadia felt that the worker, in time, would appreciate the end of the working day coming earlier.[26]

Currimbhoy Ibrahim had noticed that the men worked steadily in the evening and did not leave the mill, and so the production increased. He had evidently not bothered to investigate this matter further, but a possible answer was provided by B.H. Saklatvala, manager of the Dinshaw Petit Mills. Saklatvala felt that the 'idling habits' of the workers were partly connected with questions of temperature and ventilation. If it was cold outside they did not want to go out so much, and they remained more in the mill in the cold weather than in the hot.[27] It was left to a shop-floor worker, a retired weaving master, to raise the connection between work habits and general living conditions of the workers. He argued that the workers had very small and insanitary living quarters, where the toilets and bathing places were very dirty. There was usually little water in the taps. On the mill premises there was a comparatively ample supply of water and the toilets were cleaner. There was thus a natural tendency amongst the workers to use the mill facilities during the day.[28] N.B. Saklatwalla, director of Tata Sons, produced data on 'loitering' (i.e. absenteeism during the working day), recorded in the Swadeshi Mills . It was 14 per cent amongst the daily waged spinners, and 3 per cent amongst the piece-rated weavers. On an average, only 25 per cent of the workers were present throughout the month, which Saklatwalla attributed to the long working hours.[29] In general, the Tata Group was relatively advanced in recommending an eleven-hour day, with two half-hourly intervals.[30]

On the crucial question of the role of improved shop-floor management in productivity increases, both Currimbhoy Ibrahim and C.N. Wadia were one. Both agreed that the general level of skill had improved among the workers over a period of years. Both also deplored the fact that there had been no corresponding increase in 'industriousness' amongst them. Wadia, in fact, was quick to add the proviso that the machinery had also been improved.[31] He was sure there had been no improvement in habits of work, their idea being to earn as much as they could with as little trouble as possible. Even the evidence on behalf of Tata Sons suggested that the question of making up for 'lost time' depended as much on the quality of the cotton and the change in atmospheric conditions, as on the number of spindles worked. It does not seem to have occurred to any of these managements that industriousness was a quality to be generated by more sophisticated management practices, and was neither genetically determined nor acquired through self-improvement.

IV

It was at this time that Frederick Winslow Taylor was applying himself to the problem of increasing the 'industriousness' of North

194

American workers, so the Mumbai industrialists were perhaps not too far behind world trends. Where there was more clearly a contrast, and that with Japan, was in the understanding of the relationship between individual productivity and education, specifically with mass primary education.

Indian nationalists had raised this question as far back as 1882, when in a minute of dissent to the Education Commission, Telang had indicated its importance.[32] Subsequently, it had featured in resolutions of the Indian National Congress, and had forcefully been advocated by Gokhale. However, Gokhale's primary concern had (quite correctly) been the issue of increasing the peasant household's life skills in its interaction with the village landlord and trader/money-lender.[33]

In the more narrow terms of the relationship between education and productivity, which is the concern of this paper, the colonial authorities (even if with stability of land revenue in mind) were in the forefront. In the 1888 quinquennial resolution on education following that year's Conference of the Provincial Directors of Agriculture and Revenue, it was suggested that the Education and Agriculture Departments should work out a scheme of primary education 'which would render the agricultural population capable of assimilating new ideas and of understanding any suggestions made to them'.[34] This was a sophisticated conception of the function of primary education, which was entirely absent in the 'torrent of words' on the apparently more germane issue of technical education.[35]

The proceedings of the Indian Factory Labour Commission are important in that a specific question was asked, whether mill owners should be required by law to provide primary classes at their own expense on the factory premises. Answers to this question provide a basis for gauging the extent to which the understanding of the function of primary education quoted above, in respect to improvements in agricultural operations, in 1888, had permeated mill owners' consciousness twenty years later.

The question of the provision of primary education had been posed by the Commission in the most general terms.[36] Respondents were free to interpret it as a query as to whether it was to be a purely a philanthropic gesture by mill owners, or a non-cash wage payment, or as a means towards gaining an adult workforce with greater conceptual ability, leading hopefully to greater efficiency.[37] T.M. Nair, mayor of

195

Chennai Corporation and dissenting member of the Factory Labour Commission, had little doubt about the level of humanitarian understanding of the industrialists:[38]

> Even some of the most enlightened and educated Indian gentlemen, with whom I discussed industrial questions, had not a single word of sympathy with the labourers to express. They were all anxious to make up for lost time and to push on their industrial ventures and to accumulate wealth. But as for the workers, they were part of the machinery of production and nothing more.

Within this general framework of thought, there were some broad streams of reasoning. The most startling of these views was one that argued that the provision of primary education would be an entirely unnecessary strain on the children, and that it would deny them any time for recreation. The presumption here was that the children (half-timers) would be expected to attend classes during the 'half-time' that they were not at work in the mill.[39] It would be comforting to believe that this rationalization was, of course, expressed in 1908. However, not only was it voiced, in almost similar words, by three (Ahmedabad-based) industrialists but also by two senior British members of the Indian Medical Service based in Mumbai.[40]

More expectedly, though no less forthrightly presented, was the opinion that the responsibility should on no account be placed on the factory owners. The most articulate of these responses was from A.K. Leslie, agent of Greaves Cotton and Company. He was supported by British inspectors of factories in Ahmedabad and Mumbai, by the Bharuch district magistrate, and by an Indian (match factory) owner.[41]

Currimbhoy Ibrahim represented the viewpoint of agnosticism when he argued that elementary education was properly the function of the municipality, or the government, rather than of the mill owners. Variations on this theme were that it was desirable but should not be compulsory for the mill owners, and a plaintive note, that it had been tried but had not succeeded.[42]

N.N. Wadia, of the Bombay Dyeing and Manufacturing Company, on the other hand, agreed that the employers should be required to provide facilities as they would, in an unspecified way, find it advantageous.[43] Finally, there was a clearer viewpoint, linking an improvement in the 'habits' of the workers to the provision of free primary education, which would improve their intellectual capabilities.[44]

Conclusions

The conventional view has been that the impetus to factory legislation given by the Lancashire and, later, Dundee capitalists was an unfair use of their influence over the colonial state. The line of reasoning outlined in this paper would suggest that interventions *on factory legislation* cannot be viewed as inimical to Indian industrialization, but solely to the prevailing systems of industrial management in India.[45]

It is important to note here that the Bombay Millowners Association was established in 1875, with the objective of providing a platform for the defence of the interests of Mumbai's textile capitalists. In itself, this step would appear to be an obvious move, with little beyond historical importance. The significance principally lies in that this association arose not for the purpose of industrial solidarity vis-à-vis the workers, but against the colonial government's policies. The specific nature of this genesis had both positive and negative features for the evolution of the capitalist class's political ideology on the one hand, and of industrial management on the other.

The reduction of working hours had implications for prevailing systems of management. It brought into focus issues of shop-floor organization on the one hand, and the educational background and the derived intellectual capabilities of the workers on the other. The period covered by this paper saw the emergence of these issues as matters of public debate. Responses, as the introduction points out, took considerably longer.

Particularly in matters such as education, where the state had a major role, progress has been poor. In the post-independence period too, the Indian record of concern about primary education, let alone effective action, remains dismal. Even from the narrow point of view of industrial efficiency, there was no concern evident until the end of the third five-year plan, when the first systematic survey of educational standards amongst industrial workers was conducted.[46] It is a depressing but inevitable conclusion that matters have not appreciably changed from 1908 when T.M. Nair wrote, in his minute of dissent, that it was the workers who suffered from bad management and not the management that suffered from bad workers.[47]

Notes and References

1 The current terms, Mumbai and Chennai, have been used in this paper except when the name of an organization, such as the Bombay Millowners' Association, would make their use anachronistic.

2 For the record, it may be noted that in 1862, 1,200 workers of the Howrah railway station struck work on the demand for an eight-hour working day. Gopal Ghosh, 1966, *Maiden Strike in India*, G. Ghosh, Calcutta, p. 8.

3 Morris. D. Morris, *The Emergence of an Industrial Labour Force in India: A Study of the Bombay Cotton Mills*, University of California Press, Berkely, 1965, p. 34.

4 *Indian Textile Journal*, XXIII, No. 275, August 1913, p. 369, quoted in Morris, *The Emergence of an Industrial Labour Force in India*, p. 34, fn. 45.

5 Morris, *The Emergence of an Industrial Labour Force in India*, p. 36

6 Evidence of Bombay Millowners organization's representative in the *Report of the Indian Tariff Board on the Cotton Textile Industry, 1927*, Vol. II, p. 348 quoted in Morris, *The Emergence of an Industrial Labour Force in India*, p. 136.

7 The phrase comes from the title of William Lazonick's study of the British textile industry, *Competitive Advantage on the Shop Floor*, Harvard University Press, Cambridge Mass, 1990.

8 *Administration Report of the Cotton Department, Bombay*, for the year 1872–73, p. 6, quoted in Sukomal Sen, *May Day and Eight Hour's Struggle in India*, K.P. Bagchi, Calcutta, 1988, p. 92.

9 *The Times*, London, 7 August 1874, p. 3, quoted in S. Sen, *May Day and Eight Hour's Struggle in India*, p. 92. The other references are also from Sen, pp. 92–93.

10 S. Sen, *May Day and Eight Hour's Struggle in India*, p. 94.

11 S.G. Panandikar, *Industrial Labour in Bombay*, Longman Green and Co., Bombay, 1933, p. 119.

12 S. Sen, *May Day and Eight Hour's Struggle in India*, p. 96.

13 Ibid., pp. 95–97, 99–100.

14 Ibid, pp. 95–96; Panandikar, *Industrial Labour*, p. 119

15 Ibid., pp. 100–06

16 Ibid., pp. 105–06.

17 The strenuous opposition of the lieutenant-governor of Bengal to the proposals to make the 1881 Act effective was indicative of this. More directly, both the Bombay and the Madras Chambers of Commerce, representatives of British commercial interests, protested against an attempt by the Manchester Chamber to have the British Factories Act extended to India. S. Sen, *May Day and Eight Hour's Struggle in India*, p. 106.

18 Panandikar, *Industrial Labour*, 1933, p. 124.

19 This account is based on the evidence provided by Sassoon David before the Indian Factory Labour Commission, p. 76. [Henceforward, 'Evidence'.]

20 Fazulbhoy Currimbhoy Ibrahim, vvice-chairperson, BMA. and Sassoon David, 'Evidence' pp. 66, 68, 76. '. . . one seldom sees old men working in

factories. This, and the acknowledged fact that no human being can stand continuous work for 13 hours, and considering at the same time . . . the ignorant masses of people who for mere greed of money are often led to work 13 or 14 hours . . . lead to the conclusion that it would be advisable and necessary to protect them against their own greed, and to safeguard their health by restricting the hours of labour of adult males . . .'. N.N. Wadia of the Bombay Dyeing and Manufacturing Co., p. 112.

21 'It was spinning and not weaving that was responsible for the long hours. The weavers earned good wages, were a separate class altogether, and would not work long hours. The weaver also had to pay greater attention to his work, he worked harder than the spinner, and he would not consent to work for longer hours'. Sassoon David, 'Evidence', p. 76.

22 Currimbhoy Ibrahim, 'Evidence', p. 68.

23 'Evidence', p. 68.

24 'Evidence' of B.D. Petit, senior partner of D.M. Petit and Sons, p. 135, and of P.B. Petit, of the Emperor Edward, and the Petit Nagpur Swadeshi Mills, p. 138.

25 N.B. Saklatwalla, director of Tata Sons felt that while there might be some 'trouble at first with the workpeople over their reduced earnings'; if the hours of work were restricted by legislation, he thought that matters would 'adjust themselves', 'Evidence', p. 105. D.P. Settna, of the Maneckjee Petit Mills, p. 125, and Manmohandas Ramji, of the Indian Manufacturing Company, and the New Kaiser-i-Hind Spinning and Manufacturing Company, p. 65, supported him.

26 'Evidence', p. 94.

27 'Evidence', p. 82.

28 Written evidence by Bhiwa Ramji Nare, p. 114.

29 This was in contrast to Currimbhoy Ibrahim's confident assertion that he did not find that the men were exhausted after their day's work. 'Evidence', p. 68

30 This was based on their experience with working an eight-hour day some years previously. This having been 'forced' on the industry, the overseers were stricter. The workers, according to Saklatwalla, knowing that their earnings would otherwise be lower, had been more attentive and not wished to go out perpetually. 'Evidence', p. 105.

31 Evidence, p. 94. He was supported by H.R. Greaves, of Greaves Cotton and Company, p. 63. J.A. Wadia, director of the Currimbhoy Ibrahim Group, and of the David Mills, went further in claiming that the improvements were entirely the result of better machinery, p. 128. He, in turn, was supported by B.H. Saklatwala, manager of the Dinshaw Petit Mills, p. 82.

32 In a letter written to Ripon, governor general, in 1883, Telang had emphasized that funds for primary education should be increased, without reducing allocations for higher education. Quoted by G.K. Gokhale in his address to the 10th Annual General Meeting of the Bombay Graduates Association, 11 April 1896. D.G. Karve and D.V. Ambekar, eds., *Speeches and*

Writings of Gopal Krishna Gokhale, Vol. III: *Educational,* Asia Publishing House, Mumbai, 1967.

[33] In his 1896 address to the Bombay Graduates Association, Gokhale had stressed the importance of primary education as a means towards India's 'salvation'. Ibid., p. 166.

[34] Suggestions by subsequent provincial conferences, in 1896 and 1897, led to a resolution in 1897 on primary education by the Government of India. E. Buck, *Report on Practical and Technical Education,* Home Education A. Proceedings, no 20, quoted in Padmini Swaminathan, 'Technical Education and Industrial Development in the Madras Presidency' (mimeo), Working Paper No. 106, Madras Institute of Development Studies, Madras, 1992, p. 10.

[35] The surreal nature of the involved debate on technical education which followed the Report of the 1884 Education Commission, and carried over to World War I is due to the entire lack of interest in the matter by capitalists, both Indian and British, in the matter.

See G. Ambirajan, 'Steel Intellect and the Raj: Technical Education in South India in the Nineteenth Century' (mimeo), paper presented to the All India Workshop on Studying Problems of School Education in India in a Historical Perspective, organized by the NCERT at the Indian Institute of Education, Pune, 1984; Aparna Basu, 'Technical Education in India, 1900–1920', *Indian Economic and Social History Review,* IV, 4, pp. 361–37, 1967; *Essays in the History of Indian Education,* Concept Publishing Company, New Delhi, 1982; 'The Indian Response to Scientific and Technical Education in the Colonial Era, 1820–1920', in Kumar, ed., *Science and Empire: Essays in the Indian Context 1700–1947,* Anamika Publishers, Delhi, 1991; Saugata Mukherji, 'Some Aspects of the Policy on Technical and Industrial Education in India under Colonial Rule: From Late Nineteenth Century to Independence' (mimeo), Occasional Paper No. 123, Centre for Studies in Social Sciences, Calcutta, 1990; Padmini Swaminathan, 'Technical Education and Industrial Development in the Madras Presidency' (mimeo), Working Paper No. 106, Madras Institute of Development Studies, Madras, 1992.

[36] This is apparent from the startling response from the Ahmedabad district magistrate: 'Concerning education, Mr. Doderot did not think that the class from which these people came received, generally speaking, education, and there was no particular reason why millowners should be forced to provide it. To him there seemed no point in giving education to children who were going to work all their lives in a mill. . .'. 'Evidence', p. 2.

[37] It was clear that there was no illusion that the work currently done by the older children (it was proposed to define them as 'young adults') could not be done by adults: 'I have quoted above from the evidence given before the Commission by millowners and managers from Ahmedabad, Bombay, Agra, Cawnpore, and Sholapur. They all say that young persons could be replaced by adults, and what is more they would be so replaced. . .'. T.M. Nair, Minute of Dissent, p. 97.

200

It was equally clear that the younger children, in return for the 'apprenticeship' were expected to continue working in the mill full-time, as soon as they reached the age of fourteen. This supposition is apparent from the debate over whether there should be a medical examination before half-timers were permitted to become full-timers: 'It may be said that cases like these (children above 14 years of age who are unfit to do a full day's work) are few and constitute only a very small percentage of the total number of young adults working in the many mills in India. In other words the percentage of young adults who have ruined their health by attempting to do work beyond their strength is so small that it may be neglected. That is the frame of mind in which a manufacturer looks at damaged goods. But here we are dealing not with cotton cloths or woollen material or chemical substances but the damaged items are human beings.' T.M. Nair, Minute of Dissent, p. 110.

[38] Minute of Dissent, p. 104. The British manager of one of the Mumbai mills went so far as to confirm that the long working hours were due to pressure from the mill owners. 'Evidence', p. 80.

[39] Gokhale's private bill, intending to make primary education compulsory, advisedly had a specific clause (6) which linked the banning of (male) child labour to provision of education. Krishna Kumar, *Political Agenda of Education: A Study of Colonialist and Nationalist Ideas,* Sage Publications, New Delhi, 1991, p. 109.

[40] Evidence of Lalbhai Trikamlal of the New Manekchok Spinning and Weaving Company, p. 6; Mansukhbhai Bhagubhai of the Gujarat Spinning and Manufacturing Company, the Gujarat Spinning and Weaving Company, the Motilal Hirabhai Spinning, Weaving and Manufacturing Company, and the Purshotam Spinning and Manufacturing Company, p. 12; and Purshottambhai M. Hathisingh, p. 25. The British witnesses were the presidency surgeon of one of the districts in Mumbai, p. 45, and the personal assistant to the surgeon general, Government of Mumbai, p. 36.

[41] Evidence of A.K. Leslie, p. 59, the second inspector of factories, Ahmedabad, p. 7, the first inspector of factories, Mumbai, p. 51, the Bharuch district magistrate, p. 29, and F.F. Munshi of the Gujarat Islam Match Manufacturing Company, p. 10.

[42] Evidence of Currimbhoy Ibrahim, p. 66, and C.N. Wadia, p. 93. The first variation was represented by Mangaldas G. Parekh of the Aryodaya and Rajnagar Spinning and Weaving Company, the Bharatkhand Textile Manufacturing Company, the Victoria Mills in Mumbai, and sundry presses and gins, p. 4; Lalbhai Dalpatbhai of the Saraspur Manufacturing Company, and the Raipur Manufacturing Company in Ahmedabad, p. 14; C. Knowles, manager of the Ahmedabad Merchants' Spinning Mills, p. 15; and the executive health officer, Mumbai, p. 42. The second (plaintive) variation came from Chunubhai Madhulal of the Ahmedabad Ginning and Manufacturing Company, and the Ahmedabad Spinning and Weaving Company, p. 24; and Sorabji D. Karaka of the Ahmedabad Fine Spinning and Weaving Company, and the Hitwadhak Mills, p. 26.

43 'Evidence', p. 112. He was supported in this view by D.P. Settna of the Maneckjee Petit Mill, p. 124; the British representative of the Shorrock Spinning and Manufacturing Company in Ahmedabad, p. 4; Vaikunthbhai Ambalal Desai of the Ahmedabad Merchants' Spinning Mills Company, p. 17; Adarji Mancherji Dalal, director of cotton mill companies, p. 34; by two mill managers in Mumbai, Nowrosji Cursetji Lakriwalla, of the Saraswati Mills, p. 78; and John Taylor, of the Elphinstone Mills, p. 83.

44 J.A. Wadia, director of the Currimbhoy Ibrahim and David Mills was the most prominent exponent of this view, although his other utterances were not particularly advanced. 'Evidence', p. 128. He was supported by the Mumbai-based British managers of the Elphinstone Mills, p. 83, and the Western India Spinning and Manufacturing Company, p. 91.

45 Pressures exerted by Lancashire mill owners towards the imposition of the countervailing excise duties, levied in the 1890s, were obviously designed to retard Indian industrialization.

46 *Report on Literacy among Industrial Workers* (New Delhi), Committee on Plan Projects, Planning Commission, Government of India, 1964.

47 Minute of Dissent, p. 84.

Less-than-Total Unities
Patel and the National Movement

Rani Dhavan Shankardass

We are Indians; Unity is our strength.
Slogan on hoardings commemorating Fifty Years of Independence

Just what is this singular entity called 'Indian'? Is the suggestion in the above caption that of an entity emanating out of self-perception, or is there an implication here of objective criteria by which we could all call ourselves 'Indian'? How real is the identity that is referred to as constituting an Indian entity? How old is it? How vital is it? Does it, and how if it does, change over time? What does the above assertion wish to convey? And who is it addressing and to what effect and purpose? The answers to many of these questions lie in concerns that have engaged historians engaged with 'Nationalism as a Problem in the History of Political Ideas.'[1] Clearly, the concept of 'national unity' as a backdrop to much of our thinking about society and the polity is an issue that is far from settled and its appearance again and again is suggestive of the extent to which it would continue to form part of our agenda—political, social and economic.

Clearly too, the above slogan is intended both to exclude and include. It is suggestive of a distinctiveness derived from being different, from those who are not Indians (other 'national' entities), and from those that are smaller entities within the large 'Indian' entity, which begs the question: is there a larger Indian entity; are smaller entities constituents of it? Does the emphasis on a larger Indian entity intend to highlight commonalties that supposedly string together those differently and differentially placed within the territorial boundaries of the 'modern' institution called the nation state? In which case, just how intimately do we wish to bind the idea of Indian unity with that of the modern liberal nation-state (and still be able to boast of its

203

distinctive Indianness? The assertion at this crucial moment is also intended as a 'statement'—of self assurance, of caution and in the extreme, of a threat. This is being inferred from the emphasis in the second part of the slogan—about 'unity',—regarded as the great strength-providing virtue and by implication constitutive of an 'Indianness' that is being asserted as the hallmark of an otherwise diverse people often seen (from within and without) as different, divided and therefore disunited, even as they form part of the large territorial entity 'India'. It is, furthermore, intended also to convey a larger, more encompassing whole than some smaller units that may or may not be integral parts of which the 'whole' might be constituted.

It seems worthwhile taking stock of all these possibilities at a historical juncture when the 'nation' is celebrating the achievement of a supposedly noteworthy innings—fifty years of independence from colonial rule, an event that is serving as a vehicle for the dissemination of ideas about unity and nationalism, and possibly about 'national' direction and 'national' goals as well. That this would need some examination of the strands that made up the scenario that was a prelude to what was achieved fifty years ago by way of 'national independence', seems obvious. But which particular strands can one examine? The conflicting responses to the colonial encounter have been variously analysed in the area of the economic, the cultural and the social, and the resulting assessments have been equally contradictory: the colonial encounter has been viewed as a blessing and a curse all at once, depending on how positive and 'progressive' or how negative and 'regressive' an experience it is regarded as. Not an insignificant part of our dilemma are the neat perceptions that are invested into notions of 'progress' and persist in our sketches of oneness and unity: modern education as a hallmark of progress; or colonial institutions as 'rational'; or indeed 'rational' as universal and therefore unifying. Methodologically this essay would wish to approach the question of national unity as constituting the (nationalist) quality of being Indian in two ways: (i) as historians have seen it; and (ii) as particular historical subjects—the political/social figures of the national movement through which national attributes and events have been sought to be exemplified, have viewed it (and then acted upon it).

In either case some further questions that need to be addressed are: whether social groups and communities ('Indian' but not quite 'Indian') get stitched, merged, amalgamated or simply added together to become or to be viewed as 'Indian', and also by some process of logic or ideological objective, as united. Do they unite for any particular objective at hand (and is this the perception of the actors themselves or of nationalist historians)? What kind of unity is seen as having being achieved—is it something greater than group and community unity (and therefore superior to it), but also less than any unity beyond that of being 'Indian'? And does this make up an association called 'India', or is it an imagined political entity that we would wish to call India?

It does not constitute any part of this historical analysis to offer a *priori* definitions of what constitutes being 'Indian', being nationalist or being united (Indians with other Indians, or smaller units and entities with each other, to constitute a larger entity—'Indian' presumably). There is an assumption in the celebration of fifty years (of Indian 'freedom', or of 'independence', both having been proclaimed as the big causes to be celebrated) that a people came together as Indians, united, and thereby achieved the strength that enabled them to overthrow an oppressive outsider, to reclaim that power that all independent nations must have in order to decide their own futures and destinies. There is also a parallel assumption, sometimes contradictory to the first assumption, that this process of combat (the nationalist struggle) produced much of the substance of 'unity', or 'national unity' to be precise, and resulted in a particular unity that became a further source of strength for what was constitutive of being Indian. It is against the backdrop of this narrative (national movement, struggle for independence, transfer of power, fight for freedom, et al) that we shall analyse the process of being or getting united (and the two processes are different).

It is difficult to decide who has wreaked greater havoc with themes like unity and national identity—historians or political scientists. One thing is clear, however: there is a difference in looking at the national (nationalist) question and particularly that (strengthening) strand called unity, when it is constructed essentially from above, and/or when it is perceived in terms of the 'assumptions hopes needs longings of ordinary people' from below—which, as Hobsbawm reminds us, are 'not necessarily national and still less nationalist' even during a national movement. The latter feature is what prompts Hobsbawm (and others) towards criticism of Gellner's perspective of modernization from above ('fully industrial man') which makes it impossible to address sufficiently the view from below.[2]

As historical writing and thinking has moved away from large, totalizing, universalizing, holistic histories of nationalism, social historians have provided wholesome images of perceptions from and of those levels that had been ignored or considered irrelevant (irrelevant for what or whom was always a problematic that was addressed variously). There is now greater clarity about the 'three things' that Hobsbawm said he found were already becoming clear when he wrote about national identity:

(i) The scepticism about treating official ideologies of states and movements as a true gauge of what really motivates and activates citizens and supporters is on the increase; the desire to look beyond proclamations and rhetoric is now mixed with so much cynicism that taking almost anything at 'face value' is as obsolete as one can imagine in historical writing and interpretation.:

(ii) What is also on the increase is the acceptance that identities and 'unities' are more than national (or less than national if one is referring to some kind of continuum of unities)—Hobsbawm's 'remainder of the set of identifications' ('remainder' is a word one has difficulty with) are now treated with as much reverence and seriousness and held to be as vitally constitutive of the 'social being'.

(iii) The changing patterns of unity, national or other, over periods of time, and the unevenness with which any consciousness of that unity or identity develops in society, are also taken cognizance of by historians—except those totally crushed by the weight of their 'non-historical convictions'.

The attempt to handle the idea of 'Indianness' and of the unity that gives 'strength' to being Indian is suggestive of a 'one single people' idea that history has grappled with in one way or another at various stages of its unfolding. And yet, it has also been suggested that in a sense there really is no 'Indian' history unless it is the 'history' of its many peoples, a 'history' later strung together with some threads in order that it might be called Indian and therefore be rampant with delusions. Away from holistic, universalizing histories that were so many things all at once—too ideological, too construed, too contrived and too intellectually dishonest—there is little reason to explain why unity and nationalism might be seen not as motivating factors that caused political events but as ideas that resulted from, and were woven into, nationalist or nationalizing agendas.

At no stage do all these conflicting images from conflicting perceptions emerge as full-bloodedly as during the playing out and reporting of the national movement. In this essay the earlier (nineteenth-century) manifestations of the rise of nationalism are not being analysed for two obvious reasons. One, methodological, that we do not wish to commit the fraud of reading history backwards and ascribing processes of cementing and welding that did not constitute the self or other perceptions of the architects of the historiography and social movements of the later period. The other, that it is not the same 'nationalism' that becomes the historically-constructed, politically-assertable organizational ability to mix and match traditionalist and modernist oppositions (to colonialism) in order that a modern 'national' might be formed with unity as its hallmark. It is a complex process whose complexities remain, no matter how hard we try to disentangle them by questioning and requestioning, accepting and rejecting simplistic portrayals of the solidarity principle of community or of identity, and the presence or absence of 'otherness' or the interest-orientedness of civil society. It is all of Partha Chatterjee's rendering of Galileo's 'Crooked Line'.

Preoccupation with the theme of unity is not the prerogative of the 'nation' or of a 'national movement'. Families, communities, religious entities, social and economic organizations (and one must remember that all of them are coterminous and not mutually exclusive), almost any coming together of people for declared or undeclared goals (commonly called living), must come to terms with just how much conflict and difference exists naturally among them, how much it will 'allow', and how much consensus and 'sameness' if at all, it can or would wish to inculcate. Neither the reasons for uniting nor the forms of doing so are likely to be better understood by transferring images from one epoch to another, or one region to another, or indeed one discourse to another. Understanding that they are different partly because they are differently located is also not enough. Within the same epoch 'unity' takes on alarmingly different forms that make one wonder about the content of the concept.

This essay is about unity as it has been addressed while being located at a level called 'national' as it related historically to the pivotal context of power—primarily as sketched by the realities of colonial rule in twentieth-century India. This brings us to the particular subjects at hand: nationalism in both its manifestations, the anti-colonial and the supposedly unifying pro-indigen, and the theme of unity. Not a small part of the exercise is a focus on those nationalists that have been held out as the vehicles or instruments through which the ideas about nation and unity have either been developed, given particular shapes, or quite simply been constructed into history. Unfortunately, and despite the repeated attempts by historians to advise caution in the handling of the theme of nationalism and the unification processes and programmes associated with it in the context of the state, simplistic portrayals of events (and persons) to the exclusion of, or the selective use of, discourse have led to repetitive pseudo-theoretical assertions about nationalism. Even as the idea of homogenizing histories stands well and truly ruptured, agendas that address commonalities, excessive consensus, great unities, common pasts and common futures continue to see chunks of time, of people and of activity as 'a whole stretch of history' created in common with many others.[3]

What is being reiterated here is not just the *absence* of any total harmony in the period and movement which has been claimed (through spokespersons) as an achievement towards unity and therefore, national strength. It is also being suggested that there is clearly an implied *acknowledgement* that multi-mindedness, multi-facetedness and near-disparateness are part and parcel of the playing out of this great epic 'struggle' that goes by so many different names, and that any imposition of symmetries can only be labelled intellectual subterfuge, even as it constitutes an exercise that seems to persist. Historiography has taken so many twists and turns that looking back and looking ahead are both equally problematic. And yet, located as firmly as most of us are in a time-warp, the greatest and most yielded to temptation is that of seeking reinforcement from a historical armoury for all the shots we want to fire in the here-and-now in tackling problems of nationhood, nationality, unity and solidarity. When social harmony is desired in the present it is sought to be derived from traditional ideas of a supposed stability from the past; when identity of interests is emphasized conflict is wished away as a non-existent feature of Indian tradition.

The task of elaborating the vicissitudes that have surrounded the problem of nationalism as a paradigm have been so comprehensively handled by Chatterjee that any repetition would not only be superfluous, it would be presumptuous. Plamenatz's 'types', Kohn's distinctions, Gellner, Kadourie, Davies, Anderson; the debate about nationalist thought and the framework of knowledge that is a post-

Enlightenment legacy offering rationality and progress as universal attributes which continue to pose fundamental problems of relativism—each and all of these are adequately placed as parts of the debate. Inquiries about what all these perceptions did to the ideas about nationalism against the background (actually foreground) of the 'Great Encounter' (if one can use a take-off from the Great Event) are also referred to both for the nineteenth century and more elaborately and germanely for the twentieth century. Various nationalist positions are analysed by Chatterjee in the quest for making some headway in disentangling the complexities that surround the idea about national thought in the Indian context. Through the positions of Gandhi and Nehru we are taken towards different possibilities for different purposes in the same historical period, suggestive of attempts to come to terms with the contradictions surrounding the problematic when possible, and to gloss over them when necessary.[4]

With an implied acknowledgement of all these clarifications emerge some understandings of the 'new nationalism' which, it is suggested, might be viewed as a political doctrine, as a cultural ideal and as a moral ideal, each of these claims underwriting the other. Nationalism can thus be broadly perceived either as civic nationalism or as ethnic nationalism. Civic nationalism suggests that regardless of race, colour, creed, gender, language or ethnicity, the nation should be composed of all those who subscribe to the nation's political creed. Ethnic nationalism asserts by contrast that a person's or a people's 'attachments' are inherited. It is the 'national community' that defines the individual, not the individual who defines the national community.

Ignatieff cites India as a prominent example of a region where ethnic nationalism has flourished while the state has been formally committed to civic (nationalistic) democracy.[5] The suggestion is also made that whereas ethnic nationalism may 'have more depth' than civic nationalism, it is also more authoritarian. The question that naturally arises again and again, as history and historiography both provide shifts of emphasis, is: which nationalisms pervade at what points in the episodic canvas of a striving for unity that goes by the name of Indian nationalism?

It is against these understandings that the problems and pitfalls that surround the depictions of both the history of Indian nationalism, and of the different and differing historical personae that have provided the reinforcement for so many portrayals and misportrayals of crucial ideas about this nationalism, have to be viewed. Difficulties arise in mixing and matching the many universalizing images of unity that spring from different premises and have different agendas, but have still taken on board an idea of the nation and of unifying processes that can address nation and non-nation. Gandhi and Nehru have indeed been the 'hot favourites' in providing visions of a united India, visions albeit in many ways diametrically opposed to one another and yet capable of being brought together into the nationalist agenda as if they were of one genre and as reconcilable as any could be.

The common feature of Gandhi's and Nehru's concerns was the wish to carry 'all' of the people of the geographic unit called India with them. Gandhi did not see the post-Enlightenment legacy as sacrosanct. In the event of conflict between the harmonies that morality or nature desired, and the universalisms and uniformities that reason required, Gandhi's choices was so obviously in favour of the former that such dilemmas as Nehru faced in coming to terms with 'differences' and searching for 'universal' justice through socialist programmes and legalistic guarantees did not arise for Gandhi.

But all the ground realities, even with such intricate working-out as Gandhi and Nehru offered, were still not covered, quite simply because 'realities' were less conducive to the universalizing imagery of either sort of total vision. Holistic visions, no matter how benignly all-encompassing or scientifically all-embracing, could still not take on board what the Indian context really and realistically had to offer. Cleavages may not have been destructively divisive but they were still cleavages. Even if the attempts for total visions were of a kind that took cognizance of culture-specificity, just how many specificities could they address (or not address if they wished for 'oneness')? Some things had to be worked more mathematically and more methodically than others that had all-encompassing agendas. So we turn to Patel.

Oddly enough the chief 'architect' of a politically united and integrated India in the anti-colonial chapter of the national movement is usually identified as being Patel: odd only because his is the least universalizing, encompassing, cohesive and consensual of all the leadership images of united India, sufficiently cognizant of differences to be called disunited and splintered, and sufficiently reliant on 'control' as a means of achieving declared goals to be called undemocratic. It is nevertheless celebrated as nationalistic and his contribution is still styled as unifying and integrative. How does one explain the paradox and how does the explanation make some contribution towards a better understanding of what Indian unity is all about? Several members of the Bharatiya Janata Party have in recent times declared emphatically that if they had to settle for a 'guru' amidst the acclaimed leadership that 'fought' for independence and for a united, free India in the first half of the century, it would be Patel, not Gandhi or Nehru, who would be their choice. His were truly Indian objectives and his too, the truly Indian programme. How and why this perception pervades almost across the board amidst a party viewed with dubiety and distrust by many in the country might be better understood after the role and style of the particular leader has been assessed and analysed. It might then emerge that it is the misinterpretations and misrepresentations of Patel's reckonings that are being made to serve politically motivated objectives.

It is suggested here that the (later) invocation of Patel's 'limited' view by nationalist 'shishyas' is related to his albeit unauthorized attempt to come to grips with the recognized tensions between the two nationalisms often discussed in any treatise on the subject (rational nationalism of the Enlightenment and cultural nationalism; or civic nationalism and ethnic nationalism). It is also suggested, by implication, that the political emphasis and style of some of the nationalist leaders of the period (here, Patel) demonstrate that as long as such specific processes as could make the connections between the two nationalisms were not adequately, appropriately (and somewhat laboriously) worked out, any preoccupation with one or the other nationalism was likely to produce distorted images of the coming together of a people for causes that might themselves have been misjudged. Patel tried to actuate some bridges between civic and ethnic nationalism by giving recognition to the smaller unities, the less-than-total unities that existed everywhere in society. Some crucial questions arise: How wide could the area be in which members of smaller unities made manoeuverings for unity? Was there a 'cement' that was used to effectively bind the less-than-total unities into something nearer total unity?

Patel's encounter is acknowledged as limited and untheorized: his attitude to conflict and 'unity', or unities, is being analysed with due recognition of its emphasis on political unity, the kind of unity that he was more concerned about and engaged with at the transitional moment referred to as the 'national movement' leading to Indian 'independence'. It was Patel's view that striving for 'sameness', 'equality', 'uniformity', 'homogeneity' in social, cultural and economic spheres was a fantasy, a fiction. Political unity was the nearest one could come to by way of 'national consensus' and that was all that might be worth pursuing. Perhaps that (political area) was all he was willing to grant to a nationalism that might demand a membership in which other unities (which he believed people held dear) would need to be subordinated if not actually erased. Apart from political unity, the other kinds of 'oneness' sought by Nehru and Gandhi for instance, constitutive but not accomodative of the many existing smaller 'unities', were to Patel unreal and unachievable and therefore superfluous, given the historical moment—that of the wresting of power from the imperial 'masters' and the structuring of a free, independent India.

The burden of the argument is that despite all the limelight thrown on the Gandhian and Nehruvian visions of unity against the backdrop of a general quest for the 'national', nationalistic, or socialistically nationalistic, it is the Patelian tradition of 'larger' unity—the coming together of acknowledged smaller unities—that has informed (and misinformed) the more prevalent postures and stances adopted in the realm of political conflict and political unity in 'modern' India. These postures, with their capacity to both facilitate and hinder any total or totalizing quest for unity, contribute more realistically to our historical understanding of a wide range of images of 'unity' that have been translated into political reality, whether these images are ideally palatable or not.

Gandhi looked upon conflict as peripheral disturbances in an underlying harmony and unity in society, disturbances that were perfectly capable of being handled and resolved, particularly by a *satyagrahi* whose capacity to discover and understand this underlying harmony was greater that that of an ordinary mortal. A *satyagrahi* achieved a heightened sensitivity and understanding from the rigorous discipline and training that he underwent simply by virtue of being a *satyagrahi*. To suffer and yield were inherent parts of a *satyagrahi's* training and the outcome was always conquest and victory; the suggestion being that confrontation, social or political, could be avoided if such a method was employed.

Close as he might have been to Gandhi, these were not images that Patel subscribed to. To understand the shape and direction of Patel's images of unity we need to understand the formation of his images of 'difference', of conflict and resolution (we might call it the 'small canvas' made up of smaller unities); and then, to observe the translation or transfer of these images to the wider political arena (the 'larger canvas' with larger unities), and finally to the resulting end-product—a supposedly desired national unity. Is there a distinct tradition of some kind? If so, does it have some historical significance?

The small canvas will provide evidence of successes and failures in the quest for united action (in *satyagraha* campaigns); the larger canvas will see the lessons learnt from the small canvas put to such use as would achieve the maximum that was possible as national unity, i.e. political unity.

I

Superior Patidar, moffusil lawyer and municipal councillor—all three attributes had the cumulative effect of inculcating in Patel such qualities as enterprise, maneuverability and the ability to manipulate procedures and persons. Migrants over a large time-span, Patidars did not come to particular areas as rural elites; nor were they able to displace existing elites (brahmanical landlords) in the areas to which they migrated. Literature about Patidars particularly highlights their ability to transform from ordinary cultivators to enterprising farmers and elevate their socio-economic status by redefining a distinctive 'Patidarness' which differentiated them from other kanbis, and also produced categories of inferior and superior Patidars. Averse to ritualistic religion (from having an excessively religious father) and skilled with an understanding of community problems (from observing a pragmatic community advisor in his mother), Patel learnt the art of social handling for specific ends and explicit purposes.

Patel joined Gandhi as an apprentice rather than a disciple; there seems little evidence of a 'guru-shishya' relationship at any point. Only a few years younger than Gandhi, Patel approached him with measured reluctance and with most of his basic ideas on society and politics fairly clearly formulated. Three *satyagraha* campaigns in Gujarat—Kheda, Borsad and Bardoli—and the Flag *satyagraha* in Nagpur reveal the tactics and strategy of a political 'tailor' stitching the coat according to the material he had available.[6] The first rough-and-ready rule was a like-mindedness that might be translated simply into an agreement on immediate goals and the methods to be adopted for their procurement. A minimum similarity of approach was likely to provide an overall reduction in dissimilarities, thus reducing the area of conflict. Such disagreements as did appear were ironed out by giving the dissident the opportunity to either fall in line or quit; both choices honourable enough.

What needed to be worked out first was just how much 'like-mindedness' was needed for the supposedly anti-colonial and nationalist agenda. Starting out with some similarity of approach might result in an overall reduction in dissimilarities, assuming that other disagreements and disputes would more than likely appear along the way. Working through groups and 'followers' who shared the same regional and community background was considered one way of making the task of weeding out recalcitrants relatively easy.

A second guideline was the building of a structural framework that would hold up the scheme for achieving immediate goals by facilitating the easy exercise of authority and the provision of adequate feedback. Areas that posed problems of cooperation, unity or discipline could either be compelled to cooperate (the ways were subtle) or simply abandoned (a 'punishment' that turned out to be more damaging for groups or areas than blatant coercion). Those who 'cooperated' learnt the inherent value of falling in line and of following the 'Sardar' unquestioningly. They constituted the 'team'. In some *satyagraha* campaigns, with an easily identifiable adversary—the colonial state—and a band of ready followers, unity was easy to achieve. Others posed problems.

The *satyagraha* carried out outside Patel's home province— the Nagpur Flag *satyagraha*—threw up challenges that perplexed and frustrated Patel for a while. The province was a Hindi and Marathi (as opposed to Gujarati) speaking area; it was a Swarajist stronghold. Patel's initial response to Nagpur is worth noting: 'For the first two days nobody would come near me. Nagpur is absolutely cold. There is no response and I had to rely on outside help.'[7] Patel brought bands of his own followers from Gujarat to keep up the average of fifty volunteers available for arrest. He then requested Rajendra Prasad, with whom he worked closely, to send a steady stream of volunteers to Nagpur from Bengal and Bihar (Prasad's 'home' province). The movement received its sustenance from leaders and their followers in other regions; it was a first lesson in national networking. It was also an opportunity to observe how disadvantaged one could be, given a dearth of like-minded people, at a time when concerted action was strategically necessary: 'If only the people are united, it would be possible to make

214

the government yield within a week. But here we have an orchestra in which every player plays whatever tune he likes.'[8] The next exercise was conducted with military-like planning: a 'Commander' (Mohanlal Pandya) at the apex, a 'headquarters' at Ras and eighteen centres of control in different areas. Existing ruling elites brought in the support and meetings were conducted community-wise. Patanvadias and Baraiyas (who had turned dacoits) were treated more sympathetically than the downtrodden Ujliparaj and Kaliparaj. Appeals made to farmers emphasized their kshatriya status and their prosperous jagirdari and thakur backgrounds. The lower castes were accused of ignorance and lacking in community zeal, and appeals for unity addressed to them were considered fruitless.

The legendary no-tax campaign in Bardoli was limited in its appeal: Patidars came together to display a 'superior' status; vanias, with a financial stake in the land and in the crops trade and therefore anxious about their links with government officials, were embarrassed by the consequences of non-payment of revenue. Anavil brahmins were reluctant to support the movement, Parsis were cool and so were the Muslims. Dublas, constituting half the population of the *taluka*, were debtors and workers and saw little reason to fight. Patel's appeal was directed towards Patidars as a community and to the 6–25 acre group of landowners.[9]

Limited support was not the reason for anxiety; it was what determined the withholding of support on the part of a group of person that needed different strategic responses. Personal ambition was unacceptable and harshly handled. Community links, on the other hand, could scarcely be brushed aside and were tactfully worked around. Ideological postures, grand theories, universalizing missions brought out a political impatience on Patel's part and we know how these were handled to arrive at a unity that was nationalistic without being national. When Bose was dropped from the Working Committee in 1931 and some provinces were not represented, Gandhi voiced Patel's reservations: 'If you want work from Sardar Patel you must not put in any man on the Working Committee who might strike a discordant note.'[10] The unity of discipline was always achieved with 'orders' and 'obedience'. A crucial strategy was that of giving assurances to interest-groups. The assurance of the return of lands forfeited during *satyagraha* campaigns, and supportive comfort to mill-owners of Ahmedabad and Bombay that the movement for *swadeshi* did not imply the closing of the Bombay Cloth Market, provide evidence of some concern to protect allies. In a statement communicated to the Bombay merchants through Purshotamdas Thakurdas, a liberal reading of boycott rules was suggested: 'What Congress wants is, as is well known, the stoppage of import or sale of foreign cloth. As far as I am aware even the Bombay PCC is not against the sale of mill-made cloth.'[11] Assurances were also provided to merchants who had large stocks of foreign cloth. While dispelling any hopes the merchants might have had of selling such cloth later, after the boycott movements were suspended, Patel was still able to guarantee to them that if they had not already taken such cloth to Delhi to burn it, they ought to make an inventory of their stocks and seal them; they would be paid back every penny when a national government was established in the country. General *hartals*, he went on to say, were to be treated as symbols of protest and not as impediments to commerce and trade.

The decade of the thirties gives a clearer idea of what eventually crystallized as the idea of national unity. Discipline was used interchangeably with 'unity' alongside 'limits to democracy of thought and action'. Changes in the Congress constitution, the Working Committee, the powers of the (Congress) president and the general tendency towards centralization (all supposedly at Patel's behest), led observers (including the British officials) to believe that Patel had been given too free a hand by Gandhi and that 'the tail was now wagging the body'. Hell-bent on achieving the one goal that had received assent from most groups—capture of the legislature and the government—Patel began his programme for a unity styled in his image, not as rhetoric but as reality. Political activity itself would constitute the vehicular goal for getting the national act together. That would be the 'one voice', rather than any abstract idealism or ideological objective.

'The Congress today is absolutely of one mind', Patel asserted at the time of the 1937 elections. 'Discipline for unity', 'suppression for unity' were legitimized as methods for achieving greater goals. But what kind of unity? This is where the contradictory perceptions of Patel's goals and methods can be observed. As overseer of the functioning of Congress ministries in the provinces and of the conduct of agitation in the states, Patel did not in fact demonstrate any vision of a long-term plan for 'greater unity' or to contain differences and diversities. But, and this is crucial, while allowing for intermediary groups' affiliations as points of focus for mobilization or association, there is

216

nothing to suggest that he had any particular value for caste, group, religious or regional loyalty over and above the wider loyalty that was being sought at the time, or for that time. Smaller loyalties were neither sought to be demolished nor wished away; the idea was to use them without allowing them to become ends in themselves. Patel believed this was sound policy: it would achieve political unity and national independence; it also led to group rivalries and an insecurity in which denominations smaller than the national might become assertive.

This sandwich decade (the 1930s)—between two supposedly vision-oriented decades—was characterized by the immediacy of the political need for a structural framework that would house most of Congress's plans and policies, and a future nation's power and organization. The architect of this structural framework was Patel. But what about larger goals, the wider visions associated with socio-economic issues? Nehru once wrote to Patel that Congress had done little by way of presenting visionary goals or national programmes to the country: 'They simply cannot function in a big way'. Patel's retort was that purposeful political behaviour and power and organization in and of the polity could not be accomplished simply by 'creating a lot of enthusiasm' (as Nehru was prone to doing). Ground realities could not be wished away or pushed away: one could either work with them or against them. Patel preferred to do the former. 'In the midst of a great struggle if every soldier wants to think and act for himself the war cannot be carried or much won . . . we must accept some limits to democracy of thought and action.'[12] The first experience of Congress as government, in 1937, endeared many; it also alienated many. To the extent that it was a success story meant for British consumption, it was also a failure domestically. Congress might and power had been exhibited for all to see; that had one kind of impact on the colonial power and quite another on rival political groups whose antennae now went up out of fear, jealousy or plain insecurity.[13]

Political activity in the princely Indian states offers an insight into the internal relations between different power groups within the states. Patel drew upon this in negotiating with such 550-odd states to enable the Congress to capture the initiative of bringing them under its wing. The methods varied according to the circumstances and equations within each state. Mysore and Rajkot provided the opening lessons. The Kathiawar states set an easy pattern. Others like Limbdi who resisted were cajoled to move. Patel organized the boycott of Limbdi cotton—a commodity on which the Limbdi merchants, and through them the state, thrived. The Limbdi Prajamandal executed the boycott which was supported by Bombay magnates; Patel arranged that a committee would ensure that not one bale of Limbid cotton would reach the outside market. Even when the Congress Ministries resigned the boycott continued; Bombay cotton brokers had every intention of staying on the right side of a party and leader that had every chance of returning to power.[14]

II

For all their shared participation in a 'national movement' the essence of Indian 'nationhood' meant different things to different people, including those leaders who pooled in their resources and acumen in a supposedly common 'national' cause. Unfortunately, this difference was both quantitatively and qualitatively graded in terms of the intensity of an overarching nationalist feeling, and interpreted as less or more 'national' depending on how wide was the net that nation- al unity was able to cast. In this gradation those nationalists with prog- rammes that had an all-encompassing social support acquired a status superior to those whose appeal was directed at smaller unities, even when the object and objective of the particular action went beyond the smaller configuration.

During the phase in which the devolution of power was actu- ally worked out among and between the different parties, the large visionary goals of Gandhi and Nehru seemed inadequate as blueprints or agendas. They were unacceptable to those groups and entities that had been seen as invisible in the quest for greater visions. By March 1946 the Congress Working Committee had appointed Azad, Patel and Nehru to negotiate with the cabinet delegation. Patel had become the gauge and measure of the attitude of the Congress on political matters. This included that vital dimension of the political—the distribution of power. On the parity question Wavell and his colleagues believed that it was really Patel who was vehemently opposed to it. The reality that Patel's word could be an impediment irked the viceroy and his team.[15]

Any analysis about total or less-than-total unities in 'modern' India, particularly against the background of attaining independence or freedom, would be incomplete without due attention to that most dramatic and vital happening referred to as the partition of India, and encapsulating as many aspects of unity and disunity as one can envi-

sage. This is not the place to recount all the details of this unique, un-
paralleled and outlandish occurrence which involved the uprooting of
over ten million people from their homes to seek refuge in 'the other'
dominion. Questions of unity and nation came up in a real, tangible,
down-to-earth way, and working out the minutiae that accompanied
the occurrence was Patel's job. Not even Nehru, even as he referred to
Patel as 'the strongest pillar in the Cabinet', really understood the tight-
rope walk that was called for during the period when India supposedly
redeemed its pledge with destiny.[16] Transporting people across borders, getting adequate escorts for trains carrying vulnerable groups of
people to safe areas so that incidents of slaughter (even within Indian
boundaries) could be minimized, working out details about how refugees should be housed and whether houses vacated by Muslims in
Muslim areas should be occupied by other Muslims (as Nehru desired)
or not, division of assets and liabilities, and myriads of seemingly mundane but vital tasks—these formed the agenda of the departments Patel
was in charge of. The nature of this task was beyond 'isms', beyond
euphoric slogans and beyond spiritual or moral appeals:

> From morning till night these days my time is here fully occupied
> with the talks of woe and atrocities which reach me through Hindu
> and Sikh refugees from all over west Pakistan . . . the Press has also
> been prominently featuring these accounts with the result that
> public feeling is greatly exercised . . . people are openly clamouring
> as to why Muslims are allowed to go about in peace openly in the
> streets in Delhi and other towns, why there are Muslims at all in the
> police and civil administration . . . the people are simply not in a
> mood to listen to reason.[17]

Patel's response was a call for firm action, a request that the
Pakistan government be asked to 'make immediate attempts to put
down lawlessness with a strong hand', the strong hand being 'used not
only against the lawless elements of the general population but also
mischief makers in the various services, military, police or administrative'. Nehru toured the Punjab (west and east) on a reassurance
mission, believing that would help to calm the atmosphere. His
message to Patel was:

> Situation requires reciprocal and cooperative handling by both
> Central and Provincial governments. . . . Our joint tours have done

much good . . . everywhere Liaquat Ali Khan and Nishtar have delivered strong and good speeches. We are evolving big organizations on either side to deal with problems facing us.[18]

Patel meanwhile continued to be barraged with complaints form all sides. Yadavendra Singh, the maharaja of Patiala, expressed disillusionment on behalf of the Sikhs: there was a malicious attempt to 'paint them black', he wrote to the Sardar, and propagandists outside India held Sikhs responsible for much of the bloodshed. Reminding Patel about the promises of support that the Sikhs had been given, the maharaja pointed out that 'the Sikhs have practically been crippled economically and politically'. He urged the Sardar that something substantial needed to be done 'for this small community' and 'the immediate and powerful support of the Government of India' should be made available forthwith. Patel responded reassuringly.[19]

Many of the basic differences between Nehru and Patel surfaced, in fact, at this juncture of Indian political functioning. The sheer volume of business that had to be carried out relating to issues of majority-minority groups, fears about domination and indeed the nitty-gritty related to communal disturbances were by far the most sticky part of 'the great divide'. Constant complaints from both, indeed all three communities affected by the disturbances had to be handled each day and every day for months on end. Patel did often feel that it was not enough for the new leadership to make moral, spiritual, ethical or other kinds of high-minded speeches to bring a modicum of efficiency while fostering togetherness (unity?) among the population: 'No matter how we might wish that officials should behave immaculately without showing any partisanship based on communal or religious lines he wrote to Nehru,

> . . . we have to take note of the fact that they are human beings and it is likely that in the case of a few officials here and there their inward sympathies get the better of their discretion and they indulge in objectionable behaviour. The duty of public men of standing is, as I have made it clear to Congressmen visiting me with such vague imputations, to expose such men and to lead concrete evidence to prove their contentions. Indeed, I am first asked to suspend them and then to collect evidence. It is obvious that such an action would apart from being unfair and unjust completely throw the administration out of gear.[20]

Patel had to live down allegations of communal and religious prejudice from several directions just as Jinnah was subjected to an oft-repeated criticism that partition was the result of his vanity, disappointed ambition and intransigence. The most common criticism levied against Patel as a national leader is that he had no long-term vision that could embrace all of India, and no method that could address all Indians in the same way. It seems crucial to remember that Patel did not see himself as a visionary if 'vision' meant having a dream of an (almost) all-inclusive 'total' unity called India that did not take into account the realities of a highly differentiated, diverse society with all manner of groups and groupings whose interests were more real than any larger entity or unity. Such realities Patel believed, were hardly likely to disappear simply by being wished away by means of universalizing, equalizing magic-wands. Egalitarian goals, uniformities of procedure, universalisms—Patel saw no inherent virtue in any of these. People were different, and differentiated; between the smallest groupings and the largest (the nation-state) was a range of groupings, social and economic. In all the three decades that he worked as the architect of a meticulously constructed ('nationalistic') power structure (without which he believed no national goal could be accomplished) he harnessed support through prevalent interests and existing sub-groups. Somehow (and he decided 'how' by the measure of political unity) they had to be inserted into the political structure that he sought to build. They could scarcely be glossed over.

There is an ambivalence about the messages that might be invoked from Patel's unification policies and strategies. The same utterances and representations have, in fact, produced contradictory impulses—the need for all-encompassing national unity as well as the vitality of smaller (group) unities—both variously interpreted. And these contradictory impulses have, in turn, been further (mis) represented and misused to corroborate methods and styles that might be high-handed and indeed undemocratic, even as they profess to be 'majoritarian'. From these impulses have emerged a range of positions that depend on just how much free play might be permitted to groups and associations that take into account the nuanced cultural reality that is India, far more effectively than any overarching institution (the nation-state) bashing that is the current preoccupation of many of us.

Patel's politics brought to the surface a host of questions that face us historically and conceptually. An important component of the current debates that surround pluralism, secularism, federalism and even fundamentalism in our society is what idea of unity—abstract and real—might be 'inserted' into the issues that surround these concepts. Perhaps an overemphasis on 'inserted unities' has produced greater disunities, or assertions of disunities, in many parts of our freshly fractured societies. These questions assume an understandable importance fifty years on. An expected result is the bashing of the liberal state for ignoring or turning a blind eye to the not-so-tidy realities that form a crucial part of a society's coming together for socio-economic or political ends.

A word of caution about this dehomogenizing process seems in order. The 'unreality' of excessive national integration has indeed brought about an increasingly communitarian focus that would wish to expose and rupture the liberal state's claims as much as it would wish to assert an agenda positioned in socio-economic realities (that are a facility for some and a burden for others). It would be presumptuous for this non-total focus to assume the 'discovery' of the most appropriate way of engaging with the people of India as they are (or were). Some 'national'/'nationalist' leaders (of 'nationalist struggle' fame) did, in fact, look at Indians (with a small 'i') perceiving themselves as belonging to less-than-total unities. They viewed the desirable 'total unities' advocated by such actors as Nehru as pipe-dreams that would end in rude awakenings. Some political architects of yesterday (Patel is a prominent example) did indeed address a many-layered India as it was—regions, communities, groups (interest and other)—albeit politically, and rejected the universalisms of the radicals and the reactionaries. It is not difficult to see the ease with which they might have all too easily become icons for those who wish to demonstrate the irrelevance of a colonially imposed liberalism and its universalizing individualism.

The recognition and acceptance of smaller unities instead of a preoccupation with a quest for larger unities is not without its share of dangers. The earlier protagonists that demonstrated a degree of (political) success with such workable (smaller) unities are held up as exemplary leadership-model material. Patel is one such model. The leaders of particular political parties today hold out Patel's idea of 'unity without uniformity' as the kind of unity (and unification programme) that might be able to carry with it the essence of a larger multicultural tradition which they would wish to project as the tradi-

222

tion of the majority community, and which Patel is believed to have sought. There is a yearning in some quarters for another Patel.

This paper has sought to place Patel's ideas about Indian unity in its contextual and ideological framework—the anti-colonial national movement. It has also sought to suggest that there might be room for manoeuvre, misrepresentation and distortion in receiving and then transmitting the signals sent out by the Patelian tradition of (a less-than-total) unity; and that such misrepresentations are more than likely today, given the climate in which smaller (not inferior) loyalties, unities, interests, affiliations and allegiances are encouraged as part of the non-liberal or anti-liberal armoury that would wish to discard tow legacies—the liberal and the radical—without actually working out how the tensions between these multifarious positionings would be handled. And now that smaller unities have raised their heads seemingly over and above larger unities, the unresolved conflicts, tensions and contradictions have re-emerged.

So what does that do to our building of theoretical frameworks for nation and unity and national unity? As Chatterjee suggests, the colonial import of 'subjecthood' posed problems in converting to 'citizenship' of a nation, and Indians in colonial India constructed their national identities 'with a different narrative';[21] and this narrative 'continues to unfold to this day against the grain of that other narrative of bourgeois individualism'.

The dilemma of the devil and the deep sea remains: the fair share of dangers alluded to above are not difficult to perceive. Between the clinical unreality of larger unities such as the nation (state) and the flesh-and-blood reality of smaller unities, the 'person' or member of either entity (as opposed to the 'individual' of the liberal tradition) could be subjected to as many oppressions. The choice would only be whose oppression is more acceptable: the state's or the community's. And in the choice of the smaller unity being given pride of place as equal to or greater than any larger unity of (state) proportions, the process of selection itself might be arbitrary—between kin, clan, tribe, caste, occupation, region, religion, or race. Patel picked and chose the groups that he wished to focus on for achieving the politically motivated national unity that he considered imperative at the time. The anti-colonial backdrop helped his style of inclusion and exclusion. With that backdrop gone the groups that got excluded have their own stories to tell.

223

Notes and References

[1] Partha Chatterjee, *Nationalist Thought and the Colonial World. A Derivative Discourse*, Oxford University Press, Delhi, 1986.

[2] E.J. Hobsbawm, *Nations and Nationalism since 1780: Programme Myth and Reality*, Cambridge University Press, Cambridge, 1990; Ernest Gellner, *Nations and Nationalism*, Basil Blackwell, Oxford, 1983.

[3] Sudipto Kaviraj, 'The Imaginary Institution of India' in Partha Chatterjee and Gyanendra Pandey, eds., *Subaltern Studies VII*, Oxford University Press, Delhi, 1992.

[4] Chatterjee, *Nationalist Thought and the Colonial World*.

[5] M. Ignatieff, *Blood and Belonging: Journeys into the New Nationalism*, Chatto and Windus, London, 1993; See also John Plamenatz, 'Two Types of Nationalism', in Eugene Kamenka, ed., *Nationalism: The Nature and Evolution of an Idea*, Edward Arnold, London, 1976.

[6] Detailed accounts and analyses of these *satyagraha* campaigns can be found in Rani D. Shankardass, *Vallabhbhai Patel: Power and Organization in Indian Politics*, Orient Longman, New Delhi, 1988.

[7] Patel to Nehru,1 August 1923, *Jawaharlal Nehru Papers*, Nehru Memorial Museum and Library.

[8] Patel to Mahadev Desai, Nagpur File, *Patel Papers*, Navajivan, Ahmedabad.

[9] See R.D. Shankardass, 'Spokesman for the Peasantry: The Case of Vallabhbhai Patel and Bardoli', in *Studies in History*, Volume 2, No. 1, 1986; Shirin Mehta, *The Peasantry and Nationalism: The Story of Bardoli*, Manohar, Delhi, 1984.

[10] *Bombay Chronicle*, 2 April 1931, p. 1.

[11] Patel to Purshotamdas Thakurdas, letter published in *Bombay Chronicle*, 23 July 1930.

[12] Patel at a meeting in Matunga, *Bombay Chronicle*, 2 October 1934, p. 12.

[13] See Rani D. Shankardass, *The First Congress Raj: Provincial Autonomy in Bombay*, Macmillan, New Delhi, 1982.

[14] Files 47/1 and 47/2, *Patel Papers*.

[15] Wavell's note of an interview with Birla, 6 June 1946; and note of 12 June 1946; N. Mansergh, and P. Moon, eds., *Transfer of Power, VII*, London, HMSO, 1970–84.

[16] Nehru to Patel, 1 August 1947, *Sardar Patel's Correspondence, volume 4*, Navajivan, Ahmedabad, 1972, p. 530.

[17] Patel to Nehru, 2 September 1947, ibid., p. 318.

[18] 2 September 1947, ibid., pp. 319–20.

[19] Yadavendra Singh, Maharaja of Patiala to Patel, 2 November 1947, ibid., pp. 322–33. See also letter of 5 September 1947, pp. 324–26.

[20] Patel to Nehru, 12 October 1947, ibid., p. 299.

[21] Partha Chatterjee, *The Nation and Its Fragments*, Oxford University Press, Delhi, 1993.

Foreshadowing 'Quit India'
The Congress in Uttar Pradesh
1939–1941

Gyanesh Kudaisya

As the curtain comes down on the twentieth century and the countdown begins towards the new millenium, historians will take stock of what this century has meant for India and Indians. To name a few things we did in these hundred years: we forged a 'nation' through an epic struggle against colonial rule, became self-sufficient in food production, introduced Westminister-style democratic institutions; began producing *swadeshi* satellites, missiles, supercomputers and nuclear energy, and are now committed to becoming a major player in the globalization sweepstakes. On the debit side the record is equally dramatic: we partitioned ourselves, increased our population five-fold; fought three wars with Pakistan and one with China; allowed corruption, political violence and terrorism to undermine our polity; demolished a mosque; and subjected our natural and built environment to unprecedented exploitation and degradation.

In bringing about these outcomes several individuals and institutions have been instrumental. One such extraordinary player on the Indian scene throughout this century has been the Congress party. Indeed, political scientists have been writing about the resilience and durability of this unique political entity since the 1950s. Historians too have written persuasively about the remarkable causes and campaigns which the Congress has spearheaded in different contexts. In a sense the extraordinary career of the Congress and its peculiar brand of 'consensual' politics has, to an extent, been reflected in the writings and researches of Professor Ravinder Kumar in the mature phase of his own professional career. His seminal essays on the Rowlatt *satyagraha*, for instance, illuminated the circumstances in which the Congress emerged as a pan-Indian mass organization. His researches on politics in Bombay city in the 1920s and 1930s further explored some of the

225

dilemmas faced by the Congress vis-à-vis its constituents. His editing of one of the volumes of *A Centenary History of the Indian National Congress* and of the documents relating to momentous events of 1947 in a volume of the *Towards Freedom* series are further instances of this *affaire d'amour*. Not the least, his custodianship of the rich AICC papers during his years at the NMML and his ongoing involvement with the *Jawaharlal Nehru Selected Works* further underscore his continuing interest in the theme. With these thoughts, it is hoped that this essay on one of the lesser known, yet one of the most remarkable of the 'Gandhian' campaigns which the Congress has ever espoused, may be a suitable theme for an offering in this *festschrift*.

The Quit India movement of 1942 is widely recognized as the most dramatic of the campaigns mounted by the Congress against British Raj.[1] Official statistics give an indication of the violence that characterized the campaign as well as the scale on which it confronted the Raj. In the months following August 1942 the British were faced with a popular revolt in which over 91,000 people were arrested. Over 208 police stations, 332 railway stations and 945 post offices were destroyed in attacks on government property all over India. There were 664 bomb explosions and several thousand incidents of cutting of telecommunication wires. On 534 occasions civilian or military authorities fired upon crowds and at least 1,060 people were killed in these encounters. The British had to deploy fifty-seven and a half army battalions to restore their control and to stamp out the challenge posed by the Quit India movement. While there is consensus among historians about the dramatic and violent nature of the revolt, there are sharp differences about the role of the Congress in the direction and course of the movement. It has been suggested that the Congress organization in the period following the resignation of its provincial ministries in October 1939 had been in disarray. The leadership was confused about its political objectives in the changed context of the war, while widespread economic hardship and growing popular militancy acted to put pressure on the Congress to either seize the opportunity to confront the British or to be consigned to the proverbial dustbin of history. Gandhi, as an astute political leader, chose the path of total confrontation rather than total oblivion.

This essay looks at the activities of the Congress in the period 1939–41 in its 'political heartland'—the province of Uttar Pradesh (henceforth UP, which prior to 1947 was called the United Province of

Agra and Oudh). It focuses upon a remarkable, yet one of the least known campaigns undertaken by the Congress—the Individual Civil Disobedience movement—to look at the strength which the Congress organization enjoyed at the grassroots, the nature of the campaign of individual *satyagraha* as it evolved over the months, and the popular response it elicited. It then considers the manner in which all these foreshadowed the Quit India movement.

War, Politics and Congress Organization

The political context for the Congress was set by the outbreak of World War II in September 1939. An immediate outcome was the resignation of the Congress ministries in the provinces in protest against the viceroy's decision to commit the country to the war without consulting Indian political opinion. In UP the Govind Ballabh Pant-led Congress ministry walked out of office and the governor assumed charge of the administration under Section 93 of the Government of India Act of 1935. Meanwhile, negotiations were initiated by the viceroy, Lord Linlithgow, with Congress leaders to find a solution to the political deadlock and muster support for the war effort. Accounts of the lengthy and fruitless negotiations which took place between the Congress leadership and the viceroy in late 1939 and early 1940 are available elsewhere and need not detain us.[2]

Meanwhile, the UP government, under a new governor, Sir Maurice Hallett, geared itself to deal with its new wartime responsibilities.[3] The Congress leaders, on their part, concentrated on preparing themselves for another round of confrontation with the Raj, as negotiations with the British proved futile. Much of Congress activity after its resignation from office centred upon organizational renewal and discipline. In January 1940, when the grand annual ritual of 'Independence Day' was celebrated, the directives to subordinate Congress committees clearly emphasized the need to maintain discipline. Nehru, president of the UP Congress Committee (UPCC), told Congressmen that 'no effort should be made by Congressmen anywhere to organize a strike for any purpose on that day'. Congress activities were to be confined to *prabhat pheris*, flag-hoisting ceremonies and meetings. The highlight of the celebrations was Congress meetings in the larger towns and a hectic tour of the province by Subhas Bose. Bose, in his tour of about a dozen cities, met with enthusiastic audiences. The largest meeting took place in Kanpur where Congressmen took out a procession of over 30,000 people. Considerable enthusiasm was reported in the larger towns, particularly on the part of students, while in smaller towns and rural areas celebrations were poorly attended.[4]

After these celebrations, most of the activities of Congressmen were directed at organizing district-level political conferences. In early February 1940, the Sitapur Political Conference was organized at Mahmudabad and the Sultanpur District Conference at Kadipur. In Sitapur, uniformed Congress volunteers took Acharya Narendra Deva, the president of the Conference, in a large procession through the town. The Sultanpur Conference was presided over by Sri Prakasa, MLA, and the main speaker at both the places was Rafi Ahmed Kidwai.[5] The later part of February 1940 was dominated by the proceedings of the Ramgarh Congress session where a sizeable section of the UP delegates voted for M.N. Roy in the presidential contest.[6] Elections also took place for office-bearers of the UPCC, and the voting, as was to be expected, was along the lines of the left–right divide.[7] After the Ramgarh session, organizational activity by the Congress was stepped up. In late February 1940, for instance, district political conferences were organized in Gorakhpur and Ballia. In Gorakhpur the chief speakers were Nehru and Pant, while in Ballia Rafi Ahmed Kidwai and Sampurnanand were the principal figures. Both these conferences were well attended, and at Ballia Sampurnanand was taken through the city in an impressive procession.[8] This method of reinvigorating district-level organization by holding political conferences was pursued in the weeks to come.[9] Intelligence reports testified that these conferences were well attended and their proceedings were usually marked by much organizational activity and vigour.[10]

By early April 1940, preparations by Congressmen for another round of Civil Disobedience were in full swing. The UPCC was converted into a 'Satyagraha Council'. A series of circulars were issued to the District Congress Committees (DCCs) giving directions about the enlistment of volunteers and asking subordinate committees to send bands of activists into rural areas to explain the Congress's policy towards the war. The formal 'Satyagraha Pledge' which was to be taken by all volunteers offering Civil Disobedience was sent to the DCCs. Further, all subordinate committees were instructed to convert themselves into 'satyagraha committees' and to submit fortnightly reports of 'active' and 'passive' satyagrahis to the PCC.[11] In overall terms, much energy was displayed by the provincial Congress organization. For instance, between March and May 1940, tours and visits by 222 Congressmen from other provinces were organized in the province, more than 884 large meetings were held, and the PCC issued over 75,000 notices and pamphlets. It was reported, moreover, that the target of holding at least one meeting in every village was being fulfilled and that spinning centres were functioning satisfactorily in over ten districts.[12]

Much of this activity was coordinated by the PCC headquarters. This was reputed to be the largest and best organized provincial Congress Committee in India, with a paid staff of over 97 persons. Below the PCC there were 48 well-organized DCCs and over 2,000 subordinate (town and mofussil) committees. This entire organization was now mobilized to 'prepare' for another campaign of Civil Disobedience by enlisting volunteers willing to offer *satyagraha* at a time and in a manner which Gandhi would prescribe.

Active enlistment of *satyagrahis* began in April 1940 when the Congress 'national week' was celebrated. By the end of the month, all district-level committees had converted themselves into '*satyagraha* committees' and, according to intelligence reports, more than 5,000 *satyagrahis* has already been enrolled.[13] In its instructions to the UPCC, the AICC directed that, 'in recording the names of *satyagrahis*, there need be no anxiety to add to numbers'.[14] Emphasis was to be placed upon the moral quality of the *satyagrahis*, rather than on sheer numbers. So well prepared, however, was the UPCC that it could report that the number of 'pledged *satyagrahis*', that is those who had signed the '*satyagraha* pledge', had well exceeded 15,000 by the end of May 1940.[15]

Each DCC was at the same time asked to develop its own elaborate plan for the forthcoming *satyagraha*. Meerut district was thus divided by its DCC into fifty circles, each comprising thirty villages, each of which was placed under the charge of a trained organizer. The city itself was organized into six wards, each headed by a '*satyagraha* supervisor'.[16] Similarly, the Aligarh DCC divided its district into sixteen *kendras* (centres) each containing five or six Congress *mandals* (units). Each *kendra* was put in the charge of a *sardar* (leader) to lead a team of twenty to twenty-five *satyagrahis*. Their duties during the campaign were to be maintenance of 'order', supervision of Congress work and collection of subscriptions.[17] By the summer of 1940, the Congress provincial organization, even in remote villages, was fully geared to the project of another Civil Disobedience campaign against the government.

All this activity was supported by other important developments. After Congress's resignation from office, it had embarked upon the enlistment of 'volunteers' (as distinct from *satyagrahis*). These volunteers were uniformed members of para-Congress bodies like the Seva Dal, and their main duty was to help control crowds during meetings and processions and to train young recruits. Intelligence sources claimed that during the December 1937 deliberations of the PCC, it had been decided that at least 100,000 volunteers were to be enlisted in the province by March 1940.[18] By early 1940 B.N. Pande, a Seva Dal leader, could claim that 28,000 volunteers had already been enrolled.[19] Training camps were regularly organized in a number of districts. At the Maharajgang camp in Gorakhpur district, it was reported that efforts were being made to raise 10,000 volunteers in the district alone. At Sandila in Hardoi district, a 'Congress Sardar's Training Camp' was organized with courses in drill and crowd control, with each participant paying a fee of Rs 12.[20] In Allahabad, local Congressmen decided to revive the 'Kesari Dal' with the object of organizing Hindu communities and depressed classes. Similarly, in Bulandshahr a branch of the Mahabir Dal was organized by the local Congress and about 150 volunteers were enlisted.[21] By March 1940 training camps were reported to be functioning in Ballia, Dehradun and Ghazipur. While most of the volunteer activity took place because of the initiative shown by Congressmen, a number of instances were reported of local initiatives.[22] This momentum of organizing training camps for volunteers was continued during the early part of 1940. For instance, by the first week of March 1940 itself, three training camps in the remote villages of Agra, Ballia and Bara Banki districts were functioning. Here Congress volunteers, as elsewhere, received training in drill, methods of crowd control, first aid and even fire-fighting.[23]

In public speeches one of the key themes of Congress speakers was that Congress volunteers should now be prepared to maintain order, in view of the increasing wartime difficulties of the British Raj. For instance, at the Mathura District Political Conference, Shri Krishna Dutta Paliwa, the UPCC president, condemned the official scheme of enlisting civic guards as part of the Congress's anti-war propaganda. Instead, he urged the audience to enlist as Congress volunteers to prepare for the disorders that would result from the impending British collapse. A resolution was passed calling for the organization of a force of 5,000 volunteers to safeguard the 'internal security' of the district.[24] Similarly, in Gonda a training camp of uniformed volunteers was set up by Kunwar Raghavendra Pratap Singh to provide a defence force for the 'suppression of lawlessness'.[25] Intelligence reports of the deliberations of the Provincial Congress Volunteers' Board confirmed this tendency to organize volunteer bodies for maintaining 'order'. The Board resolved to organize a 'national defence force' in every town and village for the protection of the public in the event of internal disorder and reportedly set a target of 100,000 volunteers.[26] Soon afterwards there came reports of attempts by Congressmen to form branches of such volunteer armies right across the province; in Allahabad even 'responsible' Congressmen like Pandit Krishna Kant Malaviya and Purshottamdas Tandon made speeches calling for the organization of volunteers along paramilitary lines.[27]

Such vigorous volunteer recruitment caused anxiety to the authorities both in the districts and in Lucknow. According to official statistics, the number of Congress Seva Dal volunteers in June 1940 already stood at 30,178. What was particularly alarming was the rapid rate at which recruitment was taking place. Between January and October 1939, when the Congress ministry was in office, the monthly average rate of recruitment of Congress volunteers was 762 persons. However, after the ministry resigned, this average doubled, reaching 1,606 persons per month for the period November 1939 to February 1940.[28] Not only was the rate of recruitment alarming, but there was a growing tendency towards training of volunteers along military lines. 'A truculent spirit is growing', observed an intelligence report, 'among volunteers of all classes as a result of the aggressive propaganda . . . and of training along military lines which is being vigorously imparted everywhere'.[29] By the summer of 1940, so serious had the situation become that the government was forced to order, in August 1940, a ban on volunteer organizations or parties either engaged in military drill or wearing a distinctive uniform. The UP Seva Dal, the best organized in the country, strongly resented this order. So agitated was Nehru over it that he sought the permission of the Congress 'High Command' to launch a *satyagraha* in UP on the issue. Initially, the ban order was ignored and volunteer training camps continued their activities undisturbed. In Kanpur and Allahabad volunteers regularly organized public rallies or drills in defiance of the ban.[30] However, the Congress 'High Command' refused permission for a *satyagraha* on this issue. It simply permitted the passing of a resolution which protested that the ban 'would prevent and hamper normal activities of non-violent volunteers for social work'. As a result most training camps were disbanded and volunteer activities like drilling and parades were mainly stopped. However, Seva Dal volunteers in Allahabad and Kanpur continued to defy the ban. In Allahabad volunteers strongly resisted the order and a number of arrests were made in September 1940.[31] It was only after the 'High Command' ordered a complete stop that the Allahabad volunteers were restrained. In the months that followed many reports were received from several districts of volunteers trying to seek outlet in other activities such as shouting slogans and singing patriotic songs. In Dehradun, for instance, Seva Dal volunteers were reported to be 'very active in making regular visits to *mohallas* and villages, singing national songs and seeking funds for the Congress'.[32] With its volunteers and *satyagrahis* fully prepared, the Congress was now ready for a renewed campaign against the Raj.

Anti-War Campaign Gathers Momentum

Meanwhile a powerful public campaign against the war effort gathered momentum. Signs of such a campaign had been witnessed soon after the Congress resigned from office in October 1939. Congress activists set the tone of public attitude to the war effort by criticizing Linlithgow's arbitrary declaration making India a party to the European war. However, at that stage, speeches by Congressmen did not develop into a full-fledged anti-war campaign. The Congress leadership in Lucknow took care to restrain its local adherents and the UP government, on its part, directed its district officers not to prosecute Congressmen for anti-war propaganda while negotiations between the viceroy and the Congress over support for the war effort were still underway. Such mutual restraint was, however, short-lived. As 1940 opened local Congressmen increasingly took to criticizing the war effort more openly. Initially, the focus of their campaign was on recruitment. In Farrukhabad district, for instance, speeches were made by Ram Sarup Pande and Ambika Prasad warning villagers that, owing to the changed conditions of modern warfare, anyone who enlisted in the army would be killed and they urged their audiences to drive out recruiting agents.[33] In Azamgarh, audiences were advised not to enlist for the police or the military but instead join the 'Congress army'.[34] At more than half a dozen well-attended meetings in the district in February 1940, Jogesh Chatterjee and Jai Prakash Narain urged their audiences not to give any help to Britain in its war effort by supplying either men or money.[35] Chatterjee declared rather that advantage should be taken of 'the present opportunity' to press for immediate independence. At a separate rural meeting, Sita Ram Asthana, MLA, likewise urged his audience to take advantage of the opportunity created by the war to drive the British out of India.

The idea that British power would inevitably be weakened due to the war and that this must be used as an opportunity for action against the government soon became a frequent theme in public discourse. For instance, Swami Narain Deo, Baba Bhagwan Das and Ram Narain spoke to this effect in the course of at least seven meetings in a single week in Sultanpur district.[36] At Gorakhpur, Shyama Charan Shastri declared that the British deserved no help as they had broken their promise to grant India freedom after the last Great War. This theme was taken up by Purshottamdas Tandon when he declared to audiences of over 8,000–9,000 persons in Etawah that, for India's services in the last war, she had been rewarded with the Rowlatt Act and the Jallianwala Bagh massacre.[37] In Allahabad Damodar Swarup Seth, an important functionary of the PCC, invoked the imagery of the Jallianwala Bagh massacre to urge his audience not to help in the war effort.[38] In Azamgarh district Pandit Algu Rai Shastri, the prominent Congress leader, declared before 4,000 kisans that anyone who helped the British either by recruitment or with funds was an enemy of the country's freedom.[39] At the Ballia District Political Conference in March 1940, Rafi Ahmed Kidwai predicted that Britain was terrified of the ever-growing power of Germany and that, if the British were to win, India's slavery would continue quite indefinitely. In Aligarh, it was reported that Congressmen were conducting house-to-house propaganda against army recruitment.[40] In Rae Bareli Purshottamdas Tandon extolled the example of Japanese bravery and asked the youth to follow it, while in Sultanpur Mahendra Pratap Shastri and Chandra Bali Tewari declared that it was shameful that India's huge population should remain quiet, when the people of Poland, Hungary and China were fighting for their freedom.

The celebration of 'Independence Day' in late January, the

holding of district conferences by local Congressmen and two hectic tours by Subhas Bose galvanized public speaking against the war effort into a concerted campaign by March 1940. Bose's main message to his large audiences in about a dozen towns was loud and clear: the odds against the British Raj were rising rapidly and the time was ripe for striking a decisive blow against the government.[41] The increasing difficulties of the British were highlighted by almost all the speakers in some form or other, while many also took the opportunity to point to the growing influence of the Congress. In Sultanpur, for instance, Chandrika Prasad and Nazim Ali pointed out that whereas there were only 200 policemen in the district, the Congress had 10,000 volunteers at its command.[42] Similarly, Algu Rai Shastri, the Congress legislator, often stressed in his speeches the small numbers of the British in India as compared to the indigenous population.[43] This theme of the increasing power of the Congress vis-à-vis the weakening authority of the British was reiterated by a number of speakers.[44] A metaphor which was used widely by public speakers was to describe the position of the British Empire was that of a sinking ship.[45]

From Dehradun, an important recruitment area, reports were received of Congress volunteers carrying out vigorous anti-recruitment propaganda. Shortly before the arrival of recruiting officers, meetings were organized in villages to warn prospective candidates of the dangers of enlistment.[46] In Ballia, in eastern UP, Congress activists persisted in disturbing the work of a recruiting party by shouting slogans and distributing anti-war leaflets. In April 1940, the celebration of 'national week' by the Congress gave a further impetus to the antiwar mood. In Allahabad this was particularly marked and as many as forty-six arrests were made. Elsewhere anti-war speeches were reported from a number of districts, and there was considerable circulation of anti-war literature along with posters and graffiti. Reports of antiwar activity were received from Bulandshahr, Meerut, Mathura, Hardoi and Gorakhapur districts.[47] Of particular concern to British officials was the statement that enlistment in the army at Rs 16 a month was not worth anybody's while, and that those who decided to join would only become 'cannon fodder' of the British war machine.[48] In some places anti-war sentiments were not confined to speeches but were expressed in symbolic gestures of defiance. At Balrampur in Gonda district, for instance, Nand Lal and Gomti Prasad burnt the Union Jack before a large gathering. At a big meeting the following day, they urged their audience to refuse all help to the British in the war; to travel without tickets on railways; to burn foreign cloth; to besiege police stations; and to fill jails in the cause of independence. On the third day they repeated this performance, led a procession to the main *thana* in Balrampur and demanded that the Congress flag be hoisted. Both were then arrested under the DIR.[49]

Interspersed with this anti-war discourse were rumours about the war situation which circulated with amazing rapidity throughout the province, particularly in the eastern districts. These rumours frequently led to considerable unease and speculation among the public. For instance, rumours in Banda in May 1940 led to large withdrawals of deposits from post offices and banks. In Lucknow anxiety caused by the general atmosphere created by rumours induced arms license-holders to buy large quantities of ammunition.[50] So strong were some of the rumours that there was a run on the banks during May–June 1940. The panic to convert paper currency into silver was so widespread that scenes of disorder were witnessed outside banks and post offices in several districts. Traders began to refuse paper currency for goods sold and were persecuted for this in Aligarh, Bijnor, Dehradun and Moradabad districts, while special arrangements had to be made in Mathura and Agra districts for changing money so as to allay public fears.[51] In spite of the strict measures by the authorities, the spreading panic continued throughout June. In the eastern districts, particularly Gonda, Jhansi and Rae Bareilly, there were heavy withdrawals of currency. Although the general sense of panic abated by July 1940, confidence remained low in many districts.[52] Similarly, large purchases of ammunition were reported from Budaum, Meerut, Moradabad, Muzaffarnagar, Agra and Kanpur districts. In Bara Banki the state of excitement was reported to be such that zamindars made arrangements for a rallying post in case of trouble.[53] In Badaun rumours and uncertainty led tenants to withhold payment of rent on a large scale.[54]

Beneath this anti-war campaign lay anti-British feelings which had been fostered by months of Congress propaganda. Public speakers sketched out a scenario in which British authority would be completely subverted in very much the manner in which events took place in August 1942. For example, as early as February 1940, Rajendra Dutta Nigam advocated his 500-strong audience in Kanpur to indulge in open rebellion, which would involve the destruction of roads

235

and railways, the cutting of telegraph wires and attacks upon police stations.[55] Was this a soothsayer able to look into the future? Or was it a maverick public figure speculating about likely political developments? The evidence reveals that such scenarios were increasingly being sketched out by public speakers. For instance, Shanti Swarup, speaking in village Dari in Kheri district, asked his audience to be prepared to destroy railways, prevent the passage of military trains, destroy roads and hold up military lorries.[56] In a similar strain Ram Deo Singh urged his audience at Powai in Azamgarh district, that young men prepared to sacrifice themselves should be ready to take possession of jails and magazines, treasuries bungalows of the district magistrate and the superintendent of police, and deprive the constables of their arms.[57] In Kanpur a leaflet in Urdu, reported to be in wide circulation, urged upon the people the necessity for armed rebellion, accompanied by the looting of all police *thanas, chowkis* and *malkhanas* and setting fire to jails, telegraph offices and railway stations.[58] Weekly intelligence reports relating to this period constantly highlight this 'undertone' in public speeches, propagating an imagery of an imminent collapse of the Raj's authority.

Another important aspect of the anti-war campaign was the propagation of the idea that subscriptions should not be made to war charities or government loans. Public speakers frequently harped on allegations of coercion by government servants to take steps to promote war subscriptions. The slogan of 'no help in the war effort' (*na ek pai, na ek bhai!*) was one of the key messages which all public speakers sought to convey to their audiences. By the summer of 1940, the theme of coercion by officials in the collection of funds for the war became a powerful component of public speeches. In July the UPCC office in Lucknow declared that it had received such a large volume of complaints from almost all the districts against the forcible realization of funds, that it contemplated a massive campaign to expose the government. It then circulated one lakh leaflets alleging forcible collection of funds, giving examples of 'official excesses'.[59] For many weeks during July–August 1940, this remained the focus of Congress propaganda. In the second week of August alone, for instance, speeches alleging the use of coercive methods in the collection of war funds were made in Aligarh, Allahabad, Bahraich, Kanpur, Farrukhabad, Ghaziabad, Kheri, Prapatgarh, Pilibhit, Saharanpur and Sultanpur.[60] Pamphlets, posters and leaflets against subscription to war funds were

236

produced by local Congress committees in Bara Banki, Moradabad, Kumaon and Bijnor. From Gorakhpur reports were received that such propaganda was adversely affecting subscriptions to war funds.[61] In Mathura K.N. Katju, the former Congress minister, reminded his audience that the daily cost of the war in Europe was so staggering that India's contribution could only be very insignificant, in which case India need not contribute at all.[62] In Ghaziabad the police found cyclostyled posters condemning the war funds, which reappeared night after night on the walls of the town in spite of their constant efforts to have them removed.[63]

Allegations of coercion by officials in the realization of subscriptions were taken up by the top Congress leadership. Gandhi himself complained personally to Linlithgow about this and even furnished evidence of how local officials in Aligarh district had used high-handed methods to realize war subscriptions. His charges highlighted how the local official machinery operated in forcing people to subscribe against their will. Gandhi specifically took up the case of Babu Yadram Gupta, honorary magistrate, who complained that he had been forced by district officials—from the *tehsildar* to the district magistrate—to contribute money personally, to help with the work of the District War Committee and to use his official influence to promote the sale of war bonds.[64] Gupta alleged that when he refused to be a party to these methods, he was threatened by the sub-divisional officer with prosecution under the DIR for 'obstructing lawful collections for war purposes'. When he protested to the district magistrate against this 'excessive official zeal', he was told either to 'cooperate' or to resign his post. This particular case came to be taken up because an official functionary refused to cooperate on grounds of conscience and decided, at his peril, to complain to a Congress leader. But the evidence suggests that the 'excessive official zeal' alleged by Gupta was rampant among petty officials responsible for collecting war funds. This is amply illustrated by the work of just one local functionary of the Raj— the supervisory *kanungo*. In 1941 there were about 27,500 *patwaris* in UP who worked directly under 885 supervisory *kanungos*.[65] These men were now deployed by their district superiors to mobilize support for the war effort. In Bulandshahr district, subscriptions raised by them exceeded Rs 1,00,000. In Azamgarh they collected Rs 35,000 from the sale of proceeds of drama, *dangal* and cinema tickets, and flags and posters (in addition, they supplied over 106 recruits to the army). In

Banda the subscriptions they raised amounted to Rs 1,00,000 for war funds and a similar amount for war loans. In Rae Bareli *kanungos* raised Rs 12,000 for subscriptions, Rs 20,000 for investment in war loans and produced almost 200 recruits. In Etah they raised Rs 40,000. In Gorakhpur official zeal went to such an extent that *kanungos* collected Rs 1,14,778 from the public, donated Rs 6,822 from their own pockets and raised a further Rs 60,215 for war loans. In addition, they produced 202 recruits for the army.

Such methods yielded sums of money which were considerable from the point of view of the people who subscribed to them, but negligible in terms of the overall cost of the war. Based on figures compiled from *Annual Administration Reports*, it is possible to obtain an overall idea of the scale of wartime contributions that were obtained between 1940 and 1945. The total contributions during the five-year period to the Red Cross Society and Ambulance Association stood at Rs 77 lakh; to the King George's Fund for Sailors at Rs 16,759; to the St Dunstan's War Purposes Fund at well over Rs 353 lakh. In overall terms the total contribution made by the public in UP to war funds exceeded Rs 4.3 crore.[66] Considerable efforts were also made to realize subscriptions to war loans. These war loans were promoted by local functionaries of the state and special drives were frequently launched to set targets which the district staff had to meet.[67] Between 1940 and 1945, it is reckoned that about Rs 48 crore were raised from various war savings and investment schemes from the province.[68]

If one takes into account the figures for both voluntary subscriptions to war charities and investments in war loans, the total amount of money raised in UP over the five-year period added up to no more than two days of expenditure on the war: it was reckoned that the cost of the war was over Rs 20 crore per day. But the sum of Rs 43 crore was considerable when one sees it in the context of provincial finance. The total annual revenue of the UP government was in the region of Rs 20 crore. It is estimated that during the year 1943 alone, over Rs 1.38 crore was raised as subscription and over 10.8 crore as investment in war funds.[69] This shows that over half of the revenue of the UP government during normal times was being realized from the people as subscription and investment for the war effort. Realization of money on this scale must have meant that thousands of state functionaries exerted their 'influence' to obtain money from the people. Since contributions involved only petty sums, the number of persons who subscribed would have been extremely large. To what extent this gave rise to a 'sullen resentment' against the government is anybody' guess.

But one thing is clear. Although it was claimed that all contributions were voluntary, it was common knowledge that people paid up only when strong-arm methods were used. A close linkage existed between the willingness to subscribe to war funds and popular perceptions of the authority of the Raj. This is demonstrated quite strikingly in the timing of subscriptions. For instance, subscriptions to the Red Cross swelled from Rs 40,000 in 1942 to Rs 39 lakh in 1943. Similarly, subscriptions to the Governor's War Fund rose dramatically from Rs 38 lakh in 1942 to almost Rs 99 lakh in 1943. Likewise, deposits in war loans and savings schemes increased strikingly from Rs 2.21 crore in 1942 to Rs 10.88 crore in 1943. R.H. Nibblett, the collector of Azamgarh at the time of the Quit India movement, recorded in his diary that subscriptions to the War Purposes Fund increased twelve-fold after August 1942, and that when the governor visited the district in January 1943, purses of Rs 30,000 and Rs 1.5 lakh were presented to him at Madhuban and Azamgarh cities respectively, which just five months ago had seen the most violent ever challenges to the authority of the Raj.[70]

The Individual Civil Disobedience Movement

It was in this anti-war campaign that Gandhi launched his Individual Civil Disobedience movement. In fact, the momentum gathered by the anti-war campaign directly contributed to Gandhi's efforts. The ban on the volunteer movement in August 1940 precipitated the passage towards the inauguration of the Civil Disobedience campaign. By this time both the Congress leadership and the Raj were inevitably moving towards confrontation. As we have already seen, Congressmen energetically devoted themselves between April and August 1940 to organizational preparations such as the recruitment of volunteers, anti-war propaganda and enlistment of *satyagrahis*. The party organization was reinvigorated at the lowest level and Congress committees were converted into *satyagraha* committees. In the Congress's chequered history it was to be the launching of a campaign after the longest-ever period of preparation; for over a year Congressmen had been bracing themselves to launch what the official history of the

Congress describes as 'a model *satyagraha* unsurpassed in discipline and glorious assertion of non-violence by Gandhi and Congressmen'.[71] It further observes that 'the Congress never organized a movement more glorious in Gandhian terms than the Individual *satyagraha* . . . no Civil Disobedience Movement was more civil, more distinguished by disassociation from indiscipline and violence than this campaign.'

While Congressmen had been preparing themselves for another agitational campaign, the Raj too was making preparations to preempt a serious challenge to its authority. As soon as Linlithgow committed India to the war, the Government of India had equipped itself with emergency powers, the Defence of India Ordinance, to facilitate the war effort. The Ordinance was soon replaced by the Defence of India Act xxxv of 1939, which was enacted for the purpose of 'securing the defence of British India, the public safety, the maintenance of public order, the efficient prosecution of war, and the maintenance of supplies and services essential to the life of the community'.[72] Thus the government enjoyed extensive power of search, seizure and preventive detention—of arrest of a person by executive order in the absence of a regular trial in a court of law, and without any further right of appeal of *habeas corpus*. After the Congress ministry's resignation, district officials had been instructed 'to exercise powers vigorously and without hesitating' against those participating in 'anti-war and subversive activities'.[73] Initially, the directive was that prosecutions should be made under the preventive sections of the criminal law rather than under the extraordinary powers available under the DIR, and that important UP Congressmen such as ex-ministers and legislators could not be arrested without prior approval. In February 1940 these restrictions were removed and district authorities were empowered to prosecute under the DIR, persons indulging in 'anti-recruitment speeches including speeches designed to bring about an attitude of defeatism'.[74]

Although the government now permitted the use of special powers under the DIR, district officials were still hesitant to use them to curb anti-government activities, until they specifically related to anti-recruitment propaganda. Prosecutions were, therefore, not initiated on any large scale and many district authorities still preferred to use the ordinary criminal law rather than the emergency powers of the DIR. A full-scale initiation of the DIR regime against anti-war protest was, however, introduced by fresh orders to district authorities in April 1940. District officials were now specifically directed to use the DIR to curb anti-war activities. The powers of detention by executive order available to officials were explained, and the powers of externment of persons by removing them from the spheres of their influence were also recommended. District officers were reminded that arrests under the DIR could be made by any policeman above the rank of head constable simply on the basis of an executive order.[75] By April 1940 the broad parameters of policy within which the Raj would deal with another agitational campaign had been agreed upon.

Although district officers were given extensive powers of arrest and prosecution, these powers were not used on a large scale till the autumn of 1940. Some arrests were made under the DIR to curtail the increasing anti-war activities reported during the 'national week' in late April 1940. Initially, prosecutions were launched against speakers who made 'extreme' and 'intemperate' speeches, but care was taken to avoid important Congressmen. However, as the anti-war propaganda gathered momentum and prospects of successful negotiations between the viceroy and the Congress leadership receded, the toll of arrests, convictions and internments increasingly went up. Several important Congressmen were arrested in the early summer of 1940, including Raghubar Dayal (president, Ballia DCC), Algu Rai Shastri (MLA), B. Sanyal and Kedarnath Arya (both AICC members) and Rajendra Nigam (DCC president). In addition, the police raided Congress offices in Jhansi and searched several premises in the Kashi Vidyapith at Banaras. Earlier, two Congress MLAs in Gorakhpur had been given substantial sentences on the charge of inciting kisans and rioting.[76] On previous occasions, Hallett had contemplated persecution under DIR against ex-ministers for anti-war speeches, but refrained from action due to larger political considerations.[77] By the summer of 1940, however, both the Congress leadership and the Raj were so entrenched in their respective positions that a confrontation seemed inevitable.

Such a confrontation almost occurred in early August 1940, when Nehru and his colleagues in the UP Congress contemplated defying the ban on volunteer activities. Nehru personally took the lead in a huge procession organized by Congress volunteers in Kanpur to defy the ban, and he took to wearing the uniform of a Seva Dal volunteer.[78] Uniformed volunteers marched in hundreds and drilled through the main streets of the city. Important Congress leaders like Kidwai and Balkrishna Sharma openly declared that the ban would be resisted.[79] These activities moved Hallett to contemplate arresting Nehru, but action was deferred in view of Linlighgow's 'August offer' of making a final attempt to secure the Congress', support for the war effort.[80] However Azad, the Congress president, declined a meeting with Linlithgow to discuss the offer without even consulting his Working Committee. The die was cast and a confrontation now seemed imminent.

It was not before October 1940 that Gandhi finally made up his mind about the actual timing and the form of his campaign. The campaign he proposed was unique in many respects. Gandhi was obsessed with the desire for complete control over the course of the movement and this was reflected in the very nature of the movement, its form and its timing. Gandhi declared that only those who were designated by him could offer *satyagraha*: self-appointed agitators had no role in his present campaign. Gandhi was keen on launching a symbolic movement with a gradual tempo sustained by a slow rising tide of popular anti-war feelings. 'Gandhi was in no hurry to claim success for the Congress in the enterprise for *purna swaraj*.'[81] He was keen to highlight the element of self-sacrifice on the part of Congressmen which, he believed, would sustain popular sympathy and admiration for the Congress cause without embarrassing the British by creating situations of public disorder or seriously disrupting the war effort. He laid down that participation in *satyagraha* would be controlled solely by him and would be confined to Congressmen of his choice. Each volunteer selected for offering *satyagraha* was required to go to his (or her) own Congress committee area, home/village, and formally notify the local magistrate of the intention to break the law. He was required to indicate the time and venue of his *satyagraha*, and was not expected to organize a demonstration or *hartal* on the occasion. While offering the *satyagraha*, he was to shout: 'Do not give money to the war effort!', 'Do not give men for the war!', 'Do not give materials for the war!' If the *satyagrahi* was arrested and sent to jail, he was required to repeat the act of offering the *satyagraha* again and again. If, however, the local police decided not to arrest him, the *satyagrahi* was expected to become an itinerant preacher of the Congress programme. He was expected to proceed on foot towards Delhi in easy stages, 'keeping body and soul together by whatever food and shelter people might offer him on the way.'

By so rigidly prescribing the form of the *satyagraha*, Gandhi made the campaign completely controlled and symbolic. All activities which involved putting pressure on the authorities such as *hartals*, demonstrations, pickets, *dharnas*, *gheraoes* and flag-hoisting rituals were prohibited. While launching the movement, the Gandhian leadership had declared that:

> the Congress had no desire whatever to surround ammunition factories or barracks and prevent people from doing what they like. We want to tell the people that if they will win *swaraj* through nonviolent means they may not cooperate militarily with Britain in the prosecution of the war. This right of preaching against participation in war is being denied to us and we have to fight against this denial.[82]

Gandhi was, therefore, anxious to restrict his *satyagraha* to symbolic protest, rather than stampede the Raj with the pressure of mass agitations. He was strict about selecting only disciplined Congressmen for it; minors, unemployed and dependent persons were not to be permitted. It was to be a 'top-down *satyagraha*'. The government was relieved at having to deal with a *satyagraha* 'which does not favour any picketing, or coercive methods, or aggressive mass movement'.

The campaign in UP started with Nehru's arrest in Gorakhpur on 31 October 1940, a week after Vinoba Bhave was chosen by Gandhi to inaugurate the movement. Before Nehru's arrest the UP Congress had been fully prepared for any contingency. Fearing that Congress offices and funds would be seized, all office papers and money were removed for safekeeping with selected individuals. According to intelligence sources, contingency plans were ready for setting up one *satyagraha* ashram in each district. Communication among Congressmen by post was to be avoided, and a courier system was set up to send orders and propaganda material to subordinate committees. Nehru's arrest in Gorakhpur for anti-war speeches, for which he was punished with a severe four-year sentence, led to widespread protest in most major cities, notably Allahabad and Kanpur. Meetings were reported to be particularly large in Lucknow, Gorakhpur and Meerut.[83] Nehru's arrest for 'fomenting agrarian agitation and trying to impede the war effort' reportedly led to *hartals* in practically every district on 2 and 3 November 1940. 'The closing of Muslim shopes for Id', observed an intelligence report, 'gave a spurious air of completeness to these *hartals*.'[84]

The *hartals* galvanized the UP Congressmen into supporting the *satyagraha* campaign. The next to court arrest was Shri Krishna Dutta Paliwal, the UPCC president. The UP Congress had been very keen to make a worthy contribution to Gandhi's campaign, and Rafi Ahmed Kidwai had personally visited Wardha to consult Gandhi for finalizing the list of the UP *satyagrahis*. In the first instance, 510 volunteers were selected. These included almost all central and provincial MLAs, ex-ministers and AICC members and 243 members of the UPCC.[85]

Various district committees showed enthusiasm in submitting their own lists to the PCC. For instance, the Lucknow DCC sought approval for 265 volunteers to offer *satyagraha* across the twenty-one *mandals* (sub-divisions) into which the district had been divided. By the end of November 1940, provincial Congress leaders like Govind Ballabh Pant, K.N. Katju, Sampurnanand and R.S. Pandit had been arrested. This was followed by the arrest of Vijaylakshmi Pandit, Mohanlal Saxena and other important Congressmen. Once the campaign was in full swing, Congressmen were quite exercised by the fact that all news regarding arrest of their leaders had been censored by the government. Gandhi, however, asked Congressmen not to be disheartened by this 'news blackout'. He declared that, under such circumstances, each *satyagrahi* should function like a 'walking newspaper'. He directed that provincial committees should organize a news service to disseminate information and instructions. The PCC had already made plans for the setting up of an alternative news service to circumvent the ban. It had been decided that the PCC will issue a regular newsletter containing news and instructions for Congressmen. Intelligence sources reported that the PCC had directed subordinate committees to remit funds to help set up a regular courier service for the circulation of news and propaganda. District committees had also been directed to obtain cyclostyling equipment for the bulk reproduction of newsletters and propaganda literature. In Lucknow itself several underground presses and printing establishments were said to be in operation.

One such operation in Lucknow was carried out by Ram Kishore Rastogi—a young Congressman. Rastogi recalled during an interview how he was called by city Congress boss Chandra Bhanu Gupta one evening and given possession of an underground printing press with instructions to disseminate propaganda. Rastogi operated the press with the help of a few friends, and did everything from writing to printing to distribution. He recalled that most of what he wrote in his 'weekly newspaper' (which had various names) was the work of his own imagination rather than based upon Congress committee circulars. He conceded that most of the stories he wrote were highly exaggerated, particularly those relating to Allied reverses in the war. He believed that his newspapers helped keep the Congress spirit alive during the war years. Rastogi was able to continue the operation, despite police suspicion, for almost two years. At one time he had to move his entire press overnight in a palanquin after a tip-off from a sympathetic policeman of an impending raid on his temporary lodgings.[86] There is evidence to suggest that such underground literature greatly assisted the Congress cause, even though much of what it communicated went beyond the 'official' Congress discourse.

By early 1941 the top leaders of the UP Congress had been arrested. According to intelligence sources the total number of *satyagrahis* in the list prepared by the PCC stood at 23,0058.[87] By early January 1941, over 1,000 arrests had already taken place. By the end of March 1941, as many as 6,328 persons had courted arrest. These arrests had, however failed to cause any serious anxiety to the government. As early as December 1940, Hallett had reported that Congress activities were 'not causing any undue excitement in rural areas and rather less than at first even in urban areas'.[88] A month later he reported that 'the *satyagraha* continues its uneventful course and sill creates no sensation anywhere'.[89] And by March 1941, a typical official report from UP observed that '*satyagraha* does not worry us seriously; it is a nuisance, but on the whole our policy for dealing with it is proving successful'.[91] A month later the refrain was similar: 'the *satyagraha* movement continues in its sluggish and unpopular way'.[92]

Hallett and his officials in UP had reacted to the Congress *satyagraha* in a confident but cautious manner. Hallett maintained that Congress volunteers should be arrested under the DIR because the nature of the Congress campaign was primarily anti-war.[93] He believed that although the Congress *satyagraha* was symbolic, the sentences imposed on those arrested should be 'rigorous rather than symbolic'. He had directed his officials that:

> care should be taken to ensure that nothing is done either by undue leniency or by excessive severity to enhance the prestige of Congress

or provoke indignation against government. In other words, the object should be to keep the popular temperature as low as possible and to give the impression that the government are merely carrying out their duty in circumstances which leave them no alternative but to do so.... Shortly, the policy is to enforce the ordinary law dispassionately in the ordinary way.[94]

The law which Hallett was imposing was not ordinary, nor were the circumstances in which it was being enforced. By carrying out this 'dispassionate policy', Hallett and his men were successful in maintaining public order in the province by arresting one *satyagrahi* after another. As the numbers of the arrested Congress *satyagrahis* mounted, the Raj resorted to prematurely releasing over 2,000 'unimportant prisoners' lodged in jails for petty crimes to provide accommodation for the Congressmen. By May 1941, such was the confidence of Hallett and his officials that they now not only ignored volunteers offering *satyagraha*, but also began to release Congressmen before the expiry of their sentences. In June 1941, Hallett reported to Linlithgow that 'ignored *satyagrahis* give no trouble nor have any bad results occurred since we adopted the policy of releasing prematurely harmless *satyagrahis*. I have not figures available but I think our releases now exceed our admissions to jail.'[95]

Colonial officials found the manner in which the Congress had challenged the Raj and the methods which the government had adopted in meeting this challenge rather typical. They adopted a routine, business-as-usual approach to the Congress campaign. The following poem composed by Fredrick Graham Cracknell (ICS), then posted as district and sessions judge of Shahjahanpur, gives us an indication of their attitudes.

Song of the Satyagrahis

Back to jail again, boys,
Back to jail we go.
Pandit this and Srijut that,
And Babu so and so.

Sing it loud and sing it well,
Beat the drum and ring the bell.
Back to the old familiar cell,
Back to jail we go.

246

Back in the jail we'll be happier far,
For now we don't know where we are.
We don't like peace and we don't like war,
And we don't know what one's fighting for.

We don't care a button, we don't care a pin,
And we don't want either side to win.
We don't know why and we don't know who,
And we really don't know what to do.

But why should we worry? Why should we fuss?
In jail we'll have things done for us.
We shan't have to trouble, we shan't have to think,
We'll just have to read and eat and drink.

So back to the jail, where we're clothed and fed,
And a reading lamp is over our bed.

There we'll dream through the livelong day,
Of the glorious time (not far away).
When the people of India shall be free,
(Except, of course, the minority!).

Back to the jail again, boys,
Back to jail we go.
Pandit this and Srijut that,
And Babu so and so.

With a hearty cheer and a hip-hooray!
For Pandit Boojum, MLA!
Who can fast to death, three times a day,
Back to jail we go ![96]

Conclusion

By early 1942 as many as 12,618 *satyagrahi* Congressmen had been convicted in UP in connection with the Individual Civil Disobedience movement both under the ordinary law and the emergency provisions of the DIR. The total number of persons convicted for political or anti-war activities by then stood at 14,499.[97]

UP took the pride of place among all the provinces in India by providing the largest number of *satyagrahis*. The number of arrests made during 1940–41 were an all-time high—the number of convictions made during the Non Cooperation movement in 1920–22 and the Civil Disobedience movements of 1930–32 had been much less and this record was not surpassed even during 1942 when the Quit India movement erupted. In spite of the all-time high arrests and the considerable organizational preparations by the Congress, the Individual Civil Disobedience campaign was regarded by colonial officials as something of a damp squib. During the course of the campaign no rioting took place, no scenes of public disorder were witnessed, no attacks upon government servants were reported, no sabotage of government property occurred, no meetings or processions had to be broken, no firings took place and at no time did colonial officials feel seriously threatened by the campaign. How could a movement in which over 14,000 persons were arrested take place without a serious threat to public order? The answer to this riddle is to be found in the fact that colonial notions of what constituted public order and authority were based on collective activity. Only collective activities were perceived as constituting a threat to public order, not individual acts of protest which Gandhi had prescribed during 1940–41 to his followers. By prohibiting collective forms of activity like *hartal*, rallies, meetings, processions, *dharnas*, flag-hoisting ceremonies, Gandhi had effectively preempted a situation in which his movement could be perceived as a threat to public order by the Raj.

Even Hallett who, through liberal use of DIR, had found it remarkably easy to contain the campaign, conceded that while it was possible to suppress the Congress temporarily,

> what we must face is that we cannot destroy Congress as a political party. . . . We cannot treat Congress as a purely revolutionary organization; it is not, though possibly at times it may adopt revolutionary methods; it represents a national movement and has a vast amount of support from the educated classes.[98]

In April 1941, in a detailed analysis of the campaign, Hallett reported that the Congress campaign had little effect on the war effort or on crime, revenue collections and law and order. He reported that while most active Congressmen had been arrested, the Congress still possessed a very large number of supporters whom the party could mobilize, if it so desired, to fill the jail. 'Jail' he wrote, 'still has a less deterrent effect since the late Government and the Congress Party made it clear that no stigma attached to going to jail for "political offences" but rather that the persons acquired merit.' Reflecting on the overall nature of Civil Disobedience, Hallett wrote in his minute on the Individual Civil Disobedience movement:

> Gandhi is trying to blackmail government into conceding the Congress demand. If there are any major reverses or if and when the war is over and we are all war weary and there are the inevitable post war difficulties then he will intensify his effort. To use a homely metaphor, he is by this movement keeping his revolutionary movement simmering in the hope that a favourable opportunity will come when he can allow it to boil over.[99]

These words were to prove prophetic sooner than Hallett expected.

When a dramatic challenge to the authority of the Raj did take place in August 1942, it had already been foreshadowed by the creation of a popular mentality of revolt. It can be argued that the forms of challenges to authority, such as attacks on government buildings, cutting of telegraph lines and destruction of railways were similar —spontaneous and uncoordinated as they were—precisely because these events were foreshadowed by a continual and powerful public discourse which had assiduously called upon the people to act in the manner in which they eventually did in August 1942.

Notes and References

[1] For accounts of the Quit India movement see Francis G. Hutchings, *Spontaneous Revolution: the Quit India Movement,* Manohar, New Delhi, 1971, for an overall narrative; Chandan Mitra's unpublished Oxford D. Phil. thesis provides an account focused upon eastern UP and Bihar; and the symposium edited by G. Pandey, *The Indian Nation in 1942: Essays on the Quit India Movement,* K.P. Bagchi, Calcutta, 1988 makes available regional case-studies.

[2] See Gowhar Rizvi, *Linlithgow and India,* Royal Historical Society, London, 1976, and John Glendevon, *The Viceroy at Bay: Lord Linlithgow in India 1936–43,* Collins, London, 1971. Also see Johannes H. Voight, *India in the Second World War,* Arnold Heinemann, New Delhi, 1987.

[3] Born in 1883, he joined the ICS in 1907 and spent his early career in Bihar rising to become the chief secretary in 1930. In 1932 he joined the Government of India in the crucial position of home secretary, in which capacity he was closely involved in dealing with the Civil Disobedience movement. In 1937–39 he worked as the governor of Bihar and during 1938, officiated as the governor of UP when Haig proceeded on home leave.

4 *Provincial Abstract of Intelligence* (Weekly) (henceforth PAI), 3 February 1940 and 10 February 1940. The PAI and other related records are still in the custody of the UP police and were consulted by me at the Intelligence Headquarters at Lucknow after formal permission to do so was granted by the home secretary to the government of UP.

5 PAI, 17 February 1940.

6 The UP delegates proved to be the second largest bloc of support for Roy after Congressmen from Bengal. The considerable support for Roy showed a continuation of the UP delegates' left-wing tendency, which had earlier manifested itself strongly at Tripuri when a large number of UP delegates had voted for Bose.

7 Shri Krishna Dutta Paliwal, a right-wing Congressman from Agra, was voted president of the UPPCC, defeating Damodar Swaroop Seth by 212 to 174 votes. PAI, 24 February 1940.

8 PAI, 2 March 1940.

9 In late February, conferences were organized at Rae Bareli, Kanpur, Hamirpur, Jhanis and Kheri districts, and in early March at Bahraich, Bareilly, Mirzapur and Unnao. At Bareilly Purshottamdas Tandon was taken out in a large procession from the railway station to the *pandal*, with over a hundred uniformed Congress volunteers regulating the crowds. PAI, 9 March 1940.

10 For instance see PAI, 9 March 1940 and 16 March 1940. In early March the province was paid another visit by Subhas Bose which was marked by considerable Forward Bloc activity. Reports suggest that, even though Forward Bloc activity was not sustained in organizational terms, Bose was received by enthusiastic audiences wherever he went. For instance, in Dehradun and Saharanpur, he addressed audiences of about 7,000; in Mirzapur and Banaras the sizes of audiences were above 4,000, whereas in Allahabad, Mathura and Badaun they were said to be over 3,000. PAI, 16 March 1940.

11 PAI, 13 April 1940.

12 UPCC report in AICC, G-28 (pt 2) 1940, p. 57 cited in Bhupen Qanungo, 'Preparations for Civil Disobedience, January–September 1940', in B.N. Pande (ed.), *A Centenary History of the Indian National Congress*, Vol. III, New Delhi, 1985, p. 335.

13 PAI, 4 May 1940.

14 AICC, G-28 (pt 2) 1940, p. 59 cited in Bhupen Qanungo, 'Preparations for Civil Disobedience', p. 336.

15 This was far ahead of the other PCCs: the figures of some of the other provinces were Bihar 1,991; Gujarat 1,771; Tamil Nadu 2,765; Andhra 1,370 and NWFP 600.

16 PAI, 18 May 1940 and PAI, 1 June 1940.

17 PAI, 3 August 1940.

18 PAI, 13 Jan 1940.

19 Ibid.

20 Ibid.

21 PAI, 27 June 1940.

22 One example of such local initiative was in village Mendhapatti in district Fatehpur where about 200 youths organized themselves into 'Lal Fauj'. They adopted the uniform of red shirts, shorts and caps, with the red flag and declared their objective to be the protection of kisans from the tyrannies of policemen, *patwaris*, zamindars and canal patrols. PAI, 30 March 1940.

23 PAI, 4 May 1940 and 29 June 1940.

24 PAI, 22 June 1940.

25 PAI, 13 July 1940.

26 Ibid.

27 Tandon alleged that the British has always hindered attempts by Indian to obtain military training, as they feared that this would advance the cause of *swaraj*, and Malaviya called upon volunteers who were unable to procure arms, to train themselves with wooden guns and swords. PAI, 20 July 1940.

28 'Note on Volunteer Movement' by chief secretary, UP, in *Hallett Papers*, IOL/Mss.Eur.E251, Vol. III.

29 IB Memorandum dated 2 January 1940: Home Pol (I) 4/1/40 pp. 6–13, cited by Bhupen Qanungo, 'Preparations for Civil Disobedience', p. 339.

30 PAI, 31 August 1940.

31 PAI, 21 September 1940.

32 PAI, 15 November 1940.

33 PAI, 6 January 1940.

34 PAI, 27 January 1940.

35 PAI, 1 February 1940.

36 PAI, 3 February 1940.

37 PAI, 3 February 1940. Later in the week Tandon declared at Allahabad that, without India's help, England would have lost the last war.

38 In a rural meeting in Rai Bareilly, Seth declared before an audience of 2,000 persons that people could not expect an improvement in their conditions until the British had been annihilated. PAI, 17 February 1940.

39 PAI, 2 March 1940.

40 PAI, 9 March 1940.

41 PAI, 16 March 1940.

42 PAI, 16 March 1940.

43 For example, speeches in Fatehpur and Nawalia in Azamgarh in late February, see PAI, 24 February 1940.

44 In Hardoi, for example, Pandit Ram Swarup boasted that if every Indian threw a little dust, all the British in India would be buried. Similarly, in Fatehpur district, one Swami Bhagwan pointed out the very small number of constables in the local police station as compared to the population of the circle and urged his audience not to fear the police. PAI, 25 May 1940.

45 In Kheri Pandit Ram Asre declared British rule was fast approaching towards its end. Similarly, in village Asiwan in Unnao district, Ram Afhar and Harish Chandra Bajpai, MLA, described the plight of the British as a sinking ship. PAI, 23 March 1940.

251

[46] Ibid.

[47] See PAI, 27 April 1940 for details.

[48] For example, speeches by Ram Narain and A.P. Bajpai at village Chausana in district Muzaffarnagar. PAI, 4 May 1940.

[49] See PAI, 11 May 1940 for details of their activities.

[50] PAI, 1 June 1940.

[51] PAI, 15 June 1940.

[52] In Gonda, for instance, withdrawals from post offices were high, amounting to well over Rs 1 lakh in a single week. PAI, 27 June 1940.

[53] PAI, 29 June 1940.

[54] PAI, 22 June 1940.

[55] PAI, 10 February 1940.

[56] PAI, 13 April 1940.

[57] PAI, 4 May 1940. In a Sultanpur village Ram Pratap declared that, but for Mahatma Gandhi's orders, treasuries would already have been looted, telegraph lines cut and railways smashed. PAI, 18 May 1940.

[58] PAI, 15 June 1940.

[59] PAI, 27 July 1940.

[60] PAI, 17 August 1940.

[61] PAI, 24 August 1940.

[62] PAI, 7 September 1940. At a meeting in Kheri district a Congressman claimed that subscriptions were futile, as the cost of the war was so enormous that the contribution of the entire district could only buy, at the most, one or two bombs. PAI, 10 September 1940.

[63] PAI, ibid. In Bareilly Congress volunteers used the *Janmashtami* procession for propaganda, while in Saharanpur passengers travelling in trains were urged by itinerant speakers not to subscribe to war funds.

[64] Letter from Babu Yadram Gupta, honourable magistrate, to Dr K.N. Katju, 5 August 1940, *Hallett Papers*, IOL/Mss.Eur.E251 Vol. I.

[65] At their annual conference Percy Marsh, adviser to the governor and 'a pupil of the late Mr W.H. Moreland', who presided, described the *kanungos* as 'the Regimental Officers of the Great Army of Land Records', and added that 'your weapons and munitions are the records of the registers'. *Proceedings of the 14th Conference of the UP Supervisor Kanungo Association*, (4–5 April 1942, Lucknow), Bulandshahr, 1942.

[66] Based upon figures from *United Provinces Annual Administration Reports 1940-45*.

[67] A number of special fund collection drives were launched regularly to mobilize funds. For instance, 'War Week' was organized in March 1941; in March 1942 a 'National Defence and Savings Scheme Week' was observed; and in 1943, a 'Special Defence Savings Drive' was launched. These drives were organized at the harvest season to tap the surplus funds available with the cultivating classes.

[68] The most important of the schemes were: the Three Percent Appreciation Scheme, the Defence Savings Certificate and the Defence Savings Bank.

[69] In the following year, this trend was continued with Rs 1.35 crore as

donations to war charities and over Rs 10.8 crore to war loans; and in 1945 while donations declined to about Rs 87 lakh, loans went up to Rs 15.58 crore.

[70] R.H. Nibblett, *The Congress Rebellion in Azamgarh, August-September 1942*, Allahabad, 1957.

[71] Bhupen Qanungo, 'Preparations for Civil Disobedience', p. 306.

[72] S.K. Ghosh, *The Law of Preventive Detention in India*, Bombay, 1969. Under these emergency powers, as many as 35 entries under Chapter II of the Act were available, empowering the government to prohibit, regulate, control and restrain various activities relating to industry, explosives and vessals.

[73] Circular to District Officers by R.F. Mudie, chief secretary, 4 November 1939, *Hallett Papers*, IOL /Mss.Eur.E251, Vol. III.

[74] 'R.F. Mudie to All District Officers', 23 February 1940, *Hallett Papers*, IOL/ Mss.Rur.E251, Vol. III.

[75] 'R.F. Mudie, Chief Secretary, to all District Officers', 12 April 1940, *Hallett Papers*, IOL/Mss.Eur.E251, Vol. III.

[76] Hallett to Linlithgow, 26 April 1940, *Hallett Papers*, IOL/Mss.Eur.E251, Vol. III.

[77] For instance, see Hallett to Linlithgow, 15 March 1940, expressing concern over Kidwai's activities.

[78] S. Gopal, *Jawaharlal Nehru: A Biography*, Vol. II, London, 1972, p. 267.

[79] Nehru took a prominent role in the Kanpur proceedings. As he wrote to his daughter: 'There was a procession, a march past and speech by me to a huge crowd of about 50,000. For an hour during the procession I stood at the back of the car. Then I stood saluting while nearly 1,000 volunteers march-ed past, and then I held forth for an hour and forty minutes.' Nehru to Indira Nehru, *Jawaharlal Nehru: Selected Works*, Vol. XI, New Delhi, 1980, 11 August 1940, pp. 476–77.

[80] Hallett to Linlithgow, 12 August 1940, *Hallett Papers*, IOL/Mss.Eur.E251, Vol. I.

[81] Bhupen Qanungo, 'Preparations for Civil Disobedience', p. 396.

[82] Cited by Bhupen Qanungo, ibid., p. 406.

[83] PAI, 24 October 1940 and 8 November 1940.

[84] PAI, 8 November 1940.

[85] PAI, 22 November 1940.

[86] Interview with Shri Ram Kishore Rastogi, Lucknow, May 1989.

[87] PAI, 6 December 1940.

[88] Hallett to Linlithgow, 23 December 1940, *Hallett Papers*, IOL/MssEur.E251, Vol. I.

[89] Hallett to Linlithgow, 26 January 1940, *Hallett Papers*, IOL/MssEur.E251, Vol. I.

[90] Hallett to Linlithgow, 23 March 1941, *Hallett Papers*, IOL/MssEur.E251, Vol. I.

[91] Hallett to Linlithgow, 18 May 1941, *Hallett Papers*, IOL/MssEur.E251, Vol. I.

[92] Hallett to Linlithgow, 24 June 1941, *Hallett Papers*, IOL/MssEur.E251, Vol. I.

[93] Hallett to Linlithgow, 7 December 1940, *Hallett Papers*, IOL/MssEur.E251, Vol. I.

[94] Hallett to Linlithgow, 15 February 1941, *Hallett Papers*, IOL/MssEur.E251, Vol. I.

[95] Hallett to Linlithgow, 24 June 1941, *Hallett Papers*, IOL/MssEur.E251, Vol. I.

[96] Papers of Fredrick Graham Cracknell, ICS (UP) 1932–47, at the Archives of the Centre of South Asian Studies, University of Cambridge.

[97] *Fortnightly Report* for first half of January 1942.

[98] Hallett to Linlithgow, 7 December 1940, *Hallett Papers*, IOL/Mss.Eur.E251, Vol. I.

[99] 'Note on the *Satyagraha* Movement in UP' by Hallet, 23 April 1941, *Hallett Papers*, IOL/Mss.Eur.E251, Vol. I.

Some Reflections on the Partition of India 1947

A.S. Bhasin

Following the announcement made by His Majesty's Government on 20 February 1947 of the transfer of power into Indian hands not later than 30 June 1948, and the appointment of Lord Mountbatten as the viceroy and governor general of India, momentous developments took place in the political scene in India. Lord Mountbatten having convinced London that unless the Muslim League's demand for a homeland for the Muslims was accommodated somehow a solution to the Indian imbroglio was not possible, the British government endorsed his Partition Plan leading eventually to the transfer of power. The Partition Plan was first unfolded to the leaders of the Congress, the Muslim League and the Sikhs on 2 June, and then made public the following day. Then on the juggernaut of partition moved fast and square and there was no looking back. The country stood divided on 14 August 1947.

Was Partition Inevitable?

Was partition inevitable? This is a question that has been debated with no convincing answer for half a century. The rationale for accepting the partition was provided by Jawaharlal Nehru and Sardar Vallabhbhai Patel in their speeches at the AICC session on 15 June. Nehru, convinced of the need for a strong centralized government, felt it could not be achieved otherwise and everything else must be subordinated to this requirement. Patel, drawing on his experience of the working of the interim government for the last nine months, did not feel sorry about the partition. Acharya Kirpalani was more forthright in rejecting the Gandhian approach to the communal problem of India and said that Noakhali, Bihar and the Punjab had made

255

him feel that Gandhiji's method was no solution for the communal situation. Maulana Azad's voice of reason that the two communities were inseparable went unheeded. Therefore, the people who held the destiny of India in their hands at that crucial juncture in Indian history, for debatable and negative reasons, acquiesced in the two-nation theory without agreeing with it.

The Muslim League approached the communal problem from the wrong end of the telescope. Muslims had indeed ruled major parts of India for almost seven centuries preceding the British advent in India. Except for some over-zealous rulers like Aurangzeb, most of them were benign monarchs who treated the people as their loyal subjects and in return commanded their respect, allegiance and fidelity in keeping with the practice in those days. Non-Muslims were as good subjects as the Muslims. Both Muslims and non-Muslims fought in opposing armies in any war of conquest waged by one ruler against the other, as was ordained under the medieval polity and system of dynastic aggrandizement. Wars were not fought for religious conversions but for political and dynastic domination, territorial conquests and expansion. But Muslims were not the only or sole rulers of India at any given time. If Muslims had their rule in one part of India, non-Muslims at the same time established and defended their own sovereignty in other parts. India's size and dimensions had space for many dynasties to establish their rules in different parts and coexist either in friendship or in rivalry, as their political and dynastic interests determined. Religion played, if at all, a marginal role in determining relations among the ruling dynasties. The Muslim League's faulty theory of Muslims being the last rulers of India and hence their argument that for this reason they could not live under the 'domination' of the Hindus who formed the majority of the population, had no historical sanctity or validity. The British did not seize the empire in one go from any Muslim central authority. They conquered and annexed India bit by bit from various rulers—rajas and maharajas, kings and nawabs who followed different faiths.

Another point that had been missed altogether related to the total divergence between the objective that the League preached and the one it eventually achieved. It was the League's contention that the Muslims could not live under Hindu domination with honour. The provinces that it asked for to constitute Pakistan were, in any case, Muslim majority areas where they had a major share in governance.

They would have continued to have a lion's share of the power in those areas in any democratic system that was to follow the British withdrawal from India. The Punjab, Sind, the North-West Frontier Province (hereafter NWFP) and Bengal provided classic example. Even if the League did not form the government in Lahore, the Unionists, who were the senior partners in the Punjab government which was formed after the assembly elections in 1946, were Muslims. Similarly, if the NWFP returned a Congress government in Peshawar, it was nevertheless a Muslim-dominated government. In Bengal and Sind as well the Muslims had a majority in any case. In these areas the Muslims would have ruled always regardless of the party they belonged to. On the other hand, the United Provinces, Bihar, the Central Provinces, Bombay, Assam, Madras, etc., were all Hindu-majority areas, where the Muslims had coexisted with the Hindus for generations. It was never explained or even asked how the Mulsim-minority in Hindu-majority provinces would run away from ground realities if Pakistan was formed by putting together the Muslim-majority areas only! The Muslims who stood for Pakistan in these areas did not realize that in any Pakistan of the League's concept, it was they who would stand to lose. It is one of the unfortunate paradoxes of history that the League drew maximum support for Pakistan from areas like the United Provinces, Bihar and the Bombay Presidency. The supporters of Pakistan in these areas did not realize that the fruits of Pakistan, if any, would not fall in their lap. The Punjabi refugees from east Punjab and Bengali refugees from west Bengal were easily assimilated in west Punjab and east Bengal respectively, without much fuss. They did not suffer the fate of being permanent *Mohajirs*. The refugees from the United Provinces in west Pakistan and the refugees from Bihar in east Bengal could not be assimilated in an alien climate where political, social, linguistic and ethnic factors militated against them. Even after half a century of partition they are still suffering the consequences of being refugees in a country that was built on their political initiatives and sacrifices. Why were they discriminated against? The dominant language groups in the two wings of Pakistan could not accept them as heirs to Pakistan. Their aspirations for power were considered to be blasphemous. It was the struggle for political power between the 'refugees' and the dominant linguistic groups in the two wings that proved to be the undoing of the standard-bearers of Pakistan from the Hindu-majority provinces. Their political aspirations not only created a strong opposition to the emergence of a separate and parallel power structure, but prevented their assimilation in the local power structure as well. They, therefore, remained *mohajirs* in west Pakistan and *biharis* in east Pakistan/Bangladesh, words that are pejorative and opprobrious and that have become synonymous with second-class citizenship.

Could the Hindus have dominated the Muslims in an independent and united India after the British withdrawal, as the League feared? If only the Muslim League leaders had read their history well and with an open mind, they would have got an answer in the negative. Waves and waves of invasions came from the northwest in the long history of India, right from the ancient times until the British came by sea. Each invading army never had more than a few thousand soldiers in its camp, and yet they succeeded in vanquishing much larger indigenous armies, subjugating large populations and vast areas, and ruled over them for centuries.

Hindu society is fractious by nature and not a monolith, like Islamic society. The caste Hindus who were the bug-bear of other sections of the society, were a hopeless minority and as has been seen in the post-independence period, could be pushed around. The rajputs and the jats in the north followed a separate but antagonistic agenda. The banias had hardly any love lost with any other community except fellow trading communities. The scheduled castes had yet to acquire a constituency of their own and the tribals had not yet made their presence felt. The other backward classes were still to acquire any elan. Such a fractious society hardly had in it the ingredients or the guts to dominate a monolithic and egalitarian society such as the Islamic. Therefore the Muslim League only created the bogey of Hindu domination to achieve its own agenda of grabbing power since the Muslims in general were not sold to the League's socio-economic agenda or the need *per se* for a separate Muslim state to achieve their social or political amelioration. The League's appeal in the Muslim majority provinces was extremely limited. In the Punjab, the NWFP and Bengal, the largest of the Muslim-majority provinces, the Muslim majorities were coerced into accepting Pakistan. It did not flow from the social, religious, economic or cultural forces that determine the course of human history nor did history make it inevitable. It was the victory of the intransigence of a man who saw opportunity knocking at his door, and the British willingness to be a hostage to the obduracy, tenacity, obstinacy, steadfastness and determination with which Jinnah was laced in a generous measure.

The post-independence experience of the Muslims in India would give lie to the moribund fears that the Muslim League had deceptively tried to arouse among them. After the initial defensive posture that the community adopted as its strategy to overcome the guilt complex and trauma of partition, it has taken to the mainstream of national life in full measure. It has successfully carved out a niche for itself in the political, social, economic and cultural life of the country. On the other hand, the entire Muslim community in full strength would have been a great asset to the Indian nation and enabled it to emerge as the strongest power in Asia.

Was Bloodshed Inevitable?

If partition was indeed inevitable, as our leaders made it out to be, was the bloodshed and tragedies that accompanied partition too inevitable? Much of the bloodshed would certainly have been avoidable if the leaders of the Congress and the League had had a little foresight and if they had not been obsessed with each other. The decision on partition having been made, the leaders of the two parties drifted more and more apart and the distance between them increased by the day. The Congress considered Jinnah insufferable and Jinnah accused the Congress of being obstinate and obdurate, not wishing to accommodate another point of view. The two parties talked to each other only through the viceroy. The cabinet meetings where the top leaders of the two parties faced each other became highly acrimonious. The meetings of the high-level Partition Council on which sat leaders like Jinnah, Liaquat, Patel and Rajendra Prasad, became matches in mud-slinging. With the lives of millions of people at stake, instead of worrying about their future and devising strategies to avoid bloodshed, the great leaders who presided over the destinies of the millions were busy fighting over the division of tables, chairs, typewriters, printing presses and such other mundane things! After the decision on partition had been made, not once did the leaders of the two parties think it fit or prudent to meet together without the viceroy sitting in as an umpire, and discuss a peaceful parting. It was the viceroy who worried about the need to combat and control riots among the communities, repeatedly exhorted the Indian leaders to sit together and beseeched them to issue appeals to their people for communal harmony! When the viceroy conveyed to the Punjab governor the concern of the leaders of the two communities on the continuing communal rioting in Lahore, the governor turned around and told the viceroy that if the Indian leaders were indeed sincere about controlling the riots, they would do better to issue orders to their local units to cease rioting than complaining and asking for sterner measures that would not control the situation and indeed did not!

A lot of bloodshed could have been avoided, had the partition not been rushed through the way it was. But why was it rushed through? This is one of the questions that has repeatedly cropped up, but never been answered. The British had set 30 June 1948 as the targeted date by which the transfer of power into responsible Indian hands was to be accomplished. The actual transfer of power, however, took place on 15 August 1947, almost ten months earlier. How did the viceroy choose this date and why? Was it an arbitrary date? This date was evidently not discussed in London nor was it approved along with the plan for the transfer of power during Mountbatten's visit to London in May. When the first draft of the Indian Independence Bill was received in New Delhi on 15 June, it mentioned 1 October 1947 as the date when the British would demit power. Obviously London was still open on the date for the transfer of power and it was only the viceroy's choice. He did not pull this date out of his hat but had reasons to do so. He chose this date taking into consideration his assessment of the ground realities of the political and communal situation, legislative convenience, and finally HMG's anxiety to be of assistance in seeing the partition to its logical conclusion during the interim period. It was Mountbatten's assessment that the communal situation was getting out of control and the sooner power was demitted the better. Any pro-longed stay would mean use of force to control the ever-worsening situation that could bring the British only opprobrium and odium at the end of the Raj. Not only did he want to leave in glory himself but also to wind up the Raj in style and grandeur for the British nation and, in the process, bind India to the apron-strings of the British through the Commonwealth. India could not have been convinced to accept membership of the Commonwealth without goodwill at the time of their departure. That the British had been using their might and force to stay in power all these years was another story which he wanted to relegate to history. He did not want it to be repeated at the time of the winding up of the empire.

Imbued with this urgency, Mountbatten's calculation was predicated on the time necessary to complete legal formalities for the transfer of power. Parliament was in session in London and would continue to be in session for the next two months. The British prime minister had assured him that the Indian legislation would get 'top priority' and he had accordingly ordered the lord chancellor and the law officer of the Crown to start work on it 'at once'. When Mountbatten was still in London, Churchill, the leader of the opposition, too had given a written assurance to Attlee that the opposition, 'would facilitate the passage of this Bill'. The viceroy hoped that it would create an all-time worldwide legislative record. Hence he calculated that if the Indian Independence Bill could be passed by Parliament by the middle of July, all other formalities were inconsequential and could be rushed through and the British could divide, wind up and quit.

The need for a maximum interim period before 30 June 1948 determined the need for the earliest possible date for the initial transfer of power. In the viceroy's calculation, this could only be 15 August 1947, on the presumption that the necessary legislation would be out of Parliament by then. This date for the first time found mention in the paper 'The Administrative Consequences of Partition', that the viceroy had got updated on 2 June for circulation among the Indian leaders the next day. It was intended to be a 'shock' paper to bring home to them the adverse consequences of the partition. The paper, however, failed in its objective since the Indian leaders received it in a routine manner and it did not evoke any reaction. Even the date 15 August 1947' for demitting power did not seem to surprise them. It was taken as an earnest manifestation of the British determination to withdraw from India at the earliest. Few realized that this date had a personal significance for Mountbatten. The viceroy was full of history. He was the supreme commander of the Allied forces in Southeast Asia, a job that brought him glory. 15 August was, therefore, important because it was the date of his appointment to that job, and it was also the date when Japan announced her acceptance of the terms of surrender.

That HMG had intended the partition to be the first step towards final withdrawal of British power from India was evident from what the viceroy told the Indian leaders on 2 June, when he was unfolding the Partition Plan. He said: '. . . the British owed to the Indians, to give them all the help which they required after the transfer of power. *This could only be done if it were arranged that the transfer should take place not only before June 1948 but also as long before that date as possible*' (emphasis added). This pregnant statement of far-reaching consequences, was fortified with an assurance that the British assistance would '*not be withdrawn prematurely if it was still required*' and that '*it was the duty of the British to continue to help—not to rule—India*' (emphasis added).

The viceroy had calculated that the suggested date would fit into HMG's agenda as had been articulated by him to the Indian leaders. This was intended to leave enough time before 30 June 1948 for the Partition Plan to be taken to its logical conclusion. This idea got lost in the din that followed the announcement of the Partition Plan. Obviously it was at the back of HMG's mind that there would be an interim period after the initial transfer of power, that would not extend beyond 30 June 1948, limit fixed in the statement of 20 February 1947. There is not an iota of doubt that the idea of an interim arrangement between the initial transfer of power and the final withdrawal on 30 June 1948 had emanated from HMG. The viceroy made his presentation on the above lines to the Indian leaders within a couple of days of his return to New Delhi from London, while unfolding the HMG plan for the transfer of power. Evidently he was speaking on behalf of His Majesty's Government. Certain developments that went unnoticed fortify the presumption and the assessment that HMG did have this approach on its agenda. In a telegram dated 11 June, India Office in London informed Ismay in New Delhi that in the draft bill for Indian independence that was under preparation, it was proposed to include an enabling provision that the governor general would have certain reserve powers. These he could exercise at his discretion without the advice of the council of ministers for a certain period after the establishment of the dominions. The telegram argued that this was proposed to be done for the 'exceptional purpose of removing difficulties in the course of effecting transition to new conditions, partitioning India, dividing assets, liabilities etc.', all in the post-independence period. This provision was sought to be introduced in the bill on the presumption that the Indian Independence Act would make it mandatory for the two Dominions to have him as a common governor general. The first draft of the Indian Independence Bill indeed had a provision that 'provided that, unless and until another appointment is made, the person who, immediately before the appointed day, is Governor General of India within the meaning of the Government of India Act, 1935, shall, as from the appointed day, become the Governor General of each of the two Dominions'. That the viceroy vetoed both the proposals is another story. However, the fact that the proposals fitted into the concept that the viceroy had articulated on behalf of HMG to the Indian leaders on 2 June is a positive indication of the two-stage plan.

Why did the viceroy veto the twin proposals that were meant to enhance his position and status even after the transfer of power? The success attending the acceptance of the Partition Plan by the Indian leaders, including Mahatma Gandhi, gave Mountbatten new confidence and different ideas of his position and abilities. He was perhaps seized with a sense of self-glorification and canonization. He wanted to go down in history as the greatest viceroy with the shortest tenure who had efficiently accomplished the task entrusted to him. He wanted to be the common governor general of the two dominions not courtesy the British authorities, but with the goodwill of the two new dominions. Hence, he insisted that he would accept the common governor generalship of the two Dominions only at the request of both the parties. He was confident that the two parties looked up to him as their messiah and a request to that end would be forthcoming. Thus, he sought to put on test the popularity that he believed he had come to enjoy in the brief period he had been in India.

His initial successes whetted his appetite for still greater successes and he perceived himself capable of pushing anything down the throats of the Indian leaders, including Gandhi and Jinnah. Conceited as he was, he assured London that he saw no difficulty in the course of action he had chosen and insisted that the relevant clause in the Indian Independence Bill regarding the appointment of a common governor general was redrafted accordingly. The prime minister and his cabinet colleagues were so convinced of the viceroy's all-pervading influence and hold on the Indian leaders in New Delhi, that they ceased to question his judgement and surrendered all discretion to him. They were neither shocked nor shaken out of their complacency and naivete when Jinnah, to the viceroy's horror, refused to oblige him. HMG accepted the viceroy's alibi that Jinnah suffered from megalomania and was being cussed.

The viceroy had rejected the offer of discretionary power sought to be included in the Indian Independence Bill, apprehending that it could derail the entire process of transfer of power set in motion by him so painstakingly. He was afraid that the Indian leaders would perceive that the impending independence was only a halfway house in which the British governor general had retained the substance, transferring the shadow to them, and that they would even reject the entire initiative. He was confident that once the two dominions voluntarily invited him to be their common governor general, they would have to be more than willing to listen to him and let him enjoy certain powers, to enable him to carry out the partition process with equity, justice, impartiality and fair-play. This is the line he tried to sell Jinnah to convince him of the advantages of having a common governor general. Disillusioned and disheartened by Jinnah's attitude, Mountbatten did not make any further effort to project himself as the arbiter of Indian destiny, and as a face-saving device agreed to be the governor general of one dominion only. Mountbatten had not reckoned with the likes of Jinnah and remained under the illusion that since he had given Jinnah his Pakistan on a platter, the latter would reciprocate and oblige him. Now that Mountbatten had lost all interest in any post-independence role as an arbiter between the two dominions, HMG too did not press on with the idea of an interim administration any more. If the viceroy had been a down-to-earth man and not indulged in self-aggrandizement, and if the envisaged and implied second stage of partition had come about as a result of the Indian Independence Act, the partition would have been a smooth, peaceful, tranquil and dignified operation. As it happened, it left a trail not only of bloodshed, but rancour, hatred and enmity, that bedevilled relations between the two countries from the very beginning.

The situation too demanded that the transfer of power be effected in two stages. In the first stage, all the formalities connected with the partition, such as ascertaining the views of the assemblies of the Punjab, Sind and Bengal, a referendum in NWFP and Sylhet in Assam, reports of the Boundary Commissions, notional division of the armed forces and the civil services, division of assets and liabilities, etc., would have been completed. The first stage would have culminated in the establishment of two fully autonomous governments in the two dominions, completely free in every manner to run their administration. In the second stage, a central authority, composed of people

264

from both the dominions, under a common governor general, would have taken care of a smooth transition. The overall responsibility for law and order and control of the armed forces would have stayed with the central authority. There were the British troops stationed in India and along with the large body of the Indian army still under one authority, they were an effective and a formidable instrument for the maintenance of law and order. The armed forces were not yet struck with the communal cancer and were capable of guaranteeing the safety and security of the lives and property of the people in the two dominions. The interim period between the establishment of the two autonomous dominions and the final transfer of power on 30 June 1948 would have provided a breathing space to the people and given a chance to the two governments to establish a relationship of mutual trust and confidence. This would also have prevented the power vacuum that occurred soon after partition, for lack of effective administration in the reconstituted areas. If the people in one dominion found themselves uncomfortable and wanted to seek refuge in the other, there was enough scope to do that without having to go through traumatic experiences and communal massacres. The Indian leaders, whether of the League or the Congress, were in too much of a hurry to assume the reins of power, and failing to hit upon *modus operandi* or *vivendi*, were far too anxious to cut the umbilical cord. This had disastrous consequences for all the communities and both the countries.

Parties and Communities

After agreeing to the partition, both the Congress and the League did nothing to mitigate antagonism between the two communities. In fact, everything that was done helped to sharpen the discord that adversely impacted immediate and long-term relations between the two communities and the dominions. In allocating the defence and civil services between the two projected dominions, the approach agreed upon by the two parties was narrow and communal. It only promoted antagonism then and later. The division was effected along purely communal lines. In the defence services, while the wholly Muslim and wholly non-Muslim units were allocated to Pakistan and India respectively on a communal basis, in the mixed units, during the combing operations, everyone was given the option to choose his own dominion. In the civil services, the same principle was extended with similar results. The result was that every Muslim chose Pakistan, and every non-Muslim, India. It was soon realized that in the Punjab, when all the transfers would have been made, west Punjab with a minority of 27 per cent non-Muslims would have hardly a Hindu or Sikh official, and east Punjab with a minority of 33 per cent Muslims would have hardly a Muslim official. With Muslim officials opting for Pakistan and the Hindus and Sikhs opting for India, the minorities in the two dominions felt insecure and shaky. Since their own co-religionists had abandoned them and left them at the complete mercy of another community in that communally surcharged atmosphere, it was natural for the minorities to feel insecure. If, on the other hand, the allocation of services had been linked to the place of birth or place of permanent domicile, as per the official record at that time, both dominions would have inherited mixed services. That would have provided the much-needed sense of security and confidence.

The Congress and Mountbatten

The Congress persistence with Mountbatten as the governor general of India, after Jinnah had refused him that honour, remains a great mystery of the transfer-of-power saga. Why did the Congress stick by him? After all, the very purpose of accepting him as the link-man was knocked out once Jinnah nominated himself to that office in Pakistan. What were Congress's compulsions in not withdrawing the offer made to Mountbatten to be the governor general of India, thus mitigating the humiliation heaped on him by Jinnah? On the contrary, the Congress renewed its offer to him. The Congress leaders felt that his administrative experience, so soon after the transfer of power, would be of great value to India, and that his influence with the Indian princes would be useful in integrating the states in the union. As evidence goes, Mountbatten did use his influence both ways. While he advised the states to join one of the two dominions, taking into account their geographic location and the general will of the people of the state, he also lobbied with HMG for a policy pronouncement that if any state stood out at the time of the transfer of power, His Majesty's Government would consider granting it dominion status. The latter advice could have had most disastrous and unfortunate results for the emerging Indian Dominion but for the stand taken by the secretary of state and the Cabinet Committee on India in London, who rejected the viceroy's advice. Mountbatten's role in Kashmir too remains questionable and much of the present problems in the state can be traced to him. His advice to the maharaja to defer his decision on joining India or Pakistan until the Pakistan Constituent Assembly had been convened and his unsolicited suggestion to the maharaja that if the state joined Pakistan India would understand, relieved the latter of a lot of pressure to make a timely decision. He vehemently opposed Nehru's proposal to visit Kashmir to clinch the issue of its accession, although Nehru suffered qualms of conscience since he was anxious that his ancestral home state should be part of the new India dominion.

The apart, Mountbatten himself was not particularly solicitous of Congress sensitivities in making his decision to accept the Indian offer. He was more concerned with the advice of his people in London. He sent his chief of staff, Lord Ismay, especially to London to seek the advice of not only the government but of the opposition. It is yet another paradox of the story of partition that the British leaders, in advising him to stay on in India as India's governor general alone, did so for considerations that had hardly anything to do with the interests of India! On 7 July, Prime Minister Attlee at the meeting of the Cabinet Committee on India, articulated the view that if Mountbatten did not stay on in India 'the alternative candidate would presumably be a Hindu; in that event there was serious risk that grave differences would arise between him and Mr Jinnah'. The secretary of state for Commonwealth relations espoused the view that 'the paramount consideration must be to secure the successful transfer of power on the lines decided upon', and Mountbatten alone was qualified to accomplish this job. Lord Listowel, the secretary of state for India was more forthright and said:

> No other person could have an equal influence on Congress policy. This factor would be important for three reasons. First, it was still uncertain whether India would ultimately decide to remain in the Commonwealth. Secondly, complex and important negotiations would be necessary between His Majesty's Government and the new Dominion of India regarding future defence arrangements. Thirdly, the partition of assets between the two Dominions would in any event work out unfavourably for Pakistan; Lord Mountbatten would be in a better position than anyone else to exercise a moderating influence on Congress policy in this matter.

Mountbatten was equally anxious to seek the advice of the leader of the opposition. Lord Ismay, while still in London, called on Churchill too. The latter also advised acceptance of the offer of governor generalship of India. He predicated his advice on the ground that 'he can strive to mitigate quarrels between Hindu and Moslem, safeguard the position of Princes when that is involved and preserve such ties of sentiment as are possible between the government of Hindustan and that of other Dominions (or Commonwealth) of the Crown'. Everyone was anxious that he accept the offer that the Indian leadership had made, but for reasons which had nothing to do with India. No one in England could pinpoint the advantage that would accrue to India if he stayed on, except that it would help in the smooth transition and transfer of power, something in which Pakistan had equal if not far greater stake. Yet Jinnah had rebuffed Mountbatten. It is interesting to recall that when Mountbatten confronted Jinnah with the risks involved for Pakistan in the division of assets without a common governor general acting as an umpire, Jinnah dismissed the argument out of hand as being of no consequence to him. The Congress was so enamoured by Mountbatten, for inexplicable reasons, that it was prepared to go to ridiculous lengths to accommodate him. After the rebuff, Mountbatten was still anxious to propitiate Jinnah if he would accept him as the common governor general. He floated an idea of an officiating governor general for Pakistan whenever Jinnah was not in that country. This, he thought, would satisfy Jinnah, since most of the time he would be headquartered in Delhi. When Mountbatten put this idea to the Congress, the latter had no qualms of conscience in giving its nod. Unfortunately, to the chagrin of the Congress and the viceroy, the League rejected the idea with the contempt that it perhaps deserved. The Congress leadership stood ridiculed!

The inscrutable and vexatious behaviour of the Congress has remained a mystery even after half a century of independence. Jinnah choosing himself to be the governor general of Pakistan knocked out the very rationale of the proposition for a common governor general. But the Congress did not even think it necessary to reconsider its earlier position of having an Englishman as the head of the state on attaining independence. There were enough gibes and sarcasm hurled by the Muslim press to shame the Congress for not being able to find an able Indian to head the nation after two hundred years of colonial rule!

Some Reflections on the Partition

The Sikhs

For the Sikhs the partition was an unmitigated disaster and they stood to suffer the most. It was a Hobson's choice. They were spread over the whole of the province of the Punjab with no majority in any particular district. Therefore, they could never make out an acceptable case for a Sikh homeland. But they were united with the Hindus by inseparable ties of blood and kinship. There was hardly a family in the Punjab that was not a mixed family. There was the relationship of '*roti* and *beti*' between the two and the line dividing the two was too thin to be even perceptible. Unfortunately, between the Muslims and the Sikhs there had come to exist historic antagonism. The Sikh religion had come under pressure from the Muslim rulers during the days of its infancy and the memories of those days haunted members of the faith. If the Muslims resisted Hindu domination because they considered themselves the last rulers of India, the memories of Sikh rule in the Punjab were still fresh in everybody's mind. The restoration of Muslim domination in the land they considered their own was anathema to them. But it was their number that was their enemy and they had to struggle against this factor. If the whole of the Punjab could not be retrieved, a rescue operation was nevertheless necessary.

The Cabinet Mission Plan brought home to the Sikhs the fact that the Punjab, as then constituted, militated against their interests, and that any future battle for the Punjab had to be fought on a different plane for which they must prepare themselves. That underlined the need for the reorganization of the Punjab on administrative grounds. The Sikhs henceforth articulated the same. The proposed reorganized province would consist of Ambala and Jullundur divisions and Amritsar, Gurdaspur and Lahore districts, with a total population of 144 lakh of whom 62 per cent would be non-Muslims, mainly Sikhs and Hindus. The composition of the population by communities was to be 19 per cent Sikhs, 43 per cent Hindus and 38 per cent Muslims. It was made out that in the reorganized Punjab no single community would be in an absolute majority and hence in a position to dominate the rest. However, the Cabinet Mission Plan as a solution for the Indian problem went into limbo after the arrival of Lord Mountbatten in March 1947. The viceroy too caught the bull by the horns and made it known to Jinnah that the principle on which he wanted Pakistan would apply equally to the Punjab and Bengal, since the two provinces had substantial non-Muslim minorities. Hence the need to partition them.

The viceroy played dirty with the Sikhs, and through double-crossing talk, betrayed their cause. When he unfolded the Partition Plan as approved in London to the Indian leaders on 2 June, he invited the Sikh leader Baldev Singh in his own right as representing Sikh interests along with the Congress and League leaders, and asked for the Sikh reaction and approval. This confirmed the Sikh position as a third party in the HMG's plan. To underline the British concern for the Sikhs, he expressed HMG's sympathy with their cause and assured them how solicitous His Majesty's Government was for Sikh welfare. However, he added, since they had lost out in numbers, the notional partition 'would be entirely provisional and that the Boundary Commission on which Sikh interest would of course be represented, would have to work out the best long-term solution'. The Sikhs, in accepting the plan, made a pointed reference to the viceroy's 'anxiety' to 'help the community', and pinned a lot of hope on 'other factors' which would be taken into account to split the province. The Sikh response also underlined the fact that since the partition of the Punjab had been 'necessitated to meet the Sikh demand', clear instructions 'should be given to the Boundary Commission to ensure that as large a percentage of Sikh population as possible is included in the eastern Punjab'. No sooner had the Sikhs accepted the plan than the Viceroy lost all interest in the community and felt no compunction in turning his back on them. The very next day, 3 June, the seven Indian leaders met again to consider the responses of the three parties to the HMG plan. The viceroy brushed aside the Sikh request that the terms of reference of the Boundary Commission be spelt out at this stage itself. He now took the position that 'the terms of reference of the Boundary Commission would be drawn up in cooperation with all parties'. Thus, at the very first opportunity, he watered down the assurance of the previous day that 'the Boundary Commission, on which the Sikh interests would of course be represented, would have to work out the best long-term solution'. Once the Congress and the Muslim League formally accepted the HMG plan and the partition juggernaut was put on the rails, the Sikhs ceased to be a factor in the viceroy's scheme of things.

The Congress response to the Sikh problem was no better. Once the Congress felt assured that a slice of the Punjab was falling into the Indian lap, it too lost all interest in the Sikh predicament and left them to fight their battle alone. The Congress, while finalizing the terms of reference of the Boundary Commission, did not consider it necessary to consult with the Sikhs who were to be the most affected party. Later, when the Congress and the League were called upon by the viceroy to pledge that the reports of the Boundary Commissions would be accepted by them as 'awards', the Congress did so without consulting the Sikhs. It was only after the League and the Congress had undertaken to treat the Boundary Commissions' reports as awards that the viceroy, as a formality, verbally asked Baldev Singh to endorse the position. Baldev Singh, who was by now ingratiating himself with the Congress, did not think it advisable to go against the Congress stand. Without consulting the Shiromani Akali Dal in Lahore, he endorsed what had been proposed by the League and accepted by the Congress. The Sikh goose was cooked even before the fire was lit! Later when the Akali leadership represented by Giani Kartar Singh tried to retrieve the impossible situation, it was too late. While Giani Kartar Singh wept and sobbed in Lahore appealing to the Punjab governor for help, Baldev Singh in Delhi was busy in an exercise of self-aggrandizement, playing second fiddle to the Congress leaders for a possible role in post-independent India.

The Congress leadership too abandoned the Sikh cause after expression initial concern. At no time did the Congress Working Committee pass any resolution expressing its support or concern for the Sikhs. In their response to the 2 June plan on that day, the Congress had shown appreciation that the HMG and the viceroy himself were 'anxious to protect all legitimate Sikh interests'. The letter had stressed that it would not only be numbers alone that would determine the demarcation of the boundary in the Punjab, but 'all other factors, apart from population, will be taken fully into consideration'. The Congress response did not fail to remind the viceroy what the other factors were. It enumerated them for his benefit lest they be lost in the cacophony of competing interests later. The Congress letter emphasized that 'the Sikhs have played a vital role in developing a considerable part of the Punjab. They have been pioneers in the canal areas and have converted by their labours the desert into the richest part of the Punjab'. These were the very factors on which the Sikh case rested, and yet they were forgotten, ignored and brushed aside. The Congress never again felt it necessary to remind the viceroy that by ignoring them, injustice was being done to them. And how could they? The terms of reference that were framed by the Congress were so vague

271

and faulty that hardly any justice could have been done to the Sikh cause. None other than the Congress had to accept the blame for this. Later, when the Sikhs threatened to 'revolt' against the Partition Plan if the Boundary Commission's award was not favourable to them, the viceroy at the meeting of the Partition Council in the presence of Patel, threatened to use the might of the army and airforce to suppress them. The iron man of India did not even squeak in protest.

The viceroy, on 2 June, had promised the Sikhs that their interest would be represented on the Boundary Commission appointed to partition the province. It was expected that they would get representation on the Boundary Commission in their own right in the same way as they were represented in that meeting in their own right and not courtesy the Congress. If that were so, the Sikhs were entitled to nominate a separate representative in the Punjab Boundary Commission, apart from what the League and the Congress were entitled to. But Nehru jeopardized the Sikh chance of nominating a separate member when he assured the viceroy that of the two members that the Congress was to nominate on the Punjab Boundary Commission one would be a Sikh, and that would take care of their interests. The viceroy was relieved of the need to give them a separate representation. Whether or not a separate Sikh member on the Punjab Boundary Commission along with those of the Congress would have succeeded in swinging a more favourable award from the Commission is only conjecture at this stage. The fact of the matter is that the Congress leadership in New Delhi, without lifting a finger to help the Sikhs, arrogated to itself the role of being their spokesman. It behaved like a big brother who claimed to know best; it sacrificed the Sikh interests without at any time taking up cudgels on their behalf either in the Partition Council or with the viceroy separately. It is no wonder the Sikhs came out of the partition bruised, battered, frustrated and particularly embittered against the Congress, and that their relations with that organization always remained sore, devoid of trust and confidence.

The North-West Frontier Province

The Congress role in NWFP lacked foresight and strategic thinking. Perhaps, the NWFP being a Muslim-majority province, the Congress—having acquiesced to the division of the country on a religious basis, without admitting as much—gave it up as a lost case. If ever there was an area where the Congress creed of nationalism above religious fanaticism could have been put to test, it was in NWFP. But alas, the Congress was found wanting and a great opportunity to prove Quaid-e-Azam Mohammad Ali Jinnah wrong on his thesis of Pakistan was lost. The elections to the Frontier Legislative Assembly in 1946 were fought on the question of Pakistan. The NWFP Congress, led by Khan Abdul Ghaffar Khan and his *Khudai Khidmatgars,* gave a befitting reply to the Muslim League and settled the question of Pakistan versus India much before Pakistan was on the horizon. Later, when the viceroy adopted the Partition Plan in consultation with Nehru, the question of a referendum in the province should not have arisen. If the legislative assemblies of the Punjab, Bengal and Sind were given the right to exercise their choice on partition or joining India or Pakistan, by the same logic, the decision on the future of the province should have been left to the Frontier Legislative Assembly. Even Baluchistan, which did not have a legislative assembly, was not asked to go through the motion of a referendum. Why was a different procedure adopted for this province? The Muslim League, smarting under the great moral defeat in the elections to the Frontier Legislative Assembly the previous year, was bent upon changing the climate in its favour. The Congress victory in NWFP and the Muslim League's failure to get a majority in the Punjab were big blows to the League's claim to be the sole voice and representative of the Muslims of the subcontinent. The viceroy had left Jinnah in no doubt that if India had to be divided on the basis of Muslim and non-Muslim majorities, the same principle of division would have to be applied to the Punjab and Bengal. Both the provinces had, more or less, clearly demarcated majority areas of the two communities. With the loss of half each of the two major provinces, the additional loss of NWFP would have further truncated the moth-eaten Pakistan that the viceroy was offering Jinnah. Besides, how could Pakistan be justified with a predominantly Muslim-majority province staying out of Pakistan? The NWFP would always stand out as a sore thumb challenging the very logic of Pakistan. The Pakistan agenda impressed upon the Quaid the need for urgent steps to correct the asymmetry, both in the Punjab and NWFP. The large-scale rioting in the Muslim-majority districts of the Punjab, particularly in the Rawalpindi and Multan divisions, and the mayhem and murders of non-Muslims in its wake in March 1947, undermined the unionist coalition government in Lahore. Since the people of the Frontier Province would not play ball with the League, the same tactics would not pay dividends there. A different strategy was needed. The League infiltrated a large number of their 'volunteers' from the Punjab to the Frontier Province to sabotage not only the peace there, but also the communal harmony. To justify its action, the League created the facade of a civil disobedience movement to challenge the authority of the legally and constitutionally constituted government. The governor of the Frontier Province, Olaf Caroe, played a dubious role in giving credence to the League's propaganda that since the elections to the legislative assembly last year, the Congress government had lost the confidence of the people and the political situation had materially changed to justify a fresh look. The civil disobedience movement launched by the League, therefore, provided the rationale to the viceroy's scheme for a referendum in NWFP. Mountbatten had his reasons to accept the machinations of Olaf Caroe in Peshawar to push his agenda, but the Congress had none to fall a 'prey' at the cost of its 'sacred' principles, if sacred they were, which is very doubtful!

It was, perhaps, the viceroy's unstated logic that having accepted the principle of partition on the basis of Muslim-majority areas, excluding NWFP would be going against that very logic, particularly when the assembly as constituted was bound to opt for India. He also apprehended that Jinnah would find a part of India in his backyard unacceptable. The Afghans were also eyeing at this area covetously. The situation as it existed was quite uncomfortable for both Jinnah and the viceroy. Hence, to circumvent the existing situation, it had become logical to give a go-bye to the logic followed elsewhere. The need for a referendum in NWFP became, therefore, obvious. Jinnah was not unaware that if NWFP did not opt for Pakistan British Baluchistan was as good as lost, since the League had no roots there. Personally, Jinnah had not endeared himself to the Baluchis. It is a matter of record that later, when British Baluchistan voted for Pakistan and Jinnah wanted Mr Hugh Weightman, a retired secretary of the External Affairs Department who after retirement had settled in England, to be its governor, he declined it. Weightman, who knew Baluchistan and its people well, was aware that neither the League nor Jinnah was popular among the Baluchis and, therefore, he would find it difficult to carry out the Pakistan government's mandate in the area. When asked by the secretary of state, Listowel, to reconsider his decision and accept the offer of Jinnah, Weightman said that if he had at all to serve in India, he would do so under Nehru in the Indian dominion rather than under Jinnah in Pakistan. The Congress acquiescence in NWFP was nothing short of giving its seal of approval to the two-nation theory. That it was so was clearly borne out by the Congress reaction to HMG's proposals as they were officially unfolded on 2 June. The Congress letter of that day to the viceroy, conveying the party's reaction, instead of drawing attention to the incongruity and anachronism in the case of NWFP, asked for inclusion of the option of independence for the province, a suggestion which was also withdrawn within twenty-four hours. The viceroy simply reminded Nehru and Patel that it was the Congress which was against giving any province the option of independence, and what was not considered good generally for other provinces could not be good for NWFP alone.

There was still scope to correct this historic mistake even after the initial failure, if only the Congress had seriously applied its mind and not given it up as lost. It was a different matter that Gandhi personally remained committed to Badshah Khan and bowled one googly after another to get Jinnah to throw his wicket. Gandhi made impossible demands on the viceroy to intercede with Jinnah and allow NWFP not only internal autonomy but the right to secede later, in the same manner as Pakistan would have the right to secede from the Commonwealth. Gandhi did not ask himself the question whether Congress would allow a similar right to any of her own provinces! There were states like Hyderabad, Tranvancore, Bhopal, etc., that were on a different footing than the provinces. The states were technically being rendered sovereign and independent on the withdrawal of paramountcy, and yet Congress would not allow them any other option, not even treaty relationship, except accession to the union. How could Gandhi expect Jinnah to allow the disintegration of the moth-eaten and truncated Pakistan that he was getting, even before its birth?

A different strategy was the need of the hour, which could not have been beyond the comprehension of the Congress leaders. Unfortunately the Congress leaders, having smelt power, were so overtaken by its strong aroma that they were not willing to take the risk of considering any unconventional approach to attain what appeared lost, lest the whole process of transfer of power be derailed. They had decided to sacrifice the Muslim-majority areas on the altar of Pakistan, grab the rest, and that was that. The 3 June plan allowed the Frontier Province the option to choose between Pakistan and India through a referendum to be conducted under the aegis of the viceroy. Though London was averse to the removal of any governor at this time, when power was being demitted, Mountbatten, in order to remove the Congress apprehensions about the fairness of Governor Olaf Caroe, decided to oblige it. He replaced Caroe with Lieutenant General Rob Lockhart, who later became the chief of the Indian army on 15 August. And yet, the Frontier Congress decided to boycott the referendum. What were Badshah Khan's compulsions to do so? Why did he not go whole hog into the referendum and win it? It was apparently the painful assessment of the Frontier leaders that the induction of the Punjab Muslim 'volunteers' into the Frontier Province by the League had made the things difficult for them. A large number of the non-Muslim population of the Frontier Province had already fled to the Hindu-majority areas and the rest of them had been frightened and silenced. Most of the Muslim population had also been intimidated into accepting the logic of partition. The ferocity of the religious *jehad* let loose by the League had created fissures in the solid wall of the Pakhtoons. The ordinary people could no longer be swayed away in favour of the Congress which had accepted the logic of the League's two-nation theory. A vote against Pakistan was now perceived as a vote in favour of Hindu India. The Pathans were a simple people who could not understand the nuances of the Congress logic of accepting Pakistan, and yet not accepting a Hindu–Muslim divide. The whirlwind campaign that was needed could no longer be carried out on secular lines. A campaign on religious lines would have led to serious communal rioting among the Pathans themselves. It was precisely this that the Frontier Congress led by Khan Abdul Ghaffar Khan could not allow. The only choice was between boycott of the referendum and carrying the battle for Pakhtoonistan to another day. In retrospect, it appears that the 'boycott' of the referendum was the only way in which the *Khudai Khidmatgars* and their leaders could have avoided bloodshed and rebellion against the Congress 'perfidy'.

Was there no alternative? Perhaps, yes. In conveying its reaction to the proposals unfolded on 2 June, the Congress had asked for the option of independence for NWFP, which it withdrew the very next morning. Instead of doing so Congress should have persisted with it. An announcement that India, on attainment of independence, would be free to give independence to NWFP in the exercise of its sovereign powers, which it would acquire on 15 August or when the

Indian constitution was framed, needed to have been made. When the All India Congress Committee met on 14–15 June to endorse HMG's plan for transfer of power, the same resolution or a separate one could have formally accepted the informal announcement, if it had been made earlier. Such a dramatic gesture would have been reassuring to the freedom-loving Pakhtoons and the Pathan leaders would have at least been assured that after the initial mistake, the Congress had atoned and made sincere efforts to retrieve the situation. What Gandhi was suggesting to Jinnah, the Congress could have done itself without having to beg anyone, and thus save the Pathans from the 'wolves'.

The Congress reluctance was primarily due to the tacit acceptance by it of the principle that NWFP, as a Muslim-majority province, was a natural part of Pakistan. Secondly, the Congress apprehended that if after independence one province was allowed to secede, it could have a cascading effect on other provinces, particularly on the princely states which were technically being let off as independent and sovereign states by the British, even while India was insisting on their accession. India had ruled out, for some of the recalcitrant bigger states, the option of even a treaty relationship. But the NWFP situation was a special one and needed special treatment and a special response. To perceive the delicacy of the situation and act accordingly would have been statesmanship, which alas, our leaders failed to demonstrate!

The Congress even failed to handle the Baluchi question with the sophistication that the situation demanded. Besides British Baluchistan, the heart of Baluchi nationalism was the state of Kalat. As pointed out above, the Baluchis did not trust the League and were willing to work out a *modus vivendus* with the Congress for a post-independence scenario. At the time of the visit of the Cabinet Mission in 1946, Maulana Abul Kalam Azad, the Congress president, rejected the aspirations of Kalat for independence, fearing that the state would turn into a bastion of western imperialism on the northwestern frontier. But as independence drew closer, Kalat and Pakistan entered into negotiations for post-independence arrangements. On 11 August, after a meeting presided over by the viceroy and attended by the Khan of Kalat and Jinnah, it was announced that, 'The government of Pakistan recognizes Kalat as an independent sovereign state in treaty relations with the British Government, with a status different from that of the Indian States'. Kalat also approached India for a similar declaration. Later the state approached New Delhi for permission to set up a trade agency in

Delhi. The Government of India did not respond to either of the requests and Kalat had no alternative but to merge with Pakistan, thus killing the Baluchi aspirations for independence. It may perhaps be added as a footnote that on 27 March 1948 All India Radio announced that the Government of India had turned down the request of Kalat state for accession to India. The Khan was so incensed with this affront emanating from the official media of the Government of India, that the very next day, on 28 March 1948, he acceded to Pakistan, declaring that 'despite his [Khan of Kalat's] difference with Jinnah, he, as a Muslim ruler, could never allow his state's accession to India'. (The Government of India, however, denied the veracity of the AIR report.)

The Congress also failed to take advantage of Afghanistan's interest in NWFP by acting in concert with Kabul. Afghanistan had demanded retrocession of the Afghan areas between the Durand Line and the river Indus, seized from Afghanistan in the last century. Failing that, Kabul built up pressure on the British government, both in London and New Delhi, to get the option of independence for the province. The Afghan ambassador in Nanking had told the Indian ambassador there on 19 June that now that India was being divided, the Afghan 'sentiments and claim' on the 'Afghan portion of India' should not be ignored. He argued in favour of NWFP and Baluchistan being clubbed together to form an independent state in intimate relations with Afghanistan. While the External Affairs Department of the Government of India naturally disabused Kabul of any such hopes, surely after 15 August 1947 the position should have materially changed. If in a referendum, the NWFP and Baluchistan following suit, had opted for India, these territories could have been created into independent or semi-independent state(s) in treaty relations with India and Afghanistan. The Congress was so immersed in and obsessed with the impending dawn of independence, and anxious to tighten the nuts and bolts of the state apparatus, that it hardly saw beyond its nose, and thereby suffered no qualms of conscience in sacrificing the Pathans and the Baluchis.

Conclusions

It is one of the ironies of history that the tragedy of partition could not prevent greater tragedies later. Jinnah, like Moses, guided his people to their promised land but did not live long enough to see the emergence of the Pakistan he articulated in his speech to the Pakistan Constituent Assembly on 11 August. The forces of fundamentalism, bigotry, fanaticism and intolerance that he had unleashed during the preceding decade to achieve Pakistan could neither regress nor retreat and were to consume Pakistan itself.

Even its emergence as a sovereign state could not rid Pakistan of 'Hindu' phobia. It has, in its existence of half a century, failed to cast away the fear that India intends to grab it or destroy it. Despite the partition of the country on the basis of the two-nation theory, India continues to feel proud of its historical legacy in which the Muslim rulers, who either themselves came from outside of India or whose dynasties came with swords in their hands to subjugate the people of this country with an alien culture, settled down in India and made no mean contribution to her life. They enriched Indian art and architecture, language and literature, sartorial and culinary traditions, etc., and India is proud to recall their contributions.

Unfortunately, in Pakistan's case every attempt and effort has been made to 'liberate' its culture that is rooted in the Indian soil and has Indian moorings. It has made every effort since partition to get itself liberated from the cultural ethos that has Hindu trappings. Even history has been rewritten and placed on its head to glorify the Islamic rule, disparaging Hindu traditions and contributions. The urge for a new Islamic identity only succeeded in implanting in the Pakistani psyche hatred for its neighbour, driving India and Pakistan farther apart. And herein lies the greatest tragedy of partition!

Fifty Years On
Decolonization in Asia and Africa

D.A. Low

At the turn of the century, we were at the beginning of a twenty-year period of successive celebrations of the first half-century of independence of a large number of former colonial territories. Between 1945 and 1965, over fifty decolonizations occurred in Asia and Africa and a handful more ten years later. (Still later followed several smaller countries in the Southwest Pacific and the Caribbean.)

In view of the many studies that have now been made of the processes of decolonization in so many individual countries, it begins to be possible to offer a number of general propositions about the ways in which these proceeded; to say something about the main Asian stories—which ran largely parallel to each other—and the main African ones—which ran much more sequentially; and then offer two generalizations about the final stages in the process.

General Propositions
First, then, seven general propositions:

1. The character of the colonial encounters that led to independence varied over a wide range, form little more than robust elite mobilization at one end to bitter wars of independence at the other, with a good many variations in between.

2. Whatever some of the metropolitan-centred accounts may suggest, the growth and development of a vigorous nationalism was almost invariably the principal propellant of sustained progress towards the ending of colonial rule and the critical component in it.

3. Where, for whatever reason, nationalism developed more slowly, as in Malaysia as compared with Indonesia or in tropical Africa as compared with monsoon Asia, the onset of decolonization took

significantly longer to eventuate. This was especially the case where, as compared with neighbouring situations, there were 'native states' still extant under colonial rule: as in princely India, in northern Nigeria, in Malaya, and so on.

4. While at the climax nationalist euphoria was generally widespread, it is important to distinguish between those situations where nationalism was essentially elite-generated and those where it was populist-propelled.

5. It is important, then, to note that elite nationalism was always far easier for the imperial powers to suppress than populist nationalism. It was much easier to lock up the leadership of the Indian National Congress—even 60,000 of them—than to know which pullulating district would erupt next, as in Tanganyika (as it was then called), or Zambia, or even Uganda.

6. Two things were therefore of central importance. The character of the nationalist–imperialist encounters that occurred were principally determined by the nature of the response of the imperial power to the nationalist thrust against it; and

7. The form that nationalist activity then took was principally conditioned by the nature of the imperialist response by which it was confronted.[1]

Monsoon Asia

In the light of these general propositions one can turn to consider the main Asian anticolonial stories as something of a single group.

All but one Asian nationalist movement began by being elite-generated. The exception here is the Katipunan-led Philippines revolution against Spain in 1896, which was however, from 1900 onwards, completely overtaken by the elite-led Filipino nationalism of Aguinaldo, Osmena and Quezon against the Philippines' new imperial power, the United States of America.[2] The Indian National Congress, founded in 1885, was for a long time an elite organization (epitomized by its early leaders Ranade, Banerjea, Tilak, Gokhale, Mehta).[3] So were the early phases of Vietnamese nationalism in the heyday of Phan Boi Chou.[4] Likewise, Indonesian nationalism in the hands of Tjoakraminoto and under the inspiration of Katini;[5] and Burmese nationalism in the days of U Ba Pe.

At the end of World War I (at the time of the May Fourth movement in China, but more especially as part of the worldwide surge of nationalist demands following the promulgation of President Wilson's 14 Points on this issue in 1917) all these Asian nationalist movements became more activist. There was the expansion of Sarekat Islam in Indonesia; Gandhi's first nationalist campaign in India in 1919 and in association with the Khilafat movement in 1920–22; the Philippines' first Independence Mission to Washington in 1919; the campaign of the Buddhist Associations in Burma; and the founding of the Ceylon National Congress in what is now known as Sri Lanka.[6]

Inspired by the Russian revolution of 1917, communist parties began to spring up in Asia after World War I as well. It was not merely the Chinese Communist Party that was founded in 1921. In that year the Communist Association of the Indies was founded, which in 1924, became the Partai Kommunis Indonesie. That was eventually paralleled, after some fits and starts, by the founding of the Communist Party of India in 1927, while 1930 saw the founding of both the Indo–Chinese Communist Party and the Philippines Communist Party. Although the Communist Party of India became for a while closely involved with the labour movement in Bombay (and less dramatically in Calcutta), while both the Partai Kommunis Indonesie and the Indo–Chinese Communist Party came to be associated with peasant revolts in Indonesia and in Vietnam, all of these communist parties in Asia were also at this stage elite organizations. They were all, moreover, soon crushed by the corresponding imperial power. The Partai Kommunis Indonesie was all but exterminated by the Dutch in 1926–27, the Indo–Chinese Communist Party by the French in 1930, the leadership of the Communist Party of India was extensively imprisoned by the British (following the Meerut conspiracy case) in 1929, and that of the Philippines Communist Party by the Americans in 1933.

It is then worth emphasizing that the first mass movements in monsoon Asia were neither communist nor secular nationalist but Muslim: Sarekat Islam in Indonesia during and after World War I, and the Khilafat movement in India in 1919–22. Both, however, soon disintegrated: Sarekat Islam as a consequence of its infiltration by communists; the Khilafat movement following Gandhi's calling off of the joint Non-Cooperation movement with the Indian National Congress, when this spilled over in violence at Chauri Chaura in 1922 (and then irredeemably with the abolition of the Khilafat movement in Turkey in 1924). Crucially, however, each left behind in India and in Indonesia the sense—which was not so true elsewhere—that mass movements could be created in these countries.

The collapse of both these Muslim movements and the crushing of the communists left the field open to secular nationalist parties: Quezon and Osmena's Nacionalistas in the Philippines; Gandhi's Indian National Congress; the various nationalist parties under Sukarno and Hatta in Indonesia; and to some degree at least the VNQDD in Vietnam.

As adumbrated earlier, the nature of the conflicts between these secular nationalist parties and their imperial rulers which then ensued was principally determined by the distinctive responses of their particular imperial power to their activities; while the actions that these nationalist movements then came to take were extensively conditioned by the nature of the response of the imperial power, which they confronted towards them.[7]

In the four main cases that occurred in monsoon Asia there was a wide spectrum of circumstances. As early as 1912 the Democratic Party in the United States committed itself to Philippines' independence. By the Jones Act of 1916 the US Congress undertook to grant the Philippines independence 'so soon as stable government has been established'. During the 1920s there was some dragging of the feet by the American Republican administrations, but since empire was of no importance to the Americans, following the installation of Roosevelt as the Democratic Party's president of the United States in 1932, and as a consequence of a final pair of Philippines Independence Missions to Washington led by the Philippines' elite leaders, Osmena and Quezon, the Philippines secured internal independence in 1935 along with the promise of full independence ten years on. Independence came, in fact, in 1946; despite World War II and the Japanese occupation of the Philippines, it was only one year late in coming. It had been principally the achievement of the elite and required relatively little mass mobilization.[8]

In Indonesia the Dutch were always, in sharp contrast, quite determined to hold on to their Asian empire, believing that it was the 'cork' upon which the Netherlands' economy floated. In order to ensure that this should be so, after some uncertain toing and froing in the early 1930s, in 1933–34 they eventually deported the principal Indonesian nationalist leaders, Sukarno and Hatta, to what was called 'internal exile' on some distant island for life.[9] Although these leaders were released by the Japanese on their conquest of Indonesia in 1942–43, at the end of World War II the Dutch remained determined to recover their hold on their Indonesian empire, and showed themselves quite prepared to use force to do so. That propelled into existence a populist uprising against them which developed into the Indonesian Revolution of 1945 and the creation of an Indonesian Republican army. All of this, with international support, eventually won Indonesia its independence in 1949, following more violent struggles.[10]

In Vietnam, following an armed revolt instigated by the VNQDD in 1930 and the communist-involved peasant revolts of 1930–31, the French executed nearly 700 Vietnamese nationalist and communist leaders. The empire was crucial for them and they made it plain that Vietnamese ambitions of independence would not be tolerated, using force again and again to do so.[11] By 1945 this led to populist uprisings against the French in many parts of Vietnam,[12] which thereafter came under communist-led Vietnamese nationalist control, buttressed by the development of the quite remarkable Vietnamese guerrilla army under Giap, which eventually broke the French at the battle of Dien Bien Phu in 1954.[13]

Within this spectrum India was the anomaly. The nationalist struggle there principally took neither the form of elite negotiation as in the Philippines, nor culminated in violent conflict as in Indonesia and Vietnam. This was because the nature of British imperialism was deeply ambiguous. In contrast with the Americans, empire was of immense importance to them, while in contrast with both the Dutch and the French, there were limits to the draconian measures they were prepared to take to maintain its existence.[14] They regularly committed themselves to constitutional reform, in a way the Dutch and the French never did, but until 1942 never agreed to foreseeable independence. For the Indian National Congress all this created a very confusing situation. There seemed no chance that elite negotiation would on its own achieve its ends: the British would have to be pushed. But equally, a full-blown violent revolution was not necessarily needed either, as the British could periodically be impelled into making peaceful concessions.

It was Gandhi who saw the way forward in these very ambiguous circumstances; he thus led his three great series of largely non-violent agitational campaigns against the British—in 1919–22, 1929–

34, 1940–43—which steadily eroded their control. At the same time the Congress steadily expanded its following from its highly elitist beginnings. By the end of World War I its English-speaking elite were joined by India's merchant communities—who had few counterparts in southeast Asia where these were mostly overseas Chinese. They were of critical importance because they provided both the money and the communications network to make the Indian National Congress an effective countryside organization. And all these were joined, one by one, during the period between the two world wars, by many of India's richer peasant communities. With the slight enlargement of the franchise under the British Government of India Act of 1935, this expansion enabled the Congress to win elections in 1937 and 1946, thus demonstrating its very considerable political power. Under the sustained pressure which all this generated, the British eventually conceded, in the Cripps offer of 1942—in accord with long-standing British political traditions and their continual mouthing of promises of constitutional development—that India could have independence once World War II was over.

Once Indian independence was in the offing the British were not going to resist the Burmese national army, that developed during the Japanese occupation, in ways that both the Dutch and the French so foolishly did against its counterparts in those other two countries. Burma accordingly became independent in 1948. So did Ceylon. Here, in view of the Sinhalese majority's deep worries about the threats from India and from their own Tamil minority, nationalist impulses had generally been rather muted. However, elite negotiations, as in the Philippines, sufficed to bring it to independence in 1948. Along essentially similar lines, Malaya too gained independence nine years later.[15]

Tropical Africa

After their South Asian experience the British abandoned their ambiguity in facing nationalist opposition, and generally committed themselves to colonial independence, subject to two caveats. They would not be so accommodating where there were numbers of British settlers; and, more generally, they qualified their undertakings to grant independence in terms essentially similar to those expressed by the United States' Jones Act of 1916 which stated that this would be granted 'so soon as stable government has been established'.[16]

After their defeat at Dien Bien Phu in 1954, the policy of the French in their colonial territories in Africa became trifurcated. In 1956 independence was granted to Morocco and Tunisia. Independence for Algeria (the closest of all colonial territories to its imperial centre), however, was totally ruled out: it was conceived as being a component part of metropolitan France itself. While in the baker's dozen of France's tropical African territories local control came to be granted under the *loi cadre* of 1956, they were made firmly subject to the France-dominated French Union.

It is then of first importance to notice that, unlike Asian nationalism (at all events until towards the end), African nationalism, while having its elite leaders, was far more extensively populist-impelled from the start. A chief reason for this lay in Africa's economic circumstances.[17] Economic causes—even the 1930s' world slump—played only a partial role in Asia. They were central in Africa. They arose out of the fact that it was only generally in the late nineteenth and early twentieth centuries—with the extensive development of its tropical cash crops for sale on world markets—that Africa as a whole first moved into the cash economy. Now, cotton clothing, metal utensils, corrugated iron roofing, bicycles, and Singer sewing machines could be bought for the first time. All too soon, and for all too long, the aspirations which were thus generated came to be deeply frustrated: by the world slump of the 1930s that had such an impact on Africa because its cash economies were so overseas-oriented; by shortages of purchasable goods during World War II; by the serious inflation which then ensued; and by the switchback boom and recession during the 1950s that was tied to the global exigencies of the Korean war. All of which led to deep discontent right across the continent, most of which was soon directed against the imperial powers.

The ensuing disturbances were characteristically very localized. They were accordingly much disaggregated, and thus, far more difficult for the imperial powers to handle than by imprisoning, exiling or executing nationalist leaders, as they had done in Asia. Kwame Nkrumah (of what soon became Ghana) captured the prevailing frustration quite precisely with his arresting slogan: 'Seek ye first the political kingdom and all the rest will be added unto you.' By the 1950s all this made life exceedingly difficult for almost every colonial governor, since he could never be at all sure which of the districts in his colony was likely to erupt next.

More importantly, the fact that this frustration was continent-wide meant that many imperialist myths were rudely swept aside. That somehow French Africa could be distinguished from British Africa, and Belgian Africa from both; and that British West Africa could be distinguished from 'white settler' East and Central Africa. Under pressure from a continent-wide 'wind of change' (as the British prime minister, Harold Macmillan, called it in 1960), imperial rule in tropical Africa collapsed between 1957 and 1964 like the proverbial row of dominoes.[18]

By artfully playing off 'positive action' (i.e. agitation) against 'tactical action' (collaboration—compare Indonesia's 'diplomasi'), Nkrumah, in the aftermath of independence for the Sudan in 1956, secured Ghana's independence from the British in 1957. Togo, Cameroons and Somalia, as trust territories of the United Nations, were scheduled to become independent in 1960, as was Nigeria—delayed for three years beyond Ghana because of the need to bring along its conservative north. All of a sudden these prospects then led both French tropical African nationalist leaders, and before long their counterparts in the Belgian Congo too, to demand that they should have independence at an early date as well. France by now was involved in seeking to hold on at all costs to Algeria. It accordingly found itself embroiled yet again, as earlier in Vietnam, in a bloody and eventually disastrous colonial war. It was in no mind to court further trouble on other fronts. While it sought to corral its tropical African territories into a revamped French union called the French Community provocatively in 1958 Guinea slipped the noose. That proved to be the beginning of the end. Belgium was hamstrung by its laws forbidding the use of its largely conscript army overseas without the conscripts' own agreement. So, along with Togo, Cameroons, Somalia and Nigeria, all the eight territories of French West Africa, each of the four in French Equatorial Africa, along with Madagascar (Malagasy) and then the Belgian Congo, all became independent in one great rush in 'Africa Year' 1960.[19]

That threatened to leave the British imperial presence in their East and Central African colonies obtrusively exposed across the tropical Africa midriff. Amidst a great deal of political turmoil Britain's colonial secretary, Iain Macleod, in 1960 opened the door for all seven British East and Central African colonial territories as far south as the Zambezi—British Somaliland, Tanganyika, Uganda, Zanzibar,

Nyasaland and Northern Rhodesia—to become independent by 1964. Botswana and Swaziland followed in 1966 (Lesotho having achieved its independence in 1960).

That left the three Portuguese territories in Africa, and Rhodesia. Just as under their then dictatorship the Portuguese had been able to force their conscripts to fight in Africa, so they sought to retain their hold there. But in consequence they soon found themselves embroiled in three disconcerting colonial wars, till in 1974 their army leadership finally cracked. Thereafter Guinea-Bissau, Mozambique and Angola all became independent during the mid-1970s, and in essentially similar circumstances, Zimbabwe did so too in 1980.

The accompaniments to this collapse were, as in Asia, all largely conditioned by the responses of the imperial powers. Thus, in West Africa decolonization in both the British and the French West African territories was mostly peaceful, because of the readiness of those two colonial powers, when pushed, to grant independence to all-black governments there. By contrast, in British East and Central Africa, decolonization was punctuated by insurrections and serious disturbances—the Mau Mau revolt in Kenya more especially—because of British attempts to preserve the paramountcy of its white settlers there. In Algeria, the Portuguese colonies and Rhodesia, decolonization was scarred by war because of the determination of the dominant powers in those places—as in Indonesia and more especially in Vietnam—to try to hold on to their control at any cost.

At the End

Two broad generalizations about the final stages of the whole process can then be offered.

First, once it became clear that the colonial power was going, the key issue was no longer whether it would go, but the distribution of power upon its departure. It was this concern that generated the Pakistan movement; the delay in Malaysia's independence for some years after most of the other countries in Southeast Asia had secured theirs; the frequent need in Africa for one more election immediately prior to independence; the political splits around the time of independence in Ghana, Nigeria, Uganda, Kenya; the Congo crisis throughout the 1960s; and the protracted civil wars in Sudan, Angola and Mozambique.

288

And second, at all events in the British empire, there was often a coming together, in the last stages of empire, of the principal nationalist leader and the outgoing colonial governor. The former wanted to lay hands firmly on the levers of power. The latter wanted a smooth transfer which would rebound to his country's credit, together with an assurance that power would be transferred to a well-entrenched nationalist leadership. One can see this phenomenon at work in several of the provinces of British India as early as 1937–39; famously in the conjunction between Nehru and Mountbatten in India; but also between Senanayake and Soulbury in Ceylon, Tunku Abdul Rahman and MacGillivray in Malaysia, Nkrumah and Arden-Clarke in Ghana, Abubaker and Robertson in Nigeria, Kenyatta and Macdonald in Kenya, Nyerere and Turnbull in Tanganyika, and so on. It was such associations that so often made the 'lowering of the flag' as much a nostalgic as an exhilarating occasion.

Notes and References

[1] For one person's elaborations on these matters see D.A. Low, *Eclipse of Empire*, Cambridge University Press, Cambridge, 1991, passim.

[2] A general account is in S. Karnow, *In our Image. America's Empire in the Philippines*, London, 1990.

[3] S.R. Mehrotra, *A History of the Indian National Congress*, Vol. I, 1885–1918, Delhi, 1995.

[4] D.G. Marr, *Vietnamese Anticolonialism 1995–1925*, Berkeley, 1981.

[5] See generally, M.C. Ricklefs, *A History of Modern Indonesia*, London, 1981.

[6] On this and the following paragraphs more details can be found in Low, *Eclipse*, chapters 2 and 5.

[7] The argument here, and in the paragraphs that follow, is elaborated in D.A. Low, *Britain and Indian Nationalism. The Imprint of Ambiguity 1929–1942*, Cambridge, 1997, especially chapter 1.

[8] See also P.W. Stanley, *A Nation in the Making: The Philippines and the United States, 1899–1921*, Cambridge, Mass, 1974; T.W. Friend, *Between Two Empire: The Ordeal of the Philippines, 1929–1946*, New Haven, 1965; B.R. Churchill, *The Philippines missions to the United States*, Manila, 1983.

[9] See also J. Ingleson, *The Road to Exile. The Indonesian Nationalist Movement, 1927–1934*, Singapore, 1979.

[10] A.J.S. Reid, *The Indonesian National Revolution 1945–50*, Hawthorn, 1974.

[11] There are many surveys; see especially, J. Buttinger, *Vietnam. A Dragon Embattled*, New York, 1967, Vol. I, p. 219, and also D.G. Marr, *Vietnamese Tradition on Trial 1920–1945*, Berkeley, 1995.

[12] For a detailed account see D.G. Marr, 1995, *Vietnam 1945. The Quest for Power*, Berkeley.

[13] E.J. Hammer, *The Struggle for Indochina, 1940–1955*, Stanford, 1966.

[14] Vietnam's Ho Chi-Minh famously remarked as early as 1922: 'The Gandhis ... would have long since entered heaven had they been born in one of the French colonies.'

[15] A starting point on all this could be H. Tinker, ed., *Constitutional Relations between Britain and Burma: The Struggle for Independence 1944–1948*, 2 vols., London, 1983; K.M. de Silva, ed., *British Documents on the End of Empire* (hereafter BDEEP), Series B, Vol. 2, *Sri Lanka*, London; 1997; A.J. Stockwell, ed., *BDEEP*, Series B, Vol. 3, *Malaya*, London, 1995.

[16] On much that follows there is still little to match the two volumes edited by P. Gifford and W.R. Louis, *The Transfer of Power in Africa: Decolonization 1940–1960*, New Haven, 1982 and *Decolonization and African Independence The Transfers of Power, 1960–1980*, New Haven, 1988. But see also, for the British Empire, *BDEEP*, Series A, Gernerla Volumes edited by Ashton and Stockwell (1996), by Hyam (1992), and by Goldsworthy (1994), and Series B, Vol. 1, *Ghana*, edited by Rathbone (1992), and Vol. 4 *Egypt and the Defence of the middle east* edited by Kent (1998) passim.

[17] See especially A.G. Hopkins, *An Economic History of West Africa*, London, chapter 7, 1973.

[18] A summary account is in Low, *Eclipse*, chapter 9.

[19] See chapter 8 in Low, *Eclipse* 1.

Sovereign Subject
Ray's Apu

Geeta Kapur

The First Decade of Independence

It can be argued that the national movement, as it 'demobilizes' itself, hands over the task of cultural transformation to the state, enjoining artists to cooperate with its new institutional structure. Further, that artists, like their intellectual counterparts, perpetrate a set of self-deceptions during the period of transition to a national state; that they can be seen to use a kind of ethnic identification with extant (and idealized) traditions while gaining the upper hand through a rational-liberal discourse which is the basis of actual economic and social power in their society. An overlapping projection of (past) authenticity and (future) progress provides a formula for a democratic impulse, but it may be at the cost of the very people on whose behalf freedom was won. Both aspects of the projection have a euphoric dimension that obscures the present subaltern identity of the people in question.

Intellectuals 'always face the dilemma of choosing between a "westernizing" and a *narodnik* tendency', Ernest Gellner says,

> but the dilemma is quite spurious: ultimately the movements invariably contain both elements, a genuine modernism and a more or less spurious concern for local culture. By the twentieth century, the dilemma hardly bothers anyone: the philosopher kings of the underdeveloped world, all act as westernizers and all talk like *narodniks*.[1]

In Nehru's effort to situate nationalism within the domain of state ideology there was, as we know, a concerted effort to engage in planned development. There was an attempt to create a new framework

291

of institutions to embody the 'spirit of the age': humanism, science, progress, and their synonym, modernity.[2] Partha Chatterjee calls it a 'statist utopia'.[3] Even a cursory glance at the public institutions set up for promoting the arts after independence reveals that the cultural policy favoured a centralized and integrationist functioning.[4]

Culture was sought to be institutionalized precisely in order to carry out the overall mandate of modernization. In fact this institutionalizing process was conceived of as a way of disentangling the modern from the nationalist polemic. The latter had often to speak in the name of tradition even if it covertly strengthened the desire for the modern. While the national struggle had attempted to simulate a civilizational quest, the national state was bound to privilege culture as a means of cohering contemporaneity. In fact it would privilege culture above art as well, precisely because the intrepid claims of art always exceed, or subvert, even the more progressive rhetoric of institutionalized culture.

In India, as in other postcolonial countries (Mexico for example), artists have taken this institutional support for granted, nurtured as they have been throughout the anti-imperialist struggle on the idea of a benign national state. The nation's artists are provided with a sanctioned space in which they struggle with and resolve the riddles of language and sovereignty. For their part the artists seem to assume, even unconsciously perhaps, their responsibility to decode these terms and reconstitute them in what would be a national/ modern art. By the same logic Indian artists, while testing the existential implications of the modern in the context of the nation, have been facilitated by state patronage to gain a metropolitan identity.

If we extend the argument about the consequence of what has been called, after Antonio Gramsci, the 'passive revolution'[5] to analogous developments in the realm of contemporary arts, we find that Indian modernism has developed without an avantgarde. A modernism without disjunctures is at best a reformist modernism. The very liberalism of the state absolves the left of confrontational initiatives on the cultural front. Similarly, the very capacity of newly independent India to resist up to a point the cultural pressures of the cold war era makes it less imperative for artists to devise the kind of combative aesthetic that will pose a challenge to the Euro-American avantgarde. We know that cinema, literature and the visual arts in Latin America have revolutionized the very forms of the modern they inherited from old and new colonialisms. Whether this derives from a particular kind of a civilizational legacy, from the politics of liberalism adopted by the Indian state, or from peculiar accommodations made by the Indian middle-class intelligentsia when it moved from colonial to independent status, Indian artists have tended to avoid radical encounters with contemporary history.

All the same there is nothing to be gained from the kind of cynicism that Ernest Gellner for example uses to designate culture in the postcolonial countries. Even if art practice is ostensibly harnessed to the operation of the ideology and cultural policy of the new national state, creative practice is usually heterodox. There is a certain rebellion and also a dissembling radicalism among artists. Quite often there may be utopian formulations or, on the other hand, subversive symbols that have political import. Complemented even an episodic intransigence on the political front, it is enough to confound generalized theses on politics and culture.

Cultural Creativity

It is worth recalling that in Rabindranath Tagore's Santiniketan the romantic section of the nationalist elite led by the poet himself had encouraged an idealized aristocratic-folk paradigm for propagating a universal culture. The Santiniketan ideology in the practice of the arts was anti-industrial; with its strong craft orientation it was also obviously antiurban and emphasized environmental, ecological concerns.[6] Its vocational definition of the artist favoured a guru-shishya etiquette where the student idealized the master (Rabindranath was Gurudev, Nandalal Bose was the incontrovertible 'master moshai.') It abhorred the professional artist who was seen to demean himself by resort to the market. The modern was treated as the troubled feature of something like a civilizational project to which India, as part of the orient, would contribute its unique dynamic. This was the agenda of Benodebehari Mukherjee and Ramkinkar Baij. Indeed it was this indigenous romanticism combined with the canonical aesthetic of Ananda Coomaraswamy and the artisanal basis of Gandhian ideology which gave us the contours of a nationalist cultural discourse in the area of the arts. With the later alumni the aristocratic mentality of Tagore vanished. It had been transfigured already by the tribal persona of Ramkinkar Baij; now K.G. Subramanyan opted in favour of a transaction with the popular to arrive, through a series of modernist mediations, at a strategic notion of the contemporary.

By 1947 the course of Indian art was set *away* from Santiniketan. But if this phase of national culture was left behind in the irreversible process of post-independence modernization, the very abandonment gave rise to a permanent nostalgia for indigenist life-forms. It also led to a project for creative compensation fulfilled by an array of invented traditions.

What also got sidestepped with the advent of independence was the experiment of the cultural front of the communist movement, the most important aspect of which was of course the Indian Peoples' Theatre Association (IPTA).[7] This left another form of nostalgia, even a fierce regret, which led in turn to some major statements in art. It characterized for example the self-reflexive form of Ritwik Ghatak's cinema: the loss of a radical dream is actually thematized in his *Komal Gandhar* (1961) and *Jukti Takko ar Gappo* (1974). Ghatak, positioning himself to go beyond the so-called intermediate phase of bourgeois democratic culture, claimed modernism to be part of a logic beyond reform; indeed he positioned the logic of twentieth-century revolutionary socialism against reformist modernism. In this somewhat voluntarist exercise he provided the impetus, rather like the unorthodox genius D.D. Kosambi,[8] to see Indian tradition turned inside out, to question the assumptions about myth and reality, to problematize the nurturing potential of perennial symbols by confronting them with a historically shaped subjectivity. Precisely from this point of view Ghatak, a product of IPTA, would reject the over-determination of the aesthetic. He would pitch his expressional ambiguities beyond the westernizing/narodnik paradigm and give the interrogative mode its political edge in the contemporary.

The pan-Asian revivalism of Santiniketan as well as the people's movement of IPTA turned out to be lost causes in post-independence India. We therefore have to resume investigation of an apparently nonideological or liberal aesthetic. Clearly, it is within this discourse that Satyajit Ray's redemptive promise in the realist genre is to be located. And though this will be the basis of the critique as well— that is, his unproblematized faith in the self-emancipation of the Indian (or more precisely, of the emergent Indian middle-class) consciousness—it is because of its redemptive promise that *Pather Panchali* (1955) gains an emblematic place in the first decade of independence. Liberal discourse, privileging a realist genre with its rationally conceived possibilities of transcendence, gives *Pather Panchali* and the Apu trilogy their seminal significance in postindependence India.

Modernizing Project

Ray's choice of Bibhutibhushan Bandyopadhyaya's novels *Pather Panchali* (1928) and *Aparajito* (1931),[9] his choice of a story— set some time in the early years of the twentieth century—of the growth, travail and transformation of a young brahmin boy in the mainstream of the modern, has obvious allegorical value. The footsteps of the brahmin boy mark the transition of an impoverished but literate and gracefully poised culture of perennial India, as also the transition of 'the people' towards a subliminally perceived destiny. Narrativized with appropriate pathos, each discovery of the boy is accompanied by loss and the discovered self carries the weight of familial and social responsibility. This is a responsibility, however, that is displaced in various registers of consciousness, dodged and deferred through various stages of life. This is a story about the romance of the self and the world in the heart of Apu who passes through urban anomie like a sleepwalker, and who gains in the balanced aesthetic of Ray's cinema a life that will stand testimony as a realist document for numerous lives-in-the-making.

I will argue that by virtue of its universal success *Pather Panchali* confirmed that an Indian cultural creativity was at work to link civilizational memory with the sense of sovereignty that independence brings. There was in the making and receiving of *Pather Panchali* a hope that this cultural creativity would overcome the painful alienation of the colonial experience by turning it into a rite of passage to modernity. The colonial experience could then be marked with a before and an after: the before would be designated in terms of memory, or more properly as civilizational plenitude that yields the great imaginary. The present would move on to the destined point of arrival where the process of self-reckoning with otherness and authority, which is to say the symbolic order, has been tackled. Reality, contemporary reality, would now surface, materially replete, from its nourishing matrix. But it would also be indelibly printed with the structures of rationality gained at the collective level in the struggle for independence and revealed in the new national formation.

Pather Panchali served to provide a gloss on the civilizational trauma caused by progress; it sublimated (and displaced) the threat of modernization into a dream of autonomy. And it fulfilled the need for a newly self-regarding middle-class intelligentsia to channel its conscience. *Pather Panchali* became in the process something akin to an ethnographic allegory (built on a promise of plenitude) which denies and even seemingly undermines the politicality of a national formation (an artifice for social authority), but in fact served by deliberate default as a national allegory. That default may be seen as a way of reading one thing for another, a structure of narration corresponding to a structure of feeling. In a reticently existential film sovereignty corresponded to what one may call the political unconscious of the expressly conscious artist in postindependence India. It led 'logically' to a narrativization of the self via the nation—the most determining political paradigm delivered to the modern consciousness by the nineteenth century. Therein the nation tends to appear less as a societal struggle and more as an evolutionary trace in the consciousness, which is precisely the paradox at the heart of such a discovering mission.

The Apu trilogy is replete with symbols of colonial India in which it is temporally placed, but the colonial (like the national) consciousness is not really addressed. The village as a pristine community of precolonial India is linked directly with the sense of the historical present, Ray's own contemporary India, where the nation is the determining but invisible trajectory in the wake of which the individual can at last be valorized.

Ray's National Status

It is usual to argue that Satyajit Ray[10] belongs naturally to the Bengal heritage, beginning with the rationalized ethics of the Bengal 'renaissance' through the liberal strand of the Brahmo Samaj to which his own family belonged. And to the literary and artistic traditions reposed in Rabindranath Tagore.[11] Ray is indeed a literary filmmaker in that the developed conventions of the Bengali novel as well as its particular set of emancipatory themes are his basic material. His choice of Bibhutibhushan's novel *Pather Panchali* and its sequel *Aparajito*, which encompassed the environmental structure of the Bengali village and the destinies that ensued from it—this choice itself was significant in that it gave him through its picaresque mode, the secular space for his succinct and contemporary narrative on film.

I will argue that it is the ethics of his own version of realist cinema as this is internationally received which make Ray India's emblematic *national* artist in the decade after independence. At the biographical level the actual inscription within national culture of his first film *Pather Panchali* (1955), followed by *Aparajito* (1956) and *Apur Sansar* (1959), makes of itself a runaway story. With all the difficulties of finance Ray faced during the three years he spent making *Pather Panchali*, it was finally the West Bengal government, on the personal recommendation of the chief minister Dr B.C. Roy, that bailed the film out. No one, however, knew very much about why they were supporting the project and found justification in it being a kind of documentary. The money was granted from the account of a rural upliftment programme of the government because the film was called 'The Song of the Little Road'!

Jawaharlal Nehru had to intervene to allow the film to circulate abroad as there were objections from Indian diplomatic missions that it was too stark and pessimistic.[12] It had a prestigious opening, first at the Museum of Modern Art in New York (1955)[13] and then at Cannes (1956), where it won an award for the 'best human document'. In 1957 *Aparajito* won the Golden Lion in Venice and this confirmed Ray's international reputation. *Pather Panchali* opened commercially in London (1957) and then again in New York (1958), where it achieved huge popularity.[14] All of this was superimposed on the quick success of the film in Calcutta itself with high praise from Ray's compatriots everywhere. Thus traversing regional/national/international contexts, *Pather Panchali* became independent India's gift to the confluence of world cultures. 'Each race contributes something essential to the world's civilization in the course of its self-expression', Marie Seton quotes Coomaraswamy from the *Dance of Siva* at the head of her biography of Satyajit Ray.[15]

On seeing *Pather Panchali* and *Aparajito* Stanley Kauffman wrote that he believed Ray was determined to preserve the truth about his people and that, para-phrasing James Joyce's Stephen Dedalus, he was 'forging in the smithy of his heart the uncreated conscience of his race'.[16] The Indian intelligentsia too held it in similar regard and in terms that were not dissimilar. On the one hand it was seen as a testimony of individual conscience, and on the other as a civilizational

297

expression mediated by some form of 'racial' memory, producing symbols with contemporary aesthetic affect. This was the cultural discourse that the Apu trilogy enriched—a romantic, even orientalist discourse, shared by resurgent nationalities of the east in the first decades of this century with Coomaraswamy and Tagore as its key figures.

Tagore and Santiniketan

It is well known that it was from Rabindranath Tagore, a friend of the family and a lifelong inspiration, that Ray derived his sustaining aesthetic;[17] the need in particular to test contemporary Indian art forms on the simultaneous value of the *indigenous* and the *universal*—euphemisms in Ray's case for the regional and the international. In this sense Ray can be seen as completing India's civilizational quest as this had been articulated in renascent terms since the nineteenth century. Here, almost by deliberate default, the question of national culture was overwhelmed by preferred metaphors of perenniality.

But then *Pather Panchali* and the Apu trilogy as a cycle can also be seen as answering, in some unprecedented sense, a contemporary and most immediate need for a suitable visual solution to the question of representing everyday life in India. The perennial and the everyday: this was Ray's project. Ray imbibed this under the tutelage of Nandalal Bose and Benodebehari Mukherjee during his student days at Santiniketan's Kala Bhavana.[18]

In this sense, then, Ray was not only completing a nineteenth-century project, he was bringing two of its most distinguished cultural products across the threshold into realism: the Bengali novel in its own version of a *bildungsroman* and the pictorial language of the Bengal school, but more specifically the Santiniketan artists whose ambient imagery aspires to a kind of oriental naturalism. Now, as a film-maker, he seemed to resolve with exemplary economy the question of image, iconography and pictorial narrative—questions pending precisely since the Santiniketan project wound down in the 1950s.

Satyajit Ray's relationship to the indigenous filmmaking tradition of India, a rich and variegated tradition nearly as old as film history itself, is an area still to be properly examined. It should reveal a third and perhaps surprising trajectory running through his cultural formation. Here I want only to note that there is at work a conflation of the virtue of the camera lens (*objectif* in French) and the rest of the elaborate apparatus that goes into producing the moving image with the convention, the aesthetic, the ideology and the norm of realism. This is not the place for a critical debate on the realist genre in cinema, but it is worth remembering that this conflation initiates the viewer into a magical pact with the real whereby s/he comes to believe that the paradoxes of fantasy and perhaps even historical contradictions can at the least be visualized. The viewer moreover is led to believe that by virtue of this privileged participation in an inviolate perceptual model, a pristine cognition is also as if at hand and possibly also a universally valid resolution between nature and culture.

Ray is valorized for authenticating, in so contemporary a medium as film but yet with a commitment to the conscience of his 'race', a reforming will that befits the prevailing human conditions in India. He is also believed to have authenticated with an aesthetic modesty, the progressive aspirations of the liberal middle class. For the Apu trilogy enacts with its 'poverty of means' the painful entry of a traditional society into the historical process. It replays the rhythm of that transformation in the very narrative mode of the three films while also confirming the transcendent imagination of the author-artist: Apu, the hero of the novel and the film, is also a writer. The conspicuously placed cathartic moments of the Apu trilogy mark a patient pace and then grant the individual his process of becoming. For Apu outpaces by a finely tuned voluntarism the ritual rites of collective survival, to take his unique place in the wide world.

Death and Desire

Apu's material world is enlivened by seasonal cycles, kinship networks, children's games, adult rituals. Thus 'naturalized', simple episodes (and the film is made up of these carefully edited episodes) turn into absolutes that prefigure the fixed markers of human life: birth and death. But if all this is seen as the unmotivated truth of collective life, the very texture of a community, Satyajit Ray on his own part seems to press no strong structure on the film.

Twenty years after the film was made Akira Kurosawa,[19] the Japanese filmmaker, is quoted to have said:

> It is the kind of film that flows with the serenity and nobility of a big river. . . . People are born, live out their lives, and then accept their

deaths. Without the least effort and without any jerks Ray paints his picture but its effect on the audience is to stir up deep passions. There is nothing irrelevant or haphazard in his cinematographic technique. In that lies the secret of its excellence.[20]

Though *Pather Panchali* is manifestly episodic, actual historical discontinuity, like the experience of the colonial/national, remains an invisible feature. One has instead the fantasy of overarching continuity—from civilizational origins to the ambiguously periodized historical present. Thus the riverine metaphor, and the reception of *Pather Panchali* as a graciously easy film. But of course this is a typically realist ruse: the apparent absence of structure, of structural devices. By the time the Apu trilogy is complete one is aware of a subliminal grid placed on the natural flow of life so that it comes to be marked and narrativized as destiny.

The narrative of the trilogy is marked, for instance, by a recurring motif of death: the death of Apu's sister Durga, the death of his father and mother, and the death of his beloved wife Aparna. The death theme is worked out in the actual cinematic sequence with complete predictability, the editing of shots around the event signal separation/pain/loneliness and at the end, on Aparna's death, tragic alienation. There is a metonymic simplicity, a part-to-whole relationship of easy relay in the way life's great transitions are indicated. It is as if this loss-inducing society (colonial society?) is to be overcome by a philosophic acquiescence which is in turn overcome by a larger historical motif of survival.

Paradoxically, the deaths accelerate Apu's determined evolution. Indeed there is a flamelike sense of self that grows steadily as Apu encounters life and death and life again, and the flame is like the gleaming individuality that has been on the anvil in bourgeois literature since the nineteenth century. If separation by death sustains the romantic motif of Apu's outward journey his persistent departures make him ever more the modern exile. It is Ray's own high modernity that helps him portray Apu's introspective individuality so gracefully. Finding himself a suitable mirror image in the sanguine, clear-eyed persona of the actor Soumitra Chatterjee, he portrays the chaste urbanity of the young man, his vulnerability as he is poised on the brink of liberation and his *jouissance* as well. The terms of this idealization are predictable: the bohemian outsider within bourgeois contexts, the garret artist who will indulge himself in grand speech and creative reverie at the cost of economic gain, the poet protecting himself from reification in an indifferent city.

If this idealization of the metropolitan artist seems like vengeance for his wild sister Durga who is sacrificed to the elements in the ancestral village, it also serves as the price of selfhood in an anthropological sense—whereby indeed some of the pain of the sacrifice can be redeemed. For Durga's zest is the primitive version of the almost mystical lover that Apu is in the last part of the trilogy, when he has lost his wife as well. Then the story of a sovereign self comes full circle. He rescues his little son stalking some imaginary game in the mock-forest of his mother's ancestral home, and when he carries his son away on his shoulders the relentless succession of deaths, of loss and degradation, has been broken. We know that Apu's own selfhood is now firmly positioned vis-à-vis a future. The spoken word hinged on doubt characterizes the destinal narrative, but the final shot of *Apur Sansar*, the son perched on the father's shoulders, offers an archetypal image of doubling. The carefully wrought protagonist enters another regenerating cycle working more consciously towards enlightened desire: a typical Ray motif.

Spatial Dimensions of the Narrative

Ray transforms the harmonic structure of the novel by inscribing and then submerging a synchronous grid of life's chores. Though immured in destiny, Apu weaves in and out of the grid and in the end stretches back to repeat himself through his son, weaving another more developed pattern. Thus the narration is spatialized; thus too little Apu in all his phenomenal encounters can always gain a threshold. Ray demonstrates this in *Pather Panchali* in the way every occasion for infantile desire throws up a prospect.

In Nischindipur Durga is the little dryad who, with aunt Indir the benign witch, alleviate poverty by thieving the village harvest of fruit. Together they create a sense of pleasure against Durga's parents' persistent sense of privation. Durga and aunt Indir die in *Pather Panchali*, both wanting, desiring. The father and the mother die in the second film, *Aparajito*, entirely evacuated of desire. This symmetry gives Apu, who probably sees himself as neither poor nor rich, his turn for poetic manoeuvre. In the last film, *Apur Sansar*, he finally unlocks the grid—the balanced stasis of peasant life—and emerges as the solitary wayfinder magnetized by the horizon.

Like Apu's, the viewer's gaze is relieved by the horizons set before every turn of event. Ray's sequencing of perspectival shots, his overall editing of space, which is to say the narrative inscription of space, produces real and invisible horizons ranged in several registers to facilitate exit. Nor is this entire achievement a formal affair. The mise-en-scene of the film is crucial. It is well known that Ray insisted on shooting *Pather Panchali* out of doors in the countryside to achieve the 'true' naturalism that was preferred by Jean Renoir and the Italian neorealists whom he so admired. Not unusual in the west, this was a brave decision for Ray as he was more or less a novice without funds at the start of the project. The result of this enterprise was anyhow different from Renoir and the Italians in that with Ray nature indexed, even perhaps fetishistically signified, his commitment to an idealized reality. We will see how it is in nature, in actual space marked by his tracking camera, that he accomplished his revelatory passage into the real.

Remember the famous scene in *Pather Panchali* of the two children, Durga and Apu, in the *kash* field beyond the village, near the railway line. This is the first sequence Ray shot of the film; this is where he demonstrates naively, superbly, how cinema can accomplish an immanence of the concrete by a delicately edited figure-ground relationship. He shows how natural elements are synchronized to produce a prefiguration of destiny; how he can overcome pragmatically discrete notions of nature and history, and in an eminently spatial encounter, gain an *image* of both at once.

The children play hide-and-seek in the plumed grass, they put their ear to the strange reverberations of the telegraph poles, and then seeing for the first time the long imagined train appear on the horizon, they run towards it, Apu far in the lead. It advances like a metal dragon thundering across the landscape only to disappear swiftly leaving a trail of black cloud. How often Indian filmmakers have used the train to cut up framed space and dislocate time, creating in the wake of its disappearance primitivist nostalgia, totemic fear, sheer anticipation. But in *Pather Panchali* the train produces the kind of epiphany Ray is peculiarly capable of conjuring, an epiphany springing from a simple mise-en-scene and a stereotypical symbol. There it is, the train, invoking rustic, childish wonder and turning into the paradoxical symbol of imposed yet desired modernization. There it is, the classic cinematic miracle of the train, transposed on to the landscape in such a way that nature itself seems to herald history. And Apu witnesses this open-mouthed until the camera, now on the near side of the train, shows the speeding hulk cut across his little body, leaving him momentously and forever charged.

It is at this point that Apu first comes into his own. Here he recognizes his yearning, in the thrumming of the poles and in the silence preceding the apparition of the train. Still in thrall of his sister, he finds a signal for becoming in the *passage* of the train and advances to take responsibility, as far as possible, for his own destiny. Ray invokes a mesmeric potency in nature to gain the reality effect. Apu first tarries in the landscape and then flies like an arrow in the heart of time, signifying in both movements that here, at this spot, the child's soul and the phenomenal world fuse and become lucid, self-revealing. This is also Ray's own realization, in terms of a perfectly chosen mise-en-scene, of cinema's privileged relation to phenomenological veracity.

But equally in this early sequence Ray is at pains to translate his sense of the real so that it might, even given the epiphany, remain on the right side of realism. Everything that follows this scene in the *kash* field will build up to Durga's death, giving her a permanence of being and thereby a trace of the iconographical memory that illuminates her name. And yet at the end of *Pather Panchali* when Durga is dead and the bereaved family prepares to leave the village of Nischindipur with its destroyed ancestral home, the otherwise impractical poet-priest, Apu's father Harihar Roy, declares that *this must sometimes be done*. That departure is necessary. Moreover, while the last shot of the family departing in the bullock-cart recalls the almost ubiquitous melodramatic conventions of Indian cinema (which coincide with and sometimes assimilate what one may call Indian realism: recall similar scenes in *Devdas* and *Do Bigha Zameen*), in *Pather Panchali* it is the steady gaze of the *little* protagonist that recognizes, however bleakly, the inward journey of his life.

Having signalled the crossing over of the hero in *Pather Panchali*, having indicated Apu gently pushing fate into a space for becoming, in the next film, *Aparajito*, Ray puts tradition itself in the balance. He puts the idea of tradition as well as its generic modes of the mystical and the melodramatic in balance with the self-creating subject, the invisibly inscribed subject-in-history that is Apu.

The journey on which Apu thus embarks, moving from

Nischindipur to Benares to Calcutta and then possibly to some unknown shore, illustrates precisely like the neorealism of Italian provenance the journey that countless young men will make in India. It does so in a way that allows to be heard, like a faint but insistently repeated undertone, the rhythm of their distant figuration. It does so in a way that allows to be seen the remote emergence of these countless young men in a narrative evocation of the national story. This is what makes the Apu trilogy something of an allegory—except that if the allegory at the national level has the express purpose of exorcising superstition so as to replace it with necessity (specifically economic necessity), there is in the novel and equally in the film a further transcending step. Apu rejects the supposed perenniality of village life; he abandons the rigours of his brahmin identity but also the bondage of labour in the city, so that on the realm of necessity is mounted an ordering principle of freedom.

The Apu trilogy, then, has two overlying motifs, one devolving and the other evolving. If the first motif is a kind of sublime fatalism, the second involves the rites of passage for a modernizing young adult. Ray establishes a perfect synchrony in these two primary motifs, pivoting them on childhood adventure but seeing them prefigure the demonstrably allegorical extension to Apu's quest for knowledge and sovereignty. What I shall go on to argue is that this notion of freedom itself may produce a condition of hypostasis.

Secular Imagery

'With apparent formlessness *Pather Panchali* traces the great design of living', Lindsay Anderson said at the time of the Cannes award in 1956, adding that Ray does this while giving the impression that 'he has gone down on his knees in the dust' and 'worked with complete humility'.[21] On another occasion, as if pressing the point, Ray commented: 'I direct my films in harmony with the rhythm of human breathing.'[22]

Nearness and distance are almost as if metrically composed and then intoned by the breathing life of forms. Ray places much of his work within the formal lyric mode. At the heart of the lyric is the desire for the numen, or to put it the other way round, the lyrical is an expression of the numinous and thereby haloed. Even the occasional irony within the lyric mode must work itself around the numen and not subvert it. For that very reason I should like to see the numen residing first and foremost in the ancient aunt Indir who is, for all her little wickednesses and folly, treated with utmost tenderness.[23] She is numinous because she is the last breath, the ultimate waif of traditional society. Here is also the irony and the very mischief in it turns into grace because the errant hag's breath goes out just like that, suffusing the phenomenal world with unfinished desire. But then Indir is compressed into the soul of the younger waif Durga, whose breath is high with the passion of pure childish greed. Free from accretions, it wafts across the village ponds and groves. Taken together in intimate moments of eating and laughing, these two give us the confirmed image of the numinous in *Pather Panchali*. Then at the end of the film there is something like an apotheosis. Soon after the old aunt dies Durga dances ecstatically in the torrential monsoon rain for all the world like a mad little demon. Or an adolescent goddess. When she dies she is reclaimed by the stormy night. And yet Durga is not really canonized; indeed she is nearly forgotten as the narrative proceeds and she leaves behind only a melancholy resonance, that small *excess* of unfinished desire which is the very attribute of lyric naturalism.

In all this Ray takes his cue from his immediate literary sources, Rabindranath of course, and Bibhutibhushan who may have had a less developed notion of generic options in literature but who could, as we see, elicit from material details a fully experiential world. Ray follows Bibhutibhushan in his reproduction of splendid imagery that just stops short, deliberately, of iconographical complexities. In fact he even inverts the icon, as in the old aunt, and yet retains the numinous as simply a breathing figure imaged forth with cinematic persistence.

Ray relies on a certain romanticist faith in the image as such: the image as against symbol and icon. I have already spoken about Ray's cinematic image with its phenomenological veracity, its breathing form and numinous grace; the image in more generic terms as a focus of his lyric naturalism. I should now like to argue how, given Ray's liberal and reformist ethics, this kind of image is imbued with a secular sensibility. By disallowing any mythic overload or excessive condensation or metaphorical density to develop in the imagery, that is to say by sustaining a lean aesthetic, he strengthens its realist–modernist features. Ray places himself modestly but firmly at the juncture where romantic reverie meets with realist conscience to find formal solutions. Then, desaturating the image and allowing an ironic retake on its inescapable symbologies, he makes a gracious transition to the aesthetic of modernism. Ray offers a post-Chekhovian sleight-of-hand that brings him close to an ebullient 'realist' like Jean Renoir.[24] Also to Francois Truffaut who in turn spans Hitchcock/Hollywood and the vanguard formalism of the French 'new wave'. Ray is sophisticated, playful, witty, and for all the burden he carries in representing India, he is a cosmopolitan filmmaker.

Ray is of course quite easily situated in film lineage. I am referring to the composite, broadly realist movement in cinema signalled by Renoir (to whom Ray apprenticed himself when he came to India in 1949 to make his film *The River*) and theorized by Andre Bazin, the philosopher-critic of existential persuasion.[25] He is closer to the Italian Vittorio De Sica whose lasting intervention in cinema history via *Bicycle Thieves* (1947) influenced Indian filmmakers (Bimal Roy's *Do Bigha Zameen*, 1953, being the first evidence). With 'classical' Hollywood directors like John Ford as the baseline, Ray picks his way through several options, aligned to realism on the one hand and to the new wave on the other. Finally, however, he retracts from the logical extension of both tendencies, particularly the latter which while incorporating realism gives itself over to modernist surrealism (as in Luis Bunuel, Alain Resnais). Like the Japanese masters Kenzi Mizoguchi, Yasujiro Ozu and Kurosawa, he finds a cultural location from where he can clarify, or even rigorously demystify, the means of representation. He offers the belief that art lends transparency to history and arrives at a near-classical repose.

Ray's somewhat dissembling faith that cinematic representation in the realist genre lends transparency to history itself is complemented by his remarkable achievement in rescuing and reinforcing the secular image within his own culture. And so we return him to the tradition of the modern within this culture—its quasi-liberal ideology underwritten by a Brahmo sensibility which seeks to infuse western values within an indigenous civilizational ethic, however that may be designated (or as a matter of fact precisely as it is designated by the poet-philosopher Rabindranath). Thus individual emancipation as in the bourgeois ethos can be translated into a drive for selfhood within a purposefully interpreted vedantic logic and delivered, twice mediated, to the contemporary. Through this process of translation you receive from Ray, as also from Rabindranath, his social and cultural contribution in the form of an eminently lucid reflection on the process of 'becoming' via the very vicissitudes of everyday life. Here is a double paradigm: the heterodox values of modernity set within civilizational beliefs (such as the spiritual propensity implied by the notion of *samskaras*). Within this complex structure of values Ray is circumspect. He draws in clear, firm, but delimited contours, secular figures that are consonant with the new social formation of contemporary India.

Even as he completes his first film on a shoestring budget he proposes through its precise figuration to clean out iconographical fuzziness and correct civilizational sloth. He provides a 'pure' narrative in a mise-en-scene that is, in the Bazinian sense, the arena of lived life. Here the protagonists may not, from a necessary sense of irony or from tragic purpose, command the universe, but they see the narrative through with unassailable dignity.

Authenticating the Modern

Bibhutibhushan's splendid novel is one among the narratives that are generically categorized as *bildungs-roman*.[26] In its generic form it gives Ray the occasion to shape an elegant, allegorical tale wherein the claims of individual sovereignty and secular culture are raised. Thus, while there seems to be no overtly progressive ideology that motivates *Pather Panchali*, nor even the Apu trilogy as a whole, there is the inexorable process of growing up and knowing within the terms of modern society the truth, or rather the ethics, of survival. It is through this kind of subliminal politics that Ray inflects the historical legacy to which he belongs.

Ray does not valorize historical change either in his early classics or later. Nor does he introduce narrative disjuncture whereby the unconscious may find its formal manifestations, a language and speech which interrogate historical change itself. In other words, Ray does not stake out the contemporary as a contested space for historical forces to act in—he simply lays the ground.

It should be remembered that his mentor Rabindranath Tagore had already problematized these issues in the early decades of the twentieth century. Consider the question of Hindu male militancy in his novel *Gora*; consider the high stakes he places on the creative spirit of his female protagonist, Charulata, in *Nashta-nir*. In *Ghare*

307

Baire Bimala literally acts out the turmoil of nationalism from her niche in the home. Ray gives these protagonists a vexed consciousness that detaches itself from civilizational determinates to engage with the more ambiguously placed promises of history.

Indeed it is somewhat inhibiting to Ray's position that in cultural discourse, as in particular forms of aesthetic resolution, Tagore has already bestowed so much more complex and even painfully contradictory meanings on self and subjectivity, on love, language, race, community, people and nation—on all those emancipatory epithets of the modern which derive from the double heritage of reason and romanticism. Ray, on the other hand, can only work with the deliberate use of anachronisms, as in his early films *Jalsaghar* (1958) and *Devi* (1960). The passing away of feudalism, for instance, is established through a negative denouement of a seamless tragedy. Historical insight is in this way elided in favour of an existential truth and cultural authenticity.

Ray is not only a prime exemplar of the authentic and authenticating artist, he lays to rest the vexed debates on tradition and modernity. I refer to these debates as they have proceeded from the Indian renaissance in the nineteenth century, debates entered into by Tagore, Gandhi, and also Nehru beginning with the *Discovery of India*. For a society undergoing rapid change after independence authenticity becomes once again the redemptive sign—an illusory redemption even, but expressly functional in sustaining a national discourse. More specifically, the consolidated aspirations of the liberal middle class have to be fulfilled, and they need an art form which will emancipate them not only from the tradition/modernity debates but also from the ensuing bad conscience into which they are cornered by traditionalists and radicals alike. The middle class, favoured by the nation-state, need moreover a demonstrably secular and sufficiently classical (or classicized) art form; a 'high' art form to gain parity, via the national, with universal (international) cultural discourse.

Ray certainly gives his class an existential basis for authenticity. Deferred and even elided, the wager on the *contemporary* surfaces as a vestigial presence in the Apu trilogy. The contemporary becomes a pressure on the cinematic figuration of his narratives; it leaves traces which allow themselves to be read as secular, modern, yet systemic enough to gain a classical profile. He does this, to reiterate in a sentence the argument that has run through the essay, by handling directly and to his advantage the relation between civilizational motives and historical affect. Letting the one and then the other outpace each other, he fills the 'ideal' role of an Indian artist within the progressive paradigm of the 'first decade'.[27]

Allegorical Account

We have already seen how the Apu trilogy touches a notion of authenticity that is existentially ascertainable. More specifically, it provides a measure of authorial credibility: a nonwestern artist in the best moment of his own historical self-regard, the moment of national independence, claiming individual sovereignty. I want to conclude by moving into the more vexed area of interpretation and suggest that the Apu trilogy is, and has been taken as, or perhaps should be taken as, a kind of *ethnographic allegory*.[28] It answers the continuing need of the liberal imagination, western as well as Indian, to comprehend 'otherness' on humanistically coeval terms. It answers the need to work out a system of equations within a cultural matrix that is finally, inevitably, universal and in that universality committed to a destinal narrative—inventing that term to mean at once destiny and destination, immanent life and a metanarrative that proxies for transcendence.

Ethnographic writing is allegorical, James Clifford says, at the level of its context: in what it says about cultures and their histories, and of its form: in what is implied by its mode of textualization.[29] He goes on to say that to shift focus from ideology to ethnographic allegory in readings of culture is to suggest that the more convincing and rich realistic portraits are, the more they serve as extended metaphors, patterns of associations that point to coherent theoretical/aesthetic/ *moral* meaning.[30] Further, as a rhetorical trope 'allegory draws special attention to the narrative character of cultural representation, to the stories built into the representational process itself.'[31]

This is the point I want to stress: the allegoric/narrative character of cultural representation in a film like *Pather Panchali*. Representation interprets itself in the narrative of the film, it opens out moments of moral insight or, rather, categories of 'truth' (fictional, cinematic and social) that fulfil the most wide-ranging cultural expectation, beginning with the local and culminating in the national.

Ray decidedly belongs to an intellectual climate that respects what Clifford calls positivism, realism, romanticism[32]—nineteenth-century ingredients of twentieth-century cultural studies. But, as Clifford goes on to say, studies in rhetoric (understood in my argument to mean figures of expression and more precise linguistic decodings) have disrupted the assumption of 'presence' that underpinned the positivist-realist-romantic consensus. Meaning does not flow through seamless discourse nor does it emanate from it as numinous presence. Indeed the recognition of rhetorical moves in the quest for meaning has disrupted the inclination to valorize the symbolic (underwritten by an elaborate realist project) over allegory.[33] And the doubts generated by this disruption help us to understand that culturalist/humanist allegories[34] stand behind the fiction of 'difference' deploying exotic symbols in aesthetic discourse, even as at one time spiritual explanations used to mobilize the interpretation of other cultures towards a norm of transcendent sameness. If most 'descriptions of others continue to assume and refer to elemental or transcendental levels of truth',[35] if there is a continuing need to establish through a nexus of symbologies, human similarities over and above cultural difference, then we can know that a definite elision is at work. 'This synchronic suspension effectively textualizes the other and gives the sense of reality not in temporal flux, not in the same ambiguous, moving, *historical* present,'[36] but in retrospection that encourages the recovery of the other by way of a redemptive psychology.

Ray allows the protagonist of the Apu trilogy to *redeem himself*. He stands extra tall at the crossroads with his child on his shoulder at the end of the last film of the trilogy, *Apur Sansar*. But there is in the very courage of this verticality a break between the past and the future, and a deep-rooted regret at the alienated space of the present. This alienated space concretizes the sense of pervasive social fragmentation, the sense of a constant disruption of 'natural' relations. This, Clifford says, after Raymond Williams, is characteristic of a subjectivity inducted into city life and suffused with romantic nostalgia for a happier place elsewhere in the past, in the country.[37] The self cast loose from viable collective ties is an identity in search of wholeness; having internalized loss it embarks on an endless search for authenticity, a sign of wholeness which becomes by definition, however, a thing of the past—rural, primitive, childlike—accessible only as fiction and grasped at but from a stance of incomplete involvement. Thus there is a withdrawal from any full response to an existing society. 'Value is in the past, as a general

310

retrospective condition, and in the present only as a particular and private sensibility, as individual moral action.'[38]

If Ray is part of the positivist-realist-romantic framework, then it is my purpose to show how 'presence' is in fact used to symbolic effect; how so-called empirical evidence in the form of realism and, on the other hand, artistic spontaneity designating longing, desire, aspiration, characteristic of the romantic/lyric mode, are drawn out and yoked. So much so that the rhetoric of 'presence' is established and becomes the inescapable truth of all expression.

There has been unmitigated trust extended to Ray's conscience story via Apu. But there is also the methodological ruse one can elicit from it: the truth-effect in the inadvertent form of an ethnographic allegory that will give us the clue to ramified cultural meanings —through reverse allegorical readings that work the text against the grain with political intent. While likening the Apu trilogy to an ethnographic allegory it becomes possible then to ask what significant displacement, what civilizational subversions it introduces in our notion of the contemporary.

It may be necessary to conclude with a set of paradoxical answers. First, it is probably the refusal on Ray's part to directly address the contemporary that makes the Apu trilogy function as a national allegory. For anything more frontal would be too partisan even as it would be, paradoxically, too divisive—like the contradiction of Indian independence presented by Ritwik Ghatak in his three post-partition films: *Meghe Dhaka Tara, Subarnarekha, Komal Gandhar*, and the 'betrayal' acted out in the body and myth of a radical consciousness in *Jukti Takko ar Gappo*. Satyajit Ray prefers a subtle, submerged, subliminal treatment of the contemporary/national; he conveys it through the conduit of individual sovereignty—the artist's idealized sovereignty, rendered like a romance of the liberal imagination, with the anachronistic figure of Apu guiding it through its narrative logic.

Thus Ray tells a real story and lets it work as a national allegory or, vice versa, constructs an allegory from otherness—the priestly family in feudal India—and makes it work as a tale of self-redemption and moral sovereignty for his own class and person. In this rendering the real struggle of the 'other' life, the life of the rural boy who makes the epic journey from the country to the city, is gently appropriated with the advantage of never having to admit to a social disjuncture as such. An organic identity is posited over and against any kind of historical formation. What is more, this kind of identity can assume a secular character by virtue of its having been delivered from the imaginary order, as a gift of past plenitude. So that one may then say that Ray arrives at the secular not through demonstrable negation of faith but through an aesthetic—a realism imbued with the grace of classicism, thereby with greater illusionism—that achieves the effect of a clarified and reasonable reality.

Ray fulfils for the Indian intelligentsia (and for a sympathetic foreign intelligentsia) its need to redeem the innocent pastorale—now left behind, as can only happen in a traditional/peasant society such as India. He also achieves an authentication of the modern self engaged in the act of redeeming this recent past which slips away even as we interpret it. This is a mediatory role consisting of a conversion of the terms of allegory from ethnographic to national. The conversion succeeds because it is noncombative, because it undertakes a salvage operation, and because what is salvaged is common humanity with a glimpse of its nearly inexhaustible resources. Ethnographic data, seen as a form of material immanence, serves as a base for the nimbly placed narrative schema of a national allegory with the hope that in the end we will rationalize a lost world and even make it conform to a history that runs into the contemporary with comprehensible ease.

This too is a type of rhetoric which conceals its function and invokes instead a desire that is utopian in the historical sense. The encoding of a haunting past not only places others—the eternal peasant, or the priest, or elsewhere as in *Jalsaghar* and *Devi*, the feudal lord—in a present always slipping into the past, into ruin, it not only denies a community or a class a future, but also obstructs inventive cultural possibilities and historical change. An imaginary plenitude that nurtures and subsumes, evokes and concretizes the 'presence' we referred to above, and also in a sense loses the future.

Village boys still grow up and move from the country to the city; they suffer loss and disaffection, poetic inspiration and bruised praise for their courage. If at the end of his life in 1992 Satyajit Ray were to tell the Apu story again it could never be the same as when it was told in 1955 or else it would appear entirely disingenuous (as indeed his late films often do). The substantive element of the story is never transparent; it is better seen as a material amalgam with different levels of density and opacity and (to pursue the metaphor) with geological faults in the bedrock on which the realist narrative pattern, or the conventional form of it, is constructed. Today, when the question of identity is thrashed about on various occasions—on grounds of regional authenticity, religious fundamentalism, national culture and the hegemonic universalism of advanced capitalistic polities—life-narratives have perhaps to be denatured to be even seemingly realistic. In other words, with the concept of identity so thoroughly problematized the fictive form itself must be subjected to the disruptive demands of reflexivity.

The sublimating ethics of the Apu trilogy notwithstanding (indeed precisely because of the cultural creativity that it so appropriately puts into place in postindependent India), we must test its cutting edge along the lines of the liberal ideology on which its aesthetic is based. If on the narrative impulse of that identity there could at one time be a transference between a person's and a people's sovereignty, today it would be difficult to find a social promise (or a trope) on which its formal (that is allegorical) transfer can be conducted. Today liberal ideology itself has to construct a narrative that includes the loss of that social promise, and along with that a methodological doubt about a coherent story line. It would have to include the *absence,* and through fictive reversal and retake it would have to work towards an indefinitely delayed denouement, whether in the form of tragedy or, on the other hand, some unaccountable *jouissance* perhaps. But the discreet optimism which Ray could once command, the aesthetic of gentle closure and unstressed beginnings, that kind of narrative ease would no longer suffice.

The very progressivism in the Apu trilogy can be seen in the paradoxical form of this conclusion to become diffused, to settle into a splendid hypostasis of hope. How then shall we read the allegory that the Apu trilogy evokes: as an indelible imprint on the national conscience not yet consciously elaborated or perhaps already vanishing in that remarkably optimistic first decade?

This essay was first presented at a conference. The First Decade of Indian Independence: 1947–1957, organized by the Centre for Contemporary Studies, Nehru Memorial Museum and Library, New Delhi, St Anthony's College, Oxford University, and Centre for South Asian Studies, University of Texas at Austin, and held at all the three venues, in 1990. An earlier version was published under the title 'Cultural Creativity in the First Decade: The Example of Satyajit Ray', in *Journal of Arts & Ideas*, Nos. 23–24, January 1993.

Notes and References

[1] Ernest Gellner in *Thought and Change*, quoted in Partha Chatterjee, *Nationalist Thought and the Colonial World: A Derivative Discourse?*, Oxford University Press, Delhi, 1986, p. 4.

[2] Chatterjee, *Nationalist Thought*, chap. 5.

[3] Ibid., p. 160.

[4] The National Gallery of Modern Art, Jaipur House, New Delhi, was formally opened in 1954 by Dr Radhakrishnan, but its collection had already begun with a gift to Nehru in 1948, of a large number of paintings by Amrita Sher-Gil. Briefed to collect works from the nineteenth century, it now has a collection numbering nearly 30,000. The institution has from the start functioned under the Ministry of Education (Department of Culture). The Lalit Kala Akademi, one of three Akademis dealing with the different arts, was set up in 1954 by a parliamentary resolution initiated by Nehru and Maulana Azad, the then education minister. Though entirely state-funded, it is an autonomous organization with an all-India representation comprising artists, critics and art functionaries. Over the years, regional centres have been opened in several cities. The Indian Council of Cultural Relations, also set up by the joint initiative of Nehru and Azad in 1950 and with the vice-president of India serving as its chairperson, promotes international cultural activity. The Film Finance Corporation, later called the National Film Development Corporation, was mooted as an idea to promote good cinema in the early 1950s, but came into existence with the direct encouragement of Indira Gandhi in 1960. It functions under the Information and Broadcasting Ministry with the brief of supporting non-commercial cinema. The National School of Drama, Delhi, and the Film and Television Institute, Pune, were started in 1961 and 1959 respectively, to serve as all-India institutions for higher learning in theatre and film .

[5] Partha Chatterjee makes a qualified use of this concept throughout his *Nationalist Thought*.

[6] See K.G. Subramanyan, *Moving Focus: Essays on Indian Art*, Lalit Kala Akademi, Delhi, 1978; and *The Living Tradition: Perspectives on Modern Indian Art*, Seagull, Calcutta, 1987.

[7] Collated information on IPTA is available in *Marxist Cultural Movement: Chronicles and Documents*, Vol. III (1943–1964), compiled and edited by Sudhi Pradhan, published by Mrs Pradhan and distributed by Pustak Bipani, Calcutta, 1985. See also Malini Bhattacharya, 'The IPTA in Bengal', in *Journal of Arts & Ideas*, No. 2, January–March 1983; and Rustom Bharucha, *Rehearsals for Revolution; Political Theatre in Bengal*, Seagull, Calcutta, 1983.

[8] D.D. Kosambi, *Myth and Reality*, Popular Prakashan, Bombay, 1962.

[9] Bibhutibhushan's story of Apu and Durga was serialized in a Calcutta journal in 1928 and published as a two-part novel titled *Pather Panchali* and *Aparajito* in 1929 and 1931 respectively. Bibhutibhushan was a unique man who led a life as opposed to the lives of the privileged Tagore and Ray

families as you could get in the city of Calcutta. A village boy, he managed to get a degree in Calcutta but lived the impoverished life of a schoolteacher just outside the city and then, from 1924, in Calcutta, where he came to know other writers, among them Nirad Choudhuri. Generous and unembittered by his hard life, he became a widely popular writer and attained the status of one of Bengal's foremost authors.

When Satyajit Ray started dreaming up his filmmaking career in the late 1940s he chose *Pather Panchali* right away, recognizing that the novel was a classic in its own right and linked up with literary traditions of the world in terms of its generic structure. *Pather Panchali*, the first film, corresponded to the novel of the same name, the two subsequent films *Aparajito* and *Apur Sansar*, were a two-part extension of the novel's sequel titled *Aparajito*. The three films were together called the Apu trilogy.

10 Biographical material on Satyajit Ray is widely available. See especially, Marie Seton, *Satyajit Ray: Portrait of a Director*, Dennis Dobson, London, 1978; Chidananda Das Gupta, *The Cinema of Satyajit Ray*, Vikas, Delhi, 1980; and Andrew Robinson, *Satyajit Ray: The Inner Eye*, Rupa, Delhi, 1990.

11 Satyajit Ray's family, among the most distinguished in Calcutta, were prominent Brahmos, beginning with his grandfather, Upendrakisore Ray, who was a pioneer in the Calcutta printing industry and the author of several articles on printing technology, published in the London-based *Penrose Annual*. He was also a writer-illustrator of children's literature including, most prominently, *Mahabharata for Children* and *Ramayana for Children*. Rabindranath Tagore, a family friend, was an enthusiastic advocate of Upendrakisore's writings. Sukumar Ray, Upendrakisore's son and Satyajit's father, began writing early, producing children's illustrated literature like his father and also criticism in the field of photography, painting and literature. Returning from his studies in printing technology in London in 1913, he started a magazine for young people, *Sandesh*. This made him a household name in Bengal with nonsense rhymes such as *Abol Tabol* elaborated over several years. Although Satyajit never knew his father, the latter exerted a great influence on him. Satyajit edited, illustrated and designed *Sandesh* and made several children's films throughout his career, occasionally quoting his father's nonsense verse as in his film *Parash Pathar* (1958), even as he has filmed his grandfather's story *Goopy Gyne Bagha Byne* (1968). He also made a fictional short on his father, *Sukumar Ray* (1987).

Sukumar Ray, who was a close friend of Rabindranath Tagore, travelled back with him from London in 1913. He involved himself in passionate debates within the Brahmos—the Ray family belonged to the Sadharan Brahmo Samaj—as for example on the question of Rabindranath's affiliation to Hinduism and the objections it raised among the Brahmos, as also his salleged equivocation on nationalist issues. Sukumar Ray, prone to premonitions of death and wrapped in pessimism on the issue of faith, withdrew from the Brahmo Samaj towards the end of his short life. Tagore deeply mourned his premature death at the age of 35 in 1923, when Satyajit was only two years old. For a detailed chronicle of Satyajit Ray's family, see Robinson, *Satyajit Ray: The Inner Eye*, pp. 13–55.

12   Nehru authorized the showing of *Pather Panchali* at Cannes at the express suggestion of Marie Seton. It is also worth mentioning that Nehru invited Roberto Rossellini to make his India films in the 1950s, that he knew John Grierson personally and that he invoked the tradition of the British second world war documentary in starting the Films Division (1949). Nehru's support for *Pather Panchali* could possibly be placed with other efforts to engage Indian cultural practices with those of European contemporaries in a reciprocal way. Indeed one can conjecture Nehru's seeing *Pather Panchali* from a precisely nonorientalist point of view, wishing to show before the world that a self-emancipating India existed in the conscience of a confident *auteur* like Satyajit Ray.

13   The film was invited to the Museum of Modern Art, New York, by Monroe Wheeler on the strength of some stills he saw in 1954 while the film's shooting, begun in 1952, was in abeyance due to lack of finance. The film was to be shown in New York in 1955; in between, Wheeler asked John Huston, who was coming to India, to be his emissary and check out the progress of the film. On the basis of a silent rough-cut Huston approved the film and later wrote glowingly about his early encounter with Ray.

14   Among the numerous stories connected with the early success of Satyajit Ray it is worth mentioning that both at Cannes and Venice it was the English critics and filmmakers who supported him; the French in both cases found him by and large incompetent, as one can gauge from Rene Clair's comment—that as he had now won the award at Venice he should go away and learn how to make films. There is also the widely quoted comment by Truffaut that the film was merely 'pad pad pad about paddy fields'. However, the commercial release of the film in the Academy Cinema and the Fifth Avenue Playhouse, in London and New York respectively, was a clear confirmation of its international success. The explanation of this success in terms of the film's universal humanism and liberal progressivism is discussed in a very finely articulated evaluation of the Apu trilogy by Robin Wood (*The Apu trilogy*, Praeger, New York, 1971). A compendium of worldwide comments on Ray (and by him) is to be found in *Film India: Satyajit Ray: An Anthology of Statements on Ray and by Ray*, edited by Chidananda Das Gupta, Directorate of Film Festivals, Delhi, 1981.

15   Seton, *Satyajit Ray: Portrait of a Director*.

16   Stanley Kauffman, 'World on Film', quoted in *Film India*, p. 27.

17   Satyajit Ray had met Rabindranath Tagore only a few times while he was a student at Santiniketan. But Tagore's aesthetic continued to be an all-pervasive influence in Bengali culture long after his death in 1941. For a collection of Tagore's relevant essays, see *Rabindranath Tagore on Art and Aesthetics*, edited by Prithwish Neogy, Orient Longman, Delhi, 1961. Apart from Tagore's aesthetic as available to Ray through his family connections in Santiniketan and via his philosophic essays, there is the whole world of

Tagore's literature which is in fact the basis of several of Ray's films—*Teen Kanya*(1961), *Charulata* (1964) and *Ghare Baire* (1984). *Devi* (1960) was based on a story inspired by Tagore though written in fact by Prabhat Kumar Mukherjee. Ray also made a documentary *Rabindranath Tagore* (1961).

18 Ray studied art in Kala Bhavan, Santiniketan, 1940–42. He left without completing the course because he did not feel he had it in him to become a painter, and he joined an advertising company in Calcutta. But the experience had a lasting influence on his sensibilities and indeed on his loyalties, as his film on the artist-teacher Benodebehari Mukherjee, titled *The Inner Eye* (1972), shows.

19 Ray knew Kurosawa and held him in deep admiration. It is interesting that Ray considers Kurosawa—regarded the most western among his compatriots in Japan—in terms of an affirmative orientalism, an ideology Ray derived from Santiniketan. Indeed he placed his love of Kurosawa, in particular, and Japanese cinema in general, within the principles of an art practice learnt from Nandalal Bose, and on the ideological rendering of the eastern imagination by Okakura Kakuzo. See Satyajit Ray, 'Calm Without, Fire Within', in *Our Films, Their Films*, Orient Longman, Delhi, 1976.

20 Kurosawa, quoted in Robinson, *Satyajit Ray: The Inner Eye*, p. 91.

21 Quoted in Seton, *Satyajit Ray: Portrait of a Director*, p. 114.

22 Ray's interview with George Sadoul in *Cahiers du Cinema*, quoted in *Film India*, p. 130.

23 Ray actualizes this in the way he directs the old actress, Chunibala Devi, to literally act out her life's spent talent. The moment of Indir's death which, in the years it took to complete the shooting of the film, could have truly been Chunibala's own death, is compacted into the thud of her skull on the ground as Durga shakes her already dead body huddled by the side of the pond. Finally abondoned, the bemused witch has meanwhile been subtly enlarged by Ray's camera and she sometimes gapes into the lens, head-on, in a tight close-up, seeing blindly into our faces. This itself is part of the actualizing job, a cruel, compassionate, humorously mocking image, reflected in the mirror of the lens. But there is also a wonderful handling of the figure in profile or with her back to the camera walking away on one of her begging missions—there by denuding the numen in what is almost a parodic act of will.

24 'Renoir came in 1949', Ray says, recounting his apprenticeship with Jean Renoir when he came to India to make his film *The River*, 'and the moment I discovered that Renoir was in town, I went and looked him up. He had a feeling for nature; a deep humanism with a kind of a preference for the shades of grey, a sort of Chekhovian quality; and his lyricism and the avoidance of cliches.' He further recounts that as he already had the making of *Pather Panchali* in mind he told Renoir about it while he helped him with location hunting in the suburbs and villages of Calcutta. According to Ray Renoir said, 'It sounds wonderful, make it, I think it will make a fine film.' Satyajit Ray in an interview quoted in *Film India*, p. 123.

25 The embedding of cinematic realism within a phenomenological/existential matrix; the articulation of an ontology of the photographic image and the potential of film technology to replicate and replay lived life; the possibility of achieving a phenomenological plenitude as well as aesthetic transparency—all this makes Andre Bazin the prime theorist of cinematic realism during the 1950s. The high point of this aesthetic is Jean Renoir, with the Italian neorealists as also Bresson forming a further extension. These issues are discussed over several essays in Andre Bazin, *What Is Cinema?*, University of California Press, Berkeley, 1974.

26 For a discussion on the form and genre of Bibhutibhushan Bandopadhyaya's novel under consideration, see Meenakshi Mukherjee, 'Pather Panchali', in *Realism and Reality: The Novel and Society in India*, Oxford University Press, Delhi, 1984.

    The novel has been translated into English. See *Pather Panchali: Song of the Road*, translated by T.W. Clark and Tarapada Mukherjee, George Allen and Unwin, London, 1968; *Pather Panchali*, translated by Monica Varma, Writers Workshop, Calcutta, 1973; *Pather Panchali*, Rupa, Delhi, 1989.

27 Ray, with a moderately articulate style, answers questions that we can reconfigure into an ideological position. For a series of selected statements see *Film India*, pp. 136–39.

    'Somehow I feel that a common person—an ordinary person whom you meet every day in the street—is a more challenging subject for cinematic exploration than persons in heroic moulds, either good or bad.' (p. 136).

    'I commit myself to human beings . . . and I think that is a good enough commitment for me.' (p. 138).

    'I was closer to Nehru, I think. I admired Nehru, I understood him better, because I am also in a way a product of East and West. A certain liberalism, a certain awareness of Western values and a fusion of Eastern and Western values was in Nehru, which I didn't find in Gandhi. But, of course, as a man, as a symbol, in contact with India's multitude, he was quite extraordinary. But as a man. . .I always understood what Nehru was doing as I understood what Tagore was doing because you can't leave Tagore out of this, it's a triangle.' (p. 138)

    '. . . But you have to have the backing of your own culture very much. Even when I made my first film the awareness was there. I had a Western education, I studied English, but more and more over the last ten years I have been going back and back to the history of my country, my people, my past, my culture. . . .' (ibid.)

    'I can understand and admire Mao's revolution which has completely changed China and achieved—at a cost—the eradication of poverty and illiteracy. But I don't think I could find a place in China, because I am still too much of an individual and I still believe too strongly in personal expression' (p. 137.)

    'Well, go to Benares. Go to the ghats and you will see that communism is a million miles away, maybe on the moon. There are such ingrained habits, religious habits. I am talking of the multitude now, I am not talking of the educated, the young students, and, of course, everything falls back on education and the spread of education. . . Only through education could it happen.' (p. 139.)

28 This term and the ensuing argument is taken from James Clifford. See James Clifford, 'On Ethnographic Allegory', in *Writing Culture: The Poetics and Politics of Ethnography*, edited by James Clifford and George E. Marcus, University of California Press, Berkeley, 1986.

29 Ibid., p. 98.

30 Ibid., p. 100.

31 Ibid.

32 Ibid.

33 James Clifford refers to De Man's critique of the valorization of symbols over allegory. See ibid.

34 Ibid., p. 101.

35 Ibid., p. 102.

36 Ibid., p. 111.

37 Ibid., p. 114.

38 Raymond Williams, *The Country and the City*, quoted in ibid.

Education and Society in Post-Independence India
Looking towards the Future

Krishna Kumar

Major changes were introduced in India's economic policies at the beginning of 1990s. Although some of these changes were in the offing for at least a decade earlier, the formal announcement of a 'new economic policy' seemed rather dramatic because of the terminology used in it. The older terminology of government policy used words like 'planning', 'mixed economy', 'self-reliance' and 'socialistic pattern'. This terminology had its origins in the fifties when India's first prime minister, Jawaharlal Nehru, had opted to keep India formally non-aligned in the post-war world, standing on its own legs but leaning somewhat to the left. The new terminology of the nineties also stressed the importance of standing straight, but this time one could notice a tilt to the right. Words upholding the new climate of government policy and dominant opinion are 'liberalization', 'privatization', 'globalization' and 'market-friendliness'.

The change is not entirely of India's own making. The end of the cold war has a lot to do with the change of climate in India and elsewhere. It is also related to technological changes, especially in electronics and communication. A vast accommodation is taking place worldwide between the owners of capital and others whose main possessions are natural and human (labour) resources.[1] By many, especially in the west where reception of change is always a bit dramatic, this change is being seen as the end of history. In India, where change usually invokes the belief that this too will pass, the new policies and changes accompanying them in society and politics have aroused a passionate debate. Many people of my generation, whose memories of childhood are overshadowed by Mahatma Gandhi and Nehru, feel suspicious and bewildered. Until yesterday the state reflected our belief that India's modernization can take place without sacrificing village

320

self-reliance. Suddenly we find that the state has changed its rhetoric, that the geography of both the nation and the village has turned fluid and permeable. We feel uncomfortable teaching our children that self-reliance and moderation are myths in an interdependent world.

The present debate on the future of the new economic policies can be summarized in three scenarios. In the *first* scenario, the new policy will achieve a resounding success, fulfilling the targets set by its proponents, including the World Bank. India will achieve a high rate of economic growth by accelerating exports and attracting foreign capital. Poverty and unemployment will diminish as the benefits of increased productivity percolate to the bottom layers of society. These bottom layers, let us note, comprise no less than 60 to 70 per cent of the population. Those who inhabit these layers are landless rural labourers, peasants with small holdings, village artisans, urban workers employed in household industries, informal jobs and building construction. In the first scenario, this vast mass of the population will gradually become a literate workforce, capable of participating in a fully monetized open economy.

In the *second* scenario, this mass will form a politically restive underclass even as the export-driven economy deepens social divisions. Its fruits will be cornered by the elite minority, actively participating in the global exchange of goods and services. In this scenario, the new economic policies spell disaster. The state exhausts itself maintaining security for the wealthy so that the misery and revolt of the poor do not disturb their enjoyment and interests. India gets into a debt trap, so its already emaciated efforts in health and education deteriorate further. Speeded-up industrialization, mining, damming, forest-cutting, transport and urbanization cripple the environment's capacity to let the small-scale peasant, the artisan and the tribal subsist on it. Forced to quell frequent eruption of disorganized turmoil from among the dispossessed, the state sheds its democratic character and acts like an agent of multinational companies.

In the *third* scenario, the new economic policies will neither fully succeed nor disappear. The rich will reach western levels of consumption, and fringes of the underclass will get inducted into a peripheral relationship with globalized production and services. The rest will find political means of restraining the pace of globalization. After a brief period of higher growth rate, the economy will slow down and foreign capital will flee. The state will remain a major player in the distribution of scarce resources in addition to performing regulatory roles in the context of large-scale privatization. The outcome of the new policies will become increasingly difficult to distinguish from older trends.

The plausibility of all three scenarios is quite high, given the multiplicity of factors relevant to India, but I will defer my preference till the end. The window of education through which I am used to looking at the world is not particularly useful for making precise predictions. Education is said to be a good door to the future; it is not a good window to look at the future. For one thing, the outcome of education depends on many things we may never teach in schools—things that children and young people absorb as part of their socialization from the wider milieu. Had it not been so, British colonial education would have produced only subordinate officers and clerks, not ideologues of national freedom and others who fought for it. Similarly, the Soviet Union would have been saved by the third generation of children brought up on the belief that the Union was a wonderful achievement. In the last decade during which the so-called economic reforms have been actively applied in our country, the news in education has been particularly confusing. During this period, when the state was supposed to shed its welfare burden under the World Bank's tutorship, massive programmes of literacy and primary education have been underway. True, the latter is funded by foreign aid and loans, and the procedures followed in this as well as the literacy projects do not arouse full confidence, but one can hardly doubt that these nationwide programmes have responded to needs long neglected by the state. Similarly, the amendment in the Constitution making elementary education a fundamental right may not by itself signify a major shift in policy; but in the context of judicial activism and the growth of interest in children's education among voluntary organizations, we can expect the constitutional amendment to accelerate the demand for accountability in the system of education, particularly from its bureaucracy.

These developments do not seem very compatible with the usual rhetoric of structural adjustment and liberalization policies. Perhaps the real implications of these policies are yet to surface. For example, the claim that mass literacy and primary education have now become the state's priorities will face a test only when external funds for these areas dry up, as they must, after some time. Budget cuts in universities are an early symptom, some people argue, of the negative influence that liberalization policies will have on education. They also point towards the private universities bill which is in the offing. The strong and open salesmanship with which some foreign universities have started to lure Indian students is another symptom. However, it is hard to judge how much real change these symptoms indicate, given the strong and fairly continuous trends entrenched in the Indian system of education. These trends have been entrenched in the system since its formation in the later half of the nineteenth century. In order to assess the long-term implications of the recent changes we can fruitfully reflect on the trends which have been visible for a long time. We can focus on the shape these trends have assumed during the last fifty years of India's independence, and then speculate on how the emerging economic regime might affect them. For the present discussion I will group these trends in three broad categories.

In the *first* group we can place tendencies related to the drastic reduction on the number of children who proceed beyond the primary or the junior secondary stages. A cursory look at the number of schools in India (Table 1) suffices to convey the point that if all children enrolled in primary schools proceeded to complete eight years of elementary education, as the writers of the Constitution had desired, the junior secondary or the 'middle' schools will have a serious problem accommodating them. Compared to the 5,90,421 primary schools India has, there are only a little more than 1,71,000 middle schools. The ratio between middle and high schools is somewhat better, which means that those who survive eight years of schooling have a higher chance to stay longer, at least till they do the first public examination, to which I will refer later. Relentless elimination of children from the system takes place during the earliest grades. Official figures confirm that some 44 per cent of the children enrolled in grade one leave the school before

TABLE 1: *Number of educational institutions in India*

Primary schools	590,421
Middle schools	171,216
High schools	71,055
Higher secondary schools	23,588
Colleges (of general degrees)	6,569
Engineering and medical colleges	721
Universities	215

Source: Selected educational statistics,Government of India, 1995–96

323

reaching grade five, and those who do not reach grade eight are 63 per cent of the original population of grade one. These figures are depressing enough, but they are not accurate, and the reality is a lot worse.[2]

Collection of accurate enrolment and attendance figures has remained a chronic problem for as long as the present system has been around. And the problem has been mainly in rural India where three-fourths of the population reside. The Quinquennial Review of 1917–22 mentions how, when 100 village schools were checked in one day in the United Provinces—present-day Uttar Pradesh—the total enrolment claimed by teachers was 8,303, average attendance was said to be 5,516, and the day's actual attendance was 4,903. A visit to a village school in UP would show today's situation to be no different, and over-reporting to be much worse, considering that state documents show UP's drop-out rate to be lower than the national average, lower than that of states like Karnataka, Andhra Pradesh and Gujarat, which we know have better-functioning systems of primary education than UP has. The fact is that we cannot judge the reality of rural primary education, especially in the less literate northern Hindi belt, from any set of statistics. The gap between census figures and the ones collected by the Ministry of Education—known since the mid-eighties as the Ministry of Human Resource Development—was spotted a while ago, and recently a report has humbly acknowledged that no two sources of information seem to match.

The collection of accurate figures has received considerable international interest and funds in recent years, apparently because regional choices made by external investors of capital are likely to be influenced by the quality of available labour. The basic cause of inflated reporting continues to be neglected though it has been known since the days of the British. This basic cause is the subordinate, indeed powerless, status of the primary schoolteacher. Over the decades, higher officials have socialized and trained the teacher in dishonest record-keeping. It is on account of this training that we have grossly inaccurate knowledge of plain facts like how many children enrol, how many attend, and how many qualify for promotion to the next grade. The game of numbers goes on though everyone can see through it. We cannot have a basis for better planning of rural education as long as the teacher remains too subservient to feel free to maintain honest records of enrolment and attendance.

It is instructive to note that the heavy rate of early elimination from school has remained more or less stable over almost three decades. Old, entrenched tendencies such as the urban bias of the curriculum and school literature, the service conditions of teachers and the chronic paucity of non-salary expenditure are reflected in this stability. But it also reflects deeper socio-economic issues which have to do with the choices made in food policy in the sixties and the general pattern into which developmentalism as a global and national phenomenon has fallen since then.[3] The attempt made in the first decade of independence to link primary education with rural crafts under the 'basic' education programme inspired by Mahatma Gandhi was abandoned in the mid-sixties. The focus of the new strategy adopted then was to nurture long-term educational opportunities for owners of larger and better land-holdings. Referring to the highly inequitous distribution of land, the Education Commission of the mid-sixties calculated that

> at present there are nearly six million farms of 15 acres or more (out of 50 million farms). If we assume that ownership will change at 3 per cent a year, this means nearly 2,00,000 new farmers inherit such farms every year. It seems reasonable to think that by 1986, 1 in 50 of these may be an agriculture graduate.

The Commission endorsed the new agricultural strategy which was to enable the bigger land-owners to enhance their material opportunities. Known as the Green Revolution, this strategy aimed at making India self-reliant in the production of wheat and rice by the use of new hybrid seeds demanding heavy use of chemical fertilizers, pesticides and water. The strategy did achieve its goal, but at a serious cost. Smaller land-holders were pauperized, regional inequalities depended, and the natural environment deteriorated. The new approach depended on large-scale farmers; their political lobbies made further holes in an already weak programme of land reforms. Their dominance encouraged the populist politics and programmes of the seventies. Large-scale displacement, migration to city slums and break-up of the community and family affected an ever-growing segment of the rural population of children. The new policies had paradoxical outcomes such as lowering of child mortality, but no significant rise in nutrition and health. Absolute hunger declined, but chronic hunger and illness persisted. It was a bit like higher enrolment, but poorer attendance and early withdrawal.

Also, during the sixties, India fought three wars. Defence needs naturally gained far greater visibility and urgency, leading to the development of an impressive military-industrial complex. Literacy, rural education and health had never been high priorities; the new climate made it easier to neglect them. The Cold War perspective and the international politics of food and supply of arms provided external help in setting India on the road to redefining development as consumption and spectacular application of science and technology. About a fourth of the total population was regarded as adequate as the operative universe in which development programmes and a modern market economy could be seen as working. Enrolment statistics, despite their general unreliability for the early grades, testify to this sketch. The retention rate between grade one and eight remained almost stationary from the early sixties to the early eighties, showing that a little more than one-fourth of the children who enrolled in grade one could last in the school till grade eight. This proportion is reported to have grown to 37 per cent by the early nineties; for girls the figure was 34 per cent (Table 2).

TABLE 2: *Drop-out rates during primary and middle school years* (%)

	Grades I–V	Grades V–VIII
1960–61	64.9	78.3
1970–71	67.0	77.9
1980–81	58.7	72.7
1990–91	58.7	72.7
1990–91	44.3	63.4

Source :Selected educational statistics, Government of India, 1995–96

It is not difficult to guess the collective identities of the children who fail to survive at school. They are children of landless agricultural labourers and subsistence peasants. Caste-wise, a substantial proportion of them belongs to the Scheduled Castes who have been granted special rights in the Constitution, including reservation in higher education and representative bodies. Table 3 shows how sharply their presence at school shrinks between grade five and grade eight and there onwards.[4] The situation of children belonging to many of the Scheduled Tribes is worse, especially in the central Indian belt. Forest-dwelling tribal communities have had to bear the brunt of state initiatives in dam construction, development of tourism with the help

TABLE 3: *Scheduled Caste children in each grade as a percentage of enrolment in grade I (1986)*

	Rural schools	All schools
Grade V	40.3	43.8
Grade VIII	21.1	25.8
Grade X	10.9	14.9
Grade XII	1.8	3.6

Source: Fifth All India Educational Survey, NCERT, 1992.

of game sanctuaries and mining. Apart from such destabilizing experiences, bias against tribal cultures and languages also makes the school curriculum and the teacher a deterrant for the advancement of tribal education. Then there are rural artisans, the creators of India's glorious handicraft traditions. There are about 40 million craftspeople in India, of whom about 12 million are in the handloom sector alone. How trivial, and in that sense irrelevant and demeaning, the standard school curriculum is for the children of these craft communities, can be judged by spending just a day at Chanderi or Benaras with a craft family. No wonder, one realizes in a rather simple, unscientific way, these children stop coming to school early. Finally, the child residing in an urban slum is always a likely case of early withdrawal or elimination. The uncertainty and violence of the milieu in which the slum child lives is often combined with neglect and violence at school, in addition to the pressure of parental poverty which drives the child towards work.

The *second* dominant tendency I wish to elaborate on is the preponderance of higher education. When India became independent, the proportion of literates in the total population was 12 per cent (about 18 per cent, if we exclude children below five from the total population). Spread of literacy and primary education were rightly perceived as national priorities by the eminent leaders of that period, yet the first commission appointed soon after independence was asked to focus on university education. The second commission, appointed a few years later, was asked to focus on secondary education. Not only such official panels, but also the growth rate of enrolment and the number of institutions show that secondary and higher education expanded more rapidly than elementary education. This was consistent with the earlier trend; independence merely triggered fresh enthusiasm for the growth of institutions at the higher level. Demand for higher education had been made since the late nineteenth century in the articulate and loud voice of the literate upper-caste elites. Independence gave further strength to this voice. Starting a university or a college affiliated to it became a means of expressing political or regional clout. Thus, in the first twenty-five years of independence, the number of universities grew more than four times and then doubled itself in the next twenty-five years. As Table 4 shows, the annual growth rate of enrolment in higher education outpaced the rate at which elementary education was growing. This was true of institutional expansion too, especially in the sixties. The proportion of expenditure on higher education rose very substantially in the second five-year plan of the late fifties and remained high throughout the seventies and early eighties.

TABLE 4: *Growth of education*

	Primary	Middle	Secondary	Higher
ENROLMENT (*average annual growth rate in %*)				
1951–61	6.2	8.0	9.2	9.8
1961–71	5.0	7.1	8.6	12.6
1971–81	2.6	4.5	5.0	5.6
1981–89	3.3	5.1	6.9	5.5
INSTITUTIONS (*average annual growth rate in %*)				
1951–61	4.7	13.8	9.0	10.0
1961–71	2.1	6.2	7.8	12.5
1971–81	1.9	2.7	3.3	2.3
1981–89	1.3	2.5	4.6	1.5

Source: J.B.G. Tilak and N.V. Verghese, *Financing of Education in Inida,* UNESCO, Paris, 1991.

There is more than one way of reading this story. The obvious reading is that secondary and higher education developed at the expense of mass elementary education. In sociological terms, the culturally dominant and economically stronger sections of society used the state's resources to consolidate their hold on the expanding state apparatus of new functions and opportunities. The tuition fee was kept at minimal levels, with the justification that this would allow weaker sections to avail college education, but it mainly enabled the strong to further strengthen themselves by making their children eligible for the highest available opportunities in the job market. Who was going to college and who was not doing well even if they got there somehow?—

such enquiries established the expected truth. But it is also true that a limited number of the more tenacious aspirants for higher qualifications from relatively poorer, in some cases, rural backgrounds were able to avail higher education because the tuition fee was so heavily subsidized. They and the specially designated Scheduled Castes served as adequate means of legitimizing an arrangement which suited the post-colonial rhetoric of nation-building and attainment of self-reliance.

That last point is the gist of the second reading of the differential rates of growth we see in Table 4. Expansion of higher education, including the establishment of advanced research centres and academies, had an immediate, palpable role to play in Nehru's India—to give India a sense of presence in the post-war international order. Founding an infrastructure of basic industries was a priority of Nehru's regime. A special effort was made to establish India in the atomic and space sciences. After the war with China in 1962, these priorities stopped looking ambitious: they became necessities for a country which found itself placed in a hostile geography. Pressing requirements in transport, energy, modern agriculture and chemicals spontaneously translated into advancement of science and engineering, making them far more urgent and important aims of the unwritten education policy than the opening and maintenance of decent village schools could ever be. So while the pursuit of equality and social justice waited for political means, education became the primary means by which suitable boys and girls could be legitimately selected for higher professional and academic degrees. To maintain legitimacy for its ruthless selection devices, the system of education required an accommodating secondary school system linked to a multipurpose higher education through a public examination. High rate of failure in the school-leaving examination kept whatever check was possible on the number of college entrants, and those who entered but could not proceed to coveted professional courses, found enough room in general arts and science courses to satisfy what has aptly been called the 'diploma disease'.

The rise of a national intelligentsia, linked across geographical and cultural boundaries by English education, has been cited by historians as a prime mover of the nationalist struggle against the British. Printing technology, the transport and postal system enabled it, from late nineteenth century onwards to form civic and political associations, participate in some areas of decision-making and carve out a

329

liberal public space in which certain kinds of conflicts could be ironed out through deliberation and negotiation. Early growth of higher education and its rapid expansion after independence helped in the institutionalization of these functions. There is truth in the claim that the national intelligentsia, including the bureaucracy, the judiciary and the academia has helped India stay one, along with democratic politics and the state's coercive might. If we acknowledge this truth, we must also admit the price paid for this kind of unity in terms of neglected priorities of mass welfare, particularly in education and health. Colleges and universities trained the elite intelligentsia, while the masses alone had the franchise to train themselves to participate in the liberal institutions of parliamentary democracy. Of late, colleges and universities have produced a substantial number of activist negotiators across the state-people interface. Their role has been especially notable in the struggles for the protection of human rights, the environment and women's rights. Rather different from the men and women engaged in active politics in earlier periods, these new leaders of local action purposely elude political identity, but they are playing a widely appreciated role in redefining the scope and behaviour of older institutions like the press, the bureaucracy and the judiciary. Howsoever unjust and poor in quality, the higher education system must get the credit for training these new as well as the older players of liberal democratic games.

The *third* and last tendency I wish to discuss is that of inherent divisiveness. Multiplicity of sub-systems is hardly inconsistent with pluralism, but I am talking about a divisive tendency which protects class interests. The term 'class' sits ill with Indian social realities; it rarely implies anything more than sectional interests which seem to be moving towards the formation of a class. Thus, educational activity under the banner of religious or linguistic community which has been sanctioned in the Indian Constitution for minority groups, and caste can sometimes give the impression of contributing to a class-forming process, at other times its opposite, namely a process impeding class formation. A clearer point can be made in relation to the practice of private schooling of a kind inspired by Britain's public school model. Inasmuch as norms and rituals indicate group consolidation, the so-called public schools in India have contributed to the making of an Indian bourgeois class which forms an important and dominant segment of the national intelligentsia.[6]

Rituals which reinforce loyalty to the institution, a sense of tradition and the feeling that 'we' belong to a community of similar schools are important elements of the agenda of socialization the public schools pursue. But the core of this agenda is to impart facility in the use of the English language. Competence in English is the single most important marker of a young person's eligibility for negotiating the opportunity structure that the modern economy has made available. Those who lack competence in English have remarkably limited scope for moving into higher-income and higher-status roles. However, skill in English does not act as an isolated determinant of one's social destiny; rather, it acts as a composite indicator of long-term advantages and their numerous psychological outcomes. Early streaming into a fee-charging private school is one of the major items on the biodata of those displaying fluency in English in youth. With minor exceptions, all such schools use English as a medium of instruction in all subjects from the earliest grades onwards, in contrast to the schools that run as part of the state system which use a regional language as the medium. The medium sets the two systems apart. Public schools were rather few to begin with—about fifty at the time of independence—but the term 'public school' is not easy to define today when the original model of the British public school can at best be faintly recognized in the dozens of biodiverse forms its progeny has taken. The genotype covers more than the 3,237 secondary schools listed as unaided private schools, forming about 15 per cent of urban secondary schools in the country. Today one can see the genotype reflected in certain kinds of state schools as well as state-aided schools in the bigger villages. As a marker of distinction, both educational and economic, the English language has gained wider appreciation apart from freeing itself of the hostility it once symbolized.

Spread of the public school model and the consequent erosion of the concept of a common, neighbourhood school are expressions of a deeper tendency in the system to provide emerging or neo-elites with islands of moderate security and hope of self-perpetuation.[7] The state's inability to run a credible, universally accessible system has encouraged this tendency, but there is also a socio-cultural urge to form justifiable islands. Thus, in the early sixties a separate network was created to serve children of central government employees who are transferable throughout the country. This network has 20 schools to begin with; today there are 818. In the mid-eighties a chain of schools was proposed to serve the 'gifted' rural child, identified by means of a test for eleven-year olds. There are 359 schools of this kind now—one per district, admitting some 80 children every year in grade six. These are all residential schools, offering a kind of public school education to the children of wealthier farmers, barring the usual category of entrants from the Scheduled Castes and Tribes with reserved seats. These and a few other categories of privileged schools run by some of the state governments are all affiliated to the Central Board of Secondary Education (CBSE). At present, its network covers some 4,800 schools with about 5 million children. These include private schools. The CBSE and another privately run board conduct the matriculate and senior secondary examination throughout the country for the elite layer of schools which produce a substantial proportion of the national intelligentsia.

Exclusive schooling is a better term to name the complex social streaming that takes place in India under the auspices of private or non-government and special schools run by the government. Exclusive schooling has been on a rapid rise over the last two decades or so. It has an obvious functional rationale in a society in which less than four out of ten children are able to survive at school beyond grade eight. It also has a symbolic rationale easy to comprehend. The lotus flower, which is the seat of Saraswati, the goddess of learning, figures in the emblem of many exclusive schools, conveying the point that good learning sets its gainer apart from or above the surrounding mud of ignorance. How vast and thick this mud is can be estimated from the combined success rate of the grade ten and grade twelve examinations conducted by the provincial boards, to which the vast majority of schools are affiliated. Out of the 8.8 million students who took the grade ten or high examination in 1990, 4.1 million or about 46 per cent passed. Of them, 3.8 million took the grade twelve or senior secondary examination in 1992, in which only 1.7 million or 45 per cent passed. Thus, the two examinations left just 19 per cent of the total number of students in provincial board schools in the country who could aspire for higher educational qualifications and the jobs these might lead to. Success rates of the two all-India boards is routinely much higher although the examinations conducted by them are believed to be tougher. The CBSE is perceived as a norm-setter for the kinds of new topics or segments of knowledge that should be included in the syllabi of different subjects in provincial boards. A textbook flaunts status when it says that it covers the CBSE syllabus, just as a school announces its status by flaunting affiliation to the CBSE rather than to a provincial board, in its signboard or brochure.

I now wish to speculate on how the new economic policies are likely to influence the three tendencies I have discussed, and also how these tendencies might influence the future of the new economic policies. It is quite clear that the proponents of liberalization have been able to exercise more effective pressure in favour of mass literacy and primary education than well-meaning advisory panels or the intelligentsia have been able to at any point within the last fifty years. Literacy and schooling not only promise a more trainable and compliant workforce, but also a more brand-conscious population of consumers. The recent adult literacy campaigns and the ongoing foreign-funded programme for strengthening primary education can be expected to make some impact on the drop-out rate, especially in rural areas where a conscious demand for education has now become a reality. Also, the poor quality of school provision has been a factor more responsible for the high drop-out rate in rural areas than the use of children for labour. It is in urban areas that this latter phenomenon has greater applicability as an explanation for early school-leaving. The new economic regime is likely to worsen rather than improve the state of child labour. It is also likely to accelerate migration from rural to urban areas. Liberalization was inaugurated with a devaluation of the currency in order to boost exports. This kind of effort aimed at giving to Indian products a competitive advantage in the saturated market of consumer goods in the wealthy world inevitably implies low wages and a decline in the real income of the labouring poor—a phenomenon which has already begun to be noticed. These effects of the emerging economic policies can only sharpen the contradiction between the growth of demand and of provision for primary education on the one hand, and the incapacity of the pauperized to spare their children for schooling on the other.

Even with the decline in drop-out rates remaining largely confined to rural areas, the burden of an increased number of school survivors on secondary education is significant. Private, or rather commercial, initiative—an aspect of the new economic regime—will come forward even more than it has already done to absorb this pressure. The state's drive to invite private capital to penetrate the countryside for the exploitation of natural and labour resources is likely to be met with the demand for employing local boys and girls on a preferential basis. In the context of the recent assignment of local autonomy in decision-making, this demand may combine with a more serious assertion on territorial rights. Such assertions have been characteristic of the politics of regional and sub-regional political groups. They have forced a healthier kind of federalism on polity, but they can also slow down the pace at which private capital, domestic or foreign, might dream of striding across the Indian subcontinent.

The second and third tendencies are likely to get exacerbated in the emerging socio-economic order. The diploma disease is showing no sign of abating; in fact, the status-giving role of degrees has just begun to show its powerful lure among the educationally and economically deprived sections of society. The lure implies that these sections will compel the state to remain the major provider of higher education. The elite will increasingly look towards private and foreign institutions, but the state-supported system of college and university education will remain dominant despite the erosion of standards and norms. Over the last few years the university system has sat on choices available to it for survival in the era of structural adjustment. Budget cuts and flight of scholarship to foreign-funded research outfits and foreign universities seem to have become the order of the day in metropolitan cities. A general diminution of academic life is taking place which seems part of a global trend inimical to ideas and contemplation. Applied research, evaluative studies, monitoring and feasibility surveys are typical of the tasks left for the brighter young members of the academia to do. On the other side of the coin, one can already see student unrest taking shape in many campuses in response to the impoverished infrastructure. It appears to be certain that youth politics will absorb the energies triggered by regional and coalition politics. Unlike the sixties when campus trouble remained tied to rather trivial issues, student politics of the emerging future appears destined to mirror the issues shaping real politics.

Two kinds of issues have surfaced over the recent years. Social justice is the general theme of one kind, and collective self-identity is the main theme of the other kind. Historically, the former theme mobilized the culturally downtrodden, labouring classes, whereas the latter theme inspired the literate, upper-caste sections. Significant and sometimes startling shifts and unexpected alliances have occurred over the recent years, suggesting that the Indian political scene will continue to present complicated permutations of its two nodal themes. The politics of identity, featuring revivalist militancy, is no more as stri-dent today as it was a few years ago, but its agenda has not changed much. Redefining the content of education is a part of this agenda, and indoctrinating the young continues to be an important activity. However, the arrival of new and educationally qualified actors from among the downtrodden is speedily altering the balance of political forces, especially in northern India. How these actors will shape the details of the new political economy remains somewhat uncertain.

This picture suggests that the new economic regime will nei-ther work nor collapse. The strength of Indian democratic institutions will almost certainly wear down the initial thrust exhibited by the advo-cates of liberalization. To an extent this has already happened and one can expect the slowing down to become more manifest. The reason for this is not far to seek. Neo-liberalism and globalism have little to offer to societies in which the core struggle taking shape today is aimed at establishing the values of social justice and dignity of the human being. Among the vast sections of the Indian population who are parti-cipating in democratic processes for the first time in history today, there is no sign of boredom with modernism and with the values asso-ciated with it. Their struggle is to define modernism with autonomy and imagination. What shape this struggle will take in the immediate future cannot be predicted with precision, but one can already see that the glib saga of an emerging global culture living off internet and satel-lite television is unlikely to gain relevance beyond the well-established limits of the elite strata. Turmoil and resistance, which characterize the life and culture of the mass of India's population living in rural areas, can only intensify in response to the growing arrogance of the elites. The enormous social restiveness that India has witnessed in this century must continue, and those who choose to invest in India as part of their global initiative will have to swallow their peace of mind, much as they swallow their conscience when they invest in China.

In the context of knowledge and education, let us recall the fact that India's long traditions in these spheres did not sit well with the system and practices introduced under colonial rule. We can hard-ly expect these traditions to dissolve in the face of the new, cheap vers-ion of knowledge as electronically accessible information. The signs are that our system of education will remain in discomfort for a while to come, seeking indigenous ways to achieve a pedagogic modernism that might be compatible with old pedagogic values like rigour and memory. India is much too big to become an indistinct member of a global community of consumers served and controlled by a handful of mega-ventures. In the past, selective acceptance and application of technological choices was forced upon Indian elites, both by pressure from below to stay slow and by the pull of tradition to query the new. It seems plausible to expect that, with the advance of participatory democracy in the future, India will become more capable of reminding the west of what it misses in its own creation. I say this because the west has been and promises to remain India's major preoccupation and a source of impediment in the growth of India's imagination.

Notes and References

[1] For a comprehensive analysis of this vast 'readjustment', see Gabriel Wackhermann, 'Transport, Trade, Tourism and the World Economic System', *International Social Science Journal*, 151, 1997, pp. 23–39.

[2] In what is literally a jungle of documents on this subject, the relatively more revealing are these three: *A Handbook of School Education and Allied Statistics*, MHRD, Government of India, 1996; *Human Development Profile of Rural India*, Volume. 1, NCAER, November, 1996; *Primary Education in India—a Status Report*, Core Group on Citizen's Initiative on Primary Education, Banglore, 1997. The World Bank recently published a book-length review called *Primary Education in India* (1997). The slightly older *Education for All—The Indian Scene*, published by the Government of India on the occasion of the international conference in 1993, continues to be useful for some of the statistical information rather different from routine.

[3] For a discussion of the sixties, especially of the linkage between agricultural and educational policies carved out during this important decade, see my 'Agricultural Modernization and Education', in Shukla and R. Kaul, eds., *Education, Development and Underdevelopment*, Sage, New Delhi, 1998, pp. 79–98.

[4] See Geeta B. Nambissan, 'Equity in Education? Schooling of Dalit Children in India', *Economic and Political Weekly*, Vol. 31, Nos. 16 and 17, 1996, pp. 1011–24, for an overview of research on the subject.

[5] In a study of examination achievement, A.R. Kamat and A.G. Deshmukh (*Wastage in College Education*, Gokhale Institute, Poona 1963) found that upper-caste students enjoyed far better chances of excelling in examination. Apparently, studies of this kind which compare the performance of different castes or classes, have not been in fashion.

[6] The discussion here is based on my *Learning from Conflict* (Orient Longman, Delhi, 1996).

[7] On the rise of private education in recent times, see Geeta G. Kingdon, 'Private Schooling in India—Size, Nature, and Equity-Effects', *Economic and Political Weekly*, Vol. 31, No. 51, 1996, pp. 3306–14.

336

The Body in the Mirror
Women and Representation in Contemporary India

Meenakshi Thapan

In this paper, I am concerned primarily with the question of how gender identity is both constructed and experienced by women through the medium of visual representation and textual discourse in women's magazines.[1] I do this through examining some samples of advertisements (adverts) and fashion photography available in a particular magazine, *Femina*. It is quite clear of course that adverts have a strong commercial aspect to their production and it is apparent that a similar commercial angle dominates the production of fashion photography. Both use the female body to promote a product and the manner in which the body is packaged, displayed and eventually consumed (through the gaze) is of considerable interest. It is also the case that women readers of these magazines appropriate bodily displays and fetishize the body through the female gaze. I, therefore, particularly emphasize the role and power of the female gaze in the appropriation of women's bodies in their represented from.[2] My purpose, therefore, is twofold: to map the manner in which body images are presented and represented in women's magazines and to examine women's perceptions and experience of their bodies to understand how gender identity is constituted, in this case, through body imagery.

It is necessary to state at the outset that my concern is not with the body images of women themselves as they are presented in the discourse of women's magazines. The images serve to only highlight and reveal the ideas and practices underlying the use of particular images. The 'culture' of body imagery in itself is therefore not my central concern. It is instead, an attempt to understand and analyze the ideas, events and practices that both give rise to, and *misrepresent*, the culture of the body in the visual representation and textual discourse of women's magazines. The discourse of cultural studies, it may be

337

argued, tends to focus on representation and the decoding of the forms of representation in everyday life. It is, however, equally important to understand the lived experience of those who are partaking of this cultural discourse. This paper 'therefore' also presents the lived experience of urban women in relation to their embodied gender identity.[3]

The Lived and Communicative Body

The focus here is on the lived body, i.e., on the body grounded in experience, in everyday life, rather than on the objectified body of science. John O'Neill distinguishes between the physical body and the lived body which is 'that communicative bodily presence to which we cannot be indifferent, to which we are sensible in others as in ourselves'.[4] Our bodies, therefore, are 'the fine instruments of both the smaller and the larger society in which we live'[5]. Our bodies, as social *and* personal constructs, are thus the lived bodies of everyday life.

The lived body is located in culture and as Young points out, 'culture and meaning [are] inscribed in its habits, in its specific forms of perception and comportment'[6]. In her work on 'difference', Moore suggests the notion of 'the "lived anatomy" and of bodily praxis as a mode of knowledge that draws on an understanding of experience as a form of embodied intersubjectivity'. She argues that one's presence as an embodied subject shapes 'the ontology of experience which emphasizes the degree to which social interactions are embodied ones taking place in concrete space and time.' Experience, then, is 'intersubjective and embodied; it is not individual and fixed but irredeemably social and processual.'[7] Experience is also not a collective phenomenon but varies across cultures, races and within a culture, according to class, caste, linguistic and regional orientations. Yet, experience cannot be defined as an individual's limited perspective located in a particular milieu. It is common to individuals belonging to a particular group of similar social status and standing located in a well-defined cultural and social setting.

As Pierre Bourdieu puts it, such experience is in effect 'the habitus': it 'is necessity internalized and converted into a disposition that generates meaningful practices and meaning-given perceptions: it is a general, transposable disposition which carries out a systematic, universal application'.[8] Different conditions of existence 'however' produce different habitus and the varying practices thus engendered appear as 'configurations of properties' expressing the differences objectively inscribed in conditions of existence which function as life-styles. Bourdieu identifies 'taste' as the 'propensity and capacity to app-ropriate (materially or symbolically) a given class of classified, classi-fying objects or practices. . . .' Most importantly, it is the 'generative formula of life-style' whether seen in terms of 'furniture, clothing, language or body-hexis'.[9] The link between social class and taste, reflected in life-styles, is clear. Further, taste is *embodied* in individuals and this is evident in their life-styles. In his analysis of tastes in food, Bourdieu argues:

> Taste, a class culture turned into nature, that is, *embodied*, helps to shape the class body. It is an incorporated principle of classification which governs all forms of incorporation, choosing and modifying everything that the body ingests and digests and assimilates, physio-logically and psychologically. It follows that the body is the most indisputable materialization of class taste.[10]

Experience, grounded in and emerging from habitus, is clearly based on social class. Undoubtedly, the manner in which the body is presented and represented in social space would reflect this class awareness and appropriate forms of behaviour. Frank points out that this Bourdieuian body is really a form of capital—'physical capital'— and is thereby 'associated in its self-consciousness, predictable in its tastes, producing in its capitals, and monadic in its demonstrative value'.[11] In the end, it merely reproduces the society which it mirrors. Frank is missing a crucial point in Bourdieu's analysis, namely, that forms of capital, including physical capital, can be transformed and used for enhancing social status and even economic capital. The Bour-dieuian body is therefore not a mute reflection and reproducer of social class but has the potential for transformation and is thus imbued with agency.

This living, experiencing body located in a well-defined social space, capable of changing that social space, is also a communicative body. It mirrors aspects of society, the self, gender identity, and can also communicate its disposition to others through different forms or mediums of self-expression. This is only possible if we view the body as constantly in the process of becoming and not as a fixed static entity trapped in a particular gender identity, social class and setting. As I have argued elsewhere, in the context of the body and gender identity:

gender identity is not something fixed and immutable; it is both constructed and lived; and can sometimes also be transcended. It is, therefore, always in the making, continuously in the process of communication and exchange, evolving through the everyday life experiences of women (and men).[12]

Body Image and Self-presentation

An important aspect of gender consciousness and identity is body image. What is this body image and how do we perceive our own bodies as well as see the body of another? To see undoubtedly also simultaneously means to be seen. Vision itself implies that there is a body that is visible. This, argues Grosz, is 'the very condition of seeing, the condition of embodiment'.[13]

The limits and shape of body image are largely determined by 'space surrounding and within the subject's body'.[14] It is the 'lived spatiality of endogenous sensations, the social space of interpersonal relations, and the "objective" or "scientific" space of cultural (including scientific and artistic) representations'.[15] In everyday life, a woman's physical spatiality is shaped by both offensive and pleasurable experience in the family, home and workplace, and in the wider public arena she frequents. It is by now well-documented that across cultures women function from confined, enclosed spaces while men have access to wider, more open public spaces. Women's bodily movements are therefore restricted and, as Young points out, 'there is a failure to make full use of the body's spatial and lateral potentialities'.[16] Women's gait and stride is very different from that of men and this is nowhere more evident than on the coeducational school sports field where girls tend to concentrate on more 'feminine' sports like badminton and boys on 'macho' games like football. It is as if 'a space surrounds us in imagination that we are not free to move beyond; the space available to our movement is a constricted space. . . we lack an entire trust in our bodies to carry us forward'.[17]

A woman's physical spatiality is also influenced by representations of female embodiment in the media and theatre, in popular magazines and films, in cultural artefacts and 'scientific' worlds such as medicine. A woman's body image is therefore made visible and seen in relation to all of these, not separately perceived and identified but as an amalgamated 'social' whole which impinges on her senses and vision in many different ways rather then as separate entities.

There is no doubt that the visual and print media in any culture influence women's perceptions through the imaging of a woman's body as the 'perfect' or 'desirable' body. Images of youthful women with beautiful faces and bodies are presented to the urban Indian woman. With the advent of television and the printed word in an increasingly modern, urban India, 'the rules for femininity', as it were, tend to be 'culturally transmitted' through 'standardized visual images'.[18] Thus, 'we learn the rules directly through bodily discourse: through images that tell us what clothes, body shape, facial expression, movements and behaviour are required.'[19] Some of these images are presented to us through advertisements, fashion displays, beauty contests and their icons, fashion models, through women's magazines and so on. Undoubtedly, many of these obliquely or directly address the desirability of a woman's body in one way or another.

Modes of representing the female body in women's magazines are of particular interest as the body imagery is very strikingly conveyed to the average urban middle-class reader through fashion photography, adverts, and other forms. Fuss has pointed out that fashion photography, for example, 'poses its models as sexually irresistable subjects, inviting its female viewers to consume the product by (over) identifying with the image.'[20] The impact of much of the body imagery in women's magazines is to make women conscious of their bodies in terms of size, shape, weight, skin colour or texture, and associated characteristics. And women look at, identify with and strive to be like the images they see in an endless search for an ever-changing and elusive femininity that is constitutive of a perfect gender identity.

The other important factor that influences body imagery is the body's relationship with objects of all kinds, such as jewellery, accessories and, above all, clothing. Adornment is central to our self-presentation and indeed, as Wilson points out, 'there has never been a culture without adornment, without some modification of the raw material of the body.'[21] Clothing, according to Silverman, in an admirable paper on the subject, 'exercises as profoundly determining an influence upon living, breathing bodies as it does upon their literary and cinematic counterparts, affecting contour, weight, muscle development, posture, movement and libidinal circulation.'[22] It is in this sense that clothing becomes 'a necessary condition of subjectivity—that in articulating the body, it simultaneously articulates the psyche.'[23]

Clothing also marks the body, its position, its gait, as what one wears determines the way one walks.[24]

Fashion, it has been suggested, is 'the discourse *par excellence* which articulates the theme of women's relationship to images about themselves.'[25] The discourse of fashion forms and gives shape to gender identity, as it were, in an endless definition and redefinition of femininity. One aspect of the performativity of femininity is fashion which helps women to both display and perform their femininity in different ways.[26] A woman, therefore, makes a statement about her body image through the clothes she wears, the facial make-up and the manner in which she comports herself. In India, she is either 'westernized' or 'traditional' in her presentation of her embodied self which is a reflection of her perception of her self and gender identity according to her social status, upbringing and her inner feelings about her body image.

The body, then, does not have merely a utilitarian value; it is invested with meaning for the subject who may like and/or dislike certain parts or the whole of her body. 'It is significant', Grosz argues, 'that the investment in and the various shapes of different parts of the body image are uneven, for clearly some regions are far more libidinally invested than others.'[27] Certain parts of the body are particularly important for women in terms of body imagery.[28] These include the stomach (preferably flat), the hips, the breasts, the legs (especially if they tend to wear skirts). The concern of course is with the presentation of self so that large hips and breasts signify an inferiorized femininity out of tune, as it were, with the ideal, perfect body image. In women's experience of their erotic sexuality, as opposed to reproductive sexuality, again certain parts of the body acquire an importance in relation to their experience of it. Breasts are the most commonly mentioned and the emphasis on breasts in women's accounts appears to be related to the emphasis on women's breasts in popular literature and cinema, in women's magazines and also in contemporary fashion in urban Delhi. As Young points out, 'In the total scheme of the objectification of women, breasts are the primary thing.'[29] There is also the fact that women's breasts are 'culturally required to be exclusively "for" the other—whether as instrument and symbol of nurturing love. Or as erotic fetish.'[30]

It is also the case that women's experience of sexuality is clearly related to body image and the emotions associated with it so that if a woman sees her body as fat or out of shape, it affects her sexuality. There is a 'preoccupation with the visual image—of self and others—and a concomitant anxiety about how these images measure up to a socially prescribed ideal.'[31] The image of the perfect body is acknowledged by urban women as deriving from the media and other influences, notably western images, prevalent in India today. The concern with the presentation of the embodied self is also linked to an internalization of the gaze of the socially and perhaps sexually dominant other, which has turned the woman into a surveyed object. John Berger has suggested that 'the surveyor of woman in herself is male: the surveyed female. Thus, she turns herself into an object—and most particularly, an object of vision: a sight.'[32]

Social Difference and the Body

As earlier argued, the body is the most indisputable materialization of social class. Class differentiates bodies and this is markedly apparent in the visual representation and textual discourse of women's magazines. These magazines are clearly addressed to women from a particular social class who are educated and have the economic capital to consume both the ideas and the products advertised by the magazine. Such women are privileged to the extent that they have a choice in the kind of lifestyles they wish to pursue as well as in the manner in which they wish to present and represent their embodied selves.

There is a tendency in most analyses of the representation of the body to focus on consumption and modes of consumption in everyday life. A link is established between the ideal body image, the products, mainly related to the fashion-beauty complex, that will help in the attainment of this image, and consumption of the ideology as well as the products. However, an important and neglected area of analysis is the *production* of the goods up for consumption. This may bring us closer to an understanding of how relations of inequality and of power and powerlessness are reproduced in society. Elements of social control are clearly present both in the *production* and in the *consumption* of ideas and goods. The labouring or the working body is therefore as important as the consuming body in analyses of material culture in contemporary culture, but is outside the scope of this paper.

Social difference is present in the use of the products relating to enhancing body image. We need to ask the question, '*Who* can consume *what?*' in order to understand that there are many women in urbanareas, from poor and working-class socio-economic backgrounds, who are perhaps concerned with this aspect of heir existence in a very different way. The business of enhancing or perfecting body image for purposes of self-presentation in everyday life does not exist to the same extent as it does in the lives of upper-class women. It is therefore, not surprising that the body marked by poverty, with its attendant imagery, is absent from the public display of embodied perfection and thus outside the space of the subject's body image in women's magazines. In some fashion displays, a poor male vendor may be shown alongside the glamorous model, his dark, perhaps scarred and uneven body being presented in stark contrast to her faultless beauty. It is undoubtedly the case that the poverty, misery and social exclusion of the slum dweller in urban India lies outside the realm of body representation for the contemporary Indian woman. There is a conspicuous absence of women from a particular strata of society in this representation that suggests that the woman who is targetted for consumption is one who has economic, educational and social capital and thereby the the space for leisure, consumption and the pursuit of an appropriate life-style.

Clearly, *representation* is a problematic concept. The power of imagery lies in its ability to both produce and define the feminine in very specific ways. It is, therefore, the case that even when women think they are in control over the kind of imagery being produced abut themselves, they are, in effect, already responding to the gaze of the other in one way or another. Imagery is a form of regulation to the extent that it reflects the social relations of power: female embodiment tends to be located in a very specific form of imagery which reflects social relations in a particular culture. In urban India, these would obviously not be very conducive to the portrayal of women and their bodies in a manner that goes against the grain of social relations in everyday life. These include not only social relations within a social class or community but also relations across social classes and communities. Although this is not the focus of this paper, it becomes imperative to examine *who* gets excluded in the process of representation and the implications of this for representing the body in contemporary urban India. *Body obsession* is primarily an upper-class phenomenon in urban India to the extent that it is a reflection of a particular kind of life-style evident in the ongoing profileration of numerous 'health' and 'fitness' fads. For the middle-class woman, on the other hand, desire and aspiration are closely interlaced in the search for an appropriate body image and identity. As Bourdieu might well say, their effort is to convert economic capital into social capital by acquiring an image through forms of presentation and representation that will help in raising social status and thereby, economic and social opportunity.

Textual Discourse in Women's Magazines

To recapitulate, in this paper I am concerned with the question of how gender identity is both constructed and experienced by women through the medium of visual representation and textual discourse in women's magazines. The textual discourse vested in women's bodies through adverts and fashion displays locates, as Dorothy Smith points out, the 'social relations of a "symbolic" terrain and the material practices which bring it into being and sustain it.'[33] Smith shows us the link between this textual discourse and commercial processes so that such discourse 'creates the "motivational" structures which return the purchaser again and again' to the market in search of products to shape, adorn and maintain different parts of their bodies.[34] Textually mediated discourse is therefore not only about popular notions or opinions about clothes, body maintenance and adornment. The printed image, argues Smith, 'is interpreted by doctrines of femininity; doctrines of femininity are inscribed in printed images. Doctrines and images of femininity are inextricable from the outset.'[35] There is no doubt that socially dominant constructions of femininity as constitutive of gender identity would prevail and be influential in determining popular images and representations in women's magazines.

Magazines that address themselves largely to women are a cultural form ('mass culture' as Ellen McCracken puts it)[36] in the sense that they present attractive, pleasurable images of different aspects of femininity and construct a more or less 'women-centred articulation of the world.'[37] Magazines are also a medium for the construction of 'pleasure' for women through romance fiction, beauty tips for enhancing the body image, suggestions for improving their sex lives, their marriages, and so on.[38] Women's magazines have also been considered a form of 'escapism' and, reading them, 'women can mentally suspend themselves from the humdrum and drudgery of everyday life.'[39] Clearly, these magazines also serve a purpose that is not restricted to body imagery and narratives on the body. The 'grand narrative' of reality which is so authoritatively presented in these magazines is intended to both relate to women's everyday lives as well as take them out into the elusive, and often exotic, world of beauty, wealth, glamour and celebrity status. It does not matter if there is a conflict between the two worlds or that the second does not in fact exist for most women. The important point is to make it seem that this dream-like world is indeed attainable and accessible to every woman who wants it and decides to work for it.

One of the most commonly read magazines by middle- and upper-class women in urban India is *Femina*. Among the professional, more educated, upper-class women I interviewed, all did not claim to be readers on a regular basis but some did confess to glancing at it (carefully enough to remember specific articles and fashion displays) at neutral spaces, as it were, such as the beauty parlour, outside the home and workplace. Women clearly did not see their rational and intellectual lives being directly influenced by such a magazine which they never seemed to buy. However, middle-class women, both homemakers and working women, said they always made it a point to buy the magazine whenever it came out. They said that it was the one treat for them every month, that is buying the magazine and going through the articles; many of the issues discussed seemed very real to them, and they also developed ideas about clothes and fashion. This magazine was selected as it appeared to have some influence on women both in its absence and presence, and also because it claims to cater to those it considers 'women of substance' in modern India. More recently, *Cosmopolitan* has provided serious competition to *Femina* as it is a more glossy production and has provacative articles on beauty, sexuality and chronicles the lives of liberated women. However, it has perhaps been unable to dislodge the middle-class reader in small towns all over India who turn to *Femina* precisely because it stays within prescribed moral codes, along with other women's magazines such as *Women's Era*.

Visual Representation

As earlier argued in this paper, definitions of femininity as constitutive of identity in urban India are very closely related to the manner in which woman's body is both perceived and represented.

346

Why is visual representation so important in the construction of a feminine identity? One reason is 'the significance attached to images in modern culture and because a woman's character and status are frequently judged by her appearance.'[40] Feminine stereotypes are constructed and a woman is often judged according to whether she conforms to or deviates from this image. These stereotypes are reproduced through visual representation in women's magazines through fashion photography, advertising, the cover page, features, fiction, and other parts of the magazine.[41]

The politics of representation suggests that a woman's body is always portrayed through the ever-present male gaze. The psychoanalytic theory of 'the gaze' established by Laura Mulvey has no doubt been very influential in exploring the 'media construction of woman as spectacle, the gender of the gaze and voyeuristic pleasure.'[42] It does not, however, consider the crucial problematic of *female pleasure*, a point also made by other critics of Mulvey's position.[43]

Undoubtedly, desire is an essential component in the construction of gender identity. The discourse of femininity in a sense 'structures desire'.[44] In relation to the image, the body is always imperfect and this gap between the ideal and the real has to be rectified. Smith suggests that in this context, 'a distinctive relation to self arises: not as sex object so much as body to be transformed, an object of work, even of craft.'[45] It is in women's magazines that the ideal image is tied to information about 'how to rectify bodily deficiencies' so that women are provided with readymade recipes for body care, maintenance, as well as change. There is a solution for every sort of problem across age groups ranging from pimples, wrinkles, difficult hair, body or facial hair, body weight, and so on. In other words, 'women are sold their images in the form of commodities.'[46] There is a marked and well-defined commercial angel to the presentation of body imagery to women: certain products for 'beauty' and 'health' care are advertised along with the imagery and advice offered to readers. As Rosalind Coward has argued in this context, 'Feminine desire is to some extent the *lynchpin* of a consumerist society . . . Desire is simulated and endlessly defined. Everywhere it seems female desire is sought, bought, packaged and consumed.'[47]

There is also a link between this desire for embodied perfection, visual body imagery and sexuality, as has been suggested earlier. In fact, in contemporary representations, definitions of femininity are 'elided with the way the body is depicted as sexual entity.'[48] The sexual element becomes the focal point of body imagery whether it is fashion photography or advertising. This is done by highlighting some aspect of woman's sexuality through either blatant or subtle body display, gestures, 'the look' in the eyes of the model, and so on. It has been suggested that 'there is a continuum running from "images" to "commodities" that is determined by the fetishistic gaze'. In this sense, 'cultural fetishism takes the object and sexually energizes it, transforming it from a passive recipient of desire into an apparently active but submissive agent of desire. It seems to ask to be consumed.'[49]

While the significance of the sexual element and a certain kind of body imagery in visual representation cannot be denied, there are shifting, contradictory and often ambivalent representations of a feminine gender identity. There are no clear-cut or sharply defined body images which construct femininity in an ideal-typical way. There are many different versions of femininity, as it were, and therefore, many masks and persona available to women to acquire and use to fulfil their desires and aspirations. It would also appear that there is a break with what are considered traditional definitions of the female body. Local custom and popular practices earlier perceived a woman's body only as an instrument for the act of procreation and the pleasure of others. While contemporary representation may depict Indian women as 'modern', and her body as constitutive of self-identity to the extent that there is an excessive concern with shaping, moulding and fashioning the body, or as a career woman who may not *apparently* be concerned with her embodiment, the link with traditional definitions of femininity has not been broken. A woman may therefore be shown as a professional or as a career woman or as a modern, liberated woman, but she is simultaneously depicted as seductive and sensually appealing. In other words, such representation also emphasizes the seductive appeal and sexuality of the woman even though she may not be shown as a traditionally attired or dependent Indian woman.

Who is this middle-or upper-class urban Indian woman to whom visual representation in women's magazines is addressed? She is educated, upwardly mobile, class or status conscious, economically independent, at least to some extent, capable of taking decisions for the family, 'modern', urban, consciously middle class. More importantly, as pointed out earlier, she has the economic capacity to consume the products advertised in the magazine where beauty and body are equally emphasized, along with household/home care, through the sue of appliances, gadgets, wall paint, etc. She also has the ability to develop her culinary skills displayed in the colourful and appetizing centre-spread of the magazine, take appropriate care of her children, animal pets and garden plants, and simultaneously work hard to 'keep her man' and the marriage. She may find answers to her sexual and psychological problems in the 'Home Truths' columns or the 'Doctor's' page. Otherwise, she has to essentially rely on her wits and her imagination to survive in the world. Such a woman is *Femina's* 'woman of substance.'[50]

The woman who *Femina* addresses is no doubt a 'modern' woman to the extent that she may be a working woman, an educated professional or an educated middle class home-maker. She is interested in beauty and body care and maintenance to the extent that it helps in the embodied presentation of herself in everyday life. She is also 'traditional' to the extent that she places a high premium on certain values relating to, for example, marriage, motherhood and family life. She is, as Sunder Rajan defines her, the 'woman for all seasons', 'new' in the sense of 'having evolved and arrived'[51] in response to the times as well as being 'modern' and 'liberated'. She is also representative of the 'truly Indian' woman, as I have suggested, to the extent that she has not forsaken tradition and, in fact, her identity is tied to that. As Sunder Rajan puts it, 'She is "Indian" in the sense of possessing a pan-Indian identity that escapes regional, communal or linguistic specifications, but does not thereby become westernized.'[52]

Beauty and Glamour as Feminine Ideals

'Beauty', as sheer physical perfection in the human form, is emphasized in women's magazines like *Femina*, which seek to fulfil the female spectator's desire to gaze at representations of female embodiment and speculate on the possibilities of emulation. *Femina*, therefore, has regular features on '*Model Watch*', '*Images*', '*Faces*', '*Haute Stuff*' (about the latest in designers, clothes and accessories), '*Events*', and others, all of which address beauty through the icons of beauty, that is, the fashion models and their creators, the designers. Another section, 'Salon de Beaute', emphasizes body care and has details on body maintenance and perfecting the body.

The 'Faces' column recommends models, for example,

sixteen-years old Kavya Peerbhoy is highly recommended because of her age, her height (5 feet 8 inches), her weight (44 kg), her vital statistics (32–23–34), and her 'doe-eyed, waif-woman' look. In the accompanying photos and comments, the emphasis is on her youth, her innocence, her charming awkwardness and her incredible figure. Another model, Judi, is recommended for her dark-skinned look. Entitled 'Dark Devastation', the feature suggests an exotic element that is presented as being very different and completely disarming. She is introduced through an emphasis on aspects of her overt and subtle sexuality: 'She's got drop-dead skin, naughty eyes, a wicked smile and a seductive pout.' What is this 'drop-dead skin'? This is not explained but we have *Femina's* conclusive recommendation, '*Femina* knows the impact of the difference'. The photographer recommends her for her 'nice body which she uses really well' and concludes that 'with that face, body and attitude, . . . she'll go a long way modelling high fashion stuff'. Does her 'attitude' reflect a professionalism in her approach to modelling or is it suggestive of a liberated sexuality? This is not explained but the caption beside a particularly expressive photo perhaps tells us more: 'The song about her goes: Judi's got the lips I wanna kiss. . . .'[53] Elsewhere, in a feature on '*Haute Stuff*', a model, Cajol Sarup, is presented under a sub-title 'Exotic Species'. The selling of what might appear an exotic element in a model's sex appeal is part of *Femina's* marketing strategy. There is an exoticization of 'dark looks', 'luminous skin', 'wild mane' and so on, which are in fact, rather normal to an Indian or South Asian body. The emphasis on the normal as exotic, unusual or different, and thereby 'distinctive' and 'exclusive', only serves to highlight the magazine's astute marketing strategy. The idea is to sell beauty as a product by highlighting its most distinctive elements that can be attained through various means including the use of beauty parlours, cosmetics, clothes and accessories. The woman's body is only an object, honed to perfection by the woman herself in her search for that myth or ideal which she *herself* sees as its most perfect representation.

Glitz, glamour and partying are apparently what the models' lives are all about. This is projected by *Femina* precisely for its appeal to ordinary middle-class women who lack glamour in their everyday lives. Glamour is that elusive, inaccessible quality which is extremely desirable, and fantasizing about that glamour which offers an escape from the drudgery and dread of a woman's everyday existence. The two most well-known Indian beauty icons, Sushmita Sen and Aishwarya Rai, were ordinary young women, with images of the girl-next-door, who made it to the big world of fashion and beauty. This element gives their life stories an element of replicability, so that it is fairly simple for women to relate to them and to imagine that such a life could indeed be theirs as well.

Femina's editor applauds Sushmita Sen's victory as Miss Universe, 1994, and argues that the one area in which Indian has been 'lagging behind' the west is that of 'glamour', a gap which Sen amply filled with her victory.[54] *Femina* also glorifies the Sushmita-Sen look which is defined as one of 'naturalness', a 'smile that reaches out from the heart, into the eyes, and across the face to light it like a Diwali day.'[55] The link between the familiar, the ordinary, that is, being natural and traditional, as in the metaphor 'Diwali day', cannot be denied. Sen is also suggested as a 'role model' for 'hundreds of young, pretty hopefuls who have their sights set on the invisible pot of gold at the end of their rainbows'.

The *ordinariness* of Indian fashion models is continuously emphasized in the magazine. For example, there is a feature on twenty-years old Reshma Bombaywala, an undergraduate student in a Mumbai college, who was a semi-finalist in an international beauty contest at Costa Rica. Reshma is from a 'conservative Muslim family', studies Sociology, Political Science and English at college and also enjoys the good things of life which go with beauty contests such as partying, collecting gifts from sponsors, wearing glamorous clothes, and so on. Reshma did not win the contest but came back to modelling offers and now needs to 'convince' her parents that she has to live abroad for her work. Needless to say, *Femina* gave her the break, *Femina*, the magazine for the 'woman of substance'.

Fashion celebrities offer a more glamorous image than other models and are commonly used in fashion photography. Aishwarya Rai, for example, is presented both as a sophisticated woman of the world as well as a modern, young woman, 'very much the women in vogue', and with Sushmita Sen, as one 'chosen to lead. . . young, smart, upbeat and winners all the way'. The blurb in the corner of the photo says, 'We *aaj ki naris* [women of today] are here! Right on top of the world.'[56] *Femina* often invites its readers to participate in various beauty contests and there is a clear emphasis on post-contest privileges: 'Hollywood parties, press conferences, motorcades, meet-

ings with Heads of state.'[57] Another advert for a beauty contest emphasizes 'The Exultation, The Exhilaration. One small step for you.'[58]
While the emphasis is on the glamour and excitement of success, a
woman's vital statistics, height, weight and age are essential accompaniments in striving for this success.

The magazine offers advice for beauty care and watching body
weight which it addresses through its own columns and features as
well as through adverts. An obvious *fragmentation* of woman's body is
apparent in the advice offered. Women are advised on skin care, hair
styles and maintenance, caring for feet and hands, using appropriate
nail varnishes, focusing specially on eyes, eyebrows, nose, mouth and,
most significantly, lips, which are seen as a clear sexual symbol. There
is, in this fragmentation, an erasure of subjectivity and an objectification of woman's body. The fragmented body also signifies a fragmented identity to the extent that we tend to perceive parts of our embodied selves as particularly important, see them as constituting the
whole, and focus on them to the exclusion of others. We therefore
produce our embodied gender identity through particular aspects of
our bodies, highlighting what we consider our best features, whether
these are the legs, hair, height, waist or lips.

The adverts in the magazine also emphasize beauty as an
ideal and once again focus on parts of the body. A subtle or overt link
with a woman's sexuality is present in the text or in the model's
appearance in most adverts. In an advert for the 'Beauty Secrets' range
of cosmetics, there is an image of a partially-clad woman looking
provocatively into the camera. The text says. 'A gorgeous well-kept
body takes a lot of care and a few Beauty Secrets.' The advert highlights
three points: that a 'gorgeous well-kept body' is an ideal, that it takes a
'lot of care', and that the use of the advertised product would be helpful
in this venture. The advert also emphasizes the sexual dimension of
beauty in the model's caressing of her naked shoulder and the suggestion of her removing her bra.

An overt display of an obviously liberated sexuality is very
carefully represented. In an advert for underwear, a young woman is
shown lounging in her underwear in front of a window where the cur-
tains are not drawn. Although credits are displayed in small print at
the bottom of the page, the model's face is hidden from the viewer although she is perhaps clearly visible from the other side of the window.
Her face is not revealed so that a woman who chooses to be 'daring' in

terms of body display and her body stance, which appears to be sexually uninhibited and defiant, has to be somehow controlled, possibly by being partially hidden form view.

There is often also a focus on the contemporary woman who is neither too modern nor completely traditional. An advert for woollen shawls shows a woman wrapped in a shawl, her body, neck downwards, completely hidden from view, and says, 'Never screams for attention, never fails to get noticed. Always contemporary, always distinct'. The idea that 'contemporary' need not necessarily signify 'outrageous' but someone who is discreet and yet stylish is a clear reminder of the concept of Indian womanhood as being continuously shifting and ambivalent in its representation.

Age is a significant aspect of body representation. A woman's body in fashion photography is almost always a youthful body unless it is a special feature for older women. Adverts, however, vary as there are differences in the kind of products being advertised. There are clearly age-targetted products in the cosmetics industry. The anti-wrinkling and other 'age-defying' creams, for example, are specially targeted at a specific age-group.

The textual discourse and visual representation in the magazine, therefore, portray a certain kind of feminine ideal: an ideal that is simultaneously young and middle-aged, ordinary and glamorous, traditional and modern, daring and liberated as well as homely and family-oriented, and so on. Such an ambivalent representation no doubt appeals to every kind of woman and often becomes a part of her perception of her embodied identity.

Women's Lived Experience

Representation of woman and the attendant body imagery undoubtedly affects the way we perceive woman's body as well as our own aspirations and desires. Women often seek to *become* the image that is presented to them not so much in terms of replication but in a way which affects their self-perceptions so that they see themselves always as 'the other' which has to be perfected and presented in as ideal a form as possible to the ever-watchful gaze that is *body* male and female. Hence, the image of the body in the mirror is always that of the embodied self seen through the other's gaze. My body is no longer mine to the extent that I see myself as the other sees me or as I want the other to see me. In looking at my embodied self in the mirror I see myself as how I think or feel others see me or how I would like others to see me. In other words, although I have a material existence I exist through the gaze of the other. Gender identity is very closely enmeshed with body imagery, self-perceptions, the other's gaze and embodiment.

The narratives that follow, from my interviews with urban middle-class women, indicate that women do indeed understand the impact of the social, cultural and male representations of their bodies which to a large extent influence their own images, perceptions and knowledge of the body.[59] They however simultaneously resist the other's view by often refusing to alter their own images which may vary from those of the other. Women also express their agency in their attempt to redefine 'beauty', a strategic mode to resist conventional notions of beauty. Women therefore are often in a complex situation where they both seek and value male approval but simultaneously resist the gaze.

A forty-year-old school teacher who is separated from her hus-band and has one child says.

> The shape of my body is important. That is, to feel good about myself. Not a barbie doll figure, of course. As a particularly prog-ressive woman I might say I am not vulnerable to media images of the body but of course one is. [One] also justifies it by saying it is 'healthy' [to stay thin]. A woman's body is pleasing to yourself, to have a beautiful body. Feel more relaxed relating to somebody if I feel my body is the shape I like.

She adds,

> When men do express themselves in relation to my body's shape, it is almost as if I prompt them to say it. I nudge them to do it. Their saying 'It's wonderful' is not enough because I know it's not. [An] oriental figure: large breasts, small waist, is what I have and men might say they appreciate it because they like it. Their perceptions are different from mine in terms of what they like, for example, the western female body. But their perceptions don't convince me enough to alter myself for them.

The effect of media representations of a woman's body is ack-nowledged as well as these is an articulation of herself as someone who desires male approval of her body and simultaneously resists male constructions of the perfect female form. She perceives her need for the other's appreciation of her physical beauty which is clearly linked to her sexuality but she is also aware that she is not convinced by male notions to transform herself. There is an obvious conflict, in this case, between her perceived need and her rejection of the male gaze.

A forty-three year old, well-educated theatre personality who teaches in drama school, directs, acts and dances on stage, is married with a child, views physical beauty differently from conventional definitions,

> If I started looking very scrappy and skin full of blackheads and looking tired, I wouldn't want to go around like that. The idea of physical beauty has been very important for me—not long nails and removing hair. [It is] to do with acting. In front of a mirror, [I have] performed for hours. So it has to do with looking at an attractive and beautiful person. Mixture really of attractive and beautiful. [I have] an interest in theatre, performing another, enacting another in front of the mirror. Not just seeing yourself but also the character you are playing. So mixture of inner character, your own physical features, and the character your are playing. So when one is really into a character one's physical features can change and become beautiful as your inner character also changes. With yoga, I know we are happier, we breathe better and the blood circulates better and we look better. Important therefore to look good. Got to do also with health. [I'm] not that much concerned with wrinkles as I used to be. Now there's inner health to do with peace of mind. Now, I find, if there's beauty, then even wrinkles become part of that beauty. But having said that, I don't want my face to grow old. And when it does, to do it gracefully. Would still want to look attractive for myself. In college, it was important to look attractive to men and to my girlfriends. Now, it's important to look good for myself. [It has] also to do with the mind: thinking good thoughts, creative thoughts and then I feel beautiful, feel good, in which beauty is a part.

And then she adds, 'I don't like it when my paunch becomes loose and puffy eyes. Can't stand it.'

Although this woman has a perception of beauty that is not based on physical features, she is unable to relate it to her own experience where she has a very clear understanding of what constitutes her own agenda for her body image—no wrinkles, no paunch, no puffiness around the eyes, and so on. The conflict here is between her image of beauty and her dissatisfactory experience of her own body.

The mirror is an important instrument in the narratives. It is used both for reflecting body image as well as for constructing the image through performance and play. In the construction of the image, as seen above, the mirror is used for enhancing particular aspects of the reflected body-expressed emotions and therefore is an agential instrument. In the narrative that follows, however, the mirror is used for an assessment or evaluation of the body image, through the gaze of the other, and can sometimes result in a fetishization of the female form through a fragmentation of the body into its various parts.

A thirty-five year old university teacher, married and pregnant when I interviewed her, has a very definite perspective on her body and its physical perfection:

> I like to look good. I've always taken care of myself. I like my body to look nice. I should like my face when I look at it in the mirror. I don't like to see a tired face. I like to see a glowing face in the mirror. .. When I see my body in the mirror, I should like it, it should be pleasant for me. I don't like to see sagging breasts, don't like to have extra flesh on thighs or hips. So I like to maintain my body and eat less. I should like my body. So I don't want to have a thin body but it should look nice to me. But if I have seen it [fat], then I always do something about it. Most men don't talk about my body, that they find my breasts desirable and ravishing, etc. they talk to me, about me, as a person. My husband used to talk about my body before marriage, in letters, etc. But not later. Maybe it's not a 'ravishing body'. Maybe they don't find it attractive. Because I admire men's bodies. I like certain kinds of men's bodies.

The image in the mirror is of profound significance for this woman who judges the mirror reflection in terms of what she considers her own standards of physical perfection. She then undertakes a project to change the image and replace it with one that is more appealing to her own gaze. She is emphatic that her body image, in the mirror, should please her. This includes the physical feeling of 'sexiness'.

> I should find my body sexy too. For example, I don't like a fat stomach in my body. I also relate to my body in a sexy way. I should feel sexy looking at my body. I find my body sexy in the pregnant

state. There is an incongruity that I find attractive: the breasts are bigger. I really thought that I would hate my body when I am pregnant. But I don't. I actually quite enjoy it. I take off my clothes to look at my body and then put them on again.

The mirror becomes the instrument through which she tends to define her identity in relation to her embodied state. The image is therefore of considerable importance in her overall perception of her body, its symbolic value in her everyday life, and the uses to which she seeks to put it. Although there is clearly a narcissistic concern here with body image and the pleasures of the body, the other is nonetheless a major consideration in defining the body. She says.

I don't know if my body is "sexy" in the male definition of it; whether your [one's] lips or boobs are sexy. I'm not oozing sex. I don't have breasts that are heaving or bouncing about, so that men may not find it sexy. In my case, it's hidden but it's all there. And that in a way attracts men. I don't dress up to high light my contours, emphasize my shape, etc. I emphasize more on my personality.

There is an underlying concern here with what men desire from women's bodies and her perception of her inability to fulfil that desire in an obvious manner. She however offers the promise of fulfilling that desire through her suggestion that 'it's all there'. The body, therefore, is very much for the other and, significantly, seeks fulfillment as much from the other as through the mirror. While some women may veil their desire for male approval with descriptions of a spiritual or inner beauty or do so as a strategically resistant mode, others are rather frank in acknowledging the influence of the male gaze. In addition, their own perceptions and strategic use of feminist or alternative notions of beauty, derived form women's lived experience, the media, women's magazines and other influences, contributes to the construction of an agentially negotiated and socially constructed gender identity.

In Conclusion

This paper has attempted to example the link between the experiencing body, body image, visual and textual representation of a woman's body and identity. What is this experiencing, living body? A woman experiences her body through a collage of visual and textual representations of which women's magazines is only one trope. The presentation of the body through fashion photography, for example, is aimed at projecting both a glamorous body and a lifestyle which can apparently be achieved by any woman. The female gaze appropriates, with admiration and pleasure, a woman's body as it is projected in its glamorous and glitzy form. In other words, the female gaze looks at, desires, seeks to consume the body and its artefacts, as it is represented in its most ideal form. Woman's body is therefore not only objectified in its representation but also fetishized in its appropriation through the female gaze. It is desired by women in different ways and as modes of desire vary, so do the modes of appropriation.

Woman is desired as glamour girl, traditional yet modern or contemporary, with a 'sexy' body and therefore for the pleasures the body can provide, through the veiled sexuality or its more overt imagery. She is also 'homely' woman who strives to make her home and marriage a success. The ambivalences present in the representation of a woman's body are equally present in its appropriation. Women fetishize their own bodies as we have seen in the narrative of the woman who gazes at her body in the mirror and derives pleasure from viewing different parts of the body. In this manner, woman sees a reflection of the image and elides the image with the gaze resulting in a body which exists only through the gaze. It is therefore important to recognize that woman herself is engaged in the representation of her body and its imagery. Sandra Lee Bartky applies the Foucauldian model to the female experience of being looked at *and* looking when she argues, 'a panoptical male connoisseur resides within the consciousness of most women.'[60] This has already been recognized by John Berger when he says, 'Men look at women. Women watch themselves. . . .' and by internalizing the male gaze, look at themselves through the other's gaze.[61] It is important to emphasize, however, that this does not happen unconsciously or even unwittingly all the time but is often a strategy used by women to present themselves to the other in the most desired manner. Clearly, self-identity, to which gender identity is linked, is established and sustained very much in relation with and recognition by the other, through strategic modes of negotiation and self-definition.

Having said that, it is perhaps necessary to add that the body is often seen as a powerful medium by women who can mould, shape, use, modify the body to change their lives. Women therefore consume, make-up an image, perform an identity and see themselves always in a

358

state of becoming, never in a fixed or static form.[62] Kathy Davis argues, 'The female agent is the sine qua non of the feminine beauty system. Without agency, texts would fail to motivate women to participate in activities of body improvement.'[63] We need to, however, also consider the possibility that women are often trapped in forms of self-indulgence and may become obsessed with the material body, sexuality, and modes of self-presentation which keep them confined to a limited space of self-absorption and preoccupation with there embodiment.

Pierre Bourdieu has said, 'The social gaze is not a universal, abstract, objectifying power . . . but a social power, whose efficacy is always partly due to the fact that the receiver *recognizes* the categories of perception and appreciation it applies to him or her'.[64] If the social gaze is recognized for what it is, namely, as that which is engaged in objectifying woman's body and modes of its representation, there would perhaps be an attempt to resist such a gaze. The woman who has to 'nudge' men to comment on her body, or take the comments of the other seriously enough to make attempts to change her body image, or indulge in fantasies about whether or not men find her body 'ravishing' or 'sexy', are therefore to a large extent, *dependent* on the gaze of the other for constructing their own body image and self-identity. In a recent work Judith Butler has argued,

> Power imposes itself on us, and weakened by its force, we come to internalize or accept its terms . . . . Subjection consists precisely in this fundamental dependency on a discourse we never chose but that, paradoxically, initiates and sustains our agency . . . . Subjection [therefore] signifies the process of becoming subordinated by power as well as the process of becoming a subject.[65]

This formulation appears to have both Foucauldian and Bourdieuian resonances in its formulation of power and the reproduction of power through the subject. Butler however emphasizes the notion of 'dependency' that recognizes the subject's need for survival and the relationship the subject seeks to establish with the source of power in order to both survive and exist.

A postmodernist reading of the representation of a woman's body, and the female gaze appropriating it, might suggest, 'Women are expected to construct themselves as objects, as well as to experience themselves as subjects, and to oscillate between the subject/object dichotomy in order to maintain a notion of successful femininity.'[66]

We need to, however, pose a question: What is a *successful* gender identity? For woman, is it an enhanced or acute awareness, internalization and representation of a socially defined and self-constructed femininity? Or is it a strategic mode for defining femininity in a particular manner through performance. Perhaps, femininity does not exist at all. As Joan Riviere has suggested, femininity is a 'masquerade', a mask assumed by women to disguise their masculinity, for example, their intelligence or power.[67] This becomes significant if we consider that masquerade

> in flaunting femininity, holds it at a distance. Womanliness is a mask which can be worn or removed. The masquerade's resistance to patriarchal positioning would therefore lie in its denial of the production of femininity as closeness, as presence-to-itself, as precisely imagistic. . . . To masquerade is to manufacture a lack in the form of a certain distance between oneself and one's image.[68]

The masquerade undoubtedly destabilizes the image by accentuating femininity through a form of double representation, as it were, and confounds the masculine structure of the look. Masquerade, however ceases to be an agential mode or an act of resistance when it used only for symbolic purposes, as is often the case.

If indeed femininity is culturally, rather than biologically, constructed, then it is always about 'simulation, a simulacrum.'[69] If this is the case, then simulacrum shows that nothing exists at all. It is a superficial truth that we seek to express through different forms of display and performance. This Baudrillardian reading of femininity however denies any power to woman and has therefore been rejected by feminists. We need instead to reassess the significance of the female gaze both in the *representation* of woman's body as well as in its *construction* through the different forms that femininity might take. The female gaze is undoubtedly influenced by a social gaze but can also manipulate or use the gaze of the other, if we choose to take on an agential role, by rejecting the categories of perception and appreciation that objectify our bodies in everyday life and by asserting our own modes of looking, perception and vision.

Notes and References

[1] This paper is part of my larger work on the relationship between the body, gender and identity in everyday life in contemporary urban India. The work

is in progress and was initiated during the time I was a Fellow at the Centre for Contemporary Studies, Nehru Memorial Museum and Library at New Delhi. Different versions of this paper have been presented at a seminar on 'Gender in South Asia' at Queen Elizabeth House, Oxford University, on 21 May 1998 and at the Theory, Culture and Society Centre, Nottingham Trent University, on 10 June 1998. I am deeply grateful to the participants at these for their comments and criticism. I am also grateful to the Queen Elizabeth House at Oxford for the C.R. Parekh Visiting Fellowship in 1998, and to the Charles Wallace India Trust for supplementary support, that enabled me to work on this paper in an excellent ambience.

I would also like to express my gratitude to Professor Ravinder Kumar who gave me the opportunity to begin work on this project in 1993 and has never failed to encourage me in my intellectual endeavours.

2   The psychoanalytic discourse on the gaze in relation to film viewership tends to ignore this aspect of the power of vision in the appropriation of women's bodies. The significance of the spectator's gaze and its impact of film imagery has been emphasized and examined by Laura Mulvey in a path-breaking paper on the subject. See Laura Mulvey, 'Visual Pleasure and Narrative Cinema', *Feminism and Film Theory*, ed., by C. Penley, Routledge, London, 1988. According to this psychoanalytic theory of 'the gaze', the observer 'objectifies the subject of the gaze in the pursuit of scopophilic and voyeuristic pleasures' so that women are always represented as the object of male heterosexual desire. See Jennifer Craik, *The Face of Fashion: Cultural Studies in Fashion*. Routledge, London, 1994, pp. 12–13. However, such a view presumes the link between sexuality and 'the look' as essential and ignores other important ways of representation that may not necessarily derive from heterosexual desire.

3   See Meenakshi Thapan, 'introduction: Gender and Embodiment in Everyday Life', in *Embodiment: Essays on Gender and Identity*, Oxford University Press, New Delhi, 1997, for a consideration of the social construction and lived experience of a woman's body. See also Meenakshi Thapan, 'Gender, Body and Everyday Life', *Social Scientist*, Vol. 23, Nos. 7–9, 1995.

4   John O'Neill, *Five Bodies: The Human Shape of Modern Society*, Cornell University Press, London and Ithaca, 1985, p. 17.

5   Ibid., p. 21.

6   Iris Marion Young, *Throwing Like a Girl and Other Essays in Feminist Philosophy and Social Theory*, Indiana University Press, Bloomington and Indianapolis, 1990, p. 14.

7   Henrietta Moore, *A Passion for Difference*, Polity Press, Cambridge, 1994, p. 3.

8   Pierre Bourdieu, *Distinction: A Social Critique of the Judgement of Taste*, translated by R. Nice, Routledge and Kegan Paul, London, 1984, p. 170.

9   Ibid., p. 173.

10   Ibid., p. 190.

11   Arthur W. Frank, 'For a sociology of the body: an analytic review', *The Body: Social Process and Cultural Theory*, Mike Featherstone, Mike Hep-

worth and Bryan S. Turner, Sage, London, 1991, p. 68.

12 Meenakshi Thapan, 'Gender and Embodiment in Everyday Life', p. 26.

13 Elizabeth Grosz, *Volatile Bodies: Towards a Corporeal Feminism*, Indiana University Press, Bloomington and Indianapolis, 1994, p. 101.

14 Ibid., p. 80.

15 Ibid.

16 Iris Marion Young, *Throwing Like a Girl*, p. 145.

17 Ibid., p. 146.

18 Susan Bordo, *Unbearable Weight: Feminism, Western Culture and the Body*, University of California Press, Berkeley, 1993, p. 169.

19 Ibid.

20 Diana Fuss, 'Fashion and the Homospectatorial Look', *Critical Inquiry*, 18, 1992, p. 713.

21 Elizabeth Wilson, 'Deviant Dress', *Feminist Review*, 35, 1990, p. 68.

22 Kaja Silverman, 'Fragments of a Fashionable Discourse', in Tania Modleski, ed., *Studies in Entertainment*, Indiana University Press, Bloomington and Indianapolis, 1986, p. 146.

23 Ibid., p. 147.

24 Elizabeth Grosz, *Volatile Bodies*, p. 80.

25 Caroline Evans and Minna Thornton, *Women and Fashion: A New Look*. Quartet Books, London, 1989, p. 9.

26 Ibid.

27 Elizabeth Grosz, *Volatile Bodies*, p. 81.

28 My analysis of women's experience of their bodies is based on their accounts during my interviews with twentyfive middle-and upper-class women in 1993–94 in New Delhi. These women were selected on the basis of a snowball sample and particularly represent the category of urban Indian women who, because of their status and position in urban society, are exposed to an array of visual images and textual discourse on embodied representation in the media and elsewhere.

29 Iris Marion Young, *Throwing Like a Girl*, p. 190.

30 Susan Bordo, *Unbearable Weight*, p. 20.

31 Rosalind Coward, *Female Desire: Women's Sexuality Today*, Paladin, London, 1984, p. 75.

32 John Berger, *Ways of Seeing*, B.B.C. and Penguin Books, Harmondsworth, p. 47.

33 Dorothy E. Smith, *The Conceptual Practices of Power: A Feminist Sociology of Knowledge*, Northeastern University Press, Boston, 1990, p. 163.

34 Ibid.

35 Ibid., p. 170.

36 Ellen McCracken, *Decoding Women's Magazines*, Macmillan, Basingstoke, 1993, p. 1.

37 Ibid., p. 2.

38 Rosalind Betterton, ed., *Looking on: Images of Femininity in the Visual Arts and Media*, Pandora, London, 1987.

39 Patricia Allat, 'The Political Economy of Romance: Popular Culture, Social

Divisions and Social Reconstructions in War Time', *Sex, Sensibility and the Gendered Body*, edited by Janet Holland and Lisa Adkins, St, Martin's Press, New York, 1996, p. 37.

[40] Rosalind Betterton, *Looking On*, p. 7.

[41] It is interesting to note how all these images coalesce in the typical Hindi film where the 'vamp' is always portrayed as being westernized, sexually liberated, clothed in western attire and having being judged as being morally inferior, invariably unsuccessful in her efforts to win over the 'good man', the film's hero. She is almost always the gangster's moll. In stark contrast the 'good woman', the innocent heroine in the film, is always the traditional, devoted, virtuous Indian woman. She may be portrayed as being wayward but never sexually promiscuous, and being morally of 'good character', so to speak, is invariably placed on a pristine pedestal representative of true Indian womanhood.

[42] Liesbet Van Zoonen, *Feminist Media Studies*, Sage, London, p. 88.

[43] See, for instance, ibid. Anne Doane, whose work on film criticism takes Mulvey's work further, also argues that as female particularity or specificity is defined by proximity or sameness between women, they lack the capacity for voyeurism. For these psychoanalytic frameworks, therefore, an 'autonomous, unmediated and pleasurable female spectatorship' is perhaps inconceivable. Van Zoonen also points out that while Doane's theory suggests that the girl's close relationship with her mother forecloses distance and thereby the possibility for female voyeurism, it is also the case that it is precisely the 'pre-Oedipal bonding of the female child with the mother that facilitates the pleasurable attraction of women to each other'. The female spectator looking at woman is therefore doing so through a form of what is referred to as a 'double desire': 'an active homosexual, one, which is rooted in the bond with her mother and a passive heterosexual one stemming from her identification with woman as object of the male gaze'. See *Feminist Media Studies*, pp. 92–94.

[44] Dorothy Smith, *Conceptual Practices of Power*, p. 185.

[45] Ibid., pp. 186–87.

[46] Betterton, *Looking On*, p. 13.

[47] Rosalind Coward, *Female Desire*, p. 26.

[48] Betterton, *Looking On*.

[49] Jon Stratton, *The Desirable Body: Cultural Fetishism and the Erotics of Consumption*, 1996, p. 60.

[50] 'Woman of Substance' here, refers to the advertising line of the magazine: '*Femina* is for the Woman of Substance.'

[51] Rajeshwari Sunder Rajan, *Real and Imagined Women: Gender, Culture and Postcolonialism*, Routledge and Kegan Paul, London, 1993, p. 130.

[52] Ibid.

[53] *Femina*, 8 November 1995.

[54] *Femina*, 23 June 1994.

[55] *Femina*, 8 June 1994.

[56] *Femina*, 23 May 1995.

363

57 *Femina*, 8 November 1994.

58 *Femina*, 1995.

59 See note 28 above.

60 As quoted by L. Gamman and M. Makinen, *Female Fetishism: A New Look*, Lawrence and Wishart, London, 1994, p. 176.

61 John Berger, *Wage of Seeing*.

62 For example, Kathy Davis suggests that cosmetic surgery can, in fact, become a liberating tool for women. See her 'Remaking the She-devil: A Critical Look at Feminist Approaches to Beauty', in *Hypatia*, Vol. 6, No. 2 (Summer), and *Reshaping the Female Body: The Dilemma of Cosmetic Surgery*, Routledge, London and New York, 1995.

63 Kathy Davis, *Reshaping the Female Body*, p. 62.

64 Pierre Bourdieu, *Social Critique of the Judgement of Taste*, p. 207, emphasis added.

65 Judith Butler, *The Psychic Life of Power: Theories in Subjection*, University of Stanford Press, California, 1997, p. 2.

66 L. Gamman and M. Makinen, *Female Fetishism*, p. 216.

67 Joan Riviere, '*Womanliness as a Masquweade*', in V. Burgin, J. Donald and Cora Kaplan, eds., *Formations of Fantasy*, Methuen, London and New York, 1986.

68 Anne Doane, *Femme Fatales: Feminism, Film Theory, Psychoanalysis*. Routledge, London and New York, 1991, pp. 25–26.

69 L. Gamman and M. Makinen, *Female Fetishism*, p. 216.

Beyond State and Market?

The Indian Environment Debate

Mahesh Rangarajan

he Indian environmental debate is today at crossroads. Economic trends and deep-rooted political changes are raising new issues in a vast country. Economic liberalization has accentuated existing fissures in a deeply divided society. In particular, there are anxieties that the drive to attract investors and to increase exports will work to the detriment of the groups directly reliant on natural resources such as forests, fisheries and grazing lands. The generation of wealth would itself exacerbate conflicts between competing groups, especially when those with low purchasing power may have to pay the cost in terms of a deteriorating living space or loss of entitlements.[1] But other trends are also at work. Attempts by the government to draft a fresh law on forests have led to a concerted effort nationwide by a network of tribals, peasants and their middle-class allies to evolve a more decentralized and radical alternative.[2] Such efforts, diverse as they are in their prescriptions, have one point in common. They seek to take advantage of the political ferment in Indian society in the increasing assertion of underprivileged groups to advance an alternative vision of development. The two trends, of economic liberalization and political transformation, are often at odds with each other. The changing relationship between inequity and ecology rests, in part, on the ability of the polity to meet aspirations of hitherto marginal social groups.

The environmental debate does enable us to pose problems of wider significance. This is especially true because it poses difficult choices of how to achieve equity in a society where conflict for resources is intense. The actual model of development becomes crucial in marginalizing or empowering those who directly depend on the land and water for survival. The diversity of interests and ideas is clear even among the ranks of the environmentally concerned. The urban middle-class conservation groups often have much in common with their counterparts in developed countries in terms of wildlife preservation and other allied concerns, whether scientific or aesthetic. But a second and wider environmental concern is reflected in various currents that may be subsumed under a broad label of 'popular' movements and groups. Their critique of the development process is fundamental in a political sense, for they argue in favour of a radical change not only in the goals of development but also in the power structure. The two broad tendencies do have significant commonalities, especially in their conviction that growth in itself is not a goal. Divisions are not watertight and there have been major changes in the stances of particular individuals or groups over time. But a distinction may still be valuable for analytical clarity. The variations lie not only in terms of the elite and the popular but also within each of these camps.

The wider political context in which the debates take place is significant. The shift away from a relatively autonomous economy towards one more fully integrated with the global economy was finally brought about by the fiscal crisis of 1991. The issue is all too easily seen as lying between the state representing the quest for equity and the market as a force which promotes growth at the cost of equity. The environmental debate adds to these other dimensions which make any such easy equation difficult to sustain. By raising issues of sustainability, it points to the problems of both the role of the market and the kind of state apparatus that has existed in the country. Governmental power, after all, includes not only the institutions of representative government but also the bureaucracy. Representative systems coexist with administrative practices that often retain a colonial flavour. This is especially significant in the case of the Forest Department, which looms large in any discussion of India's environment. It is also true in a wider sense, for the essential structure of the imperial bureaucracy, originally founded to perform functions of revenue collection and law enforcement, often shows major continuities into the post-1947 era. The role of the market is more complex, but it cannot ignore the ways in which growth may actually corrode the entitlements that the poor have vis a vis common or open-access lands. This has circumscribed the scope for alternative mechanisms of cooperation and also contributed significantly in increasing the economic vulnerability of wage earners and marginal cultivators in rain-fed areas.[3] The dual impact of privatization and state control has been central to much of the environmental debate. Implicit in the critiques is the search for an alternative to both.

In the immediate aftermath of independence, these issues were rarely seen in this light by planners. Indian nationalists had articulated an agenda of autonomous capitalist industrialization by the 1880s. The raising of tariff walls to enable the growth of heavy industry and the reduction of land revenue to ameliorate the peasantry were already on the nationalist agenda. A generation later, Mahatma Gandhi knit together the issues of salt, land revenue and forest laws in the second wave of mass movements against the Raj.[4] The last were often only loosely linked to the Congress power structure, with adivasis (or tribals) and peasants in many areas going well beyond the limited forms of protest suggested by the leader. What is more crucial is that the Congress as a movement soon became an alternative party of power. By the time India became independent, the Gandhian notions of an alternative kind of development had moved to the background. Their significance has, of late, come to be of wider interest but in the main, a programme of state-assisted industrialization was carried through. It is the social and ecological impact of such growth that lies at the roots of much of the grassroots protest in contemporary India.[5] Such a sketchy account can hardly do justice to the complex and often mutually contradictory currents in Indian society. But it should suffice in setting up the background for a discussion.

Two Kinds of Environmental Concerns

The growth of environmental consciousness has largely to do with the failure of development to address such issues. The popular movements often involve those who have been 'losers' in the development process. Their initiatives sit uneasily side by side with the other narrower, but highly influential, notions of conservation that now have a mostly urban, middle-class constituency. Often, the two broad stands even mean very different things when they use the word 'conservation'. A brief look at their concerns and lineages may be helpful.

The preservationists—as the elite wildlife lobby may be conveniently labelled—form a crucial but often highly influential lobby. There are important changes and continuities with the past. The origins of imperial concerns about the depletion of forest cover grew out of a variety of anxieties, about its possible impact on agriculture and law and order, making governance difficult,[6] and somewhat later, due to the need to obtain sleepers for the railways.[7] It is well known that the colonial period saw the widespread popularization of hunting for trophies by the princes and by the British. Fear of the reduction of game led to measures to protect various species of deer, antelope and game birds to ensure an outrun of trophies and meat. Such measures were facilitated by the annexation of no less than a fifth of the land area of British India as government forest by 1900. Such lands were primarily managed to generate revenue, timber and other forest products and also to protect wild animals and birds for game. While the economic rationale of appropriating forested lands from rival resource-users was crucial, the ideological arguments advanced to buttress the claim were important. Successive generations of British and later Indian officials felt that local land-users were short-sighted and would deplete the fauna and flora. The notion of the ecologically profligate tribal was integral to elite conservation at the moment of its birth. Interestingly, the early advocates of game protection shared these prejudices, though they hoped to replace the culture of the hunt with an appreciation of nature. Organizations like the Bombay Natural History Society, founded in 1883, played a key role in advising the government on new laws. There was a remarkable continuity of perceptions of rural people as innately destructive, that was still evident in the Society's intervention decades later when it helped draft a bill for Bombay state in 1951. Despite important shifts in opinion, the broad view of the forest or wildlife question was that only governmental intervention backed by elite assistance would save endangered ecologies from the people at large.[8]

Wildlife preservation as a distinct agenda had a limited appeal until the end of the 1960s. Protection was often geared to specific ends, like saving wild elephants which were a major resource for forestry work and the British army. Reserves were also set aside to preserve certain large mammals by the Raj and also some princes to secure trophies. In independent India the wildlife advisory bodies were initially dominated by members of the *shikar* lobby, including princes, foresters, planters and elite hunters. In the break with the past, the culture of the camera swiftly deposed that of the gun. It is easy to underestimate the significance of this cultural change. But in the early 1960s it was still conventional for any distinguished foreign visitor to shoot a tiger. By 1970 the animal was protected and a nationwide project to save it and its habitats in a network of reserves was launched in 1973. In addition to older bodies, the World Wildlife Fund, India, launched in 1969, and other smaller urban groups were supported by a section of wildlife-conscious foresters.

In fact, the ideological break within the elite was more far-reaching in a host of ways. Imperial forestry as well as game management targeted certain species for local extermination. Tree species that were not commercially significant or carnivorous animals that competed for the deer with hunters were sought to be eliminated. Further, game protection was itself based on the premise that nature had to be managed in an enlightened manner to generate commodities. It did not entail a notion of preservation for its own sake. The launch of Project Tiger marked a shift in terms of consciousness among a section of officials as well as political leaders. The tiger became the flagship species for creating reserves where all species, both plant and animal, would be protected. No life-form was considered unworthy of protection within such reserves. While the broader culture and ethos of forestry was one of revenue generation, the attitude of the preservationists was to do the polar opposite. They sought not to reorder nature but to restore it to its original state. 'Do nothing and don't let anybody do anything' was the motto. In this endeavour, they were assisted by the personal intervention of Prime Minister Indira Gandhi, who pushed through the federally funded project. As a result, the very notion of success in the forester's lexicon was being redefined. By 1977 there were claims of success not only in saving the endangered tiger but in reviving the fortunes of a host of other species. The tiger stood at the apex not only of the food chain but also of a major reorientation of attitudes towards the land.[9] At present Protected Areas cover over four per cent of the land area, and the core areas where no removal of biomass is permitted, cover 1 per cent. For the preservationist this area is the key to the future of India both in ecological and cultural terms. Its existence enables the survival of myriad life-forms, from the tiger to the honey bee and the elephant to the otter. In an ideal situation the entire reserve area would be free of any human activity save for protection and study.

Yet, the process of carving out wildlife preserves itself showed clear links with the past: many were former hunting grounds of the princes or timber lands maintained by the imperial Forest Department. Conservation had involved the denial of rights; the claims of colonial

foresters were at odds with local land-users. The preservation programmes of independent India were initially more hesitant about
relocation of villages and the denial of usufruct rights. By 1973 political
backing and the notion that 'something had to be done' was strong
enough to override any such qualms. Between 1973 and 1977 villagers
from many reserves were evicted and resettled, the terms and manner
of displacement becoming one of the major grievances against the
wildlife authorities. The issue of access rights is even more friction-
prone, with one estimate—of those reliant directly or indirectly on
wildlife reserves for a living—placing the number of affected persons
at not less than 3 million and possibly as high as 4.5 million.[10] In addition to relocation and access rights, the critics would soon argue that
the idea that people and nature could be severed was itself flawed. Even
those who supported the notion that some areas ought to be preserved
totally often became critical of the manner in which officials interacted
with resident people.[11] The wildlife issue is only a sub-set of a wider
conflict over who should control the forest lands. The Forest Department, with over 74 million hectares under its sway, hopes to add to its
powers. Its opponents among popular movements wish to replace this
with one or the other form of local control.

Yet, the idea that strong centralized intervention by the Union
government could resolve problems of resource destruction was not
confined to the wilderness preservationists. The depletion of topsoil
due to erosion and other forms of degradation, and the growing losses
due to floods and droughts prompted calls for similar action to help
maintain the lifeline of agricultural production. A similar mistrust of
local-level initiatives and the advocacy of a larger regulatory authority
to mitigate the ill-effects of growth was voiced around the time of the
launching of Project Tiger. The senior civil servant B.B. Vohra's
recommendations were not heeded in a specific sense but they were a
pointer to a new rationale for centralization.[12] The wilderness preservation lobby and the scientific conservationists, as they have been
called,[13] also meshed well with the priorities of the political leadership
of the time. Mrs Indira Gandhi, Prime Minister from 1966 to 1977 and
again from 1980 to 1984, forged close links with various conservationists both in India and abroad. The transfer of forests from the States
List to the Concurrent List in 1976, in the controversial 42nd Amendment, had the support of many environmentalists. This gave the Union
government the right to override the decisions of states on forest-

related issues. The idea that the federal administration stood apart from and could override sectional interests in the interests of the future, had powerful advocates in this period.

The wider policies that contributed to denudation by giving incentives to industry, or the processes that led to the vulnerability of agricultural land to erosion, were rarely seen in depth. Outside India Mrs Gandhi won support from lobbies of ornithologists and wildlife conservation groups—she was a 'strong leader' in a developing country in whose hands the natural heritage of the world was safe for posterity.

The other kind of environmentalism started from a different set of concerns and among a very different social group. At the popular level, the denial of access and control to the rural poor over large tracts of forest land has been a form of appropriation. It has served the purposes of accumulation and industrial growth but has often been ecologically destructive. There is thus a clear lineage between such views and the peasant protests against monoculture in the Kumaon and Garhwal Himalaya in the 1920s. The replacement of the diverse broadleaf forests by conifers to meet demand for timber was at odds with peasant production which depended on vital inputs from the land. The issue of the environment emerged within the context of production and livelihood, a source rather different from the concerns of the middle class or landed gentry.[14] Similarly, the protest against the closure of access for gleaning forest products in national parks today is an echo of the myriad ways in which the Baigas or the Gonds resisted game laws in the latter half of the nineteenth century in central India.[15] The protests, whether in the moments of rebellion or in more mundane but equally significant kinds of resistance, raised issues of not only access to the forest but also took up the question of forcible labour exactions or *begar*. The common element in such protests is that they raise the possibility of a different regime of control and of styles of production geared to an agenda very different from that of the colonial or post-colonial elites. A forest with a diversity of species in the Himalaya would suit peasant production more than monoculture. A tract of land where tribals could continue to trap small game and gather forest products was at odds with the leisure interests of the colonial rulers and the princes. The differences even between these two regions should guard against any simple generalization. In central India large tracts of forest were controlled by landed intermediaries. In the western Himalaya this fissure within rural society gave way to a

371

conflict with the government over the control of forest lands. The latter had a broad majority of land-owning peasants, while in central India a large section of the agrarian population did not have clear title to the land and were either tenants or labourers. These contrasts of ecology and social structure became crucial in the kinds of conflicts in specific regions.

But it is clear that the forest meant a variety of things, depending on who was looking at it. In the timber famine that accompanied the rapid expansion of the railways, foresters tried to maximize production of wood while ensuring the reproduction of timber-tree species: the sal in central India, pines in the Himalayas, teak in western and southern India. Villagers were often at odds with this narrow view of the wealth of nature. In some areas they coppiced the teak to obtain poles for house construction. At other times they used the leaves as thatch. This conflict of end uses was even more widespread in the colonial era than conflicts over choice of species for plantation. The conflict was not simply over who would control the surplus but also about control of the production process. If poles mattered more to villagers and timber to the officials, the time at which the teak would be felled would differ considerably. The latter could succeed only at the cost of the former. It was the process of extinguishing rights that was often the spark for conflicts but it concealed a fundamental divide on who would decide what forests were for. In central India's highlands, some groups like the Baiga would also experience a deep sense of cultural loss when their earlier pattern of swidden cultivation was curbed. For other tribes like the Gonds, more familiar with the plough, such curbs were not so much of a dislocation. The broad picture was one of loss of entitlement, with the archetype of a caste Hindu cultivator being the model for the Raj.[16]

Such conflicts have intensified after independence. For instance, the use of bamboo as feedstock has been widespread with paper mills often directly competing with artisans for the resource and depleting it beyond the point of no return. Similarly, the entire subsidy and control system for water, agriculture and industry has worked to the advantage of large land-holders in lowland irrigated areas, industry and services at the cost of the economies based on dryland farming, herding and fishing. There have been important shifts for many people from one kind of occupation to another but India is still a society where over 70 per cent of all people depend on the land for a living. This broad division between winners and losers has its problems but it adequately sums up the line-up as seen by many active in grassroots movements.[17] This emphasis on forms of production such as herding and fishing, also means that a telos in which such activities gradually become extinct gives way to a more plural view of the economy. Even if such production is not sought to be frozen and preserved, it is certainly seen as a base to critically build upon for a different kind of development.

It is such dissonances that inform environmentalism from below. The ecological elements in the alternative vision rest on a view of the past directly contrary to that of the preservationists. For the urban wildlife enthusiast nature existed in the pure state until it was greviously injured by human activities. The popular version begins with a premise that there is no place that has not had a human presence. Colonial officials often vastly exaggerated the impact of tribals on the fauna.[18] In the present day this often leads to the penalizing of those who glean the forest floor for produce, even as fiscal policies actively assist in the denudation for industry. This is not only an intersectoral conflict but also one that replaces prudence with profligacy.[19] Wildlife lovers see the land as part of an ecosystem with a vital function in the cycle of regeneration and renewal. But this did not lead the preservationists (until recently) to question the manner in which conservation objectives were to be achieved. Preservation was seen as an end in itself. It was an act to help save nature for posterity. But even such preservation was a form of use, especially when it was often in conflict with livelihood.

The movements 'from below' have a very different vision. Their social composition is of crucial importance. In the western Himalayas, the centre of the famous Chipko movement, peasants have been at the forefront over the last two decades. In this region, the present strands of protest draw from a long tradition of resistance to the appropriation of the forests by the British and the princely ruler of Tehri Garhwal. The region is unusual in that upper castes make up a majority of the population. Most households own some land. Though the Chipko movement was launched around the same time as Project Tiger, it had very different mainsprings. Elsewhere, as in the Chhotanagpur plateau and in the struggle against the dams on the Narmada, it has been tribals who have been the major actors. Though there were protests against displacement as early as 1978, it was only after 1987 that the latter movement became more organized in linking together communities in various parts of the river basin.[20] Tribals are crucial in such movements but this is not a universal pattern, for the movements against displacement have drawn support from prosperous caste Hindu cultivators as in the case of the Bedthi Varahi dam in Karnataka. But broadly speaking such groups are prominent by their absence. The concerns of the upper strata of the peasantry are different, their main interest being with procurement of prices for their produce and the cost of power, water and chemical inputs. There are lively debates about the role of gender and also the need for a wider alliance with surplus-producing cultivators in Green Revolution areas.[21] But there are two key unifying issues. First, there is accord on the failure of the existing model in both its statist and market-oriented incarnations. Second, there is a search for an alternative system that would redress both social and ecological concerns. Equity and ecology are seen as inseparable, though there are differences on the precise mix of strategies to achieve such a goal.

The movements differ in scale and intensity in various parts of India. Broadly speaking, there are some whose focus is on displacement by large dams (as in the Narmada valley), against mining (as in the Gandhamardham hills, Orissa), the usurpation of common lands for urban development (the Aravalis on the edge of Delhi) and various efforts to retain or obtain rights to government-owned forests. It is easy to neglect one aspect of many such movements, namely, that they are often pitted against dominant groups at a local level as well. For instance, the Ganga Mukti Andolan in the riverine regions of Bhagalpur in Bihar has seen fisherfolk take on *pani dars* (water right holders) who have a lineage going back to the Mughal times. Similarly, the coastal fisherfolk organizations in Kerala are engaged in attempts to not only forestall trawler fishing but to enable the fishing communities to have a more central role in the power structure . In some parts of the forests and hill tracts of tribal areas in peninsular India tribal groups are aligned with radical political formations. This is especially true of parts of Andhra Pradesh, Madhya Pradesh and Maharashtra. Gandhian self-help and constructive work traditions also exert an influence, as in the case of Chipko and in parts of western India. The movement is an omnibus category. It embraces groups that are engaged in political mobilization and others who opt for constructive work. It includes the issue-based network on the Forest Bill or rehabilitation,

374

as well as more structured initiatives like the National Alliance of People's Movement.[22] The questions that divide the elite and popular movements go beyond the level of strategies and remedies. The latter, for all its internal divisions, favours a radically decentralized regime of resource control and open access over common lands. The former favours the retention of the present regime of control but often with suitable modifications to accommodate discontented groups at the lower end of the social scale. The radical argument is seen by the preservationists as populist . The conflict is seen as one between 'people' and 'nature', rather than between different classes of people. By often equating the dryland farmer or shifting cultivator with the more resource-extensive demands placed by urban or rural elites, the preservationist or the technocratic developmentalist sets the stage for the advocacy of a strong state apparatus. The popular case rests centrally on the premise that conservation cannot be separated from human livelihood.

Yet, the thrust of the populist argument is wider. It argues not for setting aside a few tracts of land but for a major overhaul of the way in which wealth is created. The poor are central as victims of the present development model and to its replacement by another one. There are two distinct but related arguments used to buttress the claim. The poor are mainly resource-intensive, while those who gain from subsidies or have higher purchasing power or own land are much more destructive. The impact of the elites on India's environment is explicitly compared to that of the developed countries on the global ecology. When the disadvantaged destroy the environment it is out of compulsions imposed on them by an unjust social order.[23] Also, many tribal and peasant traditions of conservation, such as the setting aside of sacred groves and other practices, are cited to redress the claims of their being resource-depletors. Far from being ecologically profligate, they are seen as guardians of the land.[24] Both these arguments have to be viewed in the context in which they are made. The absence of incentives for such practices is seen as the key reason for their disappearance. This does play down factors intrinsic to peasant societies that might lead to the breakdown of shared cultural norms. It may also not pay adequate attention to how certain kinds of harvesting become depletive in a new context. But the key point, that such notions allow for a very different notion of conservation, is still valid.

375

Self-reliance or Re-negotiation?

Many grassroots groups are often either sceptical of, or even hostile to, state power. They seek either to change the way power is exercised or to generate pressures which will lead to fundamental changes in the power structure. The practice of many environmental groups points to a keen ability to make use of opportunities for negotiation as they arise. This is true at various levels. The consequences of these choices are far-reaching for they may well be indicative of the evolution of a different kind of polity.

Much of the third-world rhetoric so central to the Indian political leadership for decades has now been appropriated by the environmental movement. But it is being used as a double edged weapon, not only to raise questions about the new world order but also to critique the internal ecological order. Much of the language about the desirability of the community and the role of the last person in society is directly drawn from Gandhi. The idea that the city acts as a parasitical force on the countryside has a Gandhian ring. The Mahatma of the ecological movement is not always historically accurate.[25] But that is in the logic of movements. The notion of the self-reliant village has been important for constructive workers who seek to create success stories at the micro level. Fasts undertaken by protestors against dams at Tehri are instances of using classically Gandhian modes of protest. It is also striking how prominent an older generation of Gandhians has been in specific struggles. Largely drawn from those who shunned political office and set up smaller social service institutions in hilly areas, they have at times attempted to challenge authority in ways Gandhi might have thoroughly approved of. The idea of '*Van par gaon ka adhikar*' or 'control of the forests by the village' in Uttarakhand, popularized by the Chipko movement, is a logical development of a strand in the original Gandhian project. Yet, there are many elements in contemporary movements that transcend his concerns. For instance, campaigns to achieve self-rule in tribal areas are backed by radical groups who see it as a stepping-stone to a wider programme of social change. Gandhi rarely took up the issues affecting tribals, except for briefly endorsing the violation of forest rules and blessing attempts to provide them education to achieve integration with the wider society. Such paternal attitudes, significant as they were, often fall far short of the aspirations embodied in the movements of today. Guha has described the environmental movement in India as 'a peasant movement draped in ecological colours.'[26] The tribal movements for self-rule or against displacement are then a radical or populist tendency dressed in green. This is so even in areas like parts of Madhya radesh, where radical political parties are weak and assertion takes place through the Congress itself. The point is a simple one. Gandhi's ideas have a strong moral appeal across a wide section of the ecological movement. But they have acquired significance because they mesh with aspirations of increasingly politicized sections of society.

The political system itself responds to discontent. The Narmada issue has divided voluntary groups. The notion that small is beautiful is so widespread that it is difficult to find an article about a hydel project or an irrigation scheme that does not either support or refute the notion. Even those who accept large dams on a conditional basis—that they should provide adequate relief and compensation to displaced persons—often see external influences as central to the present model of growth. This recurrent theme does draw attention to foreign linkages but fails to account for the extent of support for the present model of development, especially among those who gain from it. The Narmada movement has had to fend off not only police repression but also the charge that opponents of the project are out to thwart the emergence of a '*naya*' or new Gujarat. The environmental issue is seen as one to be resolved through growth, and protest groups as trouble-makers who have to be put in their place. Ideologues under-estimate the extent to which large projects remain a symbol of hope for a better world. One serious shortcoming of the Gandhian world-view is that it does not take account of divisions within rural society. Medha Patkar of the Narmada Bachao Andolan (NBA) was articulate about the differences between relatively less stratified tribal societies of the Bhil or Tadvi as opposed to those of caste-Hindu rural settlements. But it is not clear how a movement against displacement can tide over or confront such divisions.[27] The visions of traditional ties with nature are at odds with the aspirations of social groups who see these as thinly veiled bids to revive the caste-based social order. Dalit organizations in Maharashtra, with a base among sections once treated as 'untouchable', stood aloof from the movement against the dams.[28] What is significant is the contrast between rival visions of the future. Dalit groups see industry as positive because it breaks up the deep-rooted rural social structure. For many adivasis, the same project is a way of losing control over the land and their lives.

There were and are two clear options in the movement itself. In fact, the division between rejection and conditional acceptance are mirrored in the political leadership. While all parties in Gujarat favour the most controversial of the dams—the Sardar Sarovar—at any cost, the state with the largest number of displaced perons, Madhya Pradesh, has been lobbying for a reduction of its height to minimize displacement. This division is different from the rifts among the environmentalists. Among the latter you either favour the dam with some changes in design or oppose it outright. Among politicians, the choice is congruent with the borders of the two states: in Gujarat they favour a full-scale dam, and in Madhya Pradesh a change of design.

Yet, even this choice, false as it might appear to opponents of the project, is itself a reflection of broader political changes. In the state elections of 1993, the new legislative assembly of Madhya Pradesh saw a larger number of scheduled tribe members, especially in the Congress party. The symbolism of Gandhi is doubly significant here. The major agrarian lobby for the dam across the border in Gujarat includes the very stratum of land owning managers of cultivation, the Pattidars, who were a key constituent of his social base. But even many Gandhian activists in Gujarat and radical peasant groups in Maharashtra sought to avoid taking a rigid anti-dam stand. The fact is that while the idiom of 'the village versus the dam' worked in areas directly affected by displacement, many possible benificiaries saw the project as a blessing.[29]

The relationship with external funding agencies also turns out to have been complex. The World Bank was a major agency funding the Narmada dams till 1993. One reason for its exit was the adverse publicity generated by the movement and its own assessment of the provisions for rehabilitation. In other words, the opponents of the dam were able to lobby the World Bank and advance their own case. The negotiations between the NBA and the World Bank may have been explained away in tactical terms. But they point to a significant shift. In the coming years, the space created by external funding agencies will be exploited to the hilt by groups that have an alternate vision of development. This does not mean that the gap between the two will be bridged. The very groups who cooperated with the World Bank are at a more general level opposed to the very idea of liberalization. Their belief in self-reliance operates not only at the level of the village but extends to the nation as a whole. Increasingly, the rhetoric of opposition will be combined with a tactical flexibility that involves negotiating the structure and content of globalization. The NBA not only pointed to the impracticability of rehabilitation plans but also advanced a pragmatic criticism of hopes of irrigation. Its activists have contested the official figures as unduly optimistic. The movement was playing its own role in creating green conditionalities, though from below and not from above. In doing so, it found an unlikely ally in the World Bank team and green lobbies in developed countries. Such an idea must appear heretical to those who oppose liberalization per se. For many Gandhians, it represents the final nail on the coffin, with the consumerist ideal triumphing over the notion of a prudent society that cares for the last first rather than the gratification of each. For the radical currents, often smaller Marxist-Leninist parties with a base in tribal areas, it vindicates their view of India having a comprador ruling class. The new addition to the opponents is a section of wildlife preservationists, aghast at the failure of state agencies to withstand industrial and commercial pressures to open up wildlife reserves.

The actual practice of the actors suggests a nuanced understanding of the situation. By playing off one state government against another or the multilateral agency against the debtor nation, or by creating a situation where elected leaders take on board some concerns of the movement, the impact of pressure from below goes well beyond an all-or-nothing position. Yet, such a reading may be narrowly instrumentalist. There are now strong advocates of a rejection of the global economic order or of modern technology itself. The two are even seen as synonymous. Such views are not universally held. For instance the Kerala Shastra Sahitya Parishad, an organization that led the successful campaign to stall the construction of a hydel power project in Silent Valley in 1978–80, sees social relations as the stumbling block to achieving a just and ecologically sane society.[30] At the other end of the spectrum, the People and Patriotic Oriented Science and Technology group in Madras comes close to idealizing traditional knowledge and the hierarchies in pre-colonial society. There is a tension between a conditional or selective acceptance of scientific knowledge, or between those who see science itself as a poisoned chalice and others who stress its social context. Though their aims are often unattainable, the critiques do have a significant role to play.

In one sense, the situation is an unenviable one. Many ecology-oriented groups share a physiocratic attitude to economics. Land is seen as the repository of wealth, with little thought being given to industry. Yet, India is a society where the first rail line was laid in 1853, the first underground coal mine opened up in 1880, the first steel mill set up by an Indian industrialist in 1910. Not only is the industrial sector a major source of disequilibrium in the form of consumption of raw materials or production of effluent, it is also the lifeline of a large segment of the labour force. Utopian Gandhians would argue that industry itself is the culprit. Many critiques implicitly see a role for industry but with differences in inter-sectoral allocation and greater sensitivity to conflicts with human health and safety. Despite this, there is often a gap between land-centred ecological concerns and the industrial working class. One set of initiatives has attempted to explore if industry can be managed in alternative ways but the rich haul of ideas is not always matched in practice. The struggle of fishworkers to stop trawler fishing in coastal waters has gained support from labour unions. But this is very much an exception.[31] This remains a major Achilles' heel and requires more attention. There is little reason to believe that exhortation against industrialism will work, and a median way that is alive to Indian realities but not blind to the need for industry is required.

There are a range of popular level initiatives, ranging from Gandhian to radical, from technology-oriented groups to others who work in public education. Virtually all agree on the failure of the dominant order to redress the problems of poverty or of the environment. As critics of the state, they are not in an easy position in the debate about liberalization. Rejection of the process per se, and a call for a renewed search for self-reliance is often made. The retreat of the Indian government on issues of economic sovereignty is seen as a turning point in a negative sense. Even what scope had existed for change from below will now be more difficult due to pressure from outside. External donors, creditors and investors will increasingly supplant or buttress dominant groups within Indian society. At one level, the outlook is grim. The very diversity of opinions makes it difficult to come up with a coherent alternative of the sort that political parties, radical or parliamentary, are so often capable of.

A New Kind of Polity?

The complexity of the situation makes it possible to argue for a future other than one where the retreat of the state simply leads to the untramelled play of market forces, internal or external. The weakening of the state system need not be a negative development, provided there are strongly developed initiatives in civil society to enable a more transparent and open regime. The hub of the problem of displacement has been a lack of transparency about the siting or design of projects. Proposals for devolution of powers are varied. One stream of opinion argues for retention of rights over common and open-access resources by the village with variations depending on the local area. These would incorporate provisions to ensure a major role for underprivileged groups. In fact, they would build on existing efforts in various regions, in which a level of organization has enabled regeneration of resources without direct reliance on the government for management. These include reforestation in the Shivalik hills and water-harvesting in Ralegaon Sidhi in Maharashtra.[32]

There are specific reasons why such initiatives succeed in certain areas and not in others. In many sal forest regions in West Bengal regeneration is relatively rapid due to the root sucker system of the tree, and the diverse array of shrubs and plants enables a rapid rise in rural incomes. In other ecosystems the rates of renewal may not be as rapid. At a political level, the devolution of power to the panchayats by the democratically elected Left Front governments since 1977 enabled the rural poor, including sharecroppers and labourers, to play a central role in the process. Land reform has also made a major difference to their capability. In other regions, local institutions have broken down and even once active mechanisms for protection and regulation of common grazing lands have become ineffective.[33] The discussion here is largely focused on forests and water resources, but the scope could be much wider.

On the other hand, there are those who opt for direct struggles to ensure tribal self-rule and the extension of constitutional provisions to such areas, in the hope that once the tribal hamlets gain control over the forested lands, they will have the bargaining power to work for further reform.[34] The two visions are not incompatible, resting as they do on a common premise of local empowerment heavily slanted in favour of those with lower entitlements.

381

The response of the political leadership has been varied but it does point to a certain ability to gauge the kinds of measures that would lead to unrest. Fragmented and dispersed as such groups may be, their real strength lies in their ability to influence the political agenda. The assertion of the social groups enfranchised mostly after independence, the dalits, the other backward classes (OBCs) and women in rural local bodies, marks a major change in the power structure. Even if only at the level of representation, it does mean that the cultural and social composition of the political leadership and, to an extent, of the bureaucracy, is changing. The adivasi or tribal movements are more variegated: in addition to the Congress and more radical parties, in some regions they are the central force in movements for autonomy or statehood.

It would be logical to expect such groups to have more of an identification with the popular movements. In the southern state of Karnataka, for instance, the state government is enacting an order to give panchayats a role in conserving biological diversity and also giving them a share of taxes of produce such as non-wood forest products. In Uttar Pradesh, the centre-left ministry in power in 1993–95 was actively considering a scheme for participatory management in a national park.[35] But such measures have to set against the wider context. Successive rulers in Uttar Pradesh have pushed ahead with the Tehri dam despite continuing protests from evacuees on grounds of safety and sustainablity. The picture in Karnataka in terms of devolution is more encouraging, given the attempt to combine the skills of producers with those of the state's large pool of scientists. The strong three-tier structure of local self-government makes such a scheme eminently feasible.[36] But the rapid industrialization of the state may yet undermine many such gains. This is not unavoidable but it is taking place at a pace that will make public action to minimize ill effects very difficult. This conforms to a wider picture in which industrial growth at any cost rides over other competing objectives. A broader base for the polity makes initiatives possible, it does not guarantee success.

Participants in grassroots movements are often at odds, whether they are merely complementary to class-based initiatives or transformative efforts in their own right. There are also divisions over how radical the movements are or ought to be. But the very fact a state government could adopt part of the platform of an anti-dam movement, or that the Forest Bills proposed in 1982 and 1995 did not see

382

the light of day, was due to the effectiveness of the 'popular' strand of environmentalism.

Both the proposals mentioned above aimed at increasing the powers of the foresters at the cost of rural resource users. The fear of electorally negative consequences, especially in tribal areas, helped defeat both measures. At another level, certain local initiatives have been coopted by officials. The success of Joint Forest Management of degraded forestlands in West Bengal, in association with villagers, has not only been seen as a success but has become a model for adoption in several other states. The language of the protest movements has been adopted by not only governments—state and federal—but even by multilateral funding agencies. Are these gains or not? After all, specific victories often conceal larger defeats. Saving a patch of forest may not curb the processes that lead to denudation. The defeat of a legislative measure may well be followed up by achieving its aims by other means. Even the cession of certain tracts of forest has justifiably been seen as a limited and piecemeal reform to thwart wider changes. There are also fears that all these battles are being waged when the new international regime of property rights may take more from the basic producers in a few years than they may have lost over decades.[37] The radical fears have their counterparts among wildlife preservationists. They see new pressures in the form of industrial or urban expansion, deeper market links and population growth eating away at biological wealth.

Such anxieties are not without foundation. Piecemeal reform may divide critics and thwart basic changes. We may have an 'upstairs–downstairs' world. The foresters would retain the timber-rich lands, the wildlife authorities the major nature reserves, and the 'people' may end up with small tracts of land for self-management.

Towards a Conclusion

But it is possible to see the political changes in a cautiously optimistic way. Firstly, democracy in India has enabled the evolution of a public space vital for underprivileged groups. Most significantly, the rich debates about the future have made it possible to view development not in a narrow and economistic way but in a more holistic manner that encompasses not only different classes of humans but also the natural world. It is difficult for anyone to now publicly maintain that the peasantry is a dying class or to assert that growth always involves sacrifice of nature. These are no mean achievements. Secondly, the transformation of the debate has been accompanied by a myriad little instances of an alternative way. Whether it refers to the construction of a check dam using voluntary labour or taking over and regreening a forest patch, these have a wider significance. They demonstrate the ability of civil society to generate solutions, however transient or partial. They also point to a path that does away with an excessive reliance on the bureaucracy.

Political opportunities have to be set against the real constraints in the economic realm. In the absence of a wider change in the economic climate, it will be difficult even for a decentralized framework of powers to suffice for more effective responses to ecological questions. The changing patterns of consumption and exchange highlight a problem that lies at the root of many alternative schemes of power. Few of their advocates have begun to grasp the enormity of the challenge of the market. The logic of economic change can often undermine the most durable of political systems. The economic returns from breaking the protective network are so high that no scheme of positive incentives can possibly match it. To rely on culturally influenced notions of conservation may be more idealistic, but they too crack under strain. The change in values and in consumption patterns is presently headed towards profligacy.[38] Local control could still serve as a check as it would give direct producers direct stakes in regeneration and also provide for both livelihood and conservation, possibly by separating the kind of areas where each function is provided for.[39] But conflicts are often intense where competition is for a scarce resource. As market links have grown stronger and the number of people in each settlement larger, so have the incentives to privatize common lands. Earlier, cooperation made sense given the soil quality and uneven availability of water but now market systems provide easy, though often resource-depletive options.[40]

There is a role for the state as a mediating institution, not as a command and control authority. It would have a more limited role in direct resource control but a substantial one in terms of providing a climate in which such experiments can bear fruit. The 'ecological danger' has served as a means for officials to actually acquire wider powers. The major defence of the older system was that it sought to shield the poor from the rich. But this ignores the extent to which governmental policies and programmes have actually enabled such groups to become

384

powerful. State power is itself fractured by these tensions. Rather than use such concerns as a barrier to political reform, it would be better to incorporate them into any fresh initiatives. It is not possible to do without the institutions of government but it is essential to reform them to make them more participatory. The market is too deeply entrenched to be abolished or even regulated in the way that was attempted. The extension of its scope in recent years is not merely a result of external imposition but also represents a major shift in the views of dominant social groups. While they are not a monolith, there is a broad unity of interests. This will explain why liberalization does not involve freeing the small holder from restraints on tree-growing, or the cooperatives from the rule of the registrar.

The market too can be effectively used given a combination of disincentives in extreme cases and incentives for conservation in most. This would, however, entail a radical reworking of the institutional framework to enable greater participation. Liberalization does represent a threat because its scope has been so limited, focused mainly on industry and foreign trade. A different kind of agenda could break the deadlock in the state versus market debate.

The 'internal' dimensions of a social order weigh in a very major way on the 'external' linkages of a state. This internalist emphasis is not to lessen emphasis on the North-South aspects of the equation. But the mere creation of the artifices of economic growth or the assertion of sovereign rights over resources within the bounds of a territorial state are simply not enough to meet the aspirations of those who seek to combine equity and ecology. The kind of exclusion a democracy practices are more subtle than authoritarian systems; the limitation of scope for collective initiatives and the inequitable nature of market forces often combine to disempower or seriously limit the power of the disadvantaged. The expansion of the real alternatives they have is a major question of the day.

Notes and References

[1] A. Kothari 'Environment and New Economic Policies', *Economic and Political Weekly*, Vol. 30, 1995, pp. 924–28 .

[2] M. Gadgil and P.S.R. Rao, *A People's Health, Nature and Education Bill*, Centre for Ecological Sciences, Indian Institute of Science, Bangalore, Technical Report no. 55, February 1995; W. Fernandes, ed., *Drafting a People's Forest Bill: The Forest-Dweller-Social Activist Agenda*, Indian Social Institute, Delhi, 1996.

3   N.S. Jodha, 'Common Property Resources and the Rural Poor in Dry Regions of India', *Economic and Political Weekly*, Vol. 27, 1986, 1169–86.

4   Sumit Sarkar, *Middle Class Nationalism and Popular Movements from Below*, Centre for Social Sciences, Calcutta, 1980.

5   M. Gadgil and R. Guha. *This Fissured Land, An Ecological History of India*, Oxford University Press, Delhi, 1992.

6   R. Grove, *Green Imperialism*, Oxford University Press, Delhi, 1995. R. Guha, 'Ideological trends in Indian environmentalism', *Economic and Political Weekly*, Vol. 19, 1988, pp. 2578–81.

7   R. Guha, *The Unquiet Woods, Ecological Change and Peasant Resistance in the Himalaya*, Oxford University Press, Delhi, 1989.

8   M. Rangarajan, 'The Raj and the Natural World, The Campaign against Carnivores in Colonial India, 1875–1925', Nehru Memorial Museum and Library, Delhi, 1995.

9   K. Sankhala, *Tiger! The Story of the Indian Tiger*, Collins, Delhi, 1978.

10 A. Kothari, P. Pande, S. Singh and Variava, *Management of National Parks and Wildlife Sanctuaries in India*, Indian Institute of Public Administration, Delhi, 1989.

11 V. Thapar. *The Tiger's destiny*, Time International Books, New York, 1992.

12 B.B. Vohra, *A Policy for Land and Water, The Sardar Patel Memorial Lectures*, Publications Division, Delhi, 1980.

13 M. Gadgil and R. Guha, *Ecology and Equity: The Use and Abuse of Nature in Contemporary India*, Delhi, Penguin, 1995, pp. 110–12.

14 M. Gadgil and R. Guha, *This Fissured Land*.

15 M. Rangarajan, *Fencing the Forest. Conservation and Ecological Change in India's Central Provinces 1860–1914*, Delhi, Oxford University Press, 1995.

16 Ibid.

17 M. Gadgil and R. Guha, *This Fissured Land*, p. 36.

18 M. Rangarajan, 'The Politics of Ecology: The Debate on Wildlife and People in India 1970–1995', Occasional Papers NMML Delhi, 1995.

19 M. Gadgil and R. Guha, *This Fissured Land*.

20 A. Baviskar, *In the belly of the River*, Oxford University Press, Delhi, 1995.

21 B. Agarwal, *A Field of one's own, Gender and Land Rights in India*, Cambridge University Press, Delhi, 1995; G. Omvedt, *Reinventing Revolution: New Social Movements and the Socialist Tradition in India*, M.E. Sharpe, New York, 1993.

22 See R. Guha, *The Unquiet Woods*, A. Baviskar, *In the Belly of the River*.

23 Centre for Science and Environment, *The State of the Environment, 1982: A Citizen's Report*, CSE, Delhi, 1982; *The State of India's Environment, 1984–85, The Second Citizen's Report*, CSE, Delhi, 1985.

24 M. Gadgil and R. Guha, *This Fissured Land*.

25 Ibid.

26 R. Guha, 'Ideological Trends in Indian Environmentalism', *Economic and Political Weekly*, Vol. 19, 1988, pp. 2578–81.

27 M. Patkar, 'The Strength of a People's Movement', interviewed by G. Sen

and A.K. Roy in G. Sen, ed., *Indigenous Vision, Peoples of India, Attitudes to the Environment*, Sage, Delhi, 1992, pp. 273–99.

[28] G. Omvedt, *Reinventing Revolution*, pp. 269–72.

[29] Ibid.

[30] M. Zachariah and R. Suryamurthy, *Science for Social Revolution*, Sage, Delhi, 1994.

[31] Dunu Roy, S Seshadhri, S Ghotge, A. Gupta and A. Deshpande. *Planning the Environment*, Gandhigram Press, Madras, 1982; K. Sankhala, 'Project Tiger Revisited', *Sanctuary*, Vol. 13, 1993, pp. 16–19; Mukul, 'Labour and the Environment, Confusion, Conflicts, Closeness', *Labour File*, Vol. 2, 1996, pp. 36–42, M. Patkar, 'Interview', *Down to Earth*, Delhi, 15 July 1996.

[32] A. Agarwal and S. Narain, *Towards Green Villages*, CSE, Delhi, 1989, M. Gadgil and P.S.R. Rao, *A People's Health, Nature and Education Bill.*

[33] N.S. Jodha, 'Common Property Resources and the Rural Poor in Dry Regions of India'.

[34] *Bharat Jan Andolan, Whither Tribal Areas? Constitutional Amendment and After*, Sahyog Pustak Kutir, Delhi, 1995.

[35] A. Kothari, P. Pande, S. Singh and Variava, *Management of National Parks and Wild Life Sanctuaries in India.*

[36] Karnataka Planning Board, *Report of the Sub-group on Bio Diversity, 1996*, Govt of Karnataka, Bangalore, 16 February 1996.

[37] A. Kothari, *Conserving Biodiversity Implications of the Biodiversity Convention for India*, Kalpravrishk, Delhi, 1994.

[38] A. Agarwal, *Rough Ride Ahead in Directors Report 1994–95*, CSE, Delhi, 1996, pp. 4–6.

[39] M. Gadgil and P.S.R. Rao, 'A People's Health, Nature and Education Bill'.

[40] N.S. Jodha, 'Common Property Resources and the Environmental Context: Role of Biophysical Versus Social Stresses', *Economic and Political Weekly*, Vol. 30, 1995, pp. 3278–84.

Vocabularies of Resistance
Vocabularies of Rights

Neera Chandhoke

My investigation of the movement against the Sardar Sarovar dam has revealed a critical and a somewhat underexplored dimension of political life in India: that increasingly, the terms of the contemporary political discourse are being set by rights claims from hitherto marginalized sections of society—tribals, poor peasants, women, the urban poor. This is more than explicit when we examine the discourse of resistance to the Sardar Sarovar[1] Project (hereafter SSP) in the Narmada valley and, in particular, when we explore the vocabularies of rights that have been thrown up during the course of the struggle. Among the most crucial of these rights is the assertion of the right not to be displaced—the right to live in one's own home, among one's own community, and amidst traditional relationships with the land, resources and environment. The assertion of this right is of some import, especially when we remember that there was a time when the Nehruvian state could move people and appropriate resources as it chose, in the name of development and modernization. Today, however, practically every developmentalist project is being challenged and stymied in the name of the people's right not to be displaced, in the name of the right to habitat or what Jai Sen terms 'dwelling'.[2] The assertion of this right, as we shall see in the course of the argument, has to a large extent challenged the power of the state to do as it will with the people and with their access to resources.

I suggest that no theoretical or empirical exploration of the power of the state, or no exploration of 'politics from above' has been able to quite capture this dimension—that poor, marginal and powerless people, who have often been regarded as mere pawns on the gigantic chessboard of Indian politics, have managed to alter in crucial ways the rules of the game itself. No study of Indian politics that

388

concentrates only on elite manipulations can wholly apprehend the manner in which the terms of the political discourse—development, modernization, displacement, or compensation—have been re-tailored by people seeking to carve out a space for themselves in political agendas monopolized up to now by the elites.

In the process people, often regarded as so many manipulable units, have displayed agential capacity, the capacity to temper the best-laid plans of mice and men. But in order to understand and appreciate this facet of Indian politics we need to shift from an excessive preoccupation with the state and its institutions to studying the manner in which the people receive state policies. We have, in other words, to study the conditions of reception to these policies. Correspondingly, we have to cogitate on the ways in which these policies are rejected or modified by constituencies whom they affect in such a radical fashion. We have, in short, to grasp how state policies constitute as well as are constituted by political agendas drawn up by these struggles.[3] It is only then that we can apprehend the dialectical relationship between the state and its constituency. It is only then that we can see how the political process unfolds in ways that are often unforeseen or unplanned by decision-makers. In fact, I suggest that it is only then that we can begin to understand the complexities of the contemporary political discourse in the country.

The second implication that the vocabularies of protest carry is for the entire discourse on human rights. Whereas rights have emerged in India as the basic building-blocks of political morality—witness the proliferation of human rights organizations—the rights that have been asserted by the anti-dam movement are far richer and far broader than extant conceptualizations of rights. If we were to study the kinds of rights that have emanated from the process of people's struggles with the state, we would arrive at the conclusion that there is much more involved in the concept of what it means to be human than the dominant discourse of rights suggests. Let me clarify this. Human rights have traditionally supervened on to a concept we term human, i.e., they are targeted towards the creation of conditions within which human beings can live with dignity. Theorists call this state flourishing. Generally speaking, four sets of rights have been posited for this purpose: civil, political, economic and social, belonging to what theorists term as the first and the second generation of rights. A fresh category of rights has now emerged in the course of people's struggles—the right to live among one's own community, amidst one's own lifestyles, and among traditional relationships to natural resources—in short, the right not to be displaced. This runs contrary to the traditional conceptualization of, say, the right to work, the right to an income and the right to shelter. It is manifest that the latter sets of rights are supremely indifferent to the location of work or housing. Today people are putting forth the demand that they want to work and live in conditions of their own choice. We have come to realize that there is much more involved in the conceptualization of what it means to be human than the first and second generation of rights permit us.

Three additional implications can be gleaned from the assertion of this right. Firstly, this right modifies the classical Marxist understanding of capitalism that labour follows capital, irrespective of the location of the capitalist enterprise. Today we are being told that productive and social reproductive facilities have to come where people reside, where they want to reside. This essay is not the place to chart out the full implications of this right for capitalist theory; all I can say is that an adequate response to this demand may considerably modify the alienation of labour that arises from living in conditions which others choose.

Secondly, the assertion of this right challenges the capacity of the state to move around capital and labour in the name of developmentalism. People, as Amita Baviskar has shown, want to know why they should move to other territories in order to secure access to the basic conditions of life—health, education, work conditions, social reproduction. Why has the Indian state not delivered this facility to people who live among the forests, along the river, in cohabitation with natural resources?[4] This may provide a counterpoint to the legitimizing rhetoric of the state and of the supporters of the project, that the displaced will have access to better conditions of life in the rehabilitation and resettlement (hereafter R and R) sites.

The third implication of the assertion of these rights is equally significant. We have been led to move beyond the positivist understanding that rights are the creation of law, to the understanding that rights emanate from the struggles of people in specific conditions of exploitation. As people strive to express their own experiences, as they translate the experiential into the expressive, new rights are discovered out of the gamut of natural rights that supervene onto a category that we call human. The assertion of the right to a sound environment, to one's own lifestyle, the right to live in conditions of one's own choice or the right to an increasingly vanishing world are a case in point—all of them being rights that do not find articulation anywhere in existing discourses. These assertions have not only added to our comprehension of human nature—what human beings desire and want—they have added to our conceptualization of the conditions that are required in order for human beings to live with dignity. We have also been led to recognize that perhaps current conceptualizations of rights are both inadequate and incapable of understanding what human beings need and desire, yearn for and aspire to.

This essay examines the vocabularies of such rights. But before I do this let me chart out the context for the assertions: the unfolding of the struggle in the Narmada valley. The account is necessarily synoptic and brief, but I hope it will convey some of the historical implications of this massive struggle.

The Struggle

Although the Narmada project was initiated in 1961 by Prime Minister Nehru, much progress could not be made on the dam since the three states—Gujarat, Madhya Pradesh and Maharashtra—disagreed on the sharing of the waters. The Narmada Waters Dispute Tribunal (hereafter NWDT) was set up by the Government of India in 1969, under the Inter-State Water Disputes Act of 1956, to resolve the issue. The NWDT gave its verdict in 1979. This verdict is binding on the three state governments as well as on the Government of India. Apart from the fact that the award apportioned water among the three state governments with some success,[5] it is considered to be pathbreaking since it laid down general principles of R and R. Till then the government had followed the policy of allotting monetary compensation to the Project Affected People (hereafter PAPs). The award on the other hand laid down that, first, the oustees should improve or at least regain the standard of living they enjoyed before displacement. Second, people should be relocated among communities, village units, hamlets or families according to their preferences. Third, the government was enjoined to see that people become fully integrated into the new communities. Fourth, the PAPs should be provided with compensation and with adequate social and physical rehabilitation structures such as house sites, short-term financial protection, cash

391

compensation through grants-in-aid, and provision of civic amenities. Fifth, the award provided for the allotment of irrigated agricultural land (a minimum of two hectares per family) as compensation. Sixth, the award laid down the procedures that should govern R and R.

The award was, however, deeply flawed inasmuch as it failed to take into account the social structures of the PAPs who were largely tribals. Tribals, by and large, do not hold formal ownership of land since most of them cultivate degraded forest land under usufructuary rights. Most of them are thus labelled 'encroachers' under the Indian Forest Act of 1927. Neither did the award provide for landless people; for people whose lands would become islands (*tapus*) after submergence; or for those living downstream and whose livelihood would be affected by the construction of the project. Subsequently the three state governments instituted their own R and R schemes within the broad framework of the award. All the three sets of R and R policies were not only different from each other, they were rankly inadequate.

In the meantime, the Government of India had applied to the World Bank for a loan. The World Bank had laid down definite guidelines on R and R, but the policies of the three state governments were not looked into prior to the extension of the loan. In 1984 Dr Scudder, a World Bank expert, examined the relevant policies and found them inadequate. His report carried a harsh condemnation of the insensitivity of the three state governments. The resettlement of the oustees, he concluded, was likely to take place in a 'very unfavourable environment', and the project had been approved before the actual human costs had been estimated.

This is borne out by the fact that even before the Government of India gave conditional clearance to initiate the project in 1987, about 2,000 families from Gujarat and 90 families from Maharashtra had already been displaced and sent to resettlement sites without being consulted or given any information. In the early 1980s the tribals of the Satpura range showed little resistance to plans to raise the dam in areas inhabited by the Bhils. There was considerable resentment at the lack of information, forced evictions and displacements but the tribals, confused and bewildered as they were, were in no position to resist. A spark was needed to set off the struggle and this spark was provided by the social activists of the Arch Vahini led by Anil Patel and the Rajpipla Service Society; both concentrated on demanding a better R and R package. The Arch Vahini lobbied with the respective governments and the World Bank while the Rajpipla Service Society chose the path of judicial activism on land-related matters. These two groups were to pioneer a massive people's movement for rights in a manner that has since made history. They provided a powerful voice for the dispossessed in a way that has not been witnessed up to now in India's political history.

In 1985, Medha Patkar began to work with the Arch Vahini. Mobilization expanded as the PAPs of Maharashtra organized themselves into the Narmada Dharangrastha Samiti, which the tribals of Madhya Pradesh later joined. In 1987 the Narmada Ghati Navnirman Samiti was re-formed in the Nimad region of Madhya Pradesh to organize the non-tribal PAPs. In Gujarat, the Narmada Asargrasta Sangharsha Samiti began to organize the people in the six villages of Kevadia district. These people had been displaced to make way for the residential colony of the headquarters of the project.

The mobilization of the people and the launch of agitational politics took place in favourable conditions—an upsurge in the environmental movement and the movement against mega-developmental projects. A sympathetic press, middle-class support and advocacy of the cause by national and international NGOs gave visibility to the issue. The issues of displacement, resettlement and rehabilitation were problematized for the first time in such a sharp and sustained fashion.

In the valley, the social activists adopted two strategies. First, they highlighted the absence of basic facilities in the R and R sites and pressurized the government to adopt measures that would help the oustees tide over the traumas of displacement. Second, they mobilized the people in the villages to form self-reliant communities. These communities demanded information, oversaw the R and R policies, imparted functional literacy, instituted health facilities and set up schools. Village committees prepared comprehensive data on the amount of land possessed by potential oustees; the location and extent of submergence; the type and number of cattle and trees potential oustees owned; the quantum of produce from the land, forest and river; the size of houses; and the amount of wood and bamboo used. The data bank that was built up included information on births, deaths, and migration. Mobilizational techniques like songs conveyed information to the villagers on health care, education, self-sufficiency, self-respect and tribal independence. In a few villages the people and the government jointly conducted land surveys and prepared lists of PAPs. The tribals acquired enough self-confidence to question government officials and demand information. Expectedly the respective governments after a time found themselves unable to answer these questions. The officials accordingly began to distance themselves from the people and type them as illiterate.

Between 1985 and 1988, no change occurred in the policies of the governments of Maharashtra and Madhya Pradesh. The Gujarat government was more responsive, but it did not have sufficient land to give to the oustees of all the three states. As the government bought land from absentee proprietors, tenants and labour working on the land were evicted creating a new category of the displaced. By the mid-eighties, both the activists and the tribals were convinced that the respective governments had no clear idea of either the extent of displacement or of the gravity of the situation. They had made no serious attempts to collect information or build a data-bank for the purposes of resettlement. No attempt had been made to deal with the issue of 'encroachers' and *tapu* lands. Availability of land was uncertain. The R and R sites were deficient, lacking as they did drinking water, ration shops, schools, health care, roads and transport. No provision had been made for grazing cattle. The government simply lacked the commitment to do anything about better R and R.

In December 1987 the Gujarat government, under the combined pressure of the activists, the movement, the World Bank and NGOs, made an important announcement awarding two hectares of land to the 'encroachers' and to major sons. This was what the Arch Vahini had been demanding. The organization now turned its attention to Maharashtra and Madhya Pradesh to pressurize the governments into adopting the same policies.

But precisely at this time the other organizations changed their strategy. They were of the opinion that the Gujarat government would not honour its commitment, that there was no land available to settle the oustees and that the government simply lacked the political will to abide by the World Bank guidelines. These bodies subsequently declared themselves opposed to the dam.

In 1988 about twenty groups, among them the Narmada Dharangrhasta Samiti, the Maharashtra Ghati Navnirman Samiti, the Narmada Asargrasta Sangharsha Samiti, came together to form the Narmada Bachao Andolan (hereafter NBA). Other organizations came together in a show of support to oppose the SSP. The decision was hailed by the international NGOs. In August 1988 the NBA held rallies in the tehsil towns of Alirajpur, Akkalkuwa, Akrani and Nimad, and declared its opposition to the dam. It was announced that the dam was a developmental disaster. At the Harsud rally, the NBA vowed not to work for better resettlement but to oppose the dam itself in the name of saving the environment, maintaining the social and economic base of the people and working for suitable development. The tribals, it was declared, would rather drown in the rising waters than shift and give tacit approval to the dam by shifting. By 1988 the decision to stick to the land, river and forests had been taken.

This was the point at which the Arch Vahini and the NBA parted ways. The Vahini was of the opinion that the Gijarat government was serious about its commitments. The NBA was sceptical. 'We felt', said Medha Patkar, 'that the few resolutions by one government did not mean much since the issues were much broader. For instance, even on rehabilitation, the issues of all three states should be looked at together. Since that time the Vahini and we have had different paths to follow'.[6] The Arch Vahini was supported by other groups and individuals such as Narmada Lok Sangarsh Sahakar Samiti under Harivallabhai Parikh, Chuunibhai Vaidya, Baubhai Patel, all of whom had a record of opposing other dams. But the international and national NGOs condemned Anil Patel as a supporter of the government. This bred its own costs since funding agencies such as Oxfam stopped funding his organization.[7]

The Arch Vahini continues with its work of monitoring land purchase, seeing that the tribals are given land of their own choice and pressurizing the Gujarat government to expand its R and R package, which the latter has done. The NBA, however, refuses to work with R and R. This has had some serious consequences, for the fate of the people who have been displaced in Madhya Pradesh and Maharashtra has not been monitored by any agency outside the government. In fact, no one seems to know what happened to the oustees in Maharashtra. Anil Patel has some reservations about the strategy of the NBA. He argues that though the tribals in Gujarat in 1988 were suspicious of the government, they were keen to see the new policy implemented.

> Further, we were almost certain that the tribals in Maharashtra and Madhya Pradesh would not want to abandon their quest and

struggle for an improved R and R policy similar to that of Gujarat. And yet the battle against the SSP was declared in the name of the tribals of the valley. Bewildered and anxious we asked the organizations whether they had informed the tribals about the revolutionary contents of the Gujarat policy, and asked for their informed consent. We also raised doubts about the strength of the anti-dam case they had advanced. Only a few months earlier, these very organizations had acknowledged that the case against the SSP had to be developed, and it had decided to develop such a critique for the sake of record even though it was too late to stop its construction. In the light of this, we questioned whether it was responsible activism to keep the tribals in the front of the fight against the project'.[8]

The NBA, on the other hand, justifies its policies in the following terms:

1. Environmental studies have either not been carried out or are incomplete. The governments, therefore, are unaware of the ecological damage that will ensue through the construction of the project.

2. People will never be adequately resettled as enough land is not available.

3. The water resources generated by the dam will be cornered by the prosperous central and southern parts of Gujarat, and will not reach the water-starved areas of Kutch and Saurashtra.

4. The financial costs are escalating beyond all estimates.

5. More than a lakh and half people in the vicinity of the canal are going to be displaced, and they have not been granted the status of beneficiaries for the purpose of compensation in the form of land. They have received inadequate monetary compensation. (The NBA has a point here. It has been estimated that the Sardar Sarovar Project will adversely affect about 1,00,000 people in 245 villages who, in Gujarat and Maharashtra, are almost all tribals.[9] In Madhya Pradesh, a majority of the affected people are tribals. Also affected by the canal and irrigation plans are 14,000 farmers. People living downstream will also be affected.)

6. The fishermen living downstream have been recognized recently as PAPs but no action has been taken to ameliorate their condition.

7. The planned Shoolpaneshwar sanctuary will affect tribals living there.

8. Also displaced will be the tribals in the degraded forest land in Taloda when it is released for resettlement.

9. The status of the landless labour working on land acquired by the government has not been recognized for purposes of compensation.

10. The problems of secondary displacement have not been recognized.

The objective of the NBA is to force the government to review the SSP completely, prepare new technical, social and environmental costs and reassess the cost-benefit ratios. At the same time the NBA is recasting the internal structures of the villages by launching plans for schools, ration shops, employment opportunities, training para-medical and anganwadi workers, setting up ashrams and forcing the government to dig tube wells.

Strategically, the NBA brought pattidars, women, tribals and landless labour into a wide-ranging movement. By the late 1980s the issue of R and R had been put aside by the NBA. 1988–92 represented the highpoint of agitational techniques: morchas, demonstrations, petitions, strikes, and public confrontation. In 1990 the members agitated in front of the residence of the Prime Minister in Delhi. In December the same year, Medha Patkar and Baba Amte led 20,000 people in a march, from Madhya Pradesh to the dam site, to physically halt construction. They were stopped at the Gujarat border in Ferkuwa and confronted by 10,000 pro-dam supporters mobilized by Urmila-ben Patel. For twentyone days, the anti-dam movement confronted the pro-dam forces, matching slogan for slogan, song for song, strategy for strategy. The members of the anti-dam struggle adopted peaceful methods of resistance such as fasts and dharnas, but were met with police brutality. The people taking part in the movement returned to their villages without having accomplished their task of stopping work on the dam. Before leaving, they adopted the slogan of '*amra gaon amra raj*', charting out a new phase of people's rights.

From 1991 a new strategy, that of non-cooperation, was charted out. The villagers did not allow anyone connected with the project to enter the villages. When Manibeli in Maharashtra was due to be submerged in the monsoon of 1991, fifty families of Manibeli, activists, and PAPs of other villages waited to take *jal samadhi*. They insisted that work on the dam be stopped otherwise they would drown themselves. That year the rains were not enough to flood the village.

All this secured prestige and recognition for the movement nationally and internationally. The World Bank was forced into a review of the project, the Government of India agreed to the review provided the findings did not stop work on the dam. The Independent Review, carried out by a World Bank appointed commission, was submitted in June 1992 and came to the following conclusion:

> environmental and social tradeoffs have been made and continue to be made in the SSP, without the full understanding of the consequences. As a result [financial] benefits [of the dam] tend to be overstated while the social and environmental costs are frequently understated. Further rehabilitation of all displacees is impossible under present circumstances.[10]

The commission advised the Bank to step aside from the project and consider it afresh—a conclusion that the activists had arrived at as far back as 1988. By March 1993 it was clear that none of the tasks set for the governments by an earlier (internal) commission of the World Bank could be accomplished. The Government of India decided to ask the Bank to withdraw from the project rather than face the embarrassment of having the Bank decide to recant. This was what the NBA had wanted in the name of the internal sovereignty of the people to decide issues for themselves.

The movement intensified and its social base widened as the people who had been relocated showed disaffection with the R and R sites. In the course of the field trip made to these sites, I personally realized that the provisions were far from adequate. Whereas some of the market-friendly tribals had managed to do well, most of the oustees had been turned into wage or migrant labourers. They faced cultural problems as well since they had been resettled in alien surroundings. Discontent was rife and the oustees and potential oustees were demanding appropriate action.

In 1994 hundreds of tribals converged in Bhopal for an indefinite dharna. The displacement during the monsoons of 1994 had been immense and any further construction of the dam beyond 80.3 metres would have brought unmitigated disaster. Now that the Supreme Court has allowed the raising of the height of the dam by a further 5 metres, matters will be worse. Several reviews have brought out the severe problems involved in the course of the project, and all this are a damning indictment of the respective governments. On 21

December 1996, 4,000 people at a rally in Kasravad, Badwani in Madhya Pradesh, began the struggle for an alternative decentralized polity. On 25 April 1997, 1,000 representatives from affected villages pledged to fight against the dam at a rally in Mandaleshwar in Nimad. The Narmada Ghati Sangharsha Samanvaya Samiti coordinated all these struggles.

In the meantime, in 1994 the entire issue of the SSP was re-opened through Supreme Court intervention. The NBA had petitioned the court to undertake a complete review of the SSP with the help of experts. Construction on the project which had been stayed since May 1995 has been resumed following the raising of the height of the dam. The court, however, also ruled that adequate R and R policies should be adopted before further construction of the dam was undertaken, and that a regulatory authority should be appointed to oversee R and R. Further raising of the height of the dam, ruled the court, is dependent on the report of the authority.

From even this synoptic review of the struggle, it is clear that the gains of the anti-dam movement have been immense. In the main, the government of Gujarat has been pressurized to improve R and R facilities, the government of Madhya Pradesh has followed suit though not to the same extent. Maharashtra remains intransigent without a supervisory authority to monitor the fate of the displaced tribals. What is more important is that the struggle has problematized and brought to the forefront the issue of displacement, development, alternative strategies and the right of the people not to be removed from their homes. It is to the enunciation of these rights that I now turn. But before I begin to chronicle these vocabularies of protest and resistance, I want to point out three problem areas that inevitably crop up in research of this kind.

Three Caveats

Let me admit at the outset that, unlike other historians of subaltern resistance, I found myself at one point supremely unsure and unconfident of my ability to translate the vocabularies of protest into a language that is familiar to me and to other scholars. For the dominant languages of the public sphere constitute all of us—the languages of modernity: of rights, representation, and accountability. These safe, insipid and flat languages possessing no class, caste or gender referent, neutralize any attempt to bring the agony of people to the forefront of attention. They simply defy such a project. Therefore, when we seek to resituate languages of dissent into forms and categories that are comprehensible to us, the specificities, the anguish, the emotive content of these languages are to a large extent modified and rendered drab and indeterminate. Further, as we try to translate vocabularies of resistance into both familiar and neat concepts and terms, we tend to overlook and neglect both the grey areas and nuances of these forms of protest.

In the process, problems of representation crop up to cast doubts on the entire project. For how do we understand vocabularies that arise in situations that are specific to the people concerned and that may be alien for us? Can we even begin to understand these languages on their own terms? Are we competent to do so? A historian of the subalterns, after all, can never be a subaltern herself. She is condemned to being at best a translator but the control over translation is hers and hers alone. We, accordingly, have no way of knowing whether the subaltern speaks in her own voice, or whether the historian has translated the voice to fit categories that constitute a shared discursive universe for the scholars but which may be completely unfamiliar to the subaltern herself. This is one of the hazards of scholarship, scholarship that is so obsessed with neatness and categorization that it fails to understand that what we mean and convey may not be that which the subaltern wishes to mean and convey.

The same criticism has often been levelled against the social activist. Understandably, activists resent scholars when the latter point out that the educated, often middle-class activists speak the language of the modern public sphere, and that these languages are often imposed upon the people they wish to organize. On the other hand, activists claim that scholars feed on the experiences of the people and couch these experiences in unnecessarily academic prose that is neither welcomed by the activists nor understood by the concerned people. 'Scholars,' remarked Shripad Dharmadhikari, an activist of the NBA, to me, 'take from the people, and do not give anything back to them'. They do not even go back to the valley to present their findings to the people.

We will perhaps have to accept that these problems of translation apply to scholars as well as activists. Scholars are bound by the vocabularies of their disciplines, and activists are understandably those who speak the languages of the public sphere and who translate people's movements into idioms that find resonance in wider society. This, let me hasten to add, is not so much a comment on scholars and activists; it is the comment on the languages of our public sphere. For one, these languages are so restricted that they have no place for other languages of protest. And as our contemporary history shows us, unless a movement finds spokespersons who can translate these struggles into languages that find resonance in the modern sphere of politics, the struggles may not even be noticed. The recognition also leaves us with the uncomfortable realization that given the restricted languages of the public sphere, until and unless people who are not well versed in these languages find spokespersons who *do* speak them, we may never come to know what the people want and desire, long and aspire for.

Alternatively, even if we recognise these aspirations, precisely because we seek to couch them in terms acceptable to people like us— as we examine the struggles of people who are our own and yet not our own—ambivalances and hesitations mark the entire project of translation. For, as distinct languages spoken by the people are translated into words, terms and concepts that are acceptable by the world of modern politics, a great deal of violence is wrought on the perceptions and views of the people themselves. These languages of pain, of suffering, of exile from the *watan*, of homelessness, of communities torn apart from the familiar, are sanitized to an alarming extent.

Again and again, when I asked the tribals from Gujarat and Madhya Pradesh who have been relocated in Gujarat, what the land, forests and water meant to them in their original homes, they replied that in their villages they had the freedom to use their land, the river, the produce of their forest. Their cattle had the freedom to graze. Their lifestyles were not constrained by the stultifying restrictions that life in the resettlement colonies involves. They had to get adjusted to the idea of boundaries, the division between 'public' and 'private', not drinking in a prohibition state, women not smoking in a 'civilized' society. And certainly restrictions on gender relationships—on the nature of the marriage contract, for instance—were new to them. In all this, they had lost the freedom to live as they wanted to. There is no way in which I can translate these expressions of loss, of alienation, of bewilderment into categories that our social sciences and our politics provide us with. I have tried to do justice to them but doubts remain.

The second problem that I have constantly become aware of

is that of constituencies. We tend to assume that social movements have more or less fixed constituencies and when we study the vocabularies of these constituencies we ascribe them to all the members. It is only then that we can take a stand for or against a movement. But, as empirical research has proved, the constituency of the NBA is floating one. Many people came to the NBA because the relocation sites that they had opted for were beset with problems like water-logging or silting or non-existent facilities. Equally, many of the tribals of Madhya Pradesh opted out from the NBA, in favour of the compensation offered by the state government and for resettling in Gujarat. Not that this was done voluntarily. Many of the tribals I interviewed told me that they had no other option. Since the dam had already been constructed to a height of 80.3 metres (before the case went to the Supreme Court and work on the dam was halted), as the waters rose in the monsoons, their homes were inundated in Alirajpur tehsil, Jhabua district. People had no choice except to move.

In any case, movements widen or shrink as people choose whether or not to abide by the ideology of the movement. In the process people act as agents not only in regard to the state but also in regard to the movement. Can movements, and can we as defenders of movements, come to terms with this? We are forced into the uncomfortable realization that the aims and objectives of movements cannot be fixed for all time. Movements should logically have a second-line strategy that will allow them to be receptive to the changing scenario and the changing options of the members of the movement. This, I am afraid, has not been recognized by the NBA as it holds fast to an anti-dam position.

The third problem is constituted by the fact that the struggle in the Narmada valley is not simply one of people confronting the state. For one, we can discern at least two strains of activism—one opposing the dam and the other working for a better R and R package. And it is not as if the organizations who work for a better R and R package are mere agents of the government. Many of these activists have opposed other dams; many of them have a history of confronting the state on other issues. The Arch Vahini, for instance, has consistently worked for a better R and R package, petitioned the World Bank in earlier times, mobilized the tribals, pressurized the government to release degraded forest land for resettlement. The NBA concentrates on mobilization against the dam, hails the government policy of not releasing degraded land as protective of the environment and is opposed to external intervention. Both the movements work against tremendous odds, both are concerned with the people, but it is the NBA that has received wide publicity as the representative of the people while the Arch Vahini has been blackballed by the NGO movement. Yet it is the latter that has achieved spectacular results in widening the R and R package for those tribals who have either resettled or been forced to resettle in Gujarat. So it is not easy to dismiss organizations such as the Arch Vahini as nothing but an extension of the government.

And yet, a confrontation has erupted between social activists who adopt a 'no dam' stance and those who have been consistently fighting for better R and R. Anil Patel of the Arch Vahini, for instance, has argued that under sustained pressure from the World Bank and NGOs, in 1990 the Ministry of Environment had released degraded forest land in Taloda in Maharashtra as per the demands of the tribals and as per the agreement between the World Bank and the Government of India. The NBA, on 31 July 1990, presented a memorandum to the government of Maharashtra, stating that as a representative of 33 villages in the state it had rejected the land. The tribals, according to Patel, at 'a public meeting on 3 April 1992 . . . angrily protested to the Chief Minister of Maharashtra, questioning how his government could accept such a false claim and allow them to undermine the tribal's vital interests.'[11]

How do the people in whose name these battles are being fought view the entire issue? How do they feel about these radically incommensurable recipes for redeeming their plight? Which of these tribals was consulted and in which manner? Who represents whom? And why do the people, among whom the activists have been working for at least thirteen years, still not feel competent to develop their own organizations and their own leaderships? Are they, in other words, dependent on the spokespersons because the latter know the language of the public sphere and are able to reach national and international constituencies? Whereas I have no intention of questioning the bonafides of the leadership of the NBA, and am not in any way reducing their commitment to self-serving interaction, the problems of representation have to be raised in the interests of the tribals themselves.

It is with these caveats that I begin the discussion on the kinds of rights that have been thrown up by the movement.

403

The Vocabularies of Rights

A historian of the French Revolution made an interesting suggestion: it is not important to ask what happened to the revolution, he said, it is more important to ask how the revolution came into being in the first place. This is a question that all chroniclers of resistance need to ask. How and why do people who are too involved in the business of eking out a living, too involved in negotiating life's major and minor tragedies, rebel? What resources, what memories, what hopes and aspirations do they invest their struggle with? And yet they resist. This is of some moment when we recollect that in the heyday of Nehruvian consensualism, when there was a general agreement on mega projects, little attention was given to the rights of those who were displaced. No one asked what would happen to the people who were often dismissed with a handful of cash. No one asked what would happen to their incomes, bonds of social solidarity, community life, cultures, lifestyles or their relationship to the environment. What would happen to their perception of themselves, their sense of self and dignity, when they would have to eke out a living in the miserable shanty towns of the cities, condemned to slime and filth, whereas till then they had lived among the forests and the rivers? What does relocation do to their psyches, their standard of living, their sense of community? These questions were largely overlooked in the fascination with development. Little thought was given to the fact that these people, stripped of every vestige of self-respect, were thrown in the midst of an oppressive and intolerant market and an equally oppressive, intolerant and impersonal society.

Today, the struggle against the SSP has brought the right to live in dignity amidst one's own people to the centrestage of politics. There are various rights the movement has thrown up: the right to be consulted when decisions are taken, the right to information, the right to participation, the right to civil liberties. However, the one main right that has been thrown up by the struggle is the right to habitat. It is the assertion of this right that has launched the most important challenge to the monopoly of the state over resources and its self-perception that it can do with the people as it will. Today, people who have been till now on the receiving end of decisions and exploitative actions have stood up and demanded that their voice, their interests and their opinions be counted. That they matter and matter equally, particularly so when decisions that affect their households and survival are taken.

This is important when we remember that the history of independent India has witnessed major tragedies—the appropriation of resources wherever they are found in the name of development or public purpose; the annexation of people's modes of subsistence; the creation of a proletariat—all of which amounts to what we can call primitive modes of accumulation. The Narmada struggle has raised one basic question: can the state deprive people of their homes, tear them from their relationship to the land and forests, strip them of their livelihood, in the name of development? For, every right that every political philosopher has argued for with such passion, all the rights the Indian Constitution has granted to the people, all the rights that have come up as a product of working-class struggle, all the rights that the Supreme Court has upheld as basic entitlements, have been infringed, violated and neutralised in the name of public purpose and development till now.

And what is the attitude of the state officials to these struggles? Consider the attitude of the counsel for the government of Gujarat, Shri Nariman. In the April 1997 hearing of the case in the Supreme Court, the Justices asked the government of Gujarat what would happen to the people who had been ousted because of the dam, and whether they had been resettled well. To which question Shri Nariman replied, 'if they can't they don't. That is all'. 'The right to livelihood', he went on to say, 'gets submerged in the larger interest'. The insensitivity towards, if not outright contempt for, the people who have to pay so that others can gain, is more than evident.

Note, however, that the power generated by the movement has influenced the decision-makers to some extent. Whereas the central and the state governments argue in the court that vide Article 262 of the Constitution, the award of the Narmada Waters Disputes Tribunal cannot be reopened, the Justices of the Supreme Court argue that they are entitled to do so under article 32 that deals with the justiciability of fundamental rights.

What is more important is the fact that the right to habitat has been put on the agenda of fundamental rights—the right not to be shifted around like so much unwanted baggage, not to be removed from one's own lifestyle and places. It may be noted that the UN Commission on Human Rights, in a resolution unanimously adopted on 10 March 1993, has condemned the practice of 'involuntarily removing people from their homes against their will' and 'forced evictions' as a 'gross violation of human rights'. It may also be noted that India was a willing party to the decision.

Because this stipulation has not been heeded, the first right that has come up in the Narmada valley is the right not to be displaced, and correspondingly the right to control one's own life: '*doobenge par hatenge nahi*' is the slogan people have adopted. States have not till now recognized the trauma that accompanies the dislocation of people from their habitat—habitat which is familiar, which is dear, because it is here that people chalk out their relationship to the land, around which myths, ceremonies and histories grow up, which gives to the people a sense of history, which is a repository of memories and continuity, and where people acquire, consolidate and pass on knowledge systems. Displacement is not only a question of giving people a new home or what may even amount to a better standard of living. Displacement means the breaking up of communities, sundering their ties to the ancestral land, dividing people who may be tied by organic links, in short, making people rootless. Again and again in my conversation with the oustees resettled in Gujarat, the habitat was referred to as *watan*. People spoke nostalgically and with longing about their relationship to the land, water and forests, about their relationship to each other. It is precisely this sense of habitat that is summed up in the evocative statement of a woman in Chimalkheda, quoted by Medha Patkar, 'I will not move. I will die here. They may give land and water and whatever. But can they give me my Chimalkheda?'[12]

It is the assertion of this claim that distinguishes the Narmada movement. The people have simply staked a claim to their own homes. This rejects the idea that resettlement is an adequate option. People want to live among their own, not in a bare alienated resettlement colony where many of the oustees have become wage labour. This is more than evident in the letter written by Bava Mahalia of Alirajpur tehsil to the Chief Minister of Madhya Pradesh, Digvijay Singh:

> We are people of the river bank; we live on the banks of the great Narmada. This year, our village Jalsindhi will be the first village in Madhya Pradesh to be submerged by the Sardar Sarovar dam. Along with us four other villages—Sakarja, Kakarsila, Akadia and others— will also be drowned. We were supposed to be flooded during the monsoon this year, but now that the Gujarat government is already

closing the sluices, we will probably be submerged in the summer itself. For such a long while you have been hearing that in Manibeli in Maharashtra and in Vadgam in Gujarat, people have been ready to drown themselves. We, the first to face submergence due to Sardar Sarovar in Madhya Pradesh, will also give up our lives, but we will not move from our villages. When the water comes to our village, when our homes and fields are flooded, we will also drown—this is our firm resolve.[13]

The government, he went on to say, has coerced the tribals. It had promised them land in Gujarat where economic conditions would probably be better than in the village, but, he said, we will not move. 'We have lived here for generations. On this land did our ancestors clear the forest, worship gods, improve the soil, domesticate animals and settle villages'. The letter went on to describe the self-sufficiency of the economy, 'We grow so many different kinds of food, but all from our own effort. We have no use for money'. He went on to say, we live by livestock. In times of crisis, we can sell our goats for hundreds of rupees. People from Jhabua district have to go to Surat as labourers to feed themselves. 'We, the people of the river bank, never go to work as wage labourers'.

In Gujarat, he further pointed out, there will no grazing land for their cattle, nor forests, nor rivers. But from the forests the tribals make their homes, the forest gives them material to make their baskets, cots, ploughs, hoes, fodder, edible leaves, medicinal herbs and grass.

> The forest is like our mother, we have grown up in its lap. We know how to live by suckling at its breast. We know the name of each and every tree, shrub and herb; we know its uses. If we were made to live in a land without forests, then all this learning we have cherished over the generations will be useless and slowly we will forget it all. After the forest, how can we live in plains or in cities?

In the village, he wrote, we live with our clan, our relatives and our kin. All of us pool our labour; at weddings everyone contributes to the bride price, to the costs at funerals. The elders of the village arbitrate between quarrels. If we are uprooted from here who will arrange our ceremonies and arbitrate between quarrels? Here, if we run out of seeds or if our bullock dies then everyone, all our relatives, help us. In Gujarat, if there is no rain one year, if our seeds finish or

407

our bullock dies, then who will give us another bullock or some seeds? Our daughters' and sisters' husbands' villages are close by here, our wives' natal homes are also near. When we go away from here, then we will never get to meet our relatives. They will be dead to us. The women of our village threaten us, 'We are willing to leave our husbands; we can always find other men. But we can't get other parents; so we will never leave this place'. In Gujarat, if any sorrow or evil befalls us, to whom can we go to tell our troubles? 'You are not going to give us the bus fare and send us back, are you?'[14]

Here, he wrote, we get support because we are all alike, we share a common understanding. In Gujarat we will be strangers, we will be forced to mortgage our land to the big patidars since we will not be able to do the kind of farming we are used to. Further, he asked, if we leave our gods, where will we get our gods from? People come from all over to celebrate our festivals. We go to the market where our youth chose their own spouses—who will come to us in Gujarat?

Such, he concluded, is our life in the belly of the Narmada and in the lap of the forest. The Narmada gives joy to all who live in its belly. 'In the belly of the river we live contented lives. We have lived here for generation after generation; do we have a right to the mighty river Narmada and to our forests or don't we? Do you government people recognize that right or not?'[15] At another point, he stated forcefully, 'This is the land of our forefathers. We have right to it. If this is lost, we will only get spades and pickaxes, nothing else.'[16]

And more importantly,

> what is the state compensating us for? For our lands, our fields, for the trees along our fields. But we don't live only by this. Are you going to compensate us for our forests?. . . In the forests we have teak, bamboo, umbar, salai, mahua, anjan, palash and many more. What will be the compensation for this? Or are you going to compensate us for our great river—for her fish, her water, for the vegetables that grow along her banks, for the joy of living besides her? What is the price of this? Our livestock and the fodder—water that is essential for it—are you going to compensate us for that? How are you compensating us for our fields either—we did not buy this land; our forefathers cleared it and settled here. What price this land? Our gods, the support of those who are our kin, what price do your have for these? Our adivasi life, what price do you put on it.'[17]

The government justifies displacement by arguing that in the R and R sites the tribals will have access to modern amenities, clean drinking water, electricity and houses. But a vital question has been raised by Mahalia in this connection. We want schools and houses, electricity and irrigation, but why has all this not been given in the villages? Why has the government not given all these things fifty years after independence? You sit in Bhopal, Delhi, Ahmedabad and decide our life and death. Do you think we adivasi peasants are not human too?[18] But now, we

> have reached a collective decision. For the first time in Madhya Pradesh, land will be flooded, our villages will be drowned. All of us adivasi people are going to drown in Jalsindhi village. The land in Gujarat is not acceptable to us. Your compensation is not acceptable to us. We were born from the belly of the Narmada, we are not afraid to die in her lap. We will drown but not move.'[19]

It is this kind of protest that has been harnessed by the NBA and which forms the main plank of its agenda: 'Do we have a right to the mighty river Narmada and to our forests or don't we? Do you government people recognize that right or not?' This forms the substance of people's rights—rights that challenge the power of the Indian state to do with its people what it will, its power to stake a claim to land under the territorial jurisdiction of the country, to move people without regard for their sensibilities. And it is precisely this right that the state cannot accommodate because it is a frontal attack on its power. This is what the new assertions of rights are about—the right to not only eke out a livelihood but to do so in conditions of dignity, in conditions of one's choice, among one's family and social bondings, among familiar environments.

Conclusion

In conclusion, let me briefly point out the political clout of rights. Rights, I suggest, provide protection against calculations based on some notion of the social good, or against utilitarian computations of what is beneficial for some sections of society. They, in short, eclipse all other considerations. Correspondingly, rights as an integral part of political morality hold that individual entitlements are of such overriding importance that on no ground whatsoever can we compromise them. These entitlements cannot be collapsed into any aggregative notion of the good. Neither can the abrogation of individual rights be justified by reference to an aggregative notion of the good. Rights are, therefore, a non-instrumental and non-derivative part of morality.

It is true that we cannot guarantee that individual rights will not be violated in a given society. What we can do is to institute a norm that rights are of such primary importance, that whosoever violates them should have very good reasons for doing so. The onus of proof is on those who violate rights. Rights, therefore, perform two functions: they act as constraints on actions that violate the dignity of human beings, and they guarantee the status of human beings in society. It is in this sense that the assertion of rights in the Narmada valley has to be understood.

This paper is based upon the findings of a research project titled 'The Politics of Peoples Rights', that has been funded by the ICSSR. The report of the project is based on an investigation into two case studies—the Narmada movement and the Chattisgarh Mukti Morcha. Field trips to these areas were carried out in 1996 and 1997. This particular essay deals with the unfolding of the struggle against the Sardar Sarovar project in the Narmada valley, and chronicles the vocabularies of rights that have emanated from the struggle.

Notes and References

1 The Narmada valley development project consists of 30 major dams, 135 minor dams and over 3,000 small dams. Some of these, such as the Tawa and the Bargi, have already been built. Some—such as the Narmada Sagar and the Sardar Sarovar—are under construction while others, such as Veda, Goi, Maheshwar, Omkareshwar, have been initiated. In Madhya Pradesh, a number of dams are being constructed upstream. Central to the entire project is the Sardar Sarovar, which is the largest multi-purpose river valley project in western India. This involves the construction of a terminal storage reservoir on the Narmada. The 455-feet height of the SSP, constructed along the river in Kevadia and Navagam in Bharuch district of Gujarat, will impound water to the full reservoir level, i.e., 4.72 million acre feet, with a five-feet cushion for the moderation of floods. The reservoir is expected to submerge 37,000 hectares in three states. The diversion of 9.5 MAF into canal and irrigation schemes aggregated to 75,000 km, will submerge approximately 80,000 hectares. The canal will extend 450 km into Rajasthan.

2 I am indebted to Jai Sen for clarifying some of the aspects of the struggle for me.

3 I have dealt with this in some detail in my earlier work, *State and Civil Society. Explorations in Political Theory*, Sage, Delhi, 1995, chapter 1.

410

[4] Amita Baviskar, *In the Belly of the River,* Oxford University Press, Delhi, 1995.

[5] According to the award 9 million acre feet of water is to go to Gujarat, 0.5 MAF to Rajasthan, 0.25 MAF to Maharashtra, and 18.25 feet to Madhya Pradesh. For this the dam should be raised to 138.68 metres with a live storage capacity of 4.72 MAF.

[6] Medha Patkar, 'The Struggle for Participation and Justice: A Historical Narrative' (in conversation with Smitu Kothari), in *Towards Sustainable Development: Struggling over India's Narmada River*, edited by William Fisher, M.E. Sharpe, New York, 1995, p. 162.

[7] Interview with Anil Patel in August 1997 in Mangrol.

[8] Anil Patel, 'Resettlement Policies and Tribal Interests', in Jean Dreze, Meera Samson, Satyajit Singh, eds., *The Dam and The Nation: Displacement and Rehabilitation in the Narmada Valley*, Oxford University Press, Delhi, 1997, p. 80. Personal conversation with Anil Patel.

[9] Official figures put the displacement at 40,000, the National Institute of Urban Affairs puts it at 1 lakh, the Tata Institute of Social Sciences puts those who will be directly displaced at 1.5 lakh. Along with those who will be displaced as result of canal irrigation, people living downstream, in the back-water, zone the catchment area and the sanctuary, estites put the displaced at 2 lakh.

[10] *Sardar Sarovar: The Report of the Independent Review*, Resources Futures International, Ottawa, 1992.

[11] Personal conversation with Anil Patel. Also Anil Patel, 'Resettlement Policies and Tribal Interests,' pp. 86–87.

[12] Medha Patkar, 'The Struggle for Participation and Justice: A Historical Reconstruction', p. 158.

[13] Bava Mahalia, 'Letter from a Tribal Village', *Lokayan Bulletin*, September–December 1994–95, p. 153.

[14] Ibid., p. 57.

[15] Ibid., p. 156, emphasis mine.

[16] Ibid., p. 157.

[17] Ibid., p. 157–58.

[18] Ibid., p. 158.

[19] Ibid.

The Efficacy and Ethics of the International Political Terrorist Act or Event

Achin Vanaik

Although the above title is extremely inelegant and clumsy it seems unavoidable and is the result of some degree of careful deliberation about what the scope of the project should be. But before elaborating on this, what have been the background conditions which have stimulated the selection of this particular subject for exposition? Certainly, terrorist political acts or events throughout the world are now very much a part of our era. But there has been a more specific India spur. India is currently passing through turbulent times that promise to become even mor e so the near future. The ugly face of political Hindutva looms ever larger. More than fifty years after 1947, Indian nationalism is today more insecure and frustrated, more lacking in self-confidence than it ever was in the immediate aftermath of independence despite the traumas of partition and the assassination of Mahatma Gandhi.

An insecure and frustrated nationalism much more easily tends to become an aggressive nationalism, more willing to dispense with democratic and humanist norms in the pursuit of 'discipline' or 'stability' or 'stronger nationhood' or whatever. The Sangh Combine —as the principal embodiment of Hindutva—has both benefited from, and promoted, this trend. At this time, when the Sangh Combine has assumed central state power, there are entirely legitimate fears about the implications of this for Indian democracy and liberal, let alone socialist, values. The Indian middle class led by the professional stratum has, not unexpectedly, already progressed a considerable way in the process of making its accommodation to the Sangh and its pernicious ideology. In the name of constructing a 'strong' centre (and therefore presumably a strong India), the most sophisticated sections of the print media—the English language national dailies—are now more willing than ever to treat direct assaults on human rights and secularism as respectable alternative viewpoints and to locate such views within the *mainstream* of liberal, democratic debate.

This was strikingly revealed during the Ajit Singh Sandhu affair in the middle of 1997. Sandhu, a very senior police officer in Punjab, had been charged with severe human rights violations that had taken place under his command during the course of his counter-insurgency campaign against Sikh/Khalistani militants/terrorists. In a state of demoralization, Sandhu committed suicide, citing his deep dismay that a previously publicly designated 'hero' like himself was now being treated as an actual or possible criminal. The former police chief of Punjab, K.P.S. Gill, himself indicted for sexist behaviour in public, came to Sandhu's defence registering his own dismay at how the state was 'betraying' those whom it had once lauded for carrying out successful counter-insurgency campaigns which would not have been possible without 'occasional excesses'.

More disturbing than this, however, was the editorial response from major newspapers. One editor went so far as to demand complete immunity from legal prosecution for all personnel involved in counter-insurgency efforts. Other editorials were more cautious but it remains shocking that, by the large, they all felt that Sandhu had a point and that state 'excesses' should not be equated with the terrorism of anti-state forces, but treated more leniently. The overall thrust was to advocate a dilution of human rights considerations when the state was, in certain circumstances (protecting the 'unity and integrity of the country'), itself the violator. This was bad enough but what was worse was that such a viewpoint seemed largely in accordance with general middle-class sentiment. I have therefore felt that a clearer understanding of terrorism, its efficacy and ethics, would be a useful input into the public debate in India.

In selecting the title of this essay, I have been concerned to carefully delimit the terrain of investigation. The complexities and difficulties of understanding so multifaceted a phenomenon as terrorism, let alone of finding an adequate definition of it, are so great that without such conscious delimitation one would risk sinking into a complete and contradictory morass. Thus, I am confining myself to only looking at terrorist acts or events. Though one can also distinguish the terrorist event from the terrorist act it is not necessary to do so for the purposes of this exposition. I am referring throughout to these

413

terrorist acts which become *publicly* known and have public impact, i.e. become a public event. I avoid taking up the question of 'terrorist regimes' whose terrorism would be of an *institutionalized* type, quite distinct form the non-institutionalized by *necessarily and openly* violent form characteristic of acts usually deemed terrorist.

Even with respect to terrorist acts or events I restrict myself to *political* terrorism, excluding criminal terrorist behaviour or what some might feel are expressions of an 'economic' terrorism. Within the sphere of political terrorist acts I focus only on 'international' ones. What I mean by the distinction between domestic and international terrorism will be made clear in the course of the exposition. However, much of the discussion on the efficacy and ethics of such international political terrorist events is of general applicability to other kinds of terrorism.

At first glance, to talk of the ethics of a terrorist act might seem peculiar. Is not terrorism by its very nature ethically wrong? But it is only if a terrorist act can be defined or understood in an evaluatively *neutral* way that there can be a serious discussion of the ethics involved. There is much to be said, in fact, for just such a morally neutral definition of the terrorist act. The problems of a non-neutral definition are considerable. For example, the old saw about one person's terrorist being another person's freedom fighter is not without significant merit. How would we get out of this relativist trap? Did Shahid Bhagat Singh engage in a terrorist act or did he not? Since so many Indians are justifiably proud of Bhagat Singh, seeing him as a heroic revolutionary and martyr, the temptation would be strong for them to deny that he was a terrorist or that he engaged in what could legitimately be described as a terrorist act. However, this is a temptation that should, in my view, be resisted. It makes more sense to recognize certain behaviour, such as his, as terrorist and yet be prepared to defend it even on moral grounds. To do this is precisely to enter the terrain of discourse about the ethics of terrorism of the terrorist act.

Similarly, why should I or anyone else necessarily regard the assassination of President John F. Kennedy with moral shock or horror rather than with justified indifference or even a certain relief, if not approval? What if one believes, by no means unreasonably, that all US Presidents since World War II have behaved like political criminals in their foreign policy and bear principal responsibility for events which (in cases like Vietnam) can even be called deliberate acts of genocide?

It does not, of course, follow that one is justified in condoning or app-
lauding the assassination of Kennedy or the attempted assassination of
Ronald Reagan. The conditions under which such acts are condoned
as morally legitimate are strict, and depend also on whether the con-
doner does or does not belong to a community which is a direct victim
of immoral US policy. Moral judgment can also be influenced by the
presence of other avenues for seeking justice in that society. The point
is that there is a serious issue regarding the ethics of terrorism which
deserves more thoughtful discussion.

Defining the Terrorist Act

Perhaps the best way to begin the search for a proper definition of the terrorist act is to be clear about how *not* to define it. I started
by taking down all the dictionaries I had on my shelf and looking up
each of them for the entry 'terrorism'.[1] This was itself quite revealing.
The two early (1950s) US dictionaries I had (Webster's and Funk &
Wagnall's) were clearly reflective of the then prevailing Cold War
perspective as well as being written before the worldwide eruption of
combat group terrorist events from the sixties onwards. Here, terrorism was defined specifically with regimes—more specifically with the
'totalitarian' Soviet or communist or east bloc regimes—in mind, in
contrast to the democratic regimes of the USA and the west. Terrorism
is defined here as a negative form of governance or system of rule.
Other dictionaries (one belonging to the 1970s and the rest to the
1990s), British rather than American, did not have definitions of terrorism that linked it to any particular system of rule. Freer from Cold
War reflexes, the definitions given here are broader in character, theoretically speaking, and capable of being applied to any part of the world.
But these definitions are, in fact, too broad.

Since any sensible definition of the terrorist act must link it to
a notion of violence, defining the latter appropriate also becomes
necessary. A broad definition of violence can be appropriate in certain
contexts where we may wish to talk of the violence of poverty, racism,
sexism, etc.—of injustice itself as a form of violence. But such an
understanding is hardly helpful to the present context where we wish
to investigate the efficacy and ethics of terrorist acts or events. For our
purposes a stricter definition of violence has to be used, namely, the
exercise of force such as to physically harm, injure, pain or kill humans.

415

Such a definition excludes damage to property and is independent of the ends, intentions or subjective perceptions of the agents of such violence. It is therefore an *objective* definition appropriate to the search for an ethically neutral and objective definition of terrorism itself.

A perusal of various dictionary definitions, then, shows broadly four kinds of approaches, all of which should be rejected. Terrorism is understood as having one or a number of the following characteristics: (i) organized intimidation; (ii) violence against civilians or non-combatants; (iii) indiscriminate use of violence; (iv) illegitimate use of violence.

Each of these understandings carries grave problems. Intimidation is too loose and broad a concept. There are many kinds or forms of organized intimidation including systems or structures of psychological intimidation. Would these qualify as a form of terrorism? Terrorism need not only have civilian and non-combatants as targets. Terrorist acts can be inflicted on combatants as well. The attack on General Vaidya in Pune was a terrorist act. Similarly, when indefensible violence or extreme disproportion in violence is used against opposing combatants, such as the use of nuclear, chemical or biological warfare, this too can count as terrorism. One does not have to go so far as to use weapons of mass destruction. Simply using tanks or bombers to destroy a militant hideout, where the defenders are known to only have rifles, can also count as an indefensible terrorist act. Furthermore, certain civilians such as presidents or prime ministers, given their major responsibilities for conducting warfare, can be seen by the opposing side with justice as legitimate targets for terrorist efforts at assassination. One can sensibly describe the Officer's Plot of 1944 to kill Hitler and his senior cohorts as a terrorist attack (which failed) and even be prepared to defend and approve of it.

As for terrorism being the indiscriminate use of violence, so much of what we understand as terrorist acts or events involve very specific, indeed highly discriminate use of violence. Finally, assigning the label of terrorism to only those acts deemed illegitimate begs all questions about the legitimacy of the 'officially' legitimate wielders of violence—the state. Such an approach is far too narrow, for it definitionally outlaws even the possibility of State terrorism.

An appropriate and serviceable definition of the terrorism of an act or even then, must possess the following properties: it should be evaluatively neutral; it should not be too broad or too narrow; it should be objective. In regard to the last named property, the judgement of whether an act or event is terrorist or not should be made independently of, and without reference to, the motives or self-perceptions of the perpetrators of that act. For example, the agents of State terrorism rarely see themselves as engaged in terrorist acts. Even the more moral-minded of state officials will concede only that the state (especially if it is a liberal democratic state) is sometimes guilty of unfortunate and condemnable 'excesses' but never of terrorism. Such a view would effectively exculpate the liberal democratic state of the USA from the charge of nuclear terrorism in dropping the bombs on the overwhelmingly civilian populations of Hiroshima and Nagasaki! The untenability of such an exculpation should be obvious. Once we arrive at a definition of terrorism that is balanced, neutral and objective, we can then more intelligently discuss its efficacy and ethics.

The following can serve as a working definition of the political terrorist act or event. It is the calculated or premeditated use or threat of use of violence against an individual, group or larger collectivity in such a manner that the target is rendered physically defenceless against that attack or against the effects of that violence. What makes this a form of political terrorism distinguishing it from, say, criminal terrorism (murder), is that the act is harnessed to some political intent or purpose and carries a political meaning. The defenselessness can be the result of (a) surprise; (b) the nature of the target chosen e.g., its civilian status; (c) the nature of the weapons used; d) enormous disproportion in the violence exercised between the two sides i.e., a gross violation of the principle of *minimal or reasonable force*. The agents of the terrorist act can be the individual, the combat group, or larger entities like the apparatus(es) of the State.

Domestic and International Political Terrorism

Domestic political terrorism is easy to recognize. It is carried out by domestic agents for domestic purposes.

What about international political terrorism? Again, let us begin by pointing out what is not meant by this. Simply the fact of outside support for domestic agents does not make an act one of international political terrorism. If the February 1993 bomb blasts in Bombay were the handiwork of an outside agency, say the Inter-Services Intelligence (ISI), this would be an example of international

417

terrorism. But if there was only ISI help for domestic agents perpetrating the act for domestic purposes (for example, supposed retaliation for the police-abetted communal riots in Bombay a month or so earlier), this would not be a form of international terrorism. After all, a state can also take help form outside and use that help to carry out terrorist acts against the domestic population. The USA has helped numerous Latin American dictatorships in myriad ways and that help has been used against their own populace in the most brutal ways. But those specific acts of brutality were forms of domestic terrorism.

Further, international political terrorism cannot be identified by the mere fact that an act or event (say, the assassination of Kennedy) has international repercussions. Nor do we mean the phenomenon of the increasing international spread of terrorism.

It is the existence of any of the following properties that defines an act of international political terrorism:

1. It is carried out by 'outside' actors owing allegiance to, or residing in, another country.

2. When the cause to which the act is related is extra-national, i.e, the cause is to reorder the existing international system of states as, for example, in a war of national liberation

3. When the act is primarily directed against an external power or the act involves direct defiance of an external power or powers. This would apply to the USA's bombing of Gaddafi's palace in Libya (killing his daughter) for his alleged (the allegations were subsequently shown to be false) role in an airplane hijacking and bombing during Reagan's first tenure as President. It would also apply to the famous 1979 US hostage crisis in post-Shah Iran when revolutionary guards declaring allegiance to Ayatollah Khomeini captured the US Embassy and held its inmates hostage, or the more recent hostage crisis involving the Japanese Embassy in Peru.

While not all forms of international political terrorism are linked to perceived (by one side) 'wars of liberation', this is the most usual or frequent connection. That is to say, international political terrorist acts are very often connected to wars declared or undeclared, wars small or large, 'wares of liberation' on one side and 'counter-insurgency wars' on the other side. This connection provides important grounds for helping us to judge both the efficacy and the ethics of the international political terrorist act.

The Effectiveness of International Political Terrorism

To judge the effectiveness of terrorism generally is to ask and answer the question of how successful is the act in helping to realize the cause or overall political goals to which that terrorist act is dedicated or harnessed. This applies as much to evaluating an act of an agent like an insurgency combat group as it does to an act of the state committed to counter-insurgency operations. But important differences between state terrorism and combat group terrorism must be grasped.[2] International terrorism today is usually a form of warfare. Discussion of its efficacy must itself be located in a discussion of the nature of *modern* warfare or, more precisely, how it differs from war in the past.

Through the decades of the twentieth century there has been an inescapable trend towards the greater 'democratization of war'. What is relevant for our purposes is not so much the greater extent to which there has been citizen mobilization in the larger-scale wars of the twentieth century when compared to those of the eighteenth and nineteenth centuries. Rather, what is relevant is that the popularity of or popular support for a war has become much more important. Popular perceptions about the role and aim of a war, its continuation, and the means to be used, all have much greater impact on the conduct of the war and even on its political effects and outcome. So one important criterion for judging the effectiveness of a terrorist act related to a larger war is whether or not it increases popular legitimacy or support for the war on the side of the perpetrators of the act or acts in question. Here the differences between state terrorism and the combat group terrorism of its opponents become important.

State terrorism has no flexibility. It has one primary aim: to cow down the opposition, to show through promoting a 'fear of consequences' of fighting such a war, the *futility* of the cause to which its opponents are attached. State terrorism can even alienate further the popular base of the enemy force form the state in question, but the latter is prepared to pay this price if it feels it has more than compensated for this through its success in getting its message of futility across. State terrorism is also relatively inflexible in being directed primarily at the enemy population or armed rebels. Such terrorism has no message directed at the home population. Thus the state has no interest in that kind of publicity fir its terrorist acts which might create alarm

419

or reservations about its 'humanity' or respect for rights amongst its home population. The more democratic the country of the state in question, the more worried that state is likely to be about such publicity. It usually makes every effort to cover up such acts from public scrutiny (domestic or foreign), to deny the existence of such acts, to minimize the degree to which human rights have been violated if such acts become public, or to attack the patriotic credentials of those who uncover or are horrified by the revelation of such acts. Such routine reflexes have, of course, been very much in evidence with regard to the Indian state's reaction to critics of its human rights behaviour in Kashmir and Punjab.

The contrast with combat group terrorism is striking. This is politically aimed not only at the enemy population or strike force but also at its home population. The primary purpose of the terrorist act here is symbolic and the last thing the combat group wants is for the act not to be known to a wide public, for it to remain a secret. In most cases the combat group or movement or front responsible for the act wants to make that responsibility publicly known. However, in some cases where the primary purpose is revenge and the perpetrators fear negative political repercussions, e.g., a weakening or loss of legitimacy even among the home population, responsibility may not be acknowledged. This might well have been the case with regard to the assassination of Rajiv Gandhi and the behaviour of the LTTE, if it was responsible for the assault. But as a general rule, combat group terrorism wants public awareness of its act because the act is aimed simultaneously at enhancing the legitimacy and support for its cause amidst the home population and demoralizing the enemy force and its popular support base.

Revolutionary Marxists have hit the nail on the head when they say such terrorist acts are 'propaganda by the deed' or 'reformism with a gun'. The traditional Marxist critique of terrorism is not on moral grounds but on tactical/strategic grounds. The Marxist tradition has been critical of terrorism because it does not believe that it is, on balance, efficacious. Terrorism is condemned because it is seen as an individualist or small group substitution for mass activity or for efforts to generate such mass activity. It is further condemned for being based on a false premise—that the elimination of supposedly key individuals can somehow bring about a dramatic transformation of the system or of a government's basic orientation or policies.

The Marxist view, then, makes two claims arising out of its assessment of the inefficaciousness of terrorism: (a) terrorism is the politics of the weak; (b) it perpetuates this weakness. However, this view is not fully correct and needs to be substantially qualified. Terrorism is often the weapon of the strong, e.g., of the strong counter-insurgency state. The stronger side can and does resort to terrorism although the weaker side is more likely to make of terrorism (regular terrorist acts) a matter of strategy rather than just tactics. This does not, of course, preclude the stronger side from resorting to systematic and regularized terrorism.

One obvious but nonetheless very important distinction between state terrorism and combat group terrorism is that the *scale* of terrorism perpetrated by the former can be and so often, is much greater than when perpetrated by the latter. Although the state has much the greater and more powerful means for engaging in large-scale terrorism, the issue of 'availability of means' is not the primary reason why the scale of state terrorism is so much greater. It is the contrasting ends and goals between states and other much smaller entities that is the determining factor. For example, for all the talk over the decades—talk which has become louder after the end of the Cold War and the break-up of the USSR—about the danger of combat group nuclear terrorism, there is the highly awkward yet extremely stubborn historical fact that there has not been any serious evidence that any non-state terrorist group has sought to make, acquire, use or consider using weapons of mass destruction like an atomic bomb, chemical or biological agents. Even much more easily available capacities to cause mass destruction, like poisoning water supply, have not been exercised. This is in striking contrast to the scale of mass killings of civilians perpetrated by states, form the killing fields of Kampuchea to Hiroshima-Nagasaki to USA's indiscriminate, saturation bombings and use of chemical warfare in Vietnam, or the chemical warfare in the eight-year war between Khomeini's Iran and Hussein's Iraq.

For the combat group the terrorist act is a *dramatized statement of political intent or commitment* and/or has a very specific purpose such as release of prisoners or fulfilment of specific and limited demands. Therefore, there has to be a strong relationship of *proportionality* between the ends sought by that act and the means used in it. The act itself should never be of such a nature as to alienate popular home support or to rationalize or justify enemy state retaliation against

421

its home population on a scale involving thousands more. This is precisely what a terrorist act involving weapons of mass destruction would invite or do.[3] In short, there is inherent in the very political character of combat group terrorism a powerful factor of self-limitation regarding the means to be used. It has never made sense for the combat group or its side to even think of competing with states in upping the scale of destruction threatened or carried out!

This brings us to the nub of the issue. It is only the pursuit of 'grandiose' objectives that can justify or rationalize the possession, use or threat of use of 'grandiose' means, like weapons of mass destruction, or justify a very large scale of killings in a single act. A struggle for national liberation, to which combat group terrorism is often harnessed, is certainly a grand ultimate objective but each particular act of terrorism has much more limited and specific objectives even as it is part of the larger pursuit of a final grand goal. It is states alone that can most convincingly claim to be pursuing such supposedly grandiose objectives as a matter of *regularized routine*.

These can range form the claim of 'defending the security of the nation' to 'defending the free world' to 'defeating world imperialism' to 'behaving like a world power' to wanting to 'shift the balance of power in one's favour' by sending a political message to one's perceived rival(s) (almost certainly the main purpose behind the USA's dropping of nuclear bombs on Hiroshima and Nagasaki), to whatever other 'grand' aim the state sees as its cause, role or responsibility. That so many people should nevertheless not wish to face up to the potential and actual dangers of state terrorism by preferring to see the state as capable only of 'excesses', represents a deep insensitivity to universalist and state-transcending principles of human rights.

But before coming to the issue of ethics, we have still to properly dispose of the issue of efficacy. Here, contrary to the traditional Marxist claim about the inefficacy of combat group terrorism, such acts can, and have been politically effective. (This is true also of state terrorism). The Marxist failure to adequately factor in the dimension represented by the 'democratization of warfare' leads to a characteristic underestimation of the importance of the symbolic dimension and, therefore, of the potential possessed by the terrorist act. The Marxist tradition simplifies the relationship between the generation of mass consciousness in the home population and the terrorist act as an external stimulus to it. It also underestimates the potentially demoralizing

422

or delegitimizing impact it can have on the direct enemy agency and its relationship to its own support base.

There are numerous post-World War II historical examples that confirm this. But before looking at an arbitrary selection of them, it should be said that states have also learnt something in the course of the history of modern counter-insurgency operations world-wide. They have become more intransigent when faced with terrorist demands. This seems particularly so in hostage scenarios where an attritional strategy of 'waiting it out' is seen as providing the best chances to the side (the state) opposing the hostage capture and authorized to negotiate with the captors. In short, most states have greater resources to deal with even strongly implanted and well-armed liberation movements and though unable to inflict decisive defeats in the short or medium term, are more confident of success in the longer term through the pursuit of sustained and prolonged attritional warfare.

From the late seventies onward, states began to engage in, and learn from, their prolonged counter-insurgency operations. Usually, though not always, the prolonged passage of time and the ensuing war-weariness has a stronger negative effect on the more weakly armed side even when it enjoys deep and wide political support form its home population. This is true of the Naga struggle for independence. It is also a factor in the LTTE struggle for Tamil Eelam. This general trend has also had its impact in diminishing the political value of the terrorist act when carried out by the combat group. But this is not to say, however, that we have reached the stage where such acts are never or only rarely efficacious. Precisely because we live in the era of mass communications and in a context where popular perceptions have become more important than ever, the temptation to engage in 'symbolic politics' or to pursue the 'low cost' and potentially 'high-impact' politics of terrorism, has become stronger. Terrorism is here to stay for a long time to come. Nor should we forget or ignore the durability of state terrorism.

Five Examples

1. The first example is not one of international terrorism, strictly speaking. It has to do with an internal civil war situation where the overthrow of an existing dictatorship and not a war for national liberation or separation of part of the country was at issue. If I have

423

nonetheless included it here, it is only because it is a very striking example of how the terrorist act can be enormously efficacious in certain cases. This was the 1978 Sandinista capture of the National Assembly in Nicaragua and the holding of its legislator members as hostages. The ultimate outcome was the capitulation of the Somoza regime to the specific demand for release of certain Sandinista prisoners and their safe passage (along with the Sandinistas involved in the National Assembly capture) by airplane to Cuba in return for the release of the hostages at the airport.

The symbolic and general political impact of the deed was enormous. It not only catapulted the Sandinistas to national awareness but emphasized dramatically their new national-level authority in a way which the previous years of prolonged guerrilla struggle had not. It was a most dramatic example of outright and open political defiance of the Somoza regime right in the very heart of (symbolically) one of its most important seats of power. This act also catalysed a spontaneous and open exhibition of mass popular support for the Sandinistas as never before. The road from the Assembly to the airport was literally packed on both sides for miles with people cheering and waving their support for the Sandinista rebels as they and their hostages were escorted to the airport. This act thoroughly demoralized the Somozaist regime and paved the way for the final successful armed insurrection in 1979 which overthrew the Somoza regime.

2. Palestinian commando raids on various (including civilian) targets between 1967 and the Israeli invasion of Lebanon in 1982 is another important example. Before the 1967 war there was hardly any Palestinian military presence that was independent of the control of neighbouring Arab states. Till 1964 the Palestinian political leadership had been largely subordinated to one or the other of the Arab governments. It is only after 1964 that an independent Palestinian political leadership emerged and only after 1967 that an independent armed wing developed significantly and came to prominence primarily through (a) a series of terrorist acts in Israeli territory and (b) through growing control in internecine fighting in Lebanon. At one point in the mid-seventies, Palestinian forces and Lebanese leftists controlled over 70 per cent of Lebanon. This was only overturned when Syria (with the approval of both the USA and Israel) entered militarily into this civil-war situation to establish it area of substantial control.

But in regard to the commando raids and terrorist acts in

Israeli-controlled territory, in a period when Israel had established effective dominance over the other Arab states especially after the separate peace with Egypt, this was the one way in which the political issue of Palestine was repeatedly kept publicized and retained on the global political agenda.

3. The third example is of the Iran hostages crisis of 1979–80. The capture of the US Embassy and of its inmates for a prolonged period of many months had two political effects. Internally, it served to greatly unify pro-government (pro-Khomeini) forces to the detriment of his opponents such as the many Leftist groups which had in fact played a major role in the insurrection that finally toppled the old regime. Externally, the prolonged symbolic defiance of US power had a major demoralizing effect on the Carter administration and was probably the single most important reason for his failure to be reelected.

4. In Reagan's second term, despite his 'strong USA' rhetoric, the bomb attack in Lebanon which killed 250 US marines probably played a decisive role in Washington's decision not to involve itself directly or militarily in the Lebanese quagmire.

5. The last example is the 'Battle of Algiers' (1956–58) which was essentially a series of calculated bombings and armed assaults on police, military and civilian targets by a secret and tightly organized network of activists in Algiers owing allegiance to the National Liberation Front (FLN) leading the struggle for Algerian independence form France. Though this network was ultimately destroyed (with the use of state terrorism) and armed activity then shifted to the countryside, this 'Battle of Algiers' had a major and positive political impact in mobilizing popular support, defiance by Algerians of France and in helping to convince the French of the enduring hostility of native Algerians to anything short of full independence and freedom from French colonial rule.

The Ethics of International Political Terrorism

Here there is less need to make a distinction between international and domestic political terrorism. Much of what will be argued for in this section will have general relevance. But focusing on international political terrorism does make matters a little easier since so much of this kind of terrorism is linked to wars of liberation. In so far as domestic political terrorism can be linked to 'righteous' revolutionary struggle to overthrow oppressor regimes, the discussion of ethics would apply to these cases as well. Clearly, in talking of the ethics of such kinds of political terrorism we are operating very much on the terrain of the age-old discourse about the relationship between ends and means.

To begin with, any possibility of claiming that a terrorist act is just and should therefore be supported, must assume that the cause to which that act is harnessed is itself good and just. This is a necessary, even if not a sufficient, condition for one to claim that such an act is to be defended. If the cause is itself not believed to be just, as one side will usually consider it not to be, then the act cannot be justified. The justice, then, of using terrorist methods is related to the justice or justness of the cause itself. Indeed, to rebel against an 'unjust' system can itself be considered a fundamental right of the individual in the Lockean sense. But even when we accept this, it still doesn't answer the question of how to rebel?

There are two ways of justifying all violence in the aid of a supposedly just cause or one perceived to be so. The first way is to do so in the name of efficacy. Here the question of what means or methods are to be used in pursuit of the given end is not a moral but a practical one. It is a question of effectiveness, of tactics and strategy. This is how revolutionaries usually rationalize the use of terrorist threats or acts of violence. Since the end striven for constitutes such a profound trans-formation of existing society and its values, including its moral ones, why then should the struggle against it be bound by such values, the revolutionary asks, especially when the enemy will not feel bound, even by existing values, in defence of its power? Of this last point there are many examples but a particularly important one was the 1973 US-supported military coup in Chile to overthrow and crush the demo-cratically elected Popular Unity government of Salvador Allende.

Chile had perhaps the longest history of representative democratic government of any third world country. Nonetheless, although Allende was reelected in 1973 with a bigger mandate than in 1970 and had committed himself to the use only of peaceful and constitutional methods of political activity, this did not prevent the ruling classes who felt deeply threatened by his policies to resort to the most brutal and undemocratic methods to overthrow him. Allende refused to listen to his own supporters who, in anticipation of the coup and in clear recognition of the turmoil in the country, were clamouring for the arming of the general civilian public to prevent the coup which so many recognized was obviously coming.

The point, then, is not a trivial one. It is what lies behind, for example, Malcolm X's famous dictum concerning the liberation of black people in the USA: 'by any means necessary'. That is to say, such revolutionaries claim there should be no weakening of their struggle to achieve a just end by a renunciation *in advance* of the means to be used.

The second way of justifying all violence in the name of a just cause is through an approach that Barrington Moore Jr has aptly called the 'calculus of suffering'.[4] Here the claim is that the oppression of the oppressor is so great that no amount of terrorism by the oppressed can change the overall balance-sheet of suffering. In the remarkable film by Gilo Pontecorvo, *The Battle of Algiers*, this particular approach to justifying terrorist violence was dramatized most effectively. The French authorities had captured one of the principal leaders of the FLN, Ahmed Ben M'Hidi and were parading him in front of an international press conference. One reporter of a French newspaper asks him that if he thinks the cause of Algerian independence is so just, then what kind of cause is this which can justify the placing of home-made bombs in baskets which are then put in public places to blow up innocent French women and children? M'Hidi replies that yes, it is terrible that French women and children are killed in this way but then goes on to remind the reporter and the others at the press conference that French planes which fly over Algerian villages and drop their bombs kill many, many more Algerian women and children. He then goes on to exclaim, 'I tell you what, give us your planes and we will give you our baskets'.

However, neither of the two rationalizations given (whether of efficacy or of a balance-sheet of suffering) can be fully acceptable. To do so begs a crucial question. Does this mean that everything or any form of violence such as cruelty, torture, killing of children can be justified? Merely to ask the question should, one hopes, be enough to elicit the proper reply. No, it cannot. 'By all means necessary' is an utterly unacceptable dictum. One must accept that there are individual rights and that some of these are all but inviolable. That is to say, certain rights (e.g., no cruelty to children, no torture) are, if not absolute, near-absolute. If we accept this, as we should, then it becomes possible to formulate general rules regarding the use of permissible or acceptable means in pursuit of just ends.

However, much discussion in India on the relationship between means and ends has been strongly influenced by the Gandhian tradition whose approach has been insufficiently subtle, to say the least. Ends, we are repeatedly reminded, cannot justify means. Good ends cannot justify bad means. But another question is rarely if ever asked within the Gandhian tradition: do means justify ends? Do good means justify bad ends? Does the building of schools and hospitals justify or even lessen the evil end of maintaining colonial rule?

The idea that means must prefigure ends has to be handled carefully. There is genuine merit in the view that the goodness or worth of ends achieved bears some significant relationship to the goodness of means used in pursuit of those ends. But what is this relationship? To what extent can means prefigure ends? Any claim that means *must* prefigure ends, which is the basic thrust of the Gandhian approach, is ridiculously and unjustifiably rigid. For means cannot only reflect or presage their ends, they also unavoidably reflect their beginnings. Means are doubly determined, both by their putative goals and by their starting point, the prior situation of injustice (in variable forms of brutality and repression) confronting victims. In the struggle to overthrow slavery or fascism, for example, to expect that the means used will not bear some definite relationship to the character and system of this repression is quite unrealistic. Such means can certainly differ significantly from those used to overthrow other kinds of oppression operating in much milder contexts of physical repression and brutality.

There is, however, another claim within the Gandhian tradition. Terrible or unacceptable means, it is argued, can negate or nullify ends. What are we to make of this line of argument? Clearly, it depends on what we mean by negating or nullifying ends. All too often this is misunderstood to mean that the very *justice* of the end sought can be negated or nullified by the injustice of the means used in pursuit of that cause but is determined independently of those means. This may be a trivial point of logic but it is surprising how often it is forgotten. Nor does this mean that a sympathizer or supporter of that cause cannot condemn or oppose the use of a whole range of means. Of course, one can. But this is to insist that, for example, the justice of the Palestinian cause cannot be negated or nullified or even altered in any way by the iniquity of means (however terrible) that may be used in its pursuit. This does not mean, however, that the justice of that cause stands eternally. That justness is historically constituted and can there-

428

fore by historically altered, in that it might no longer become a meaningful cause whose value must be adjudicated or placed on the political agenda. So it is historically and theoretically conceivable, for example, that at some future time, few Palestinians may remain concerned about securing a Palestinian nation.

If, however, by negating or nullifying, one means that the *worth* of achievement or of the realized form taken by the goal desired can be diminished, sometimes greatly so, or even fully nullified by the character of the means chosen to pursue it, then this is obviously correct. If the overthrow of the South African apartheid regime had resulted in the institutionalization of say, a reverse apartheid, then many would certainly question the value of the form that the final achievement—the overthrow of apartheid—had taken. The value, many would feel, was significantly diminished even if not fully negated. Or, to take another example, the use of nuclear weapons in the service of some cause could easily and fully nullify the value of that final achievement, however just the goal and the struggle for it might be.

Any judgement of the possible indefensibility of the use of certain means is connected not so much to the concrete effect of those means on the form in which the just cause is realized but on the grounds of other general principles, ethical principles concerning individual human rights. This is the basis of the well-known and very important distinction between the justice of a war and justice in the conduct of a war. Even if opposing sides cannot agree on the justice of a particular war as seen by the other side, e.g., the Indian state and its supporters are not likely to accept the justice of the Naga struggle for independence, both sides can still accept the necessity of justice in the conduct of that war. Thus there can be certain *rules of warfare* which pertain to even terrorist acts, that can be accepted and respected by all.

Two such rules seem particularly pertinent in this regard.

Rule 1

There has to be a distinction between legitimate and nonlegitimate targets. This does not have to correspond strictly to the distinction between civilians and non-civilians. Certain kinds of civilians, depending on the particular context, have real responsibility for the conduct of warfare on one side and from the perspective of the other side are entirely legitimate targets. There is, moreover, an unavoidable

429

grey are or twilight zone, e.g., blowing up an ordnance factory can result in killing of nearby civilians but that does not mean the factory is not a legitimate target. But despite the inescapable generality of this rule it can still serve as an important guideline to proper moral beha-viour. It is one thing to target a Golda Meir for assassination or to target a senior defence official or to attack a military or strategic instal-lation. It would be another thing altogether, and quite unacceptable, to bomb a public space wherein ordinary Israeli citizens will be killed or injured or threatened with grave physical harm. However, for one who supports the Irish Republican cause, IRA public bombings which damage property and cause severe disruption in everyday life but are preceded by adequate prior warning to the relevant British authorities to clear the targeted site of people, need cause no serious moral dilemma or anguish.

Rule 2

Even for legitimate targets there have to be rules for *how* they are attacked. Certain vital principles have to be respected. One is that only minimum or reasonable force be applied. You don't use a ham-mer to kill a fly. Or, to put it another way, every effort must be made to avoid the imposition of gratuitous suffering. A serious and genuine commitment of this kind would outlaw forms of torture or the inflic-tion of humiliation or the use of unwarranted interrogation methods. There may be exceptional circumstances in which such restraint does not apply but these are much more likely, and frequently, to be found in the abstract peregrinations of moral philosophers or in the fiction of films and books than in life. Brutal interrogation methods used by the police and army on captured suspects or militants/terrorists as a matter of routine are not justified by the argument that extraction of information from such captives in necessary to preserve the larger good extraction of information form such captives is necessary to preserve the large good and to protect the public over which the state exercises its sovereignty.

A second principle to be upheld is that there has to be a distinction between the combatant who can be attacked and the 'person' whose rights have to be respected. One can attack a combat-ant, even kill him or her. In a combat situation one can hardly avoid this. But this does not give a right to calculatedly disfigure or maim an opponent. Moreover, once the situation changes and the status of the opponent is no longer that of being a combatant, then his or her new role must be recognized and the rights associated with that new role, or those rights associated with him or her being a 'person', must be respected. Thus prisoners, for example, have definite rights to be fully respected once a former combatant becomes a prisoner.

Of course, the rules we are talking about are general. They can hardly be expected to cover all contexts, contingencies or situations. But they nonetheless provide real practical guidelines. When so much of current practice, even in democracies like India, constitutes a standing violation and contempt for even these very elementary principles, we will be accomplishing a great deal if we can generalize respect for such principles and institutionalize their practice regardless of whether our support and loyalty is extended to the combat group in question or to its opposing State or to other power structures.

Notes and References

1   *Webster's New School and Office Dictionary,* 1957: 'Terrorism: a system of Government by terror; intimidation'; *Funk & Wagnall's Standard Home Reference Dictionary,* 1957: 'Terrorism: a system that seeks to rule by terror; the act of terrorizing'; *Chamber's Twentieth Century Dictionary* 1957: 'Terrorism: an organized system of intimidation'; *The Concise Oxford Dictionary of Current English* 1990. 'Terrorism: the use or favouring of violent and intimidating methods of coercing a government or community'; *Cobuild (Collin's Birmingham University International Language Database) English Language Dictionary,* 1991. 'Terrorism: is the use of violence, especially murder, kidnapping and bombing, in order to achieve political aims or to force a government to do something'; *Collin's Gem English Dictionary* 1993. Terrorism: use of violence and intimidation to achieve political ends'.

2   The distinction between combat group and state terrorism is obviously artificial since the state has its own combat groups. But making the distinction between these two types of agencies, one state and the other non-state, is essential.

3   Most alarmists, warning about the danger of nuclear terrorists, have combat groups, not states in mind. For a fuller treatment of why this is unwarranted alarmism, see Achin Vanaik, 'Nuclear Terrorism' in *The Hindu,* 27 October 1997. Such alarmism had three objective effects: (1) It helps to justify the possession of nuclear weapons by states, for example, to provide deterrence against such non-state nuclear terrorism; (2) It diverts attention away from the behaviour, attitudes and thinking of state elites. The implicit assumption that such terrorists are frighteningly irresponsible when compared to those who run states or influence its policies is simply

431

nonsense and belies all historical evidence; (3) It lets the mindset of nuclear deterrence advocated, defended or practised by state elites off the hook. Deterrence is simply a way of rationalizing the adoption of a fundamentally terrorist way of thinking about nuclear weapons. It is not some distinctive breed of footloose or insane nuclear terrorists but the routinized and disguised terrorism of deterrence thinking by ordinary, sane and in other ways humane and moral-minded people that is the source of the greatest nuclear danger.

4 Barrington Moore Jr, *Reflections on the Causes of Human Misery,* Penguin, Harmondsworth, 1972, pp. 25–28.

5 Chapter 2 titled 'Our Morals' in Naoman Geras, *Discourses of Extremity,* Verso, London, 1990, carries an excellent summary discussion of the ethical problems pertaining to revolutionary violence. I have drawn heavily on it for my presentation here. The notion of pre-figuration is also taken up at some length in Naoman Geras, *The Legacy of Rosa Luxemberg,* Verso, London, 1976, pp. 133–73.

Contributors

ROMILA THAPAR is Emeritus Professor of History at Jawaharlal Nehru University, New Delhi.

UMA CHAKRAVARTI teaches history at Miranda House, University of Delhi, Delhi.

RAJESWARI SUNDER RAJAN will shortly be joining the English faculty at University of Oxford, Oxford.

KUMKUM SANGARI teaches English at Indraprastha College, University of Delhi, Delhi.

SUSAN VISVANATHAN teaches sociaology at Jawaharlal Nehru University, New Delhi.

MEENA RADHAKRISHNA is an ICSSR Fellow at Nehru Memorial Museum and Library, New Delhi.

DLIP M. MENON teaches history at University of Hyderabad, Hyderabad.

NASIR TYABJI is a Nehru Fellow and visiting professor at the Centre for Science Policy, Jawaharlal Nehru University, New Delhi.

RANI DHAVAN SHANKARDASS is an independent researcher and Secretary General of the Penal Reform and Justice Association of India.

GYANESH KUDAISYA teaches at the School of Arts at Nanyang Technological University Singapore.

A.S. BHASIN, former diplomat, is engaged in academic research on South Asia at Nehru Memorial Museum and Library, New Delhi.

D.A. LOW is an eminent historian at Australian National University, Canberra.

GEETA KAPUR is an independent art critic and curator based in Delhi.

KRISHNA KUMAR teaches at the Department of Education, University of Delhi, Delhi.

433

MEENAKSHI THAPAN teaches at the Department of Education, University of Delhi, Delhi.

MAHESH RANGARAJAN is an independent researcher and commentator on ecology and politics based in Delhi.

NEERA CHANDHOKE teaches political science at University of Delhi, Delhi.

ACHIN VANAIK is an independent researcher and political commentator based in Delhi.

Index

435

Index

Index

Index